DORDOGNE, BORDEAUX
AND THE SOUTHWEST COAST

DORDOGNE, BORDEAUX
AND THE SOUTHWEST COAST

CONTENTS

DISCOVER 6

EXPERIENCE 58

NEED TO KNOW 252

Front cover: Sweeping vista of the Saint Cirq Lapopie town
Left: Colourful beach tents in Biarritz
Previous page: Vineyards of Saint-Émilion

DISCOVER

Rooftops of Bordeaux, capital of the Gironde

WELCOME TO DORDOGNE, BORDEAUX AND THE SOUTHWEST COAST

Nestled in the southwest corner of France is this wonderfully unhurried region. Its beautiful landscapes - verdant green hills, meandering rivers, attractive coastline - are a beacon to visitors seeking rest and recreation. The many villages and cities sprinkled throughout, meanwhile, are equally appealing, each one tracing France's storied history. Whatever your dream trip to Dordogne, Bordeaux and the Southwest Coast includes, this DK travel guide is the perfect companion.

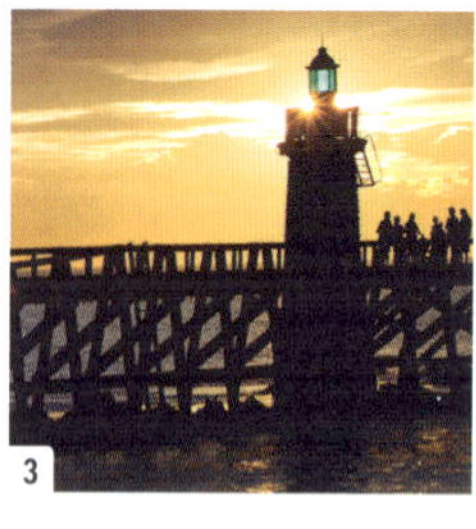

1 A sample of regional specialities.

2 Pic du Midi d'Ossau in the Vallée d'Ossau.

3 A lighthouse in the old port town of Capbreton.

4 The Old Town in medieval Sarlat-la-Canéda.

The landscapes of southwest France offer something for everyone. History buffs will be moved by the prehistoric caves at Lascaux, where humanity's palaeolithic ancestors felt compelled to create images of the beasts that used to roam these parts. Nature lovers, cyclists and hikers will find themselves spoiled for choice between country lanes, thick forests and rolling hills, while massive dunes and soft sandy beaches on the Atlantic will keep sun-seekers and surfers content for days.

Even the urban spaces retain the relaxed, countryside atmosphere, all of them bursting with character and history. A stroll around the city of Périgueux reveals the legacy of its early Roman conquerors, whose bridges and amphitheatre are still part of the cityscape. Bordeaux – France's elegant wine capital – is the belle of the ball, with exceptional architecture, outstanding museums and classic French cafés perfect for people-watching. Tiny towns and rural villages are also a delight to explore, as each one is full of its own local charm, with unique festivals, speciality foods and traditional buildings surrounding old town squares.

With so much to appreciate, you won't want to miss a single thing. We've broken this region down into easily navigable chapters, with detailed itineraries, expert local knowledge and colourful, comprehensive maps to help you plan the perfect visit. Whether you're staying for a few days, weeks or longer, this DK guide will ensure that you see the very best of the region. Enjoy the book and enjoy southwest France.

REASONS TO LOVE DORDOGNE, BORDEAUX AND THE SOUTHWEST COAST

Rich historical heritage. A civilization steeped in culture. World-famous cuisine and wines. Ask anyone from southwest France and you'll hear a different reason why they love this region. Here, we pick a few favourites.

WINE COUNTRY *1*

Bordeaux's wines are known around the world, bringing fame to the region since the age of the Roman Empire. Sip for yourself at one of the many vineyards throughout Gironde.

BASQUE HERITAGE *2*

The unique language, cuisine and architectural style of the Pays Basque is most evident between the chic beach resort of Biarritz and the port city of Bayonne *(p46)*.

3 MOVING DUNES

Fly a kite from the top of a massive sand dune, like those in the Arcachon Basin *(p86)*. Then settle down with a picnic to watch paragliders riding the winds.

CAFÉ CULTURE 4

Lounge away an afternoon with a pastry and a coffee. Soak up the relaxed atmosphere on a rooftop terrace or choose a street-side spot to people-watch.

ROCAMADOUR 5

Dramatically etched into the cliffside, this venerated town offers a humbling climb up steps that have been walked by pilgrims since the 12th century *(p120)*.

FANTASTIC FLAVOURS 6

Fresh oysters from the ocean, black truffles from the forests and seasonal produce from the farms. The richly flavoured treasures here are perfect for foodies looking to indulge *(p30)*.

HISTORIC CATHEDRALS 7

Marvel at the majesty of Gothic, Romanesque and Baroque cathedrals, whose intricate designs chart the region's changing architectural tastes across the ages.

SURF'S UP 8

All along the coastline the sounds of the crashing waves of the Atlantic promise excitement further out to sea, where great swells challenge surfers of every level *(p49)*.

9 CLIFF TOP CASTLES

Once standing guard over the lands of French nobles, many of these castles now have museums demonstrating life as it used to be behind those impenetrable ramparts.

PADDLING THE DORDOGNE 10

For the quintessential Dordogne experience, take to the water. Pack a picnic lunch, hire a canoe and drift along the serene river on a warm summer's day.

PREHISTORIC PAINTINGS 11

Dappled horses, charging bison and hulking mammoths are just a few of the life-sized beasts depicted on the walls of the caves at Lascaux *(p140)*.

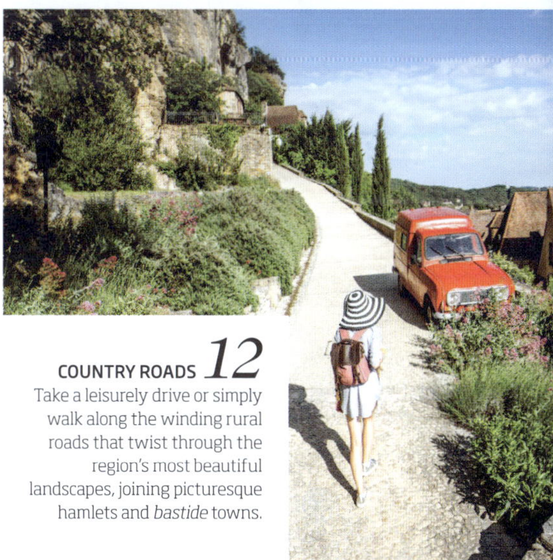

COUNTRY ROADS 12

Take a leisurely drive or simply walk along the winding rural roads that twist through the region's most beautiful landscapes, joining picturesque hamlets and *bastide* towns.

EXPLORE

DORDOGNE, BORDEAUX AND THE SOUTHWEST COAST

This guide divides Dordogne, Bordeaux and the Southwest Coast into seven colour-coded sightseeing areas, as shown on this map. Find out more about each area on the following pages.

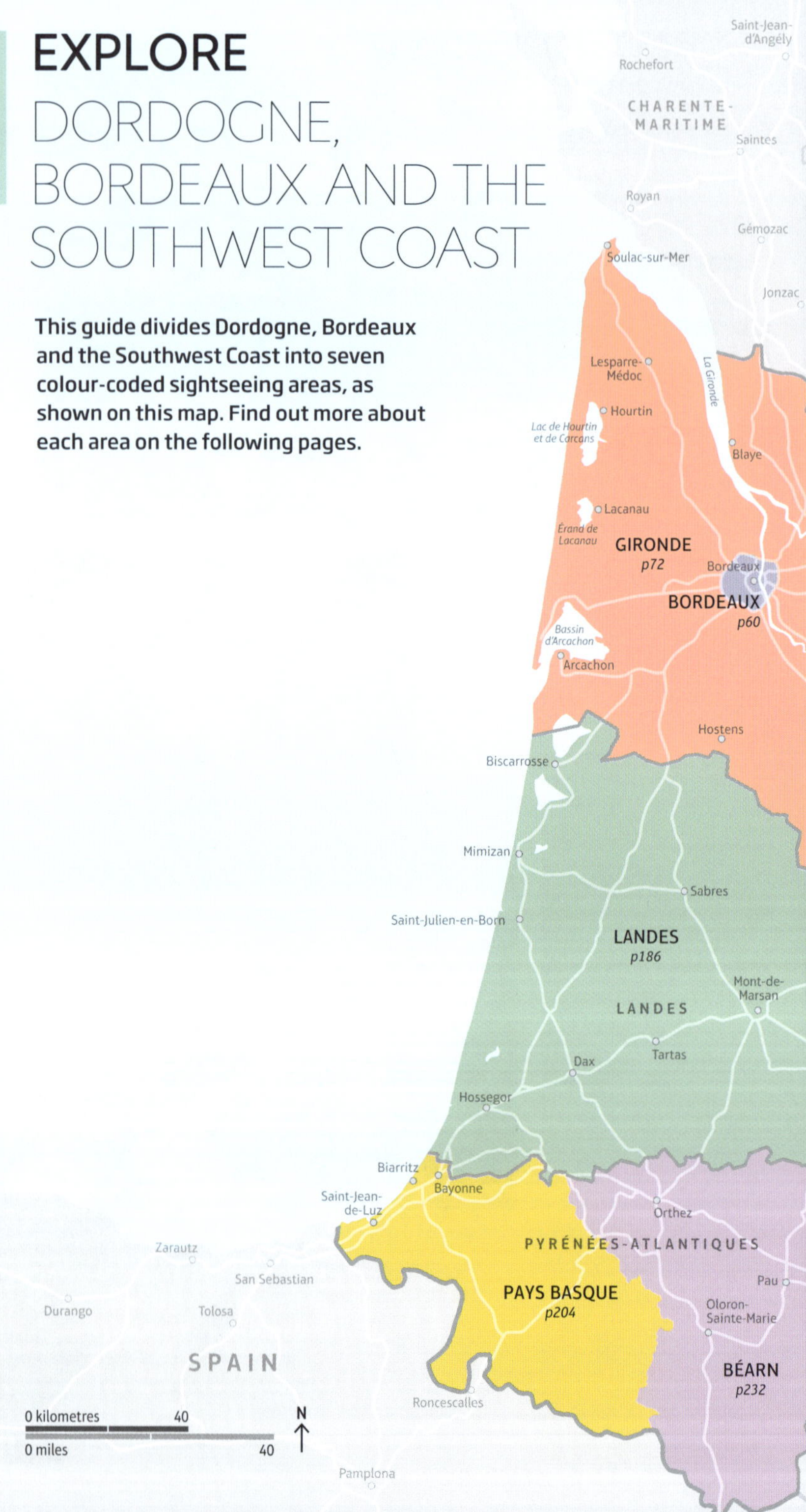

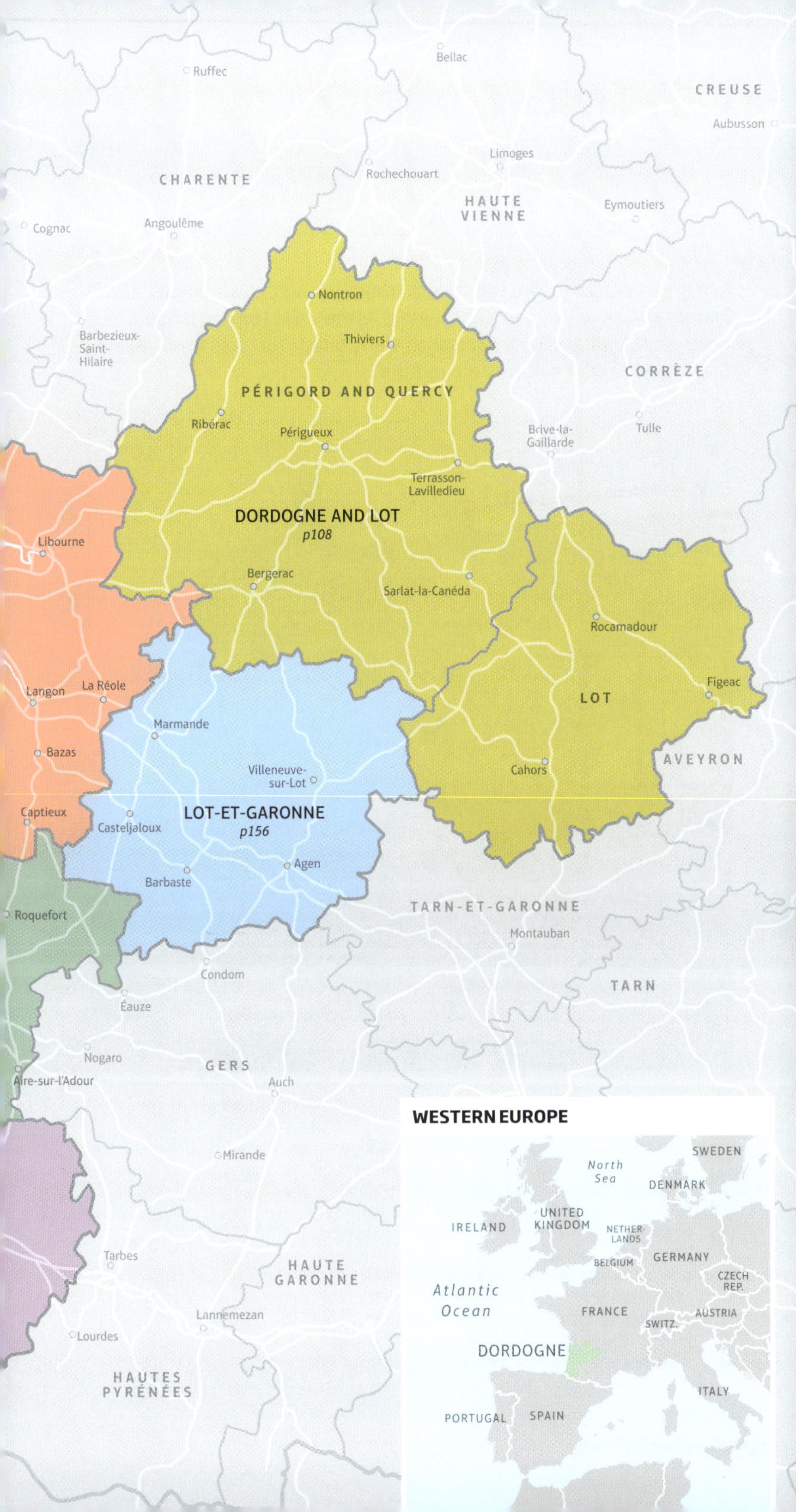

Bellac
Ruffec
CREUSE
Aubusson
Limoges
CHARENTE
Rochechouart
HAUTE VIENNE
Eymoutiers
Cognac
Angoulême
Nontron
Thiviers
Barbezieux-Saint-Hilaire
CORRÈZE
PÉRIGORD AND QUERCY
Ribérac
Périgueux
Brive-la-Gaillarde
Tulle
Terrasson-Lavilledieu
DORDOGNE AND LOT
p108
Libourne
Bergerac
Sarlat-la-Canéda
Rocamadour
Langon
La Réole
Figeac
LOT
Marmande
Bazas
AVEYRON
Villeneuve-sur-Lot
Cahors
Captieux
LOT-ET-GARONNE
p156
Casteljaloux
Agen
Barbaste
Roquefort
TARN-ET-GARONNE
Montauban
Condom
Éauze
TARN
Nogaro
GERS
Aire-sur-l'Adour
Auch
Mirande
Tarbes
HAUTE GARONNE
Lannemezan
Lourdes
HAUTES PYRÉNÉES
WESTERN EUROPE
North Sea
SWEDEN
DENMARK
IRELAND
UNITED KINGDOM
NETHER-LANDS
BELGIUM
GERMANY
CZECH REP.
Atlantic Ocean
FRANCE
SWITZ.
AUSTRIA
DORDOGNE
ITALY
PORTUGAL
SPAIN

GETTING TO KNOW DORDOGNE, BORDEAUX AND THE SOUTHWEST COAST

A region for any season, southwest France is a land of stunning natural beauty and ancient townscapes. Amid its mountain peaks, languorous valleys and endless golden beaches stand beautiful towns and villages that are alive with culture and tradition.

PAGE 60

BORDEAUX

A port city on the Garonne river, Bordeaux has been attracting visitors for centuries, most notably wine-lovers who come to sample the exquisite reds and whites that have been produced here since Roman times. Aside from the many wine bars, the magnificent architecture makes the city a great place to explore on foot. Stroll along the grand boulevards lined with UNESCO Heritage-listed medieval and Neo-Classical buildings. On the way, pop into one of the old riverside warehouses that have been turned into welcoming cafés, and take some time to explore the city's museums.

Best for
Architecture, wine and fine cuisine

Home to
Grand-Théâtre

Experience
Exploring the world of wine at the ultramodern La Cité du Vin, ending with a tasting session and views over the river

PAGE 72

GIRONDE

A wealth of vineyards makes this a must-see destination for œnophiles, who can enjoy wine tastings at stately châteaux all over Gironde. But there's far more to this *département* than its grapes. The verdant countryside is dotted with historic *bastide* towns, which have a relaxed, rural atmosphere that makes southwest France such a rejuvenating leisure spot. If you want to get active, or simply enjoy the outdoors, head to the Arcachon Basin inland sea, home to Europe's highest dune, or to the nearby resort town of Arcachon for seaside fun and oysters.

Best for
Wine country tours and water sports

Home to
Château de Roquetaillade, Saint-Émilion, Château de Cazeneuve, Arcachon Basin, Phare de Cordouan

Experience
Kiteboarding, paragliding and surfing at Arcachon Basin

→

PAGE 108

DORDOGNE AND LOT

The *départements* of the Dordogne and Lot are two of the most beautiful areas in the country, replete with all the experiences you could ask for on a dream vacation in France. Hop in a canoe and drift along the Dordogne river; take a road trip down charming country lanes to sample fine wines and cheese in *bastide* towns and old châteaux; stroll through the medieval city centres of Périgueux and Bergerac. Adventurous travellers can explore ancient caves, while culture and history lovers admire ethereal prehistoric paintings gracing the walls inside.

Best for

Nature, prehistoric cave paintings and medieval towns

Home to

Périgueux, Gardens of the Manoir d'Eyrignac, Les Eyzies-de-Tayac, Rocamadour, Château de Hautefort, Figeac, Château de Castelnaud, Bergerac, Grotte du Pech-Merle and Sarlat-la-Canéda

Experience

Cruising the Dordogne in a traditional wine cargo boat

PAGE 156

LOT-ET-GARONNE

Built upon its limestone plateaux, Lot-et-Garonne is renowned for being home to some of France's most alluring towns and countryside vistas. It's impossible to pass through without making detours to explore some of the many wonderful old *bastide* towns such as Villeréal, enjoy the verdant valleys of the Pays du Dropt, or visit a historic castle like the Château de Bonaguil. Wherever you find yourself, make sure to stop and enjoy all the local delicacies on offer, including decadent truffles and fine wines from local vineyards.

Best for

Countryside, bastide *towns and indulgent food*

Home to

Château de Bonaguil and Agen

Experience

Feasting on truffles on a café terrace in Agen

PAGE 186

LANDES

Known primarily for its beautiful landscapes, Landes' outdoor adventures are bursting with an exciting array of holiday fun. The inland region is dominated by vast pine forests crisscrossed with routes for hiking and cycling, while the coastline is paradise for surfers and sunseekers, who come here for the rolling waves and sweeping sandy shores of Europe's longest string of beaches – the Côte d'Argent. Picturesque villages such as Labastide d'Armagnac appear like a tableau from a storybook, and their markets and restaurants offer up gastronomic treasures like sea bream and goat's cheese.

Best for

Beaches, forests and spas

Home to

Parc Naturel Régional des Landes de Gascogne

Experience

Relaxing in the thermal springs of Dax

→

PAGE 204

PAYS BASQUE

There's a bit of everything on offer to entertain you in the Pays Basque, whether you're after the perfect waves for surfing, a pristine beach for sun-lounging or a glamorous casino for an evening of thrills. This is also France at its most proudly independent, with traditions, festivals and food that make the region's towns fascinating places to explore. Take in trendy Bayonne or stay a while in the chic surf city of Biarritz with its six golden-sand beaches. Absorb its culinary and cultural influences from Gascony and Spain – a blend of heritage and history that makes this region unique.

Best for

Basque culture, seaside resort towns and regional cuisine

Home to

Bayonne, Biarritz

Experience

Sampling the famous jambon de Bayonne *(melt-in-your-mouth cured ham)*

PAGE 232

BÉARN

One of the most sparsely inhabited parts of the country, Béarn contains some of southwest France's most magnificent natural sights. At its centre are the three valleys of Barétous, Ossau and Aspe, with their endless opportunities for biking, hiking, climbing and soaking up breathtaking mountain views in summer. In winter the region becomes a popular place for off-piste skiing. There's even more to see in Béarn's urban landscapes, such as the capital city of Pau, whose grand château, inspiring art museums and grand villas will delight culture and history lovers.

Best for
Mountain views, outdoor adventures

Home to
Pau and Vallée d'Ossau

Experience
Taking the Train d'Artouste up the valley for views of the distinctive Pic du Midi d'Ossau mountain peak

1

3

2

4

←

1 Splashing in the Miroir d'Eau at place de la Bourse.

2 La Cité du Vin.

3 Inside the Grand-Théâtre.

4 Dessert at Le Bouchon Bordelais.

Spend some time in southwest France and you'll find the very best of the country's landscapes, food and culture all in a single region. These itineraries will inspire you to make the most of your visit.

2 DAYS *in Bordeaux*

Day 1

Morning Start at the majestic Cathédrale Saint-André *(p68)* where Eleanor of Aquitaine (one of the most powerful French women of her time) married her first husband, French King Louis VII. Climb its bell tower, the Tour Pey-Berland *(p69)*, for views of the city below. Stroll north along boulevards lined with fine 18th-century buildings, passing by the stone Porte Cailhau *(p67)*, the city's historic gate, built in 1495. Continue on, with the 14th-century Église Saint-Pierre on your left and stop at place de la Bourse, Bordeaux's most popular square *(p66)*, with its famed Miroir d'Eau (Water Mirror, *p67*) sitting beside the Garonne river's edge – a lovely place for a rest and a few photos.

Afternoon After a morning admiring the city's magnificent historic sights, immerse yourself in contemporary art at CAPC *(p71)*, Bordeaux's modern art museum, stunningly located in a former wine warehouse. Treat yourself with a typical Bordelais sticky treat, *canelés*, at the rooftop terrace of the Café du Musée *(cafesdemusees.fr)*. Walk or take the tram line up to La Cité du Vin *(p68)* for one of their themed tours to learn all about the global wine industry.

Evening Return south via the tram to the columned, 18th-century Grand-Théâtre *(p64)* for a dinner of fine regional French cuisine at the on-site Le Quatrième Mur *(quatrieme-mur.com)*, followed by an opera or ballet performance.

Day 2

Morning Wander around the ruins of Palais Gallien *(p66)*, left behind by the Romans who took over Bordeaux in the first century BCE. Grab a picnic breakfast from one of the supermarkets nearby and then walk to place des Quinconces, a grand city square, to take part in the quintessential French pastime of people-watching. Continue your history lesson of Bordeaux and the surrounding region at the Musée d'Aquitaine *(p67)*, which has exhibits dating back to the city's ancient Gaulish inhabitants.

Afternoon To get even better acquainted with Bordeaux wine, book a tour or drive out to one of the many beautiful wineries around the city. The historic Château Pape Clément is a great spot for its wonderful red and white wines *(chateau-pape-clement.fr)*.

Evening Dine at Le Bouchon Bordelais *(bouchon-bordelais.com)*, the perfect Bordeaux bistro to round off your visit, offering a diverse menu of local dishes in a friendly and cosy atmosphere (reservations are recommended). If you're up for a nightcap, head to place du Parlement, a lovely square in the historic heart of Bordeaux, brimming with lively bars and cafés.

1 Bayonne's Old Town.

2 Shale cliffs at Pointe de Sainte-Barbe, outside Saint-Jean-de-Luz.

3 Bayonne ham market stall.

4 Espelette peppers.

3 DAYS

in the Basque Country

Day 1

Morning Start your Basque adventure in Bayonne *(p208)*, beginning with the area around 13th-century Cathédrale Sainte-Marie, known as Notre-Dame-de-Bayonne. Stop for a glass of hot chocolate at one of the many *chocolateries*. Then cross the Nive river to Petit Bayonne to visit the Musee Basque *(p209)*, where you can learn about this vibrant cross-border culture.

Afternoon Enjoy lunch at Tarte Julie *(18 rue Thiers)* then head to Biarritz and spend the afternoon at the Jo Moiraz surf school *(jomoraiz.com)* on the Grande Plage.

Evening Sample the local ham at the Auberge du Cheval Blanc *(au-cheval-blanc.fr)* in Bayonne. Then head to the pier to stay in one of the spacious cabins aboard Péniche Djébelle *(17 quai de Lesseps)*, a small bed-and-breakfast in a barge.

Day 2

Morning Arrive in Saint-Jean-de-Luz *(p214)*, and browse the buzzing market (held on Tuesdays and Fridays) for its charcuterie, cheese and seafood, then wander to the Église St-Jean-Baptiste to admire its glittering altar. Take care to look up – the wooden ship hanging from the ceiling was a gift from Empress Eugénie who was almost shipwrecked off the coast nearby.

Afternoon Cross the Charles de Gaulle bridge to the village of Ciboure *(p228)* and stroll its narrow, hilly streets lined with red-and-white Basque architecture.

Evening Walk up to Pointe de Sainte-Barbe *(p214)* for sensational sunset views, then on to dinner at La Réserve *(1 rue Gaëtan de Bernoville)*. Spend the night in one of its luxurious rooms overlooking the water.

Day 3

Morning Pass through Ainhoa *(p218)* – one of France's official Most Beautiful Villages – on your way to the lively village of Espelette *(p223)*, which is famous for its eponymous red peppers.

Afternoon Visit Saint-Jean-Pied-de-Port *(p224)* – the last French town on the Camino de Santiago de Compostela pilgrimage route. Climb the town's old ramparts for panoramic views and to see the pilgrims trooping up towards the mountains.

Evening Linger in Saint-Jean-Pied-de-Port for a sunset apéritif and then dine at Café Ttipia *(2 place Floquet)*.

1 Medieval Rocamadour.

2 Dining alfresco in Bergerac.

3 Cave paintings at Lascaux.

4 Charcuterie at a market stand in Sarlat-la-Canéda.

5 DAYS
in Dordogne

Day 1

Morning There's no more dramatic way to start a tour of Dordogne than at the stunning town of Rocamadour *(p120)*. Climb all 216 steps of the Grand Escalier to explore the cliff-side Cité Religieuse.

Afternoon Make your way to the Gouffre de Padirac *(p142)*, where a boat trip takes visitors along a stream to the subterranean Lac de la Pluie (Lake of Rain).

Evening Drive to the hilltop town of Domme *(p155)*. The terrace at L'Esplanade hotel-restaurant *(esplanade-perigord.com)* affords wonderful countryside vistas.

Day 2

Morning Set off early to Sarlat-la-Canéda *(p132)*, where each Saturday, the town square fills with market stalls laden with locally grown vegetables and specialities such as walnuts and truffles *(p31)*.

Afternoon Travel into the tranquil Vallée de la Vézère *(p136)*, famed for its prehistoric art. Marvel at the spectacular cave paintings of horses, bison and deer in Lascaux *(p140)*.

Evening Stop for a tasty dinner, pool and spa at Les Glycines *(les-glycines-dordogne.com)*, a bijou hotel in the glorious countryside on the way to your next stop.

Day 3

Morning Just a short drive northwest lies Périgueux *(p112)*, where you can strike out on foot to explore the town's Roman remains as well as a Byzantine-style cathedral.

Afternoon Sample regional favourites at Bistro Le Troquet *(4 rue Notre Dame)*, in the heart of the old town, which offers a great lunchtime menu.

Evening Have an apéritif before heading to La Table de Pouyard *(table-pouyaud.com)* to try truffles and aubergine caviar.

Day 4

Morning Drive west to Brantôme *(p138)*, also called the "Venice of Dordogne". Stroll along the banks of the river Donne and lunch at the renowned Le Moulin de l'Abbaye *(moulinabbaye.com)* at the water's edge.

Afternoon Canoe downriver to Bourdeilles, and stop for lunch at a café in this lovely old village.

Evening Catch a taxi back to Brantôme and dine at Charbonnel *(hotelrestaurant charbonnel.com)*, which offers regional dishes.

Day 5

Morning Journey south to the market town of Bergerac *(p128)*, surrounded by vineyards. The Maison des Vins gives a glimpse into the local wine industry.

Afternoon Drive south to sample more fine wines at the idyllic 16th-century Château de Monbazillac *(chateau-monbazillac.com)*.

Evening Return to Bergerac and visit L'Imparfait *(imparfait.com)* for a *café liégois* (coffee ice cream topped with Chantilly cream) – an indulgent house speciality.

1

2

3

5 DAYS
on the Coast

Day 1

Drive up the Gironde estuary past the fabled vineyards and grand Châteaux of the Médoc *(p106)*, stopping at Château Lamothe Bergeron *(lamothebergeron.com)*, a fairy-tale-like castle dating from the 18th century. Ask for the "tasting and picnic" option for a tour of the castle, followed by a delicious lunch to be savoured right on this lovely estate. Drive north to Le Verdon-sur-Mer and take a boat out to the remarkable 17th-century Phare de Cordouan *(p88)*, a lighthouse known as the "Versailles of the Sea". Head to Soulac-sur-Mer *(p90)* and visit the Romanesque Basilique-Notre-Dame-de-la-Fin-des-Terres. End the day with a seafood dinner and ocean views at the Le Grill Océan *(legrillocean.eatbu.com)*.

Day 2

Tour around the charming 19th-century villas in the Ville d'Hiver in Arcachon *(p86)* and catch a trans-basin boat to see the fascinating birdlife, oyster huts and cabins on stilts in the Arcachon Basin *(p86)*. Take food with you as you climb the golden Dune du Pilat *(p97)* and join the other picnickers at the top for lunch. Drive south down the country roads to enjoy the view along the "Silver Coast", named for its long line of beaches. As well as the glistening ocean to the west, this region is crisscrossed by many waterways – known as *courants* – making their way to the sea. Stop at Étang de Léon *(p193)* and take a tour along this maze of rivers on a *galupe*, a traditional flat-bottomed boat propelled by punt *(bateliers-courant-huchet.fr)*. End your day in Hossegor *(p192)*, where annual surfing competitions are organized on the great waves of the Atlantic Ocean. Watch the sunset and slurp on fresh oysters at one of the shacks on the northern end of Lac d'Hossegor.

Day 3

Double-back and head up north again for a relaxing morning in Mimizan *(p192)*, which has beautiful woodlands with miles of cycling routes for a refreshing morning ride, as well as plenty of pristine beaches for swimming and sunbathing afterwards.

1 Château Lamothe Bergeron.

2 Seaside terrace at the Arcachon Basin.

3 Les Halles market in Bayonne.

4 Surfing in Hossegor.

5 Rocher de la Vierge, Biarritz.

6 Port at Saint-Jean-de-Luz.

When you've soaked up some sun, head down to Bayonne *(p208)* and enjoy a leisurely tea or coffee with a sweet pastry at Mokofin *(mokofin.com)*. Bayonne is a great place to explore on foot, with vignettes of history and character found all over – from the ruins of Château-Vieux to the cosmopolitan Quartier Saint-Esprit. Enjoy tapas and drinks at the riverside Le Bistrot Itsaski *(lebistrotitsaski.com)* to round off your evening in this attractive inland port city.

Day 4

The covered market of Les Halles along the river is overflowing with Basque Country goods for breakfast. Walk off a full belly along the old city ramparts, which have been converted into pretty gardens. Next, head south to explore the Art Deco splendours and beautiful coastline in glitzy Biarritz *(p216)* – one of Europe's most popular resort towns since the days of Napoléon III. Take a stroll along the beachfront promenade to see L'Église Sainte-Eugénie, the casino, chic boutiques and oceanside cafés for a lunch of *fruits de mer* (a platter of fresh seafood and shellfish). End your walk at the Phare de Biarritz, a lighthouse located in the middle of a park, that makes the perfect setting for a gorgeous sunset view. For an indulgent Basque dinner – such as lobster-stuffed pasta with truffle sauce – try Iqori at the Regina Biarritz hotel *(hotelregina-biarritz.com)*, which has direct views of the lighthouse nearby.

Day 5

Start your morning with a walk from the Rocher de la Vierge, a rocky point reached via a metal footbridge. Then surf the waves at Biarritz's famous Grande Plage – or pretend to surf with a virtual reality headset at Cité de l'Océan *(citedelocean.com)*. Then hop in the car and carry on south along the coast to Hendaye *(p214)*, and the spectacular Château d'Abbadia, which is open till late in the summer and hosts regular evening events. Later, join the queue of locals at the Grillerie du Port *(quai du Maréchal Leclerec)* in Saint-Jean-de-Luz *(p214)*, for grilled sardines freshly caught that morning.

FARM VISITS

Caviar de Neuvic
La Grande Veyssiere
caviar-de-neuvic.com
Tours of the sturgeon-breeding facilities and caviar tastings.

Ferme de Cor
Saint-Avit-Sénieur
fermedecor.e-monsite.com
A 100-year-old, family-run organic farm specializing in saffron and walnuts.

Terre d'Escargots
Puybazet
05 53 53 73 14
A farm tour dedicated to the quintessential French delicacy: snails.

Fresh oysters, a delicacy of the Arcachon Basin

FLAVOURFUL FOOD

Southwest France might be famous for its wines, but for foodies it is a gastronomic paradise. Whether in a rustic farmhouse or a sumptuous Michelin-starred dining room, you'll find delectable dishes and regional specialities to indulge in for every meal of the day.

From the Farm

It's true farm-to-table dining in this region, with vast green pastures making up a huge portion of the landscape. Lamb often comes from Pauillac *(p93)* and is slowly braised and stewed; ducks and geese, mostly for *confit de canard*, are raised in Landes; and *jambon de Bayonne* is produced from pigs that roam around the Adour river basin in the Basque Country.

Thinly sliced *jambon de Bayonne* (Bayonne ham), a speciality from the Pays Basque

Fruits de Mer

"Fruits of the sea" is the perfect description of the ocean and freshwater harvests from this region. All the French classics are in abundance, but keep an eye out for menus offering local delicacies. Oysters are gathered from the pure, clear waters of the Arcachon Basin *(p86)*. Sturgeon, which thrive in the estuaries, are farmed for eggs to produce caviar. And in the Pays Basque, small squid are stuffed with spicy, sweet red peppers.

INSIDER TIP
Truffle Hunting

Sarlat-la-Canéda's truffle market is held on Saturday mornings from November to early March. Here, you can shop and enquire about good recipes; however, the vendors keep the truffle locations a closely guarded secret.

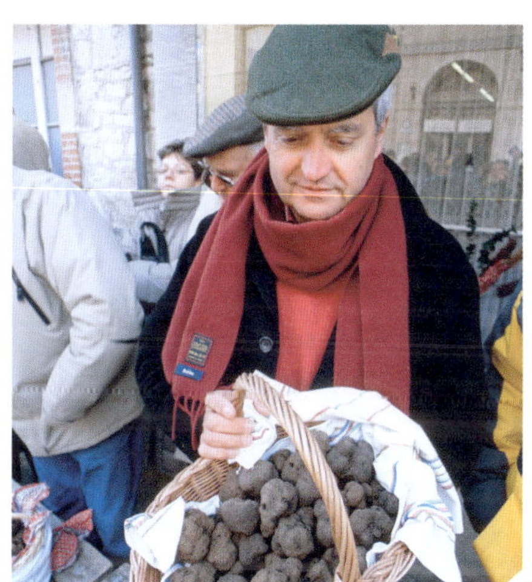

Black Diamonds

The black Périgord truffle, a native species of the forests of the Dordogne, is a highly prized aromatic mushroom coveted by chefs and locals alike. Its complex flavours are used to enhance local dishes such as roasted meats or omelettes topped with truffle shavings. During truffle season, from November to March, these little black treasures are sold at markets in villages such as Lalbenque *(p151)* and Sarlat-la-Canéda *(p132)* at astronomical prices.

Truffles at a market in the village of Lalbenque

Room for More

While the region is best known for its savoury dishes, there are plenty of sweet treats on offer, too. Local desserts include *canelés de Bordeaux* - small fluted cakes with a soft, moist centre and caramelized shell - and ewe's-milk cheese from the Vallée d'Ossau *(p240)* served with black cherry jam.

→

Delicious and moist *canelés de Bordeaux*

Did You Know?

Research suggests that spotted horses, painted at Pech-Merle, were alive during the Ice Age.

PREHISTORIC ART

Southwest France is home to some of the best-preserved prehistoric art on the continent, especially in the Vallée de la Vézère. The paintings and sculptures on display at Lascaux and Les-Eyzies-de-Tayac offer a remarkable insight into how these early artists viewed their place in the world.

Incredible Carvings and Sculptures

Discovered in 1909, the rock shelter of Abri du Cap Blanc, just outside Les Eyzies-de-Tayac *(p118)*, is home to a life-sized frieze of horses sculpted in the rock. Flint tools found at the site are on display at the on-site museum, which also shows a replica of the Magdalenian Woman and several "Venuses". Nearby in Laugerie Basse, the Visitor Centre displays finely carved throwing spears found in the area, and children can borrow a tablet to have a virtual "excavation" as they roam the site.

Frieze of a grazing horse, Abri du Cap Blanc

Inspiring Cave Paintings

Southwest France boasts an extraordinary concentration of prehistoric art, some around 20,000 years old. Visit a reconstruction of the Lascaux cave *(p140)*, where interactive displays re-create the original decorated cave's atmosphere and paintings. At Grotte du Pech-Merle *(p130)*, the "spotted horses" and handprints make the artists seem spine-tinglingly close. Learn the context at the Musée National de la Préhistoire *(p118)*.

← Exploring cave paintings in the lit-up Lascaux cave replica

ART FOR ART'S SAKE?

No one knows the exact significance of the cave paintings. They were once believed to be part of a ceremony to invoke a successful hunt, but the common view now is that they were painted in a trance as part of a shamanic ritual. Or they may simply have been attempts to capture fleeting beauty.

→ A room of reconstructions of Lascaux cave

Epic Etchings and Sketchings

Etchings, carvings and sketchings, created by the stroke of a few lines, are seen in stunning detail at Grotte de Pech-Merle *(p130)*. Look out for etchings of female silhouettes and mammoths, and footprints chiselled into the rock. The Grotte de Rouffignac in the Vallée de la Vézère *(p136)*, meanwhile, is ideal for those with children: an underground electric train journeys through the caves, stopping at various points to reveal 13,000-year-old engravings, many depicting mammoths. The highlight is the final chamber, the ceiling of which is decorated with animals.

↑ Line drawing of a woolly mammoth at the Grotte de Rouffignac

▷ Tranquil Rivers

More than 3,000 km (1,860 miles) of rivers and streams crisscross the region, so take to the water for a fun way to see the countryside from a new perspective. The Dordogne stretches through some of the most beautiful villages in France, and the Vézère tributary forms a valley that includes some famous prehistoric sites *(p136)*.

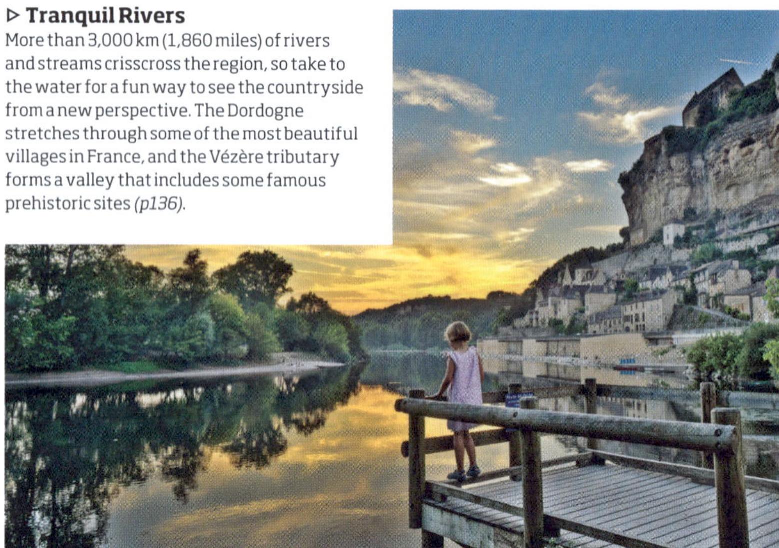

STUNNING LANDSCAPES

Vast forests stretching out beside pristine beaches, broad rivers meandering through sleepy valleys, and medieval villages clinging to the slopes of the Pyrénées – observing the ever-changing scenery is one of the real pleasures of a stay in southwest France.

◁ Verdant Forests

This region is renowned for its beautiful, peaceful forests. Soak up the dappled sunlight under the greenery while enjoying a simple picnic lunch or – even better – a full-blown camping trip. For truly unspoiled nature, visit the Parc Naturel Régional des Landes de Gascogne *(p190)*, a vast protected area of forest, wetlands and coastline.

Did You Know?

The Forêt des Landes is the largest human-made forest in Western Europe.

▷ Windswept Dunes

The sand dunes along the Atlantic coast stretch over 200 km (124 miles), rising and falling past sandy beaches, marshy basins and lush forests. The most prominent among them is the Dune du Pilat *(p97)*, the highest and largest dune in Europe. Picnic on the peak and watch how the sea breeze moulds the ever-shifting sands.

◁ Small-Town Charm

The towns dotted across the landscape seem just as much a natural part of the land as the rivers and forests. The weathered stone buildings and cobblestone streets feel organic and alive with history and personality. Some, such as Les Eyzies-de-Tayac *(p118)*, look like they're formed right out of the surrounding stone cliffs, while others, including Pujols *(p168)*, are recognized as some of France's "Plus Beaux Villages" (Most Beautiful Villages).

▷ Beckoning Coastline

The Atlantic Ocean meets France along a diverse coastline. The Cap Ferret headland curls around the Arcachon Basin *(p86)*, creating an inland bay surrounded by tiny towns, marshes and oyster farms. An almost unbroken line of white sandy beaches runs from Biscarrosse *(p192)* to Capbreton *(p195)* - some of them deserted, and others bustling with surfers, bathers and world-class resorts built in the dunes.

◁ Breathtaking Mountains

Adventurous travellers can hike up into the Pyrénées for incredible views across the Vallée d'Ossau landscape *(p240)*. But for those who don't want the trek, the mountains' distinctive peaks can be seen from as far away as Pau *(p236)*, and there are hilltop views all over the region, with castles such as Château de Castelnaud *(p126)* perched high above the valleys they once ruled.

Rainy-Day Fun

If the weather lets you down, there's still plenty of fun to be found indoors. The Aquarium du Périgord Noir and L'Aquarium Biarritz are excellent choices, tying in exhibits on local geography and wildlife with all the fun of an aquarium. The region's many fascinating prehistoric sights are also a highlight in any weather, as are accompanying museums such as the cliff-hugging Musée National de la Préhistoire *(p118)* with its life-size mammoth displays.

→

L'Aquarium Biarritz, with exhibits on local marine life

FAMILY FUN

It might be all wine tastings and fine art museums for the grown-ups, but kids can have just as much fun in southwest France. With a mild climate, fascinating history and beautiful natural environments to explore, this region is packed full of adventures to discover together.

Time to Unwind

When you're exploring the towns of southwest France and your little ones need a break, you'll have a choice of beaches, green river banks, public gardens and old town squares where they can let off some steam. Even in the busy city of Bordeaux, the Miroir d'Eau on place de la Bourse *(p67)* is great for splashing around in on a hot day, while the Jardin Public has lakes and a vintage carousel.

→

Relaxing in Bordeaux's Jardin Public

INSIDER TIP
Market Meals

Evening summer markets like those in Sarlat-la-Canéda are great for picking up family meals of fresh local food - just be sure to bring your own utensils, plates and cups to enjoy your feast.

Exciting History Lessons

Fabulous castles from every era are perched on hilltops across southwest France. While adults can enjoy the architecture, furnishings and history, there's also lots to entertain the kids – such as knights in shining armour and live catapult demonstrations at Château de Castelnaud *(p126)*. For an even earlier history immersion, Préhisto Parc in the fascinating Vallée de l'Homme *(p137)* has giant dioramas of Neanderthals and ancient beasts, as well as hands-on workshops in constructing stone tools.

← Catapults on the ramparts at Château de Castelnaud

FAMILY CAMPSITES

Cabanes de la Romaningue
Pompignaci
cabanes.laromaningue.fr
Glamp in a wooden caravan, zipline-accessed treehouses and bubble tents.

Camping le Paradis
Saint-Léon-sur-Vézère
le-paradis.fr
Luxury safari-style tents and cosy cottages set around a swimming pool by the Vézère river.

Camping Aux Couleurs du Ferret
Lege-Cap-Ferret
campingcapferret.com
A forested campsite with stilted cabins near the Atlantic coast and Arcachon Basin.

↑ Bathers enjoying the pristine sandy beach and waves at Hossegor

Back to Nature

The Dordogne is wonderful for wading, with safe, accessible beaches to be found up and down the river. There are also many boat companies in the area if you want to head out on the water. For seaside destinations, you'll be spoiled for choice, but for something picturesque with local character, visit Hossegor *(p192)*.

↑ La Cité du Vin in the wine capital Bordeaux

Celebrating the Wine Region

When touring the wine country in southwest France, you'll come across many old estates, such as the Château Lanessan *(p92)*, where the historic and prosperous story of the wine industry is evident in the beautiful old buildings that overlook local vineyards. But for a modern twist on the region's wine legacy, visit the jaw-dropping La Cité du Vin *(p68)*. Home to tasting laboratories and workshops, this building on the Garonne river looks like a slosh of wine poured into a champagne flute.

AMAZING ARCHITECTURE

Encompassing châteaux, grand cathedrals, Art Deco icons and modern masterpieces, the architecture of southwest France embodies the heart and soul of the region, and an architecture tour is both an adventure through history and an introduction to local life and culture.

Lords of the Castles

This region is full of beautifully preserved castles perched on hilltops high above the lands over which they once presided. The châteaux here are a unique blend of both English and French styles and history, as the region changed hands between the two throughout the Middle Ages. Château de Bonaguil *(p160)* was the last fortified castle built during the region's English era, while Château de Hautefort *(p122)* is a classic French design. In both cases, the fairy-tale-like feel is evocative of the history and splendour behind each estate.

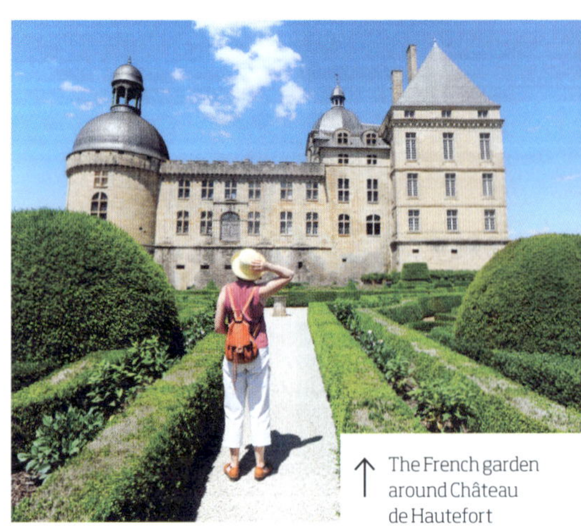

↑ The French garden around Château de Hautefort

18th-Century Bordeaux

In 2007, UNESCO protected almost half of Bordeaux *(p61)* because of its intrinsic architectural value – the world's first city of its size to be awarded this distinction. The city is full of remarkable structures, meaning a straightfoward stroll can end up feeling like a photoshoot as you try to snap the perfect picture of each sight. The Pont de Pierre bridge is a good place to start, before enjoying the Quays, the Port de la Lune and the shopfronts of the old town. Visit the Grand-Théâtre *(p64)* in the evening to see it illuminated in a golden glow.

The Neo-Classical Grand-Théâtre, a highlight of Bordeaux

The Art Deco City

When it comes to early 20th-century architecture, few places capture the imagination like Biarritz *(p216)*. It may have a fabulous string of beaches, but the real pull is in the stylish hotels and venues constructed in the late 19th century. To enjoy the city's Art Deco magic, check in to the Regina Biarritz *(hotelregina-biarritz.com)* for a Belle Époque vibe.

Art Deco buildings along the coast in Biarritz

Bastide Towns

Southwest France is scattered with old fortified towns known as *bastide* towns. Locals are passionate about preserving their medieval townscapes, so there are dozens of examples still to be found across the region - such as Monflanquin *(p172)* and Eymet *(p149)* which have ramparts, arcades, half-timbered houses and picturebook-pretty cobblestone squares.

Traditional half-timbered houses in an old town square in Monflanquin

Listen Up

For many, Nouvelle-Aquitaine nightlife revolves around music. There are concerts to be discovered almost every night at big city venues such as Pau's modern temple to the arts, Zénith de Pau *(zenith-pau.com)*. But you'll also find events popping up everywhere from small churches to the gardens of the Médoc's wine estates. For festivals, don't miss Le Grand Pruneau Show in Agen *(p162)*, a music festival to honour the plum harvest, and Nuits Lyriques de Marmande, a grand singing competition in Marmande *(p176)*.

Florent Pagny performing at Zénith de Pau

CAPTIVATING CULTURE

Never mind the history and outdoor pursuits – this region is just as great for exciting nightlife and cultural events. Head to the vibrant coastal casinos or explore a stunning art gallery. There are myriad bars and nightclubs, of course, but it's also a hotbed of fun festivals, concerts and live music venues.

Hey, Big Spender

Casinos here are different to the glorified arcades of Las Vegas. The chic and glamorous venues on the Atlantic coast evoke the atmosphere of the 1920s when these resorts began to boom, and also showcase some of the area's finest buildings. Come to Arcachon *(p86)* for a casino inside a 19th-century seafront castle, and stop by Casino Barrière in Biarritz *(p216)* for Art Deco glamour.

→

The seafront Casino d'Arcachon

The World's a Stage

There are so many performing arts festivals in this region that it's hard to know how to make time for all the highlights. Some of the biggest and best events are held in July, such as Le Festival des Jeux du Théâtre in Sarlat-la-Canéda *(p132)* - a hotbed of amateur dramatics. Mimos *(p51)*, also in July and August, is Périgueux's fun, contemporary mime festival, with circus and clown acts for people of all ages. Likewise, Le Festival Arte Flamenco in Mont-de-Marsan *(p199)* welcomes first-timers and wannabe dancers with open arms. Check online before you go to find out what events are taking place near you during your stay.

Performers at the Mimos festival in Périgueux

TOP 3 JULY JAZZ FESTIVALS

Jazz in Sanguinet
A four-day festival that focuses on all types of jazz, but also includes blues, gospel, rock and soul music *(jazzin sanguinet.fr)*.

Jazz in Souillac
This week-long festival, which hosts big jazz names, will celebrate its 50th year in July *(souillacenjazz.fr)*.

Andernos Jazz Festival
The Bassin d'Arcachon provides the backdrop for this three-day event. All concerts are free *(andernos-jazz-festival.fr)*.

Admiring classical paintings in Bordeaux's Musée des Beaux-Arts

Glorious Galleries

France's artistic legacy is world famous, and no trip here would be complete without some time spent perusing its incredible galleries. For some of the best, you'll want to visit Bordeaux. Here, the Musée des Beaux-Arts *(p67)* provides a wonderful overview of art from the Renaissance to the modern era, while the Musée d'Aquitaine *(p67)* celebrates the region's ancient art scene, with Roman statues and prehistoric sculptures.

FOR HISTORY BUFFS

Delve deeper into this corner of southwest France to discover a long and colourful history. Stories abound at every turn, from cave art created by our ancient ancestors to vestiges of wars fought long ago. Take a tour, spend time in a museum or simply follow your feet to find out more.

TOP 3 HISTORY TOURS

Bordeaux
bordeaux-guided-tours.com
Splurge on this guided tour of the city's viticulture history and beautiful architecture.

Les Eyzies-de-Tayac
There are archaeological sites here dating back 400,000 years, and many of them offer tours *(p118)*.

Lascaux
The most dazzling prehistoric cave art in Europe, with tours offered at Lascaux II and Lascaux IV *(p140)*.

Magnificent Museums

No matter what era of French history sparks your curiosity, you'll undoubtedly find a museum to enjoy somewhere in the region. Castles often include exhibits and original decor from their heyday, while even rural towns may have a venue to regale visitors with stories of local history and culture, such as the Musée du Béret in Nay *(p247)*. For a great all-encompassing history tour, Périgueux's Musée d'Art et d'Archéologie du Périgord *(p113)* underlines the region's rich prehistoric legacy.

→ Artists sketching replica tombs at the Musée d'Aquitaine in Bordeaux

War-time Memorials

Southwest France has seen more than its fair share of wars over the centuries *(p52)*, and there are many battlefields and memorials for those keen on military history. Croix de Mouguerre, near Bayonne, is dedicated to the soldiers who fought with Napoléon in 1813. For World War II sights, BETASOM in Bordeaux was a submarine base built by the Axis Powers *(bordeaux.fr/o271/base-ousetmarine)* and Oradour-sur-Glane was where civillians were brutally killed.

→ Commemorating a tragic World War II massacre in Oradour-sur-Glane

↑ Navarrenx, a *bastide* town in the southern region of Béarn

Step Back in Time

History in southwest France isn't limited to museum displays. Head outside and walk along the streets of a fortified medieval town such as Navarrenx *(p245)* to get a feel for what the region was like in the Middle Ages. You may find Roman ruins popping up unexpectedly in modern city streets, as at the Palais Gallien in Bordeaux *(p66)*. Prehistoric cave paintings abound in the Dordogne, and further south on Monte Argibel *(p222)* there's a stone circle whose purpose is shrouded in mystery.

Did You Know?

Only about 10 per cent of the wine produced in the region is white.

Red-wine tasting in a beautiful vineyard setting ↑

WINE LOVERS' PARADISE

Southwest France is famous for its wines, with Bordeaux widely regarded as the wine capital of the world. Œnophiles will have plenty to discover here, as each area produces a unique character and flavour according to the blend of grapes, the soil, the climate and local processes.

Brilliant Whites

Complex and full of character, with both dry and sweet options, the crisp, white wines produced in this region come from a blend of Sémillon, Sauvignon Blanc, Muscadelle and Sauvignon Gris grapes. White Bordeaux are served cool but not too cold, and are often sipped as an apéritif or to accompany fresh seafood dishes. To learn more, there's no better starting point than Château Haut Brion *(haut-brion.com)*, which has been involved in wine production since Roman times.

→ A glass of Château Carbonnieux, from the Pessac-Léognan subregion of Graves

Legendary Reds

Intense and bold, with rich aromatic bouquets, the reds produced in the Bordeaux region come from a blend of several grape varieties whose names are now world famous, including Cabernet Sauvignon, Merlot and Malbec. The blend varies depending on whether the winery is located on the left bank or the right bank of the Garonne estuary. Red Bordeaux are decanted for about half an hour, served slightly below room temperature, and are perfect companions to roasted lamb and duck dishes, or even just with a slice of Ossau-Iraty cheese. For a lesson in Bordeaux reds, book a tour and wine tasting at Château Pichon Baron *(pichonbaron.com)*. This grand estate, complete with a turreted castle, has been producing some of the finest red wines since the 17th century.

←

Vines of Cabernet Sauvignon grapes in Bordeaux

A WINE LOVER'S ITINERARY OF THE GIRONDE

A tour of some of the Gironde's top wineries will leave you with a better understanding of these world-famous wines. Start at the historic Neo-Gothic Château Pape Clément *(216 avenue Dr Nancel Penard, Pessac)* for their 5 Senses Tour, which will take you all around the stunning winery and vineyard. In the afternoon, pay a visit to the 16th-century Château de Reignac *(38 chemin de Reignac, Saint-Loubès)* to complete your first lessons in œnology. Tastings are held here in a glasshouse built by Gustav Eiffel, the designer of the Eiffel Tower in Paris.

And for Dessert

Produced from Sémillon, Sauvignon Blanc and Muscadelle grapes, Sauternes is the region's famous sweet white wine. A type of fungus causes the grapes to shrivel and sweeten, and notes of apricot, caramel and citrus can be expected. Enjoy after a meal with fruit tarts and cheeses.

→

A classic French dessert of cheese, nuts and grapes, accompanied by a glass of white wine

BASQUE CULTURE

The Basque people possess an intriguing blend of culture, tradition and language that's utterly their own. In a region long squabbled over by their Spanish and French neighbours, red is the colour of their spirit of independence, and you'll see it everywhere.

Fêtes de Bayonne

The capital of the French Basque Country is Bayonne *(p208)*, and each July the city comes alive with five days of festivals that see the red-and-white-clad locals party hard. Join the throngs lining the streets to watch parades through the city, dance and sing along at concerts, cheer on pelota matches (a Basque ball game) and rejoice at the eruption of fireworks each night.

Locals celebrating the Fêtes de Bayonne

Bastions of Basque Life

For a true Basque experience, start with Bayonne *(p208)*, the capital of Basque culture and home to the Musée Basque *(p209)* for an overview on local tradition and history. Then dip into one of the border towns such as Ainhoa *(p218)*, or visit one of the fishing villages that dot the coast, such as Saint-Jean-Pied-de-Port *(p224)*, to dine on bowls of *marmitako* (fish stew, typically tuna), eaten to the sound of pelota balls being smacked across a court. If there is only time to visit one Basque town, make it Saint-Jean-de-Luz *(p214)*. This proud fishing port, with its red timber-framed architecture set against the breathtaking backdrop of the Pyrénées, is a quintessential Basque gem.

←

Fishing and pleasure boats bobbing in front of Saint-Jean-de-Luz's charming and colourful harbourfront

PELOTA

A traditional Basque ballcourt game, pelota pits players against each other using their bare hands, different kinds of bats or a *chistera* - a narrow curved basket on the end of a glove. It can be played in a number of ways, generally against a wall, like a cross between squash and handball; you'll see a high-walled court or *fronton* in most Basque towns and villages.

→

Axoa aux piments d'Espelettes, a typically spicy Basque veal stew

Zingy Cuisine

The food in this region is distinctly different from the rest of French cuisine. Basque dishes are generally spicy, with their central ingredient being the *piment d'Espelette*, a variety of red pepper. You'll see strings of these peppers adorning buildings in the region, but most evidently in the village of Espelette *(p223)*, from which they take their name.

→

Stringing Espelette peppers into *ristras* (chains) to dry

Pic du Soum Couy on the cross-country GR10 footpath in the Pyrénées

Hit the Road Jacques
With over 100 hiking trails and around 80 pilgrimage routes, it's well worth packing your hiking boots when you head for south-west France. For hardened hikers, there are four soul-stirring stages of France's cross-country GR10, taking those with an unbendable spirit from the Pays Basque to Béarn. Easier routes along the coast include a hike from Hendaye *(p214)* to Saint-Jean-de-Luz *(p214)*, or ambling along the cape around the Arcachon Basin *(p86)*.

THE GREAT OUTDOORS

To make the most of this region's sweeping beaches, mountain peaks and river-streaked forests, you'll need to get active. Be it surfing, backcountry skiing, cycling or paddling the languid turns of the Dordogne, it's never been easier or more fun to head back to nature.

The Alternative Tour de France
With an enviable backdrop of epic hills and deep valleys to discover, it's no surprise the French have a love affair with mountain biking and road touring in southwest France. A standout for those seeking a lesser-known playground is the Vallée d'Aspe *(p248)* in the Pyrénées, where hire shops and self-catering *gîtes* are particularly well set up for those on cycling holidays. Other highlights include a trip from Pau *(p236)* to the Col du Tourmalet (a Tour de France favourite) and from Bordeaux *(p60)* to Pauillac *(p93)*, with a well-earned break in Médoc's vineyards.

Cycling the Col du Tourmalet, a mountain pass in the Pyrénées

Mountain Heights

While the rest of France descends upon Mont Blanc and the Alps, savvy locals keep the Pyrénées to themselves. Climbers, hikers, skiers and stargazers all have reasons to adore the Pic du Midi d'Ossau *(p241)*, home to one of the world's highest observatories and accessible by cable car from La Mongie. Surprises lie in store elsewhere, particularly for off-piste skiing at lesser-known La Pierre-Saint-Martin or Artouste, and at Gourette for cycle tours, trail running and via ferrata climbing in summer.

INSIDER TIP

Hiking Trails

Be sure to plan ahead before exploring new terrain. Local tourist offices are a great resource, so ask there for trail maps, route ideas and advice on weather and terrain.

Off-piste skiing on the Pic du Midi d'Ossau

On the Water

There's a perfect marriage of expert thrills and beginner excitement on Nouvelle-Aquitaine's coastline, where you can hop from scuba kit or sea kayak to surf gear or kite board. For those who don't want to deal with the Atlantic waves, the massive Arcachon Basin *(p86)* has calmer waters for enjoying a bit of seaside fun.

Surfing on the Atlantic coast in Gironde

The River Less Travelled

Hire a canoe for a few hours and it's easy to see why there's an obsession in the Dordogne with getting out for a paddle under the dappled shade of the river banks. Upstream is far wilder than the more mellow, châteaux-strewn curves towards Beynac-et-Cazenac. For a guided tour, book a trip on a traditional *gabare* (flat-bottomed cargo boat) - particularly around Bergerac *(p128)*.

Paddling on the Dordogne past the town of La Roque-Gageac

A YEAR IN DORDOGNE, BORDEAUX AND THE SOUTHWEST COAST

JANUARY

△ **Maskarada** *(1st Sun in Jan–1st Thu in Lent).* The Pays Basque's odyssey of drama, dance and poetry.

Truffle Festival *(mid–late Jan).* The black Périgord truffle is celebrated in its home town of Sarlat-la-Canéda with huge feasts.

FEBRUARY

△ **Jumping International de Bordeaux** *(early Feb).* Top-level equestrianism, show jumping and plenty of horsing around.

Fête des Boeufs Gras *(last Thu before Lent).* A cattle beauty contest in Bazas, followed by a 13th-century-style feast before Lent.

MAY

Festival Jazz Pourpre Périgord *(early–mid-May).* Get ready for a string of concerts, dinners and dancing at this jazzathon in Bergerac.

△ **Fête de l'Agneau** *(mid-May).* Wine by the barrel, award-winning grilled lamb and sheep dog demos in Pauillac.

JUNE

Pride *(mid-Jun).* Cities around the region, including Biarritz and Bordeaux, host LGBTQ+ Pride events.

△ **Fête du Fleuve** *(late Jun).* Ships ahoy on Bordeaux's Garonne river, with fireworks, concerts and masted brigs to explore.

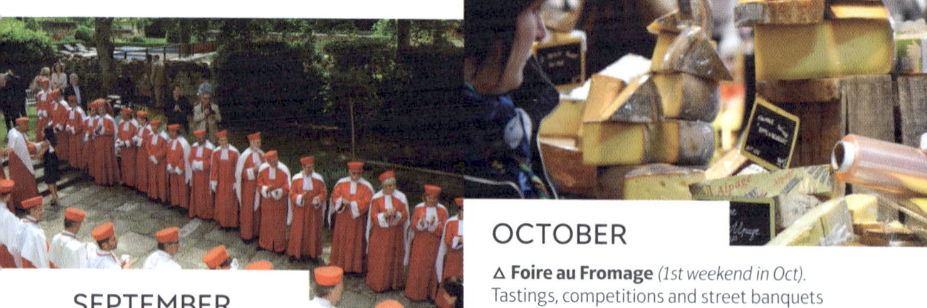

SEPTEMBER

△ **Jurade** *(late Sep).* A festival of wine in Saint-Émilion, celebrating harvest vintages chosen by the town's wine council.

OCTOBER

△ **Foire au Fromage** *(1st weekend in Oct).* Tastings, competitions and street banquets dedicated to Laruns' zingy sheep's cheese.

Fête du Piment *(late Oct).* Espelette goes all out for its sweet chilli pepper during this two-day festival.

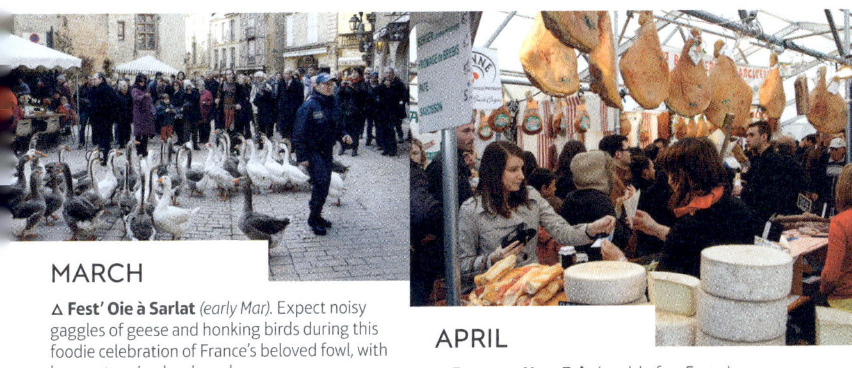

MARCH

△ Fest' Oie à Sarlat *(early Mar)*. Expect noisy gaggles of geese and honking birds during this foodie celebration of France's beloved fowl, with banquets using local produce.

Bi Harriz Lau Xori *(late Mar)*. Film, music and theatre, all delivered in the Pays Basque's unique tongue – Euskara.

JULY

Festival d'Art Flamenco *(early Jul)*. Mont-de-Marsan embraces its Spanish influence with classical guitar jams and moonlight dance-offs.

△ Fêtes de Bayonne *(late Jul)*. France's largest festival features five days of dances, parades and fireworks.

Mimos *(Jul–Aug)*. Circus acts, clowning and puppetry at the Périgueux mime festival.

NOVEMBER

△ Festival du Film de Sarlat *(early Nov)*. A cinema celebration focusing on the next generation of film-makers.

Festival International du Film d'Histoire à Pessac *(mid-Nov)*. Films, documentaries, debates and discussions all focused on one thing: history.

APRIL

△ Bayonne Ham Fair *(week before Easter)*. Expect four days of feasting on one of France's most famous hams.

Fête des Soufflaculs *(after Easter)*. The Nontron carnival sees nightgown-wearing locals chase spirits away – using medieval bellows.

Festival des Vallées et des Bergers *(late Apr–early May)*. Concerts in Oloron-Sainte-Marie to celebrate the Béarnese dialect.

AUGUST

△ Caraïbos Lacanau Pro *(mid-Aug)*. Surf's up! The five-day World Surf League is held in Lacanau.

Féria de Dax *(mid-Aug)*. Parades and concerts in Dax, plus plenty of red scarf waving (a local festival tradition).

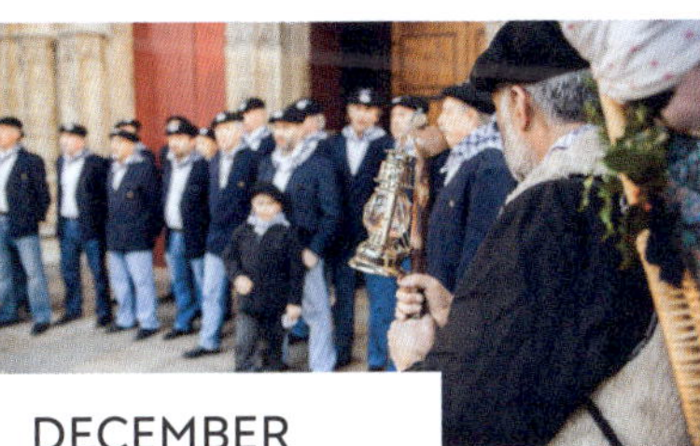

DECEMBER

Journée Portes Ouvertes en Jurançon *(mid-Dec)*. Join 50 estates, 50 winemakers and 50 parties for this annual Pyrénées spectacle.

△ Olentzero *(24 Dec)*. The festive figure of Olentzero drops off gifts for children – an inseparable part of Basque Christmas culture.

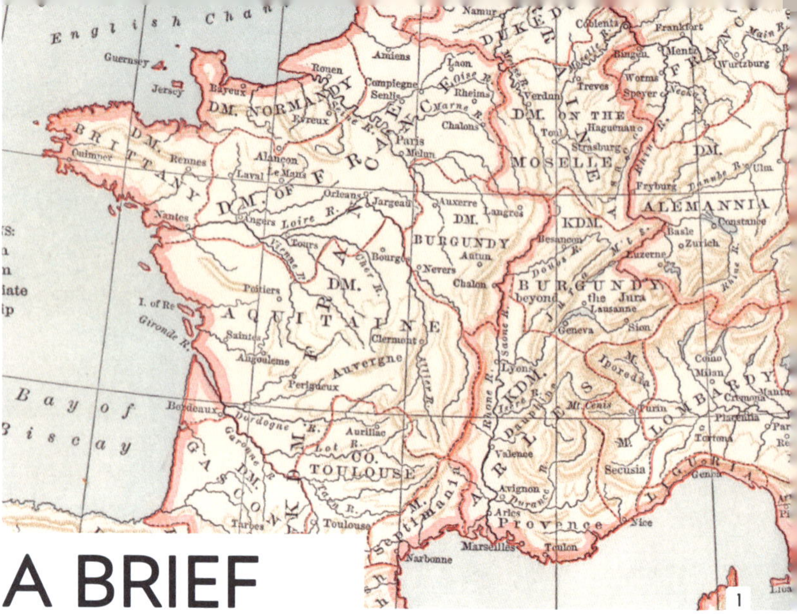

A BRIEF HISTORY

This region's history can be traced back to its first settlers in 400,000 BCE. There are many places where history lives on, existing side-by-side with the 21st century: the ancient cave paintings of Lascaux, medieval fortified towns, and the millennia-old Basque culture and language.

Early Years

In the early 3rd century BCE, the Celtic Gauls began to settle in southwest France, in a region known as Aquitania. Their leaders established trade links with a Roman province in southern Gaul, but in 52 BCE the Romans took over after victory in the Battle of Alesia, marking the beginning of their dominance in the region.

Did You Know?

Under English rule, Aquitaine was known as Guyenne.

Invasions and Unrest

The end of the 3rd century CE saw the first of many invasions by Germanic tribes from the east. The citizens of Aquitaine took refuge behind hastily constructed town ramparts, and a turbulent

Timeline of events

c 300 BCE

The first Celtic group (the Gauls) settle in southwest France.

c 107 BCE

The Gauls defeat the Romans in the Battle of Burdigala (the early name for Bordeaux).

52 BCE

More conflict between the Romans and Gauls; the Romans are victorious, and take control of Aquitania.

284–305 CE

Ramparts are built to defend Bordeaux and Périgueux from invasion by Germanic tribes.

481

A series of invasions leads to the Visigoths making the region part of their kingdom.

period of history began in the region as a succession of groups attacked from the 3rd century through to the late 9th century. Some of these groups only had short-lived victories, but others were more successful, claiming land or ravaging existing towns. After centuries of turmoil in the region, the Gallo-Roman civilization was broken and gradually withered away.

The Middle Ages

During the 11th and 12th centuries, political stability returned. Christianity spread, and more land was cleared in order to build abbeys and monasteries. For much of the Middle Ages, Aquitaine was under English rule, after Eleanor of Aquitaine – a duchess and former wife of King Louis VII of France – married Henry II of England. Defending this position against French claims to the territory led to almost continuous conflict, and the construction of many castles. Each of these great fortresses belonged to a lord, who was either under the protection of the king of France or the king of England. At the same time, the rapid population expansion that occurred in the 13th and 14th centuries caused towns and cities to double in size.

1 Map of France showing Aquitaine during the Carolingian Empire.

2 A depiction of the Battle of Alesia between the Romans and Gauls.

3 Illustration of the Visigoth's invasion in the early 5th century CE.

4 Eleanor of Aquitaine, one of the most powerful women in France during the Middle Ages.

580

The Vascons from the Pyrénées invade, settling in an area between the Garonne river and the mountains.

late 7th century

The Duchy of Aquitaine is established under the Franks.

781

The former Duchy of Aquitaine becomes part of the Carolingian Empire.

950

Pilgrimages to Santiago de Compostela begin, travelling through southwest France.

1152

Duchess Eleanor of Aquitaine marries the Duke of Normandy (later King Henry II of England).

1

2

3

French Rule

During the Hundred Years' War (1337–1453), the kings of England and France fought over French territory, and Aquitaine was eventually seized by King Louis VI of France. This marked the beginning of the *Ancien Régime*, an administrative system through which the monarchy ruled with absolute power and the nobility carried incredible influence. After many years of relative calm, strife broke out in the mid-17th century, first among peasants who revolted against rising taxes and excessive authority, followed by a rebellious movement led by members of the wealthy middle class. The trouble was suppressed by the ruling powers, and the first half of the 18th century was an era of enlightenment rather than rebellion.

The French Revolution

Members of Bordeaux's parliament were the first to question royal power in the late 18th century, so, in August 1787, King Louis XVI ordered them to be exiled to Libourne. In Bordeaux, this decision marked the first stirrings of the French Revolution (1789–99) which brought an end to the *Ancien Régime*. A political faction of Aquitaine deputies, known as the Girondins, became

↑ King Louis XVI, the last king of France before the French Revolution

Timeline of events

1337
King Philip VI of France confiscates Aquitaine from the English.

1441
The University of Bordeaux is established.

1498
The introduction of printing to Périgueux.

early 1500s
Marguerite de Navarre becomes a patron of the arts.

1562–98
Wars of Religion between Catholics and Protestants.

instrumental in campaigning for the end of the monarchy. When the Revolution began to spiral away from their initial goals, the Girondins tried to bring it to an early end, but found themselves the target of other politicians who supported the ongoing Revolution. When power passed to their opponents, many Girondins were arrested or guillotined, ushering in the Reign of Terror (1792–4).

Aquitaine Against Napoléon

Although the political situation stabilized during the subsequent era of the French Empire (1804–14), the upper classes remained hostile to its ruler – Napoléon Bonaparte – as his blockade against Britain made trading from Bordeaux difficult. In March 1814, English troops arriving to combat Napoléon's forces were favourably received by Bordeaux's inhabitants, who welcomed the end of the Napoleonic Wars. When Napoléon attempted to return to power during the Hundred Days period (20 March–8 July 1815), Marie-Thérèse Charlotte, the Duchess of Angoulême, made a stand against him in Bordeaux.

1 French troops during the Hundred Years' War.

2 Bordeaux in 1750.

3 Monument to the Girondins, Bordeaux.

4 Duchess of Angoulême rallying the citizens of Bordeaux.

Did You Know?

The Duchess of Angoulême was the eldest child of King Louis XVI and Marie Antoinette.

1637–53

Rebellions among peasants, aristocrats and parliamentarians.

1743–57

Marquis de Tourny lays out Bordeaux's elegant squares.

1789–99

Aquitaine's economy collapses during the French Revolution.

1792–4

The Reign of Terror during the French Revolution.

1815

The Duchess of Angoulême rallies the troops of Bordeaux against Napoléon Bonaparte, who is seeking to regain power.

Rise of Aquitaine

Although the economy of the southwest struggled after the French Revolution, the region blossomed during the Second French Empire (1852–70). In line with the huge increase in the region's wine exports, the ports of Bordeaux and Bayonne expanded and, with the development of the coastal resorts of Arcachon and Biarritz, tourism grew. Aquitaine become a magnet for an elite who sought to emulate the Emperor and Empress, who came to visit the region several times.

1 Empress Eugénie, who brought fame to Biarritz.

2 Parliament in session in Bordeaux's Grand-Théâtre.

3 A World War II-era submarine base, Bordeaux.

4 The beach at Hendaye.

Late 19th and early 20th Centuries

During the Franco-Prussian War (1870–1), fears of a German invasion led the seat of government to be moved from Paris to Bordeaux. The city became the capital of France again under similar circumstances during World War I (1914–18) and World War II (1939–45). After the Armistice of June 1940, southwest France was bisected by a demarcation line and, until 1942, Bordeaux and the whole Atlantic coast was occupied by Germany. The French Resistance gradually came together, but the Gestapo and the French militia harshly cracked down on it.

Did You Know?

Wine was introduced to Bordeaux by the Romans in the 1st century CE.

Timeline of events

1852–70
Empress Eugénie visits the Basque coast and Pyrenean spa resorts.

1871
Bordeaux's Grand-Théâtre is requisitioned as a makeshift parliament.

1914
The French government once again moves to Bordeaux.

1939
France and Great Britain declare war on Germany, commencing World War II.

1940
A young man discovers prehistoric cave paintings at Lascaux while walking his dog.

3

4

Fearing an Allied landing, the Germans installed a string of military bunkers, known as the Atlantic Wall, all along the coast. World War II eventually drew to a close in 1945, but political and economic unrest continued to plague southwest France until the mid-1970s, when tourism took off once again and brought new life to the region of Aquitaine.

Dordogne, Bordeaux and the Southwest Coast Today

The area's natural beauty and historic towns are a source of local pride that continue to charm millions of tourists every year. Faster trains from Paris and beyond are also introducing this mesmerizing region to more visitors than ever before. The area underwent significant change in 2014, when three *départements* merged together to form Nouvelle-Aquitaine, the southern half of which contains Dordogne, Bordeaux and the southwest coast. Given this revitalization and renewed interest in the area, the renaming and birth of a new, larger region feels particularly symbolic, ushering in a new chapter in this region's long and fascinating story.

↑ Wines from Bordeaux, one of the best wine regions in the world

1940–42

The Atlantic coast is occupied by Nazi Germany.

1954

The discovery of natural gas at Lacq and of oil deposits at Parentis helps to boost the southern region's economy.

1997

France declares Pays Basque an official *pays* - a special cultural territory.

2014

Aquitaine merges with two other regions to form Nouvelle-Aquitaine.

2019

Biarritz hosts the G7 summit.

EXPERIENCE

Riding the waves at Plage Santocha

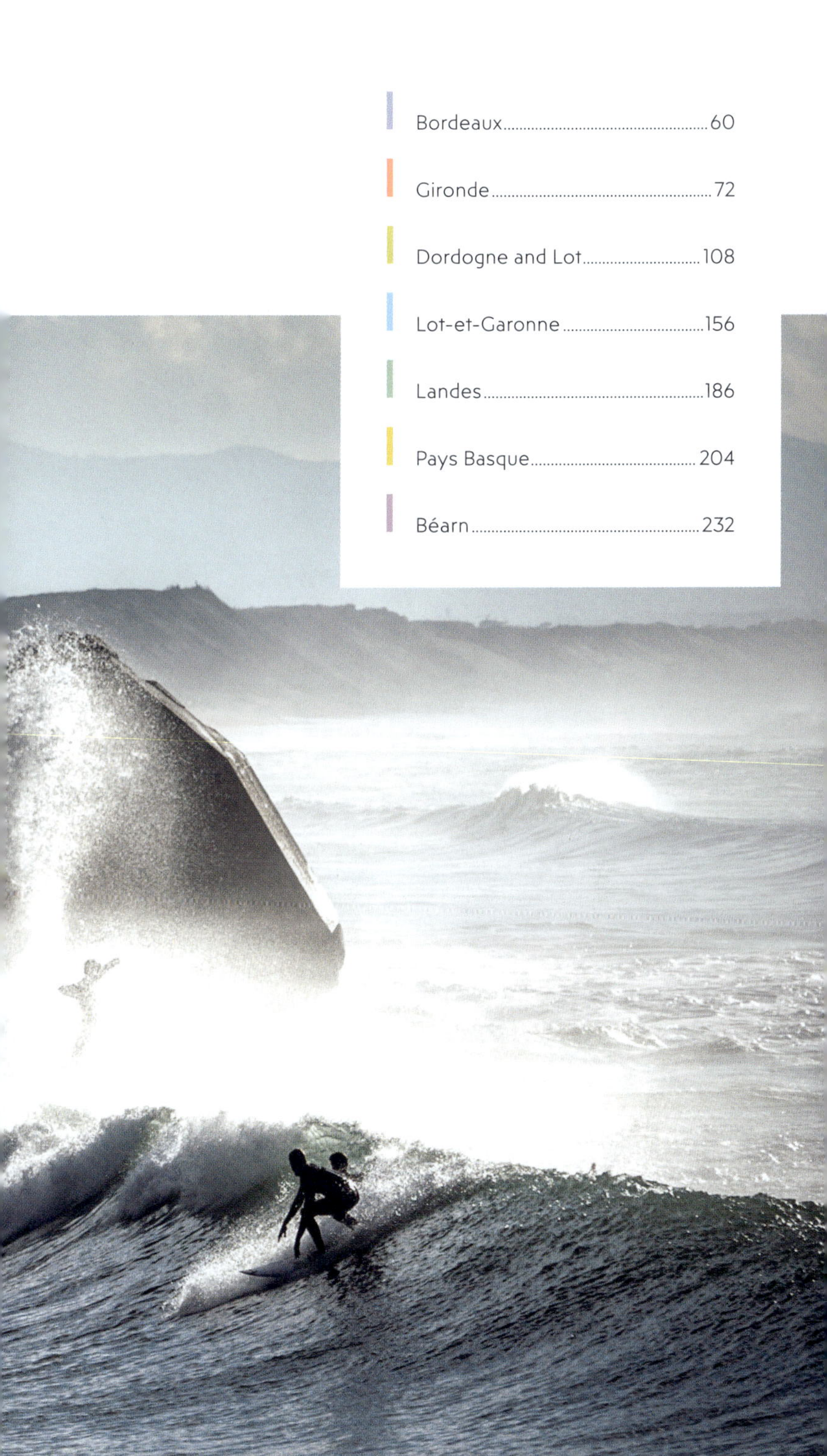

Enjoying the evening sunshine on place de la Bourse

BORDEAUX

With its strategic location on the Garonne river, Bordeaux – once known as Burdigala – has been a major hub of trade since the 3rd century BCE. Along with its prosperity, Bordeaux's prominence also made it a key setting during turbulent periods of French history – being torched by Normans in 848 CE, passing from English to French rule in the Middle Ages and suffering under Napoléon's Continental blockade. Yet through these difficult periods, Bordeaux's busy port, and its influential politics, culture and art, made the city the crowning jewel of Aquitaine.

Meticulous restoration has enhanced the many splendours of Bordeaux: the richly decorated façades of its majestic buildings; the glorious Gothic churches that hint at its importance in medieval Europe; entire quarters that have been pedestrianized; and quays that offer long riverside walks. All these invite the visitor to explore the city's riches, and with modern trams and a network of bike lanes to aid travel, it's a pleasure to seek out the highlights of this captivating city.

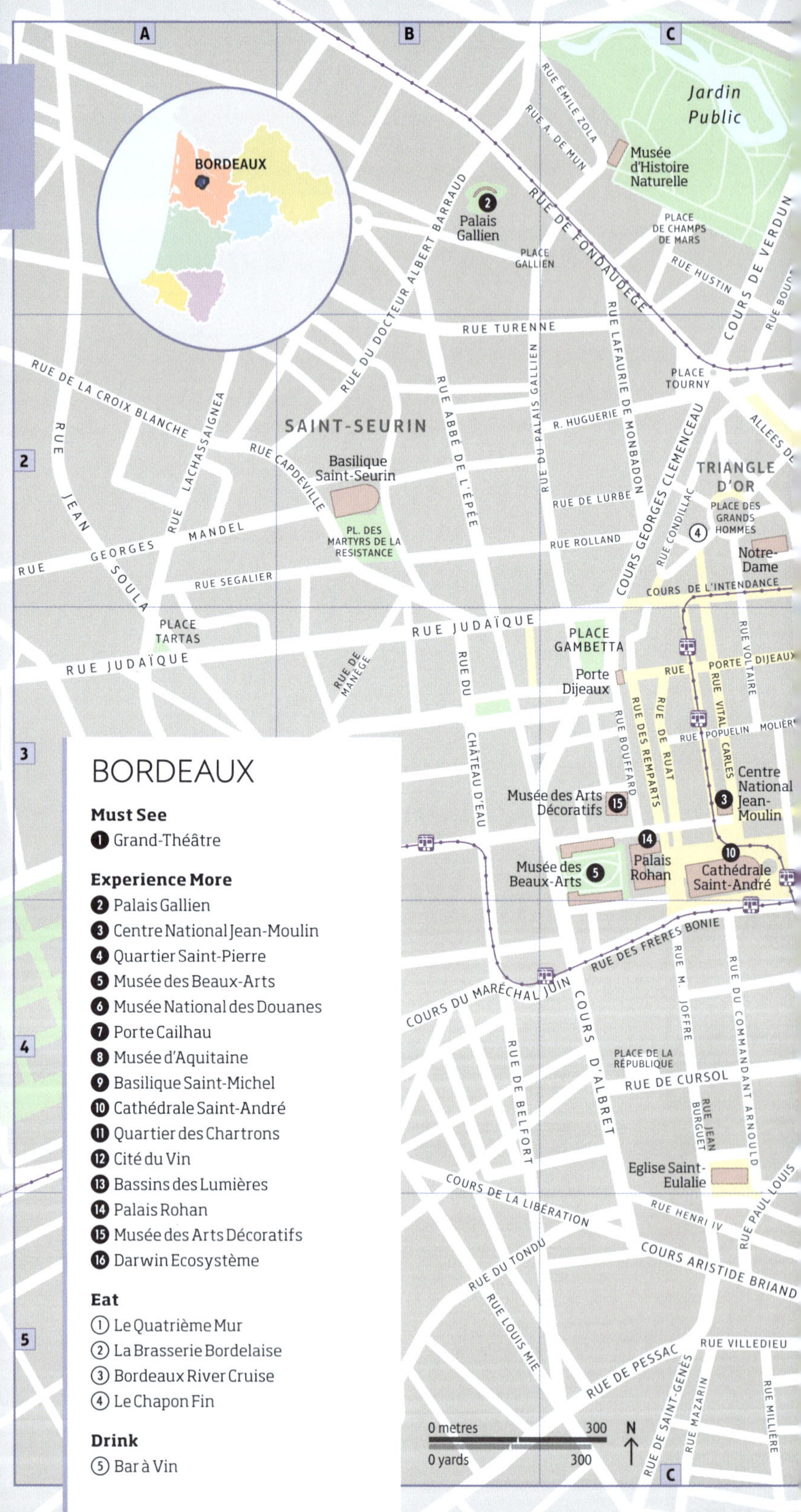

A
B
C
2
3
4
5
BORDEAUX
Jardin Public
Musée d'Histoire Naturelle
RUE ÉMILE ZOLA
RUE A. DE MUN
PLACE DE CHAMPS DE MARS
RUE HUSTIN
COURS DE VERDUN
RUE DE FONDAUDÈGE
2 Palais Gallien
PLACE GALLIEN
RUE ALBERT BARRAUD
RUE DU DOCTEUR ALBERT BARRAUD
RUE TURENNE
RUE LAFAURIE DE MONBADON
PLACE TOURNY
ALLÉES DE
RUE DE LA CROIX BLANCHE
RUE LACHASSAIGNEA
SAINT-SEURIN
RUE ABBÉ DE L'ÉPÉE
RUE DU PALAIS GALLIEN
R. HUGUERIE
COURS GEORGES CLEMENCEAU
TRIANGLE D'OR
RUE JEAN SOULA
RUE CAPDEVILLE
Basilique Saint-Seurin
RUE DE LURBE
RUE CONDILLAC
PLACE DES GRANDS HOMMES
4
Notre-Dame
RUE GEORGES MANDEL
PL. DES MARTYRS DE LA RESISTANCE
RUE ROLLAND
RUE SEGALIER
COURS DE L'INTENDANCE
PLACE TARTAS
RUE JUDAÏQUE
RUE DE MANÈGE
PLACE GAMBETTA
RUE VOLTAIRE
RUE PORTE DIJEAUX
Porte Dijeaux
RUE DU CHÂTEAU D'EAU
RUE BOUFFARD
RUE DES REMPARTS
RUE DE RUAT
RUE VITAL CARLES
RUE POPUELIN
MOLIÈR
Centre National Jean-Moulin
3
Musée des Arts Décoratifs
15
14 Palais Rohan
10 Cathédrale Saint-André
Musée des Beaux-Arts
5
RUE DES FRÈRES BONIE
COURS DU MARÉCHAL JUIN
RUE M. JOFFRE
RUE DU COMMANDANT ARNOULD
COURS D'ALBRET
RUE DE BELFORT
PLACE DE LA RÉPUBLIQUE
RUE DE CURSOL
RUE JEAN BURGUET
Eglise Saint-Eulalie
COURS DE LA LIBÉRATION
RUE HENRI IV
RUE PAUL LOUIS
COURS ARISTIDE BRIAND
RUE DU TONDU
RUE LOUIS MIE
RUE VILLEDIEU
RUE DE PESSAC
RUE DE SAINT-GENÈS
RUE MAZARIN
RUE MILLIÈRE
0 metres 300
0 yards 300
N
BORDEAUX
Must See
1 Grand-Théâtre
Experience More
2 Palais Gallien
3 Centre National Jean-Moulin
4 Quartier Saint-Pierre
5 Musée des Beaux-Arts
6 Musée National des Douanes
7 Porte Cailhau
8 Musée d'Aquitaine
9 Basilique Saint-Michel
10 Cathédrale Saint-André
11 Quartier des Chartrons
12 Cité du Vin
13 Bassins des Lumières
14 Palais Rohan
15 Musée des Arts Décoratifs
16 Darwin Ecosystème
Eat
① Le Quatrième Mur
② La Brasserie Bordelaise
③ Bordeaux River Cruise
④ Le Chapon Fin
Drink
⑤ Bar à Vin

Around the city centre
13 Bassins des Lumières
Cité du Vin 12
LE BOUSCAT
CHARTRONS
GRAND PARC
11 Quartier des Chartrons
PAUL DOUMER
Darwin Eco-système 16
ST-SEURIN
LA BASTIDE
BORDEAUX
Garonne
area of main map
ST-GENÈS
0 km 1
0 miles 1
N
Temple de Chartrons
Cours Xavier Arnozan
Centre d'Art Plastique Contemporain
Rue Ferrère
Allées de Chartres
Allées de Bristol
Esplanade des Quinconces
Monument aux Girondins
Allée de Munich
Quai Louis XVIII
Maison du Vin
Tourny
Rue Condé
Rue Lafayette
Les Platanes des Quais
Rue Esprit des Lois
R. Mautrec
Place de la Comédie
1 Grand-Théâtre
Palais de la Bourse
Cours du Chapeau-Rouge
Rue Saige
Place de la Bourse
Rue Saint-Rémi
Place du Parlement
6 Musée National des Douanes
Garonne
4 Quartier Saint-Pierre
Rue Margaux
Place Saint-Pierre
Promenade Sainte-Catherine
Rue Sainte Catherine
Rue de la Devise
Rue de la Cour des Aides
Rue du Chai des Farines
Quai de la Douane
Rue Guiraude
R. du Pas St-Georges
Rue Arnaud Miqueu
Rue des Trois Conils
R. de la Merci
Rue de Cheverus
Porte Cailhau 7
Place du Palais
Rue Ausone
R. de Cerf Volant
Rue du Loup
C. d'Alsace et Lorraine
Quai Richelieu
Pont de Pierre
Rue Léonce Motelay
Allée Serr
Quai des Queyries
Rue des Ayres
Rue de la Rousselle
Rue Bouquière
Rue Buhan
Rue Neuve
Rue St-James
Place de Bir Hakeim
Quai des Salinières
Rue Renière
8 Musée d'Aquitaine
Grosse Cloche
Cours Victor Hugo
Rue Sainte-Catherine
Rue des Faures
Rue Maubec
Cours Pasteur
Lande
Rue du Mirail
Rue Saint François
Rue de Marengo
Rue des Menuts
Basilique Saint-Michel 9
Quai de la Monnaie
Rue Carpenteyre
Parc des Sports de Saint-Michel
Saint-Michel
Rue Magendie
Rue Leyteire
Rue Clare
Rue Planterose
Rue des Bouviers
R. des Fours
R. Camille Sauvageau
R. Le Reynart
Rue Andronne
R. Porte de la Monnaie
Quai Sainte-Croix
Rue Augustins
Rue Permentade
Rue des Vignes
Rue Mérigean
Rue Saincric
Rue Henri IV
Rue S. de Pomiers
Rue Saint-Benoît
Rue Paul Broca
Rue du Bigot
Rue du Hamel
Rue du Portail
Place de la Victoire
Victoire
Rue Élie Gintrac
Abbatiale Sainte-Croix
Rue Sauteyron
Rue des Douves
Cours de l'Argonne
Cours de la Somme
Rue Leberthon
Rue Bergeon
Cours de la Marne
Parc André Meunier
Rue Beaufleury
D
E
F
1
2
3
4
5

1

GRAND-THÉÂTRE

D2 Place de la Comédie B, C Many buses Hours vary, check website opera-bordeaux.com

At the centre of Bordeaux stands the Grand-Théâtre, one of the oldest and most beautiful 18th-century concert halls in the world. Designed by Victor Louis, the building's dramatic architecture and brilliant colours enhance the venue's stunning performances.

The theatre was commissioned by the Maréchal-duc de Richelieu, who was governor of Guyenne (the former name for Aquitaine). A fine example of the Neo-Classical style, it was constructed between 1773 and 1780 on the site of a Gallo-Roman temple, known as the Piliers de Tutelle. Built to a rectangular plan, the building is surrounded by vaulted galleries and faced with 12 Corinthian columns. Inside, the grand foyer is a homogeneous example of the style of the Second Empire (1852–70). The auditorium, which is renowned for its acoustics, is still decorated in its original colours of blue, white and gold. A host of productions are held throughout the year, including both classic and contemporary ballet, operas and jazz concerts.

Did You Know?

In World War II, the theatre was used by the National Assembly for the French Parliament.

EAT

Le Quatrième Mur
A decadent restaurant inside the theatre, featuring beautifully plated local dishes such as grilled seafood.

D2 Place de la Comédie quatrieme-mur.com

DRINK

Bar à Vin
This bar, located in a Neo-Classical building near the theatre, is ideal for a glass of Bordeaux wine before a show.

D2 3 cours du 30 Juillet baravin.bordeaux.com

The façade is surmounted by statues of the goddesses Juno, Venus and Minerva, and the nine Muses, carved by Pierre-François Berruer (1733–1797).

Grand Foyer

The building is faced with 12 Corinthian columns. The arcaded galleries on either side once housed small shops.

Atrium

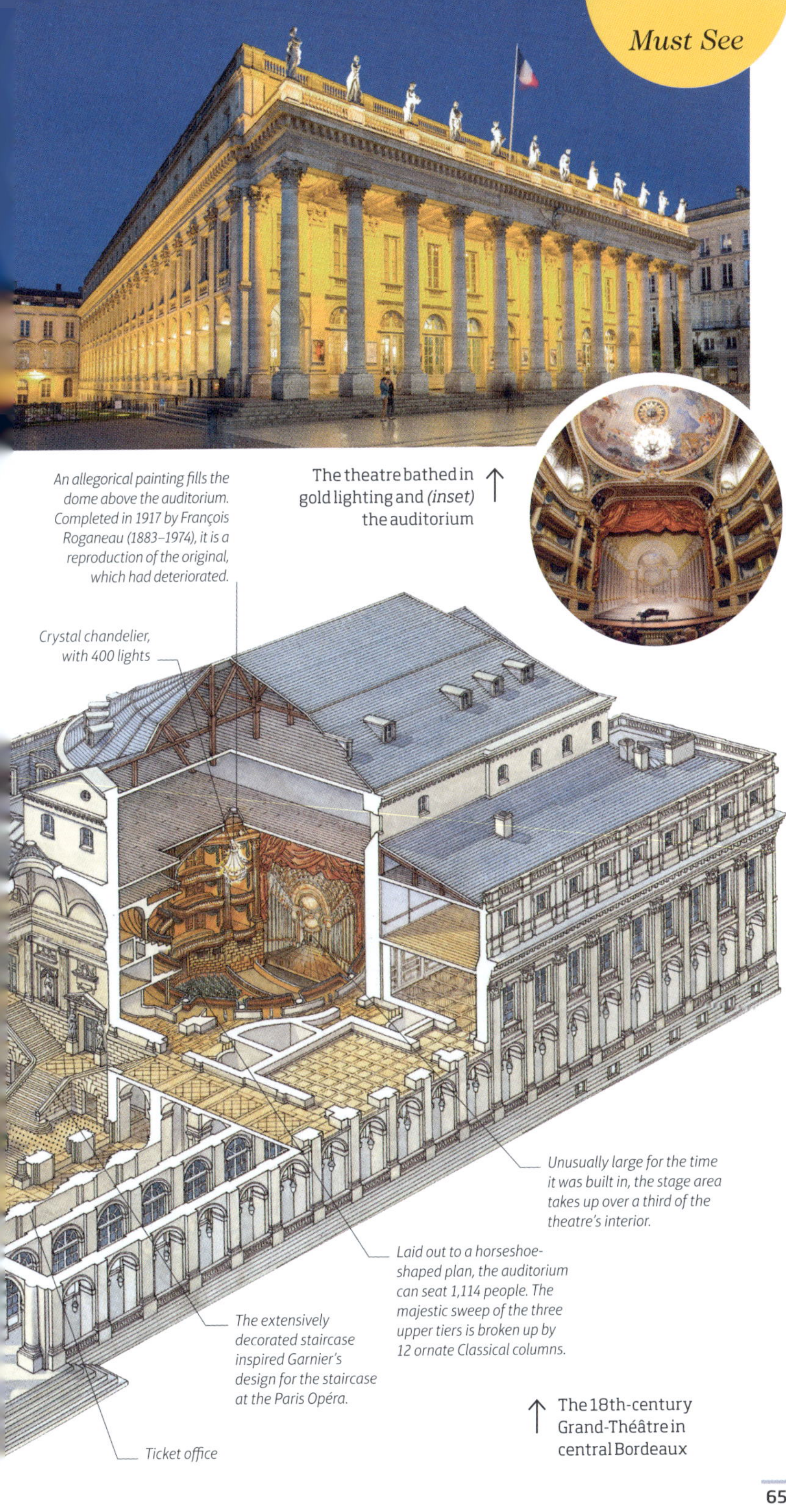

↑ The theatre bathed in gold lighting and *(inset)* the auditorium

↑ The 18th-century Grand-Théâtre in central Bordeaux

EXPERIENCE MORE

Palais Gallien

B1 Rue du Docteur-Albert-Barraud 05 56 00 66 00 24 hours daily

The late 2nd-century Palais Gallien is the only vestige of ancient Burdigala, as Bordeaux was known in Gallo-Roman times. About 130 m (425 ft) long and 110 m (360 ft) wide, this ancient amphitheatre could seat 15,000 people. Gutted by fire during the barbarian invasions of 276 CE, it was also partly destroyed during the French Revolution (1789–99).

Centre National Jean-Moulin

C3 Place Jean Moulin 05 56 10 19 90 For renovation until 2026

This war museum, established in 1967, is devoted to the French Resistance, the deportation of France's Jews and the wartime role of the Free French.

MASKS OF STONE

Many of the façades of Bordeaux's houses are decorated with carved masks. While the earliest date from the 16th century, they are more typical of the 18th century. Legendary gods and mythological beings are chosen to tie in with the location they watch over. Mercury, the ancient Roman god of trade, surveys the harbour traffic from place de la Bourse, while Bacchus, the Roman god of the grape harvest, evokes the wealth that wine brings to the city.

Quartier Saint-Pierre

D3 Place Pey-Berland Place du Palais

Located between the Garonne river and the city centre, this quarter was once enclosed by walls, which were demolished in the 18th century. Now beautifully restored, it is a pleasant area to explore on foot. What is now place de la Bourse was laid out by the Gabriels, a father-and-son team of architects, in 1729–55. On its north side is the Palais de la Bourse (now the Chamber of Commerce) and on the south is the Hôtel des Fermes, its upper storey set with columns on ornate pediments. In the square's centre is the Fontaine des Trois-Grâces, erected in 1864. Lined with restaurants and cafés, place du Parlement – commissioned by Tourny in 1754 – is a masterpiece of architectural harmony. Louis-XV townhouses surround a paved courtyard, containing a Neo-Rococo fountain that dates from 1867. On place Saint-Pierre is the Église Saint-Pierre, built in the late Middle Ages and remodelled in the 19th century.

Musée des Beaux-Arts

C3 20 cours d'Albret Hôtel de Ville, Palais de Justice, Château de Hâ 11am-6pm Wed-Mon musba-bordeaux.fr

The north and south wings of the city hall – added to the building by Charles Burguet in 1878–81 – now house this museum. Almost the entire history of Western art, from the Renaissance to the late 20th century, is covered by the collection on display including works by artists such as Titian, Van Dyck, Picasso and Matisse. Also represented are the Italian and Flemish Schools, Romantic painting, Impressionists and modern works.

PICTURE PERFECT

Miroir d'Eau

Between the Garonne river and ornate 18th-century façades sits the largest reflecting pool in the world, the Miroir d'Eau (Water Mirror), at place de la Bourse. It's an ideal location for photos, day or night.

Musée National des Douanes

E3 1 place de la Bourse Place de la Bourse 10am-6pm Tue-Sun musee-douanes.fr

Occupying a part of the Hôtel des Fermes that formerly served as a customs house, this museum – the only one of its kind in France – traces the history and work of French customs officers. Exhibits include a fine painting by Monet, *La Cabane du Douanier, Effet d'Après-midi* (1882).

Porte Cailhau

E3 Pl du Palais Pl du Palais 10am-1pm & 2-6pm daily

This city gate offers lovely views of the north bank of the Garonne. The gate was built in 1495 to honour a victory won by the French king in Italy. Its design is a unique mixture of decorative features (such as the conical roofs) and defensive elements (including a portcullis and a crenellated gallery).

↑ The fairy-tale-looking Porte Cailhau, a defensive city gate

Musée d'Aquitaine

D4 20 cours Pasteur Musée d'Aquitaine 11am-6pm Tue-Sun musee-aquitaine-bordeaux.fr

The museum's Prehistory and Protohistory collections highlight the region's ancient legacy. The Gaulish items include a hoard of gold from Tayac *(p118)* and a bronze figure of Hercules.

Also on display is a varied Modern Era collection, which explores Bordeaux's history through the 18th century, with a focus on its prosperous port and the history of enslavement in the region.

The Miroir d'Eau on place de la Bourse, in Quartier Saint-Pierre

Inside the Basilique Saint-Michel, with its beautiful stained-glass windows

EAT

La Brasserie Bordelaise
Choose from over 700 wines to pair with a delicious Bordelais meal.

D3 50 rue Saint-Rémi brasserie-bordelaise.fr

Bordeaux River Cruise
Dine on regional dishes on board a boat while cruising the Garonne river. Includes stops along the way and exceptional views.

D1 2 quai des Chartrons bordeaux-river-cruise.com

Le Chapon Fin
Dating back to 1825, this fine-dining spot has a fabulous Rococo interior and an excellent wine cellar.

C2 5 rue Montesquieu Sun-Mon chapon-fin.com

Basilique Saint-Michel

E4 Place Cantaloup Saint-Michel 10am-5:30pm Mon & Sat, 2-5:30pm Tue-Fri, 11am-3pm Sun

The Basilique Saint-Michel is in a colourful antiques dealers' district, where there is also a lively market on Mondays and Saturdays and a flea market on Sundays.

While its construction began in the 14th century, the church was completed 200 years later in the Flamboyant Gothic architectural style. The Chapelle Saint-Jacques within was built for the use of the city's brotherhood of pilgrims.

Cathédrale Saint-André

C3 Place Pey-Berland Hôtel de Ville Hours vary, check website cathedrale-bordeaux.fr

A UNESCO World Heritage Site, this is the finest of all Bordeaux's churches. The nave, built in the 11th and 12th centuries, was altered in the 1400s. Depictions of the apostles, bishops and martyrs, and of the Last Judgment, adorn the west and north doors and the entrance to the southern wing of the transept (built in the 13th–14th centuries).

Quartier des Chartrons

F1 Many stops

This is the historic hub of Bordeaux's wine trade, which dates back to Roman times. Here the city's wealth was amassed and dynasties of wine merchants were established. The **Musée du Vin et du Négoce de Bordeaux** is located in three 18th-century vaulted cellars not far from the quai des Chartrons. The multimedia exhibits relate the history of the wine trade at the Port of Bordeaux.

Musée du Vin et du Négoce de Bordeaux
41 rue Borie
10am-6pm daily
museeduvinbordeaux.com

Cité du Vin

F1 Esplanade de Pontac, 134 quai de Bacalan & La Cité du Vin Hours vary, check website laciteduvin.com

Housed in a striking contemporary building on the river bank, this excellent museum explores the history and traditions of viticulture around the world. The visit culminates with wine tasting on the eighth floor, offering spectacular views across the city and the river. The Cité du Vin also hosts wine-themed seminars, shows and movie screenings, and receives over a million visitors each year.

The dynamic design of the Cité du Vin and a display of wine *(inset)*

Bassins des Lumières

F1 Impasse Brown de Colstoun 10am-7pm daily bassins-lumieres.com

This former World War II submarine base has been converted into the largest digital art space in the world. Visitors can walk along a series of interconnecting bridges to experience a spectacular, immersive sound-and-light show reflected in the water.

Palais Rohan

C3 Place Pey-Berland Hôtel de Ville 05 56 10 20 30 8:30am-5pm Mon-Fri, 9am-noon Sat

Dating from 1771–83, this was built as the residence of Archbishop Mériadec de Rohan. Since 1937, it has housed the city hall. Note-worthy features include its lavish dining room and the grand staircase.

Musée des Arts Décoratifs

C3 39 rue Bouffard Gambetta Until 2026 madd-bordeaux.fr

This museum is housed in the Hôtel de Lalande, a refined townhouse built in 1775–9. Several rooms evoke the opulence typical of Bordeaux townhouse interiors in the 18th century. On display are paintings, miniatures, prints, sculptures and furniture.

Darwin Ecosystème

F1 87 quai des Queyries Stalingrad & Jardin Botanique Hours vary, check website darwin.camp

Darwin, built in the former military barracks, has rapidly emerged as the city's coolest music venue and urban culture centre. It has a skate park, co-working spaces, restaurants, a dance studio and a riverside bar.

TOP 3 CHURCH TOWERS

La Flèche
The belfry at Basilique Saint-Michel. Built in the 15th century, it was restored in the 19th century and separated from the basilica.

Tour Pey-Berland
The bell tower at Cathédrale Saint-André was built in the mid-15th century in the Flamboyant Gothic style.

Église Sainte-Croix
This church has two imposing squared bell towers. While they look similar, they were built around 800 years apart.

A SHORT WALK BORDEAUX

Distance 2.5 km (1.5 miles) **Time** 30 minutes
Nearest tram stop Grand-Théâtre

Built on a curve of the Garonne river, Bordeaux has been a major port since pre-Roman times, although you'll see little evidence of this history as you walk around the city. Always a progressive place, Bordeaux underwent a radical transformation in the 18th century. Today, its industrial and maritime stretch is scattered around a mix of grand boulevards and noble, Neo-Classical squares that are a joy to explore on foot. Facing directly onto the waterfront lies the place de la Bourse, flanked by a row of elegant wine merchants' houses, originally built to mask the medieval slums that once lay behind. The magnificence of the Esplanade des Quinconces sweeps down to the river, offering a fine view of the lavishly decorated Monument aux Girondins from the quayside. Also striking is the place des Grands-Hommes, a rare example of town planning in Bordeaux at the time of the Revolution.

The stunning Baroque ***Église Notre-Dame*** *was completed in 1707.*

START

COURS DE L INTENDANCE

RUE MAUTREC

Did You Know?

Many of Bordeaux's buildings were once black due to pollution.

The façade of the ***Grand-Théâtre*** *(p64) is decorated with statues of the nine Muses, and the goddesses Juno, Minerva and Venus.*

RUE SAINTE-CATHERINE

PL. DE LA COMÉDIE

FINISH

RUE SAINT-RÉMI

COURS DU CHAPEAU ROUGE

A masterpiece of architectural harmony, ***place de la Bourse*** *is flanked by two buildings, the Bourse – old Stock Exchange – and the Hôtel des Fermes – now the Musée National des Douanes (p67).*

PL. DE LA BOURSE

←

Outside the elegant Neo-Classical Grand-Théâtre in the heart of Bordeaux

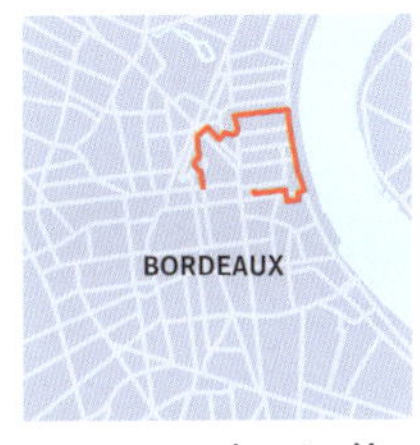

Locator Map
For more detail see p62

↑ Fountains around the Monument aux Girondins, symbolizing the Triumph of Concord and the Republic

Bar à Vins (p64) *and* **École du Vin du CIVB** *hold professional wine tastings.*

Fountains in the form of statues flank the **Monument aux Girondins***, dedicated to the deputies who suffered during the Reign of Terror* (p55)*. It is crowned by a statue of Liberty breaking free of her shackles.*

0 metres 100
0 yards 100
N →

Surrounded by trees and set with statues of Montaigne (p149) *and Montesquieu* (p102), **Esplanade des Quinconces** *was laid out during 1827–58.*

Les Chartrons (p68) *area, once inhabited by wine merchants, has been restored. Its fine townhouses are highly sought after.*

CAPC *(Musée d'Art Contemporain) is one of Bordeaux's best modern art museums. It is housed in an early 19th-century port warehouse.*

Paragliders soaring over the Dune du Pilat

GIRONDE

The Romans were among the first to exploit the Gironde's potential. They laid out vineyards on the hillsides, where they built sumptuous villas. Pioneering medieval monks erected prestigious abbeys and English rulers established the *bastide* towns such as Monségur and Sauveterre-de-Guyenne. The late 19th century witnessed the discovery of the healthy benefits of the sea air at Arcachon and Soulac, and the advent of the railways, making the region accessible.

Today Gironde has plenty to tempt travellers. The great waves crashing on to the sandy beaches of Gironde's Atlantic seaboard offer surfers and other water sports enthusiasts near perfect conditions. Similarly, the banks of the Gironde estuary are a paradise for anglers, and are also lined with a succession of prestigious wine-producing châteaux and some magnificent Romanesque and Gothic architecture.

GIRONDE

Must Sees

1. Château de Roquetaillade
2. Saint-Émilion
3. Château de Cazeneuve
4. Arcachon Basin
5. Phare de Cordouan

Experience More

6. Saint-Ferme
7. Phare de Grave
8. Libourne
9. Soulac-sur-Mer
10. Blasimon
11. Sainte-Foy-la-Grande
12. Fort-Médoc
13. Blaye
14. Bourg
15. Pauillac
16. Entre-deux-Mers
17. Castillon-la-Bataille
18. Rauzan
19. La Sauve-Majeure
20. Étang de Lacanau
21. Margaux
22. Lesparre-Médoc
23. Moulis-en-Médoc
24. Barsac
25. Dune du Pilat
26. Sauveterre-de-Guyenne
27. Lac d'Hourtin-Carcans
28. Monségur
29. La Réole
30. La Brède
31. Saint-Macaire
32. Graves
33. Cadillac
34. Bazas
35. Château de Villandraut
36. Uzeste
37. Sauternais

Atlantic Ocean

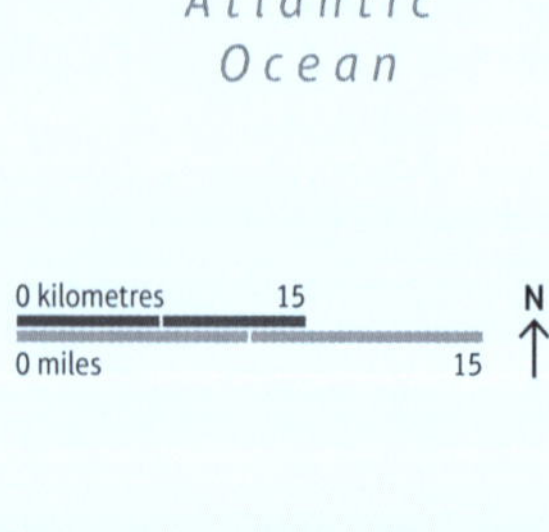

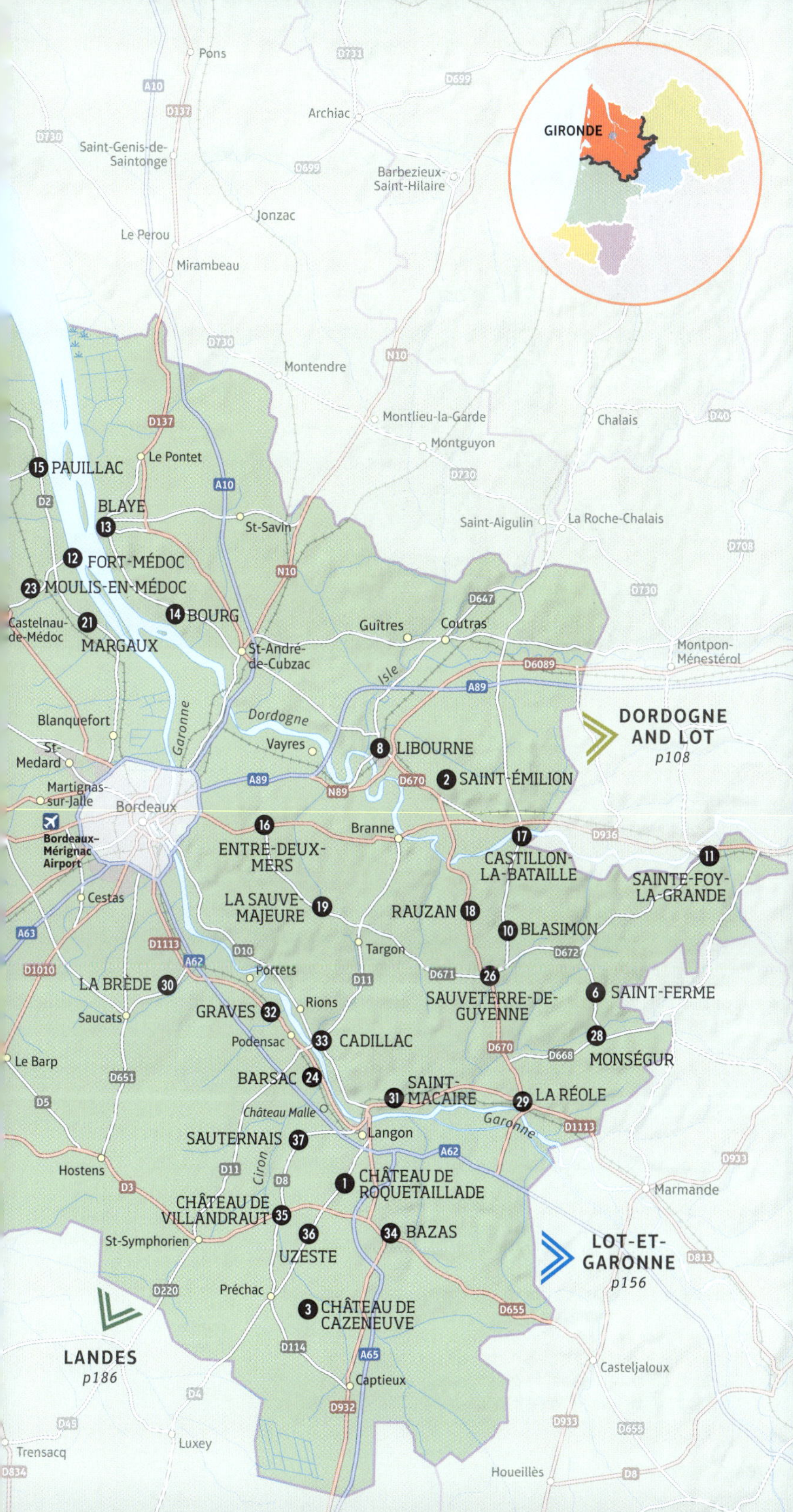

GIRONDE
Pons
Archiac
Saint-Genis-de-Saintonge
Barbezieux-Saint-Hilaire
Jonzac
Le Perou
Mirambeau
Montendre
Montlieu-la-Garde
Montguyon
Chalais
Saint-Aigulin
La Roche-Chalais
Montpon-Ménestérol
15 PAUILLAC
Le Pontet
BLAYE
13
12 FORT-MÉDOC
23 MOULIS-EN-MÉDOC
14 BOURG
Castelnau-de-Médoc
21
MARGAUX
St-Savin
Guîtres
Coutras
St-André-de-Cubzac
Isle
Dordogne
Garonne
Blanquefort
Vayres
8 LIBOURNE
2 SAINT-ÉMILION
St-Medard
Martignas-sur-Jalle
Bordeaux
Bordeaux-Mérignac Airport
16
ENTRE-DEUX-MERS
Branne
17
CASTILLON-LA-BATAILLE
11
SAINTE-FOY-LA-GRANDE
DORDOGNE AND LOT
p108
Cestas
LA SAUVE-MAJEURE
19
RAUZAN
18
10 BLASIMON
Targon
Portets
LA BRÈDE
30
26
SAUVETERRE-DE-GUYENNE
6 SAINT-FERME
Saucats
GRAVES
32
Rions
Podensac
33
CADILLAC
28
MONSÉGUR
Le Barp
BARSAC
24
Château Malle
31
SAINT-MACAIRE
29
LA RÉOLE
SAUTERNAIS
37
Langon
Ciron
Hostens
1
CHÂTEAU DE ROQUETAILLADE
Marmande
CHÂTEAU DE VILLANDRAUT
35
36
UZESTE
34
BAZAS
LOT-ET-GARONNE
p156
St-Symphorien
Préchac
3
CHÂTEAU DE CAZENEUVE
LANDES
p186
Captieux
Casteljaloux
Luxey
Trensacq
Houeillès
A10
A89
A62
A63
A65
N10
N89
D731
D699
D137
D730
D40
D647
D6089
D708
D670
D936
D1113
D10
D11
D1010
D671
D672
D668
D651
D5
D3
D8
D933
D813
D220
D655
D114
D932
D4
D45
D834
D8

1

CHÂTEAU DE ROQUETAILLADE

C3 Mazères For tours only; hours vary, check website roquetaillade.eu

An imposing fortress built by Charlemagne once perched here above the forest. The estate now consists of two castles and a chapel, exquisitely decorated in the Neo-Gothic style of Viollet-le-Duc, and has been owned by the same family for over 700 years.

Set in extensive parkland full of centuries-old trees, this is one of the most astonishing castles in the Gironde *département*. It perches high over a series of troglodyte caves, a perfect position for striking at would-be invaders. The castle consists of two main parts, one being the ruins of the 12th-century Château-Vieux (Old Castle), with its fortified gatehouse, guardroom and keep. The other is the better preserved Château-Neuf (New Castle), built by Cardinal Gaillard de La Mothe – nephew of Pope Clement V – in 1306, with the permission of King Edward I of England (then ruler of Aquitaine). Still owned by the Cardinal's family after more than seven centuries, it boasts six towers and an impressive central keep that give it the air of a true storybook castle.

Tours of the castle and the grounds must be booked in advance. As well as stunning interiors to admire in Château-Neuf, the estate is also home to a farm and a vineyard.

THE FATHER OF NEO-GOTHIC

The Mauvesin family commissioned Eugène Viollet-le-Duc (1814-79) to restore the Château-Neuf in the 19th century. A great exponent of Neo-Gothic architecture, Viollet-le-Duc turned the castle into a highly romanticized medieval jewel. Work began on the exterior in 1865, but the elaborate interiors - in a style that anticipated Art Nouveau - were sadly never finished.

←

The fabulous Pink Room, decorated by Viollet-le-Duc and Edmond Duthoit; and *(inset)* the 14th-century Château-Neuf

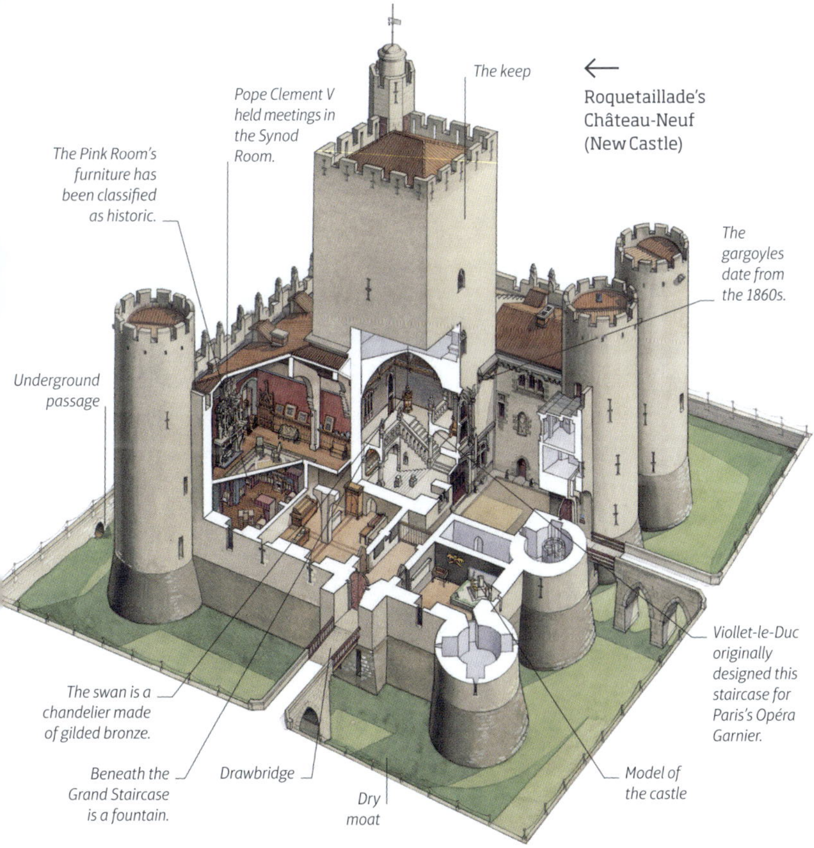

The keep

Pope Clement V held meetings in the Synod Room.

The Pink Room's furniture has been classified as historic.

The gargoyles date from the 1860s.

Underground passage

Viollet-le-Duc originally designed this staircase for Paris's Opéra Garnier.

The swan is a chandelier made of gilded bronze.

Beneath the Grand Staircase is a fountain.

Drawbridge

Dry moat

Model of the castle

←

Roquetaillade's Château-Neuf (New Castle)

2

SAINT-ÉMILION

D2 **Doyenné (Deanery), place des Créneaux; saint-emilion-tourisme.com**

Saint-Émilion traces its past back to the Romans, who introduced wine to the region, and to the monks who built extraordinary underground churches here. The UNESCO designation "Cultural Landscape" perfectly describes the charming medieval architecture and heritage that is displayed here.

Église Monolithe

Place de l'Église-Monolithe 05 57 55 28 28 For guided tours only, book in advance

This church sits in the heart of Saint-Émilion in the place de l'Église-Monolithe, with its ancient covered market and several restaurants. A troglodyte building, it was dug out of the surrounding limestone rock in the 12th century, and is unique in Europe. It has a 12-m- (39-ft-) high nave decorated with relief carvings and a 14th-century doorway with a tympanum that features depictions of the Last Judgment and the Resurrection of the Dead. Excavations have brought to light drainpipes that the monks installed to enable the rainwater to be rerouted.

The church's tall bell **tower** rises 68 m (223 ft) above place de l'Église-Monolithe and is one of the finest sights in Saint-Émilion. Climbing the 196 steps to the top is certainly a challenge but the breathtaking views of Saint-Émilion and its surrounding vineyards is reward enough.

Beyond the entrance to the Église Monolithe is an underground passage, which leads to a space containing several burial niches, which are dug directly into the rock. Its dome above forms the base of a well whose walls enclose a spiral staircase. Archaeologists studying this area have documented that these **catacombs** may have been originally used as an underground graveyard.

GREAT VIEW
Tour du Roy

A symbol of royal power in Saint-Émilion, this fortress was built in the 13th century. Climb the 180 steps to the top for magnificent views of the city. The Fêtes de la Jurade, a festival organized by a committee of Saint-Émilion wine tasters, takes place here *(p50)*.

Tower and Catacombs

Place de l'Église-Monolithe 05 57 55 28 28 By appointment (call ahead)

A distant landmark, the Église Monolithe and its bell tower

Abbey Church and Cloisters

Church: rue des Écoles; Cloisters: via tourist office 05 57 55 28 28 Daily

The church's 12th-century nave, in the Romanesque style, has Byzantine-style domes that are supported by stone pillars. Traces of frescoes remain, including an image of the Madonna and the martyrdom of St Catherine. The choir dates from a later phase of construction in the 14th century. By the vestry door is a statue of St Valéry, who local vinegrowers consider their patron saint. The Romanesque cloister was modified in the 14th century.

Place de l'Église-Monolithe

Once place du Marché, this central square is lined with restaurants. The original Tree of Freedom, planted in the centre during the Revolution, died and has been replaced.

Rue de la Cadène

From place de l'Église-Monolithe, this road leads to Porte de la Cadène, once the access point between the upper and the lower town. A 15th-century wooden house is built onto it, with charming features such as turrets, mullioned windows and a polygonal tower.

Ramparts

Surrounded by a dry moat, the ramparts encircled the upper part of the town. They were pierced by six gates. The Romanesque Porte Brunet, on the southeastern side, the Tour du Guetteur, to the south, and L'Éperon, a lookout tower at Porte Bouqueyre, still stand.

Ermitage de Saint-Émilion

Place de l'Église-Monolithe 05 57 55 28 28 By appointment (call ahead)

The Ermitage de Saint-Émilion is supposed to be where the monk Émilion spent his days. The spring water that flows from the rock nearby is said to have therapeutic powers.

A SHORT WALK SAINT-ÉMILION

Distance 1.5 km (1 mile) **Time** 15 minutes
Nearest station Gare de Saint-Émilion

In the 8th century, a hermitage was set up here by Émilion, a monk from Brittany. Fortifications began to be built in the 12th century, and throughout the Middle Ages, houses, chapels and monasteries were added. This rich history, along with its famous vineyards, have earned Saint-Émilion and its outlying villages a place on UNESCO's World Heritage List, making it a fascinating place to stop for a walk. The town's architectural heritage is almost without equal, and the ochre-coloured stone buildings, complete with pinkish-red roof tiles, make Saint-Émilion a picturesque place for a stroll.

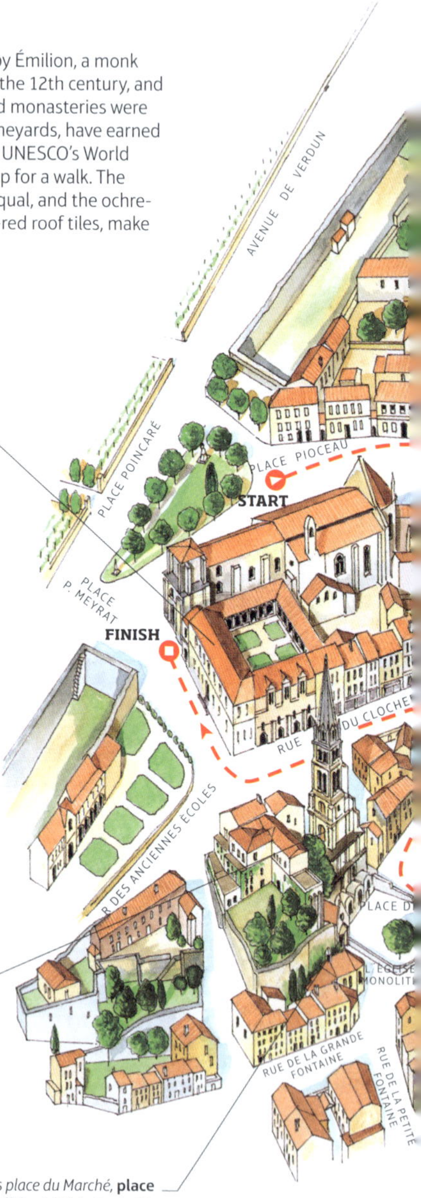

The cloisters of the ***Abbey Church*** *(p79) are 30 m (98 ft) square. Built originally in the Romanesque style, they were rebuilt in the Gothic period.*

Sunlight filtering through the cloisters of the abbey church

A remarkable sight in Saint-Émilion is the ***Église Monolithe's*** *bell tower (p78). It is the second highest in the Gironde after the spire of the Basilique Saint-Michel in Bordeaux (p68).*

Previously known as place du Marché, ***place de l'Église-Monolithe*** *(p79) is lined with restaurants. The original Tree of Freedom, planted in the centre during the Revolution, died and has been replaced.*

AVENUE DE VERDUN
PLACE POINCARÉ
PLACE PIOCEAU
START
PLACE P. MEYRAT
FINISH
RUE DU CLOCHER
R. DES ANCIENNES ECOLES
RUE DE LA GRANDE FONTAINE
RUE DE LA PETITE FONTAINE

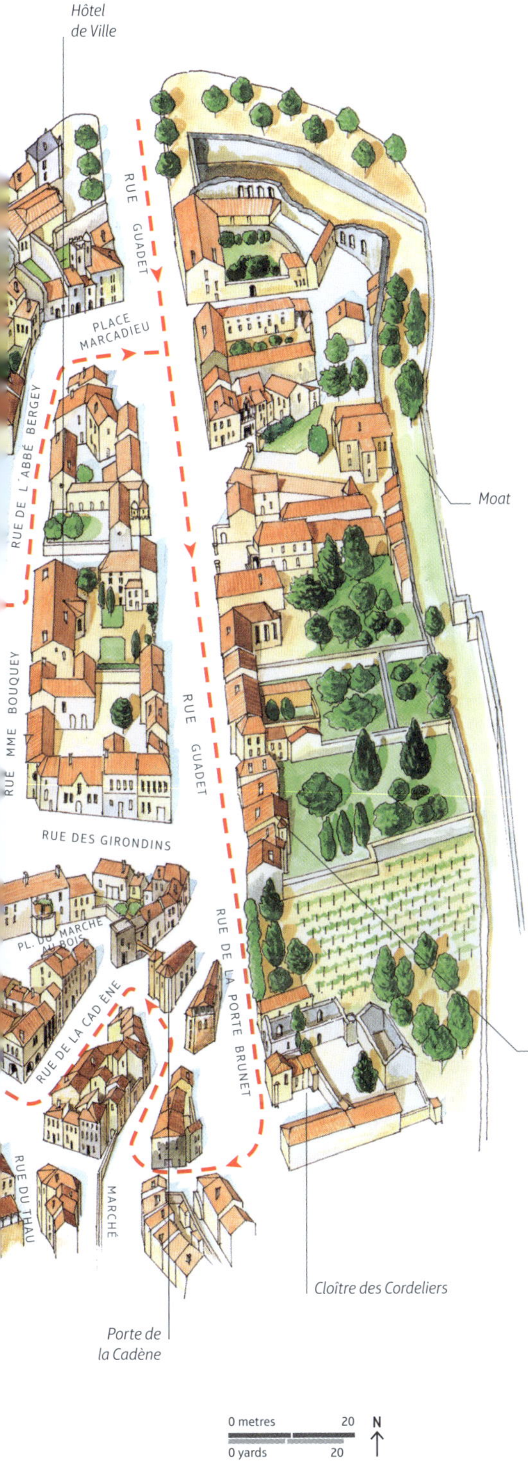

Hôtel de Ville

RUE GUADET

PLACE MARCADIEU

RUE DE L'ABBÉ BERGEY

Moat

RUE MME BOUQUEY

RUE GUADET

RUE DES GIRONDINS

PL. DU MARCHE AU BOIS

RUE DE LA PORTE BRUNET

RUE DE LA CADÈNE

Main part of the house, built in the 15th century, with the access staircase added in the 18th century.

RUE DU THAU

MARCHÉ

Cloître des Cordeliers

Porte de la Cadène

0 metres 20
0 yards 20
N

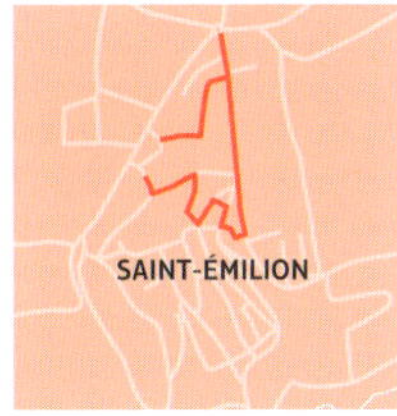

Locator Map
For more detail see p79

↑ Dining in place de l'Église-Monolithe in Saint-Émilion

Did You Know?

The monk Émilion is said to have performed miracles, earning him many disciples over the years.

A DRIVING TOUR SAINT-ÉMILION

Length 100 km (60 miles) **Starting point** Saint-Émilion **Stopping-off points** Wine tastings abound in this area, so pick up some brochures from the St-Émilion tourist office

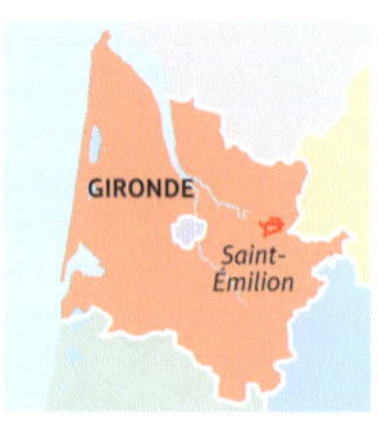

Locator Map

The Saint-Émilion area is dotted with picturesque villages that have fallen under the town's jurisdiction since 1289. In 1999 the whole area was declared a UNESCO World Heritage Site, and there are historic towns and beautiful architecture to admire on your drive. The land itself is crossed by winding country roads, and with colours that change with the seasons it is a strikingly beautiful place for a drive at any time of year. Beyond the natural beauty and pretty towns, it is the vineyards of Saint-Émilion that are the highlight for many tourists. Viticulture was brought here by the Romans, and the exceptionally favourable climate and vine-growing soil have resulted in it becoming one of the most prestigious wine regions in the world.

Saint-Émilion *(p78) is one of the oldest wine-growing areas in France.*

At **Pierrefitte***, near the village of Saint-Sulpice-de-Faleyrens, is a prehistoric menhir (standing stone). At 5 m (16 ft) high, it is made of limestone, widely found on the Saint-Émilion plateau.*

Vignonet's *economy is based entirely on vine-growing, with vineyards right up to the banks of the Dordogne river.*

D122
D243
Guadet
Bord
Beau
START
Saint-Émilion
Magdeleine
Les Grandes Versannes
Pierrefitte
D670
La Gaffelière
La Chapelle de Lescours
Grand Bigaroux
D19
D670
Saint-Sulpice-de-Faleyrens
D19e1
Dordogne
Ruisseau de Canterane
D670
D122
D19
VC7
Estey du Gréan
D122
Dartus
Vignonet
Dordogne
Le Port de Branne

← Vineyards growing around the town of Saint-Émilion

End the drive with wine tasting in **Saint-Laurent-des-Combes**. *Even this small village has multiple wine estates – try Château de Candale, which also serves meals.*

At the top of the hill above Saint-Christophe-des-Bardes stands **Château Laroque**, *a grand cru classé wine estate.*

↑ The 17th-century castle of Château Laroque, famous for its Merlot and Cabernet Franc

At the heart of the charming village of **Saint-Étienne-de-Lisse** *is a 12th-century church in the shape of a Latin cross. Above the village stands the Château de Preyssac, built by the English in the 15th century and later remodelled.*

A twisting road leads up from the Dordogne valley to **Saint-Hippolyte**, *an ancient village set in the middle of vineyards. It had a château from the early years of the Ancien Régime and a Romanesque church. The views from this town are spectacular.*

Spread out on either side of the road from Libourne to Castillon, the town of **Saint-Pey-d'Armens** *is named after St Peter ("Sent Pey" in Gascon), to whom its church is dedicated.*

→ Romanesque church tower in the town of Saint-Hippolyte

3

CHÂTEAU DE CAZENEUVE

C4 Préchac Hours vary, check website
chateaudecazeneuve.com

The 11th-century Château de Cazeneuve was once a place of exile for Margaret of Valois – wife of King Henri IV and queen consort of Navarre and France. Built by Amanieu VII d'Albret, the medieval castle was completely rebuilt in the 17th century and continues to be lived in by the same family.

Set high above the deep, picturesque gorge carved by the Ciron river, the castle is fronted by vast acres of wooded parkland. Although this elegant building has a unified look, its appearance today is the result of several successive phases of building. The castle grew out of a simple keep built on a motte in the 11th century. Three hundred years later it had become a fortress and in the 17th century it was converted into a sumptuous residence. The buildings, which are still inhabited, are arranged round the main courtyard. An extensive tour takes visitors through the castle's various stages of development and brings to life famous visitors and inhabitants, including Henri IV of France, who owned it, and his queen, Margaret of Valois.

HIDDEN GEM
Historic Park

The park surrounding Château de Cazeneuve is well worth exploring after the castle. The grounds feature a bamboo forest, pond and waterfall, and a cave system known as the Queen's Cave.

QUEEN MARGARET

An intelligent and cultivated woman, Margaret of Valois' life was torn between duty and family, politics and art. Despite her many accomplishments, she was banished to Cazeneuve by her husband Henri IV when she was unable to produce an heir. She later moved to Paris, where she died in 1615.

Light streams into the large, vaulted chapel through the seven windows. The nave is flanked by aisles.

Dating from the Middle Ages, the cellars are stacked with barrels of highly prized Bordeaux wines.

Merovingian tombs

The lower courtyard leads to the pool and to the medieval wine cellars.

← Château de Cazeneuve set in beautiful grounds

→ Barrels in the wine cellar below the château

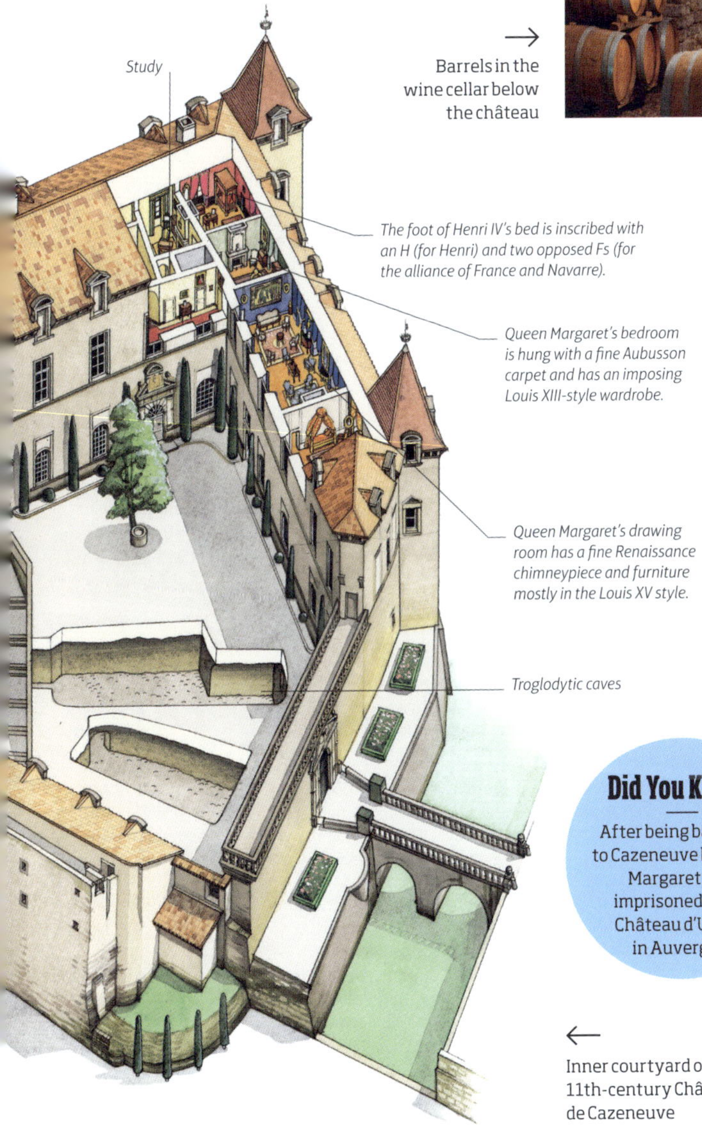

Study

The foot of Henri IV's bed is inscribed with an H (for Henri) and two opposed Fs (for the alliance of France and Navarre).

Queen Margaret's bedroom is hung with a fine Aubusson carpet and has an imposing Louis XIII-style wardrobe.

Queen Margaret's drawing room has a fine Renaissance chimneypiece and furniture mostly in the Louis XV style.

Troglodytic caves

Did You Know?

After being banished to Cazeneuve by Henri, Margaret was imprisoned in the Château d'Usson, in Auvergne.

Inner courtyard of the 11th-century Château de Cazeneuve

4

ARCACHON BASIN

 B3 **MA.AT, Esplanade Georges Pompidou, 22 boulevard du Général Leclerc, Arcachon; arcachon.com**

Only 50 km (31 miles) from Bordeaux, the Atlantic Ocean leaps and creeps into France through the Arcachon Basin. Oyster-farming ports, sandy beaches, pine forests, and a string of towns and villages surround the basin to create a unique maritime culture.

1

Arcachon

 **21 avenue Général de Gaulle arcachon.com**

It was thanks to Napoléon III that Arcachon began to develop as a coastal resort. This was completed by the arrival of the railway in 1857. Arcachon is one of France's largest towns, covering 200 sq km (77 sq miles) and almost merging with the neighbouring La Teste-de-Buch.

A marina was built in the 1960s, and the pier on the seafront is now the town's meeting place. Looking onto the coast road above Arcachon is the Ville d'Hiver, with 300 different 19th-century villas. Grab a map from the tourist office and set off on a self-guided tour of the area.

2 

Parc Ornithologique du Teich

Maison de la Nature du Bassin d'Arcachon Daily reserve-ornithologique-du-teich.com

This 1-sq-km (half-a-sq-miles) nature reserve, sitting on the basin's wildest shores along the Eyrre Delta, was created around the brackish waters of abandoned salt meadows. Up to 260 species of migratory birds can be seen here throughout the year. Herons, wild ducks, egrets, storks, swans and bluethroats may be observed in a natural setting, with salt-loving plants such as false willow and tamarisk growing nearby.

3

Gujan-Mestras

37 avenue de Lattre-de-Tassigny; 05 56 66 12 65

This small town with seven harbours produces 55 per cent of all the oysters farmed in the basin. The **Maison de l'Huître**, an information centre, is located in Larros harbour. *Pinasses*, long slender boats made of Landes pine, are anchored in the channels here.

Maison de l'Huître

Rue du Port de Larros 05 56 66 23 71 Jul & Aug: daily; Sep-Jun: Mon-Sat

EAT

Pinasse Café

Indulge in an array of seasonal dishes and an extensive wine list at this waterfront spot. The venue also has a sushi bar and small café for lighter meals.

2 bis, avenue de l'Océan, Lège-Cap-Ferret pinasse-cafe.com

Houses on the sandy coastline stretching along the Arcachon Basin

Île aux Oiseaux

Lying 3 km (2 miles) north of Arcachon, this island is named for the many seabirds that flock here. The island is also an oyster-farming centre, and is popular with hunters, who lie in wait for their prey in hides. Raised on stilts, these wooden huts are known as *cabanes tchanquées*, from the Gascon word *tchanque*, meaning "stilt".

Lège-Cap-Ferret Peninsula

1 avenue du Général-de-Gaulle; 05 56 03 94 49

Sandy beaches stretch for 22 km (14 miles) along the western side of this thickly wooded peninsula. On its eastern side there are beaches at Claouey, Grand-Piquey, Petit-Piquey and Piraillan. At the oyster-farming villages of Canon and L'Herbe, most of the tiny cottages are now second homes. The Moorish-style chapel at L'Herbe is all that remains of the grand Villa Algérienne. The peninsula's smartest resort is at **Phare du Cap-Ferret**, where the lighthouse has a curious red lantern.

Phare du Cap-Ferret
Rue de la Poste Apr-Sep: daily; Oct-Mar: Wed-Sun
phareducapferret.com

Domaine de Certes

Audenge; 05 57 70 67 56

The fish-farming shallows at Certes consist of large expanses of fresh and salt water interconnected by the odd patch of dry land. Sea bass, grey mullet and sea bream are farmed here. A footpath runs along the coast, and bird-watchers can see a variety of species in their natural habitat.

Andernos-les-Bains

Esplanade du Broustic; 05 56 82 02 95

This resort is nestled on the northeastern shore of the basin. There is no water here at low tide, but when the tide is in, its many small beaches are ideal for relaxing. The resort also has an oyster farm and a marina at Le Bétey.

Did You Know?

Pinasses boats are designed to safely navigate the waters concealing the basin's sandbanks.

PHARE DE CORDOUAN

B1 Le Verdon-sur-Mer, Royan Apr–Oct: hours depend on the tides, check website phare-de-cordouan.fr

Originally manned by a religious hermit, the Phare de Cordouan has been watching over the Gironde estuary and its turbulent tidal waves for over four centuries. The "King of Lighthouses", with its domed chapel, is a UNESCO World Heritage Site.

The lighthouse's elegant silhouette rises up against the skyline to the west of Pointe de Grave. A boat can take you part of the way, but you must wade the last part of the journey to visit the lighthouse and explore the beautiful tower interiors. Work began in 1584, although 10 years later Henri IV had the original plans altered. In 1611, a Renaissance-style tower was added. The lighthouse was declared a historic monument in 1862 and, because of its restrained classical style, soon became known as the "Versailles of the Sea".

The lighthouse was declared a historic monument in 1862 and, because of its restrained classical style, soon became known as the "Versailles of the Sea".

↑ The Phare de Cordouan at low tide

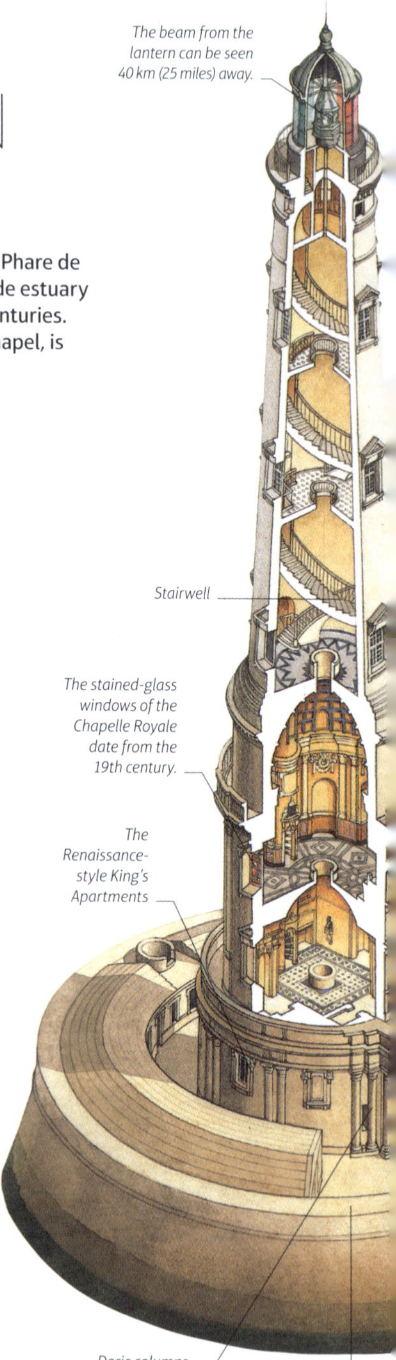

The beam from the lantern can be seen 40 km (25 miles) away.

Stairwell

The stained-glass windows of the Chapelle Royale date from the 19th century.

The Renaissance-style King's Apartments

Doric columns frame the monumental portico.

Parapet

The spiral staircase inside the Phare de Cordouan

301

The number of steps to get to the top of the lighthouse tower.

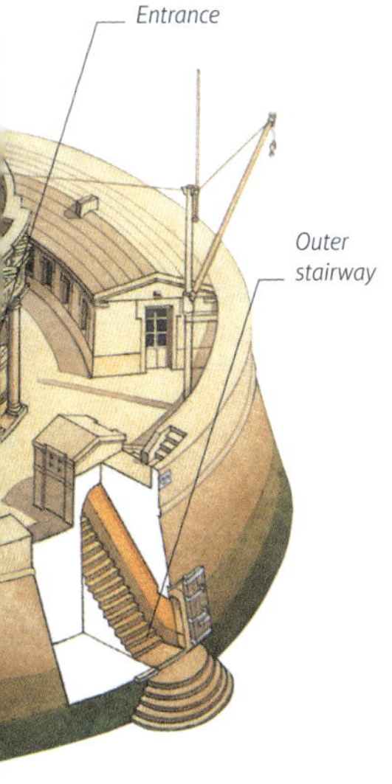

The elegant Phare de Cordouan tower and beautiful interiors

EXPERIENCE MORE

6

Saint-Ferme

B1 Place de l'Abbaye; 05 56 61 69 92

This small town is almost overwhelmed by the great Abbaye de Saint-Ferme, which was founded in the 11th century. Being near the Dropt – the river marking the border between French and English territory – it was fortified. The wealthy abbey was run by enterprising monks, who took in pilgrims on the road to Santiago de Compostela *(p226)*. It was sacked during the Hundred Years' War (1337–1453) and again during the Wars of Religion (1562–98).

The 12th-century **abbey** church is crowned by a small dome, and its Romanesque capitals have magnificent carvings of Daniel in the Lions' Den and other biblical scenes. The old **monastery** buildings now house the town hall. Entrance is free, but there is a fee for guided tours.

Abbey and monastery
33580 Saint-Ferme
Daily abbayesaint ferme.jimdo.com

7 

Phare de Grave

B1 2 allée du Sémaphore, Le Verdon-sur-Mer 05 56 09 00 25 Apr-Jun & Sep-Nov: 2-6pm Fri-Mon; Jul & Aug: 11am-7pm daily

This lighthouse, at Pointe de Grave, has a museum, with exhibits illustrating the life of a lighthouse-keeper. The 108 steps of the 28-m- (92-ft-) tall lighthouse lead to a platform with panoramic views of the Phare de Cordouan out at sea and the port at Le Verdon.

The little fishing harbour and marina at Pointe de Grave

Libourne

C2 40 place Abel-Surchamp; tourisme-libournais.com

Lying at the confluence of the Isle and the Dordogne, this *bastide* town still has portions of the old ramparts. The 15th-century town hall houses the **Musée des Beaux-Arts**.

Libourne is a great base from which to explore other interesting towns in the area, many of which are known for their wines. In Périssac, 17 km (10 miles) northwest of Libourne, is **Domaine de la Chataignière** which houses a wine museum. The collection documents the workings of the vineyards at Fronsac, which produce robust, full-bodied red wines. (Call ahead to make a reservation.) To the north lie the vineyards of Pomerol. The fine wines that are produced here owe their smoothness to the iron oxides in the local soil. This is particularly true of Château Pétrus, the most highly prized of them all.

At Guîtres, 15 km (9 miles) north, is the **Abbatiale de Guîtres**, a Romanesque abbey, dating from the 11th to the 15th centuries. At the **Musée Ferroviaire**, which has a small railway, visitors can relive the age of steam and diesel trains. The **Train Touristique de Guîtres** operates a steam-train service that covers a 14-km (9-mile) circuit of the countryside between Guîtres and Marcenais and stops off at a pleasant rural café-restaurant. Visitors can also explore Guîtres using the marked walks or indulge in a little wine tasting at a wine *chai* (warehouse).

Musée des Beaux-Arts
42 place Abel-Surchamp
05 57 55 33 44 Tue-Sat

Domaine de la Chataignière
1 les Grandes Terres, Périssac 06 85 52 26 88

Abbatiale de Guîtres
Guîtres 05 57 69 10 34
Jul-late Aug: daily; late Aug-Jun: by appointment

Musée Ferroviaire
Gare de Guîtres 05 57 69 10 69 May-Oct: Sun (Jul & Aug: also Wed)

Train Touristique de Guîtres
Gare de Guîtres 05 57 69 10 69 May-Oct: Sun (Jul & Aug: also Wed)

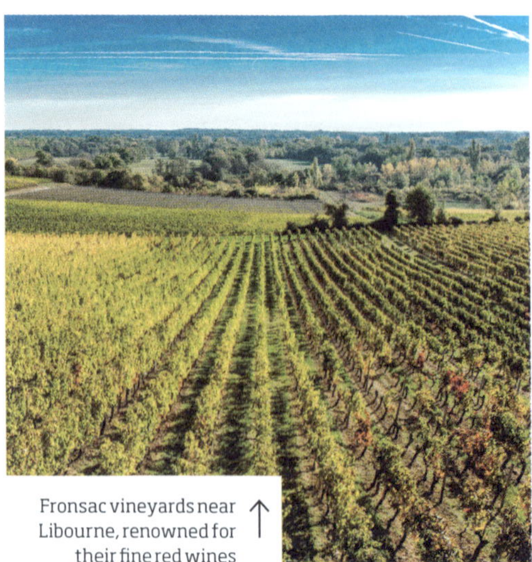

Fronsac vineyards near Libourne, renowned for their fine red wines

Soulac-sur-Mer

B1 68 rue de la Plage; medoc-atlantique.com

Soulac-sur-Mer developed as a resort when the railway line was built nearby during the Second Empire (1852–70). Attractive villas sprang up in the late 19th and early 20th centuries along Soulac's fine sandy beaches, including Plage Amélie and Plage la Négade. The latter is a nudist beach.

A UNESCO World Heritage Site, the **Basilique Notre-Dame-de-la-Fin-des-Terres** lies on the route taken by pilgrims travelling from Britain to Santiago de Compostela *(p226)*. This great 12th-century

Did You Know?

Soulac's basilica is named after its proximity to "the end of the earth" at Pointe de Grave.

←
Soulac's beautifully austere Basilique Notre-Dame-de-la-Fin-des-Terres

church has superb modern stained-glass windows and carved capitals.

The nearby **Musée d'Art Contemporain de Soulac** contains modern and contemporary paintings and sculptures by Aquitaine artists. The museum's archaeological pieces are from the prehistoric, protohistoric and Gallo-Roman eras in the Médoc.

Basilique Notre-Dame-de-la-Fin-des-Terres
33780 Soulac-sur-Mer
Daily

Musée d'Art Contemporain de Soulac
1 avenue El-Burgo-de-Osma 05 56 09 83 99
Apr–Jun: Fri–Sun; Jul & Aug: daily; early–mid-Sep: Wed–Sun

10

Blasimon

D3 Mairie; 05 56 71 52 12

Founded in 1273, Blasimon became a *bastide* town in 1322 on the orders of King Edward II of England, when the area was under his rule. Nestling in a small wooded valley alongside the Gamage river is Blasimon's stately **Benedictine abbey**. Built in the 12th and 13th centuries, it was owned by the abbey of La Sauve-Majeure *(p95)*. The two-tier façade looks beautiful at sunset, when it is bathed in golden light. The doorway and the arches that frame it are decorated with some of the most delicate Romanesque carvings in the Gironde.

On Wednesday evenings in July and August, there is a market, featuring locally grown produce and craft items.

Benedictine abbey
Quai Pascal Elissalt
Inner courtyard: all year

11

Sainte-Foy-la-Grande

D3 102 rue de la République; 05 57 46 03 00

This 13th-century *bastide* town on the banks of the Dordogne was founded by Alphonse of Poitiers, brother of Louis IX. After 1271, it stood in English territory, but was retaken by the French in 1453. By the 16th century, it had become a centre of trade and was one of the most dynamic of all Huguenot towns.

Of the medieval town, only four towers survive, now converted into houses. There are also several half-timbered dwellings from the 15th–17th centuries and a number of fine 18th-century townhouses.

At Port-Sainte-Foy is the **Musée de la Batellerie**, a fascinating museum of river craft, with models of *gabares*, wide flat-bottomed boats that sailed down the river as far as the Atlantic.

Located at Montcaret, 13 km (8 miles) west of Sainte-Foy-la-Grande, are traces of a Gallo-Roman villa dating from the 1st to 5th centuries CE. Although little of the structure remains, the outline of the main eating area and the thermal baths can be seen. Highlights include the mosaic bath floors, which depict fish and other marine animals.

Musée de la Batellerie
6 rue Notre-Dame
05 53 22 24 10 Mid-Jun–mid-Sep: Tue–Sat; mid-Sep–May: by appointment

↑ A vibrant, festive market street in Sainte-Foy-la-Grande

12 

Fort-Médoc

C2 Avenue du Fort Médoc, Cussac-Fort-Médoc Feb, Mar & Nov: Sat & Sun; Apr-Oct: daily bordeaux-tourisme.com

This fort was built by prolific military engineer Vauban in the late 17th century and, together with the citadel at Blaye and Fort-Paté, it formed part of the Gironde estuary's defences. The Porte Royale, a gateway whose pediment is filled with a relief of the sun, symbolizing Louis XIV, leads through to a courtyard. Beyond are the surviving elements of the fort, which include the guardroom and the battery platform. Based on a rectangular plan, the building is set with four corner bastions. One of these, overlooking the Gironde, offers wide views of the estuary and opposite bank.

The **Château Lanessan**, 2 km (1 mile) away, welcomes visitors to its wine cellars, where Haut-Médoc wines are matured. It also has a Musée du Cheval devoted to horses.

Château Lanessan

 Cussac-Fort-Médoc 05 56 58 94 80 Daily (by appointment)

13

Blaye

C2 Rue Couvent des Minimes, La Citadelle; bbte.fr

Blaye is of interest chiefly for its citadel, which was made a UNESCO World Heritage Site in 2008. It was built in 1689 and is set with star-shaped bastions. Overlooking the Gironde, the citadel offers breathtaking sunset views, especially from the Tour de l'Aiguillette. Guided tours of the citadel's old underground tunnels are available from the tourist office. In summer, the citadel is filled with artisans selling arts and crafts, as well as local produce and wine.

Next to place d'Armes, the Manutention – which once used to be a prison and later a bakery – houses the **Musée d'Histoire et d'Archéologie du Pays Blayais**, tracing the history of Blaye and its citadel.

Just south of Blaye lies the **Villa Gallo Romaine de Plassac**. Three villas, built from around the 1st to 5th centuries CE, have been carefully excavated and reveal details of the prosperous people who once lived here. Imported marble was used for much of the construction and the floors had underground heating.

Musée d'Histoire et d'Archéologie du Pays Blayais

Rue de la Manutention 06 82 34 72 66 Daily

PICTURE PERFECT
Estuary views

In and around the town of Bourg there are several good viewpoints (dubbed *Les fenêtres sur L'Estuaire*) over the Gironde estuary, ideal for watching river vessels and the local fishermen at work.

Villa Gallo Romaine de Plassac
 5 allée de la Mairie, Plassac Mar-Oct: daily villagallo romaine-plassac.fr

14 Bourg

C2 Hôtel de la Jurade, place de la Libération; bbte.fr

Built from local limestone, Bourg was a fortified town in the Middle Ages. Set on a steep slope, the town offers fine views over the Gironde river below, and can only be visited on foot. Today it is known for its local Côtes-de-Bourg wines.

In the upper part of the town is the **Château de la Citadelle**. This elegant folly, built to an elongated plan and surrounded by gardens, was once the summer residence of the archbishops of Bordeaux. It now houses the **Musée des Calèches**, a museum devoted to the horse-drawn carriage. The upper and lower town are separated by Porte Batailleyre, a 13th-century gate carved out of the surrounding rock.

A prehistoric cave, **Grotte de Pair-non-Pair**, lies 4.5 km (3 miles) east of Bourg on the D669. Discovered in 1881, its walls feature engravings of animals, including mammoths, ibexes and horses. It is the only decorated cave in the Gironde open to the public.

The main street in the Citadelle de Blaye, and *(inset)* views over the Gironde

Château de la Citadelle
Parc du Château Daily

Musée des Calèches
05 57 68 23 57 Mar-May & Oct: Sat & Sun; Jun-Sep: daily Nov-Feb

Grotte de Pair-non-Pair
 Prignac-et-Marcamps Tue-Sun (book ahead) pair-non-pair.fr

15 Pauillac

C2 La Verrerie; pauillac-medoc.com

The marina at Pauillac is very popular in summer and a common stopping place for sailing boats to de-mast before taking the river to the Canal du Midi.

While Pauillac is well known for its lamb, which is enjoyed all over France, it is more famous as the capital of Médoc winemaking. Three of the five Bordeaux *grands cru* vineyards (the highest level of red wine classification) lie around Pauillac - Lafite Rothschild, Mouton Rothschild and Latour. The **Maison du Tourisme et du Vin** here sells local *grands cru* wines and organizes tours of the region's châteaux, with opportunities to meet the growers.

Northwest of Pauillac is Vertheuil. The Abbaye des Prémontrés was founded here in the 11th century, but all that remains is an 18th-century building. The abbey church, the **Église Saint-Pierre**, which also dates from the 11th century, is a Romanesque church with a nave flanked by aisles. It has two bell towers, one dating from the Middle Ages. On the north side, the moulding round a restored doorway is carved with scenes from the life of Jesus Christ.

↑ Sailing boats docked at the tranquil marina in Pauillac

The Gironde estuary is dotted with a number of islands. One of them, the Île Patiras, lies just off Pauillac and can only be visited through a boat trip with **Bordeaux River Cruise**. They offer a range of different trips, such as wine cruises and a visit to the island's restored lighthouse. The Refuge de Patiras, located next to the lighthouse, is the former caretaker's home and is now a restaurant, also accessible via the boat cruise.

Maison du Tourisme et du Vin
Vinothèque La Verrerie Daily pauillac-medoc.com

Église Saint-Pierre
Vertheuil Daily Sun

Bordeaux River Cruise
bordeaux-river-cruise.com

Did You Know?

Pauillac's lamb pairs well with the local claret.

The vineyards of medieval Château de Monbadon, near Castillon-la-Bataille

Entre-deux-Mers

C2 4 rue Issartier, Monségur; entredeuxmers.com

In spite of its name, the area known as Entre-deux-Mers ("Between Two Seas") lies in fact between two rivers, the Dordogne and the Garonne. It consists of a large plateau cut by small valleys that are covered with meadows, fields and woodland. Human settlement here goes back far into prehistory. Entre-deux-Mers also has a rich heritage of *bastide* towns, Romanesque churches and fortified mills.

Vayres, situated high above the Dordogne, is the gateway to the region. The 13th–17th-century **Château de Vayres**, with its beautifully landscaped formal gardens and mixture of medieval and Renaissance architectual styles, was owned by Henri IV.

The vineyards of Entre-deux-Mers cover 15 sq km (6 sq miles), with 250 vine growers producing a fruity dry white wine. Visitors can enjoy diverse tastings at the **Maison des Vins de l'Entre-deux-Mers**.

Château de Vayres

63 avenue de Libourne
By appointment via website
chateaudevayres.com

Maison des Vins de l'Entre-deux-Mers

16 rue de l'Abbaye, La Sauve Jun-Sep: Mon-Sat; Oct-May: Mon-Fri vinsentredeuxmers.com

Castillon-la- Bataille

D3 5 allée de la République; tourisme-castillonpujols.fr

Castillon-la-Bataille is named after the decisive battle fought between the French and the English on the Plaine de Colly in July 1453. General Talbot was killed by Charles VII's troops, under the command of the Bureau brothers, and his 8,000-strong army was decimated. This defeat of the English marked the end of the Hundred Years' War and led to Aquitaine and the southwest being restored to the French Crown.

Vestiges of the town's eventful past include the 11th–12th-century gate, the Porte de Fer, a 17th–18th-century Baroque church and the Église Saint-Symphorien. The town hall, a former inn in the form of a rotunda, was built with funds provided by Maréchal de Turenne.

The Côtes-de-Castillon wine *appellation*, created in 1989, covers 30 sq km (12 sq miles) of vineyards and includes about 366 vine growers. Get a chance to sample some 60 different wines from Castillon and around at the **Maison du Vin Castillon Côtes de Bordeaux**.

At Petit-Palais-et-Cornemps, some 17 km (11 miles) north of Castillon-la-Bataille, is the beautiful Église Saint-Pierre. It is located just behind the cemetery and its façade is one of the best examples of Romanesque architecture in southwestern France. It has three superimposed arcatures supported by four sets of double columns. The doorway has spectacular carvings of lions and human figures, including a Spinario (a boy removing a thorn from his foot), based on the famous Roman statue.

Did You Know?

In the summer, the Battle of Castillon is re-enacted at Château Castegens, in Belvès de Castillon.

Maison du Vin Castillon Côtes de Bordeaux

6 allée de la République castillon-cotesdebordeaux.com

GREAT VIEW
Rauzan Castle

Although Rauzan castle is now in ruins, visitors can still climb to the top of the keep, which stands at 30 m (98 ft) high and offers a wide panorama of the town and the surrounding countryside.

Rauzan

D3 12 rue Chapelle; 05 57 84 03 88

Rauzan is best known for the atmospheric ruins of its fortified medieval **castle**. The castle in its present form was built by the Plantagenets in the 14th century. Restored in Gothic style after the Hundred Years' War, it then passed to the Durfort de Duras family. It was acquired by the municipal authorities of Rauzan in 1900. Built on a limestone plateau, the castle still has some impressive features, such as the keep, the main living quarters and the central tower. Access is over a bridge that leads to a massive gateway.

The **Grotte Célestine**, an underground river, which was discovered in about 1845, is open to visitors. Boots, protective clothing and helmets with headlamps must be worn and are provided.

Castle
12 rue de la Chapelle
Hours vary, check website
chateau-fort-rauzan.fr

Grotte Célestine
8 rue de Lansade
Apr-Aug: daily; Sep-Mar: Tue-Sat (by appointment)
grotte-celestine.fr

La Sauve-Majeure

C3 62 boulevard Victor-Hugo, Créon; 05 56 23 23 00

The Benedictine **Abbaye de la Sauve-Majeure** was founded by Gérard de Corbie in 1079, in an area that the monks gradually cleared of trees. Located on the pilgrim route to Santiago de Compostela, the abbey became a dynamic centre of religion and trade, and counted 70 priories in its sphere of influence.

Reduced to ruins by wars and the unrest during the French Revolution, the abbey has undergone several phases of restoration since 1952 and was made a World Heritage Site in 1988.

The abbey's majestic Romanesque and Gothic ruins stand in beautiful, mostly open countryside. The choir has Romanesque capitals carved with strikingly expressive biblical scenes. Next to the church are the remains of the 13th-century cloister, the chapter room and the refectory. A museum displays pieces found during excavations of the abbey.

Fine 13th-century frescoes can be seen in the Église Saint-Pierre, in the village.

The **Maison de la Poterie** in Sadirac, 10 km (6 miles) west of La Sauve-Majeure, displays a range of pottery, made in a style that has been traditional in Sadirac since antiquity. The museum is built around an old 19th-century kiln. Two hundred archaeological pieces are on display, while temporary exhibitions focus on more contemporary ceramics.

Abbaye de la Sauve-Majeure
05 56 23 01 55
Jun-Sep: daily; Oct-May: Tue-Sun

Maison de la Poterie
Feb-Dec: 2-6pm Tue-Sat
maisonpoteriesadirac.fr

→ The graceful arches of the Romanesque abbey at La Sauve-Majeure

The calm waters of Étang de Lacanau's natural lake, perfect for boating and water sports

Étang de Lacanau

B2 Place de l'Europe, Lacanau-Océan; medoc-atlantique.com

Covering 20 sq km (8 sq miles), this lake in between the coast and the town of Lacanau is ideal for sailing and sail-boarding. For over 20 years, this "Lacanau-Océan" has hosted a stage of the world surfing championship. It also has a large number of early 20th-century seaside villas.

The Étang de Cousseau, 5 km (3 miles) northeast of Lacanau, is a serenely tranquil lake with a nature reserve.

EAT

Le Wine Bar Margaux

At this bar, in a legendary wine village, choose from a wide range of salads or hot dishes from the daily menu. There's an outside terrace, too.

C2 12 rue Georges Mandel, Margaux 09 67 68 32 90

Margaux

C2 Route du Port, Lamarque; margaux-tourisme.com

The charming village of Margaux on the banks of the Gironde river is a portal to one of this area's best wine regions. Together, the vineyards around the villages of Arsac, Cantenac, Labarde, Margaux and Soussans produce the wines officially classed as "Margaux". Wine-lovers should make a point to stop at **Château Margaux**, which produces one of the great *premier grand cru classé* wines. Its fine oak-beamed cellars are open to the public, although sadly tastings are not available. The **Maison du Vin**, on the edge of Margaux, is an informative visitor centre for those interested in the great local wines.

Château Margaux

Margaux Mon-Fri, by appointment only Public hols, Aug & grape harvest chateau-margaux.com

Maison du Vin

7 place de la Trémoille Mon-Sat margaux-tourisme.com

Lesparre-Médoc

B1 7 place du Maréchal-Foch; lesparre-medoc.fr

This wine village is dominated by a square tower, **La Tour de l'Honneur**, which is all that remains of the 14th-century castle of the Lords of Lesparre. Inside, there is a museum devoted to local crafts and viticulture. Visit the rooftop terrace, for a lovely view over the town and woodlands.

Also of interest is the Neo-Gothic Saint Trélody church, built on the site of a former Benedictine monastery, and the 19th-century Notre-Dame de l'Assomption, which houses a Wenner organ dating from 1881. Both are open only during services or by appointment.

In the first weekend of August the town hosts La Fête du Vin et de la Gastronomie. This three-day event show-cases the region's wine and food and also features concerts and shows.

La Tour de l'Honneur

7 rue Pierre Curie Jun-Sep: Tue-Sat tour-de-lhonneur.jimdofree.com

The ever-shifting Dune du Pilat, one of France's most impressive natural wonders

Moulis-en-Médoc

C2 La Verrerie, Pauillac; 05 56 59 03 08

This village has a grand 12th-century Romanesque church that features an imposing Gothic bell tower and sculpted capitals. The **Maison du Vin de Moulis** here organizes tours of the châteaux within the Médoc *appellation* area.

By taking the D5 northwards, you will arrive at the picturesque **Port de Lamarque**, on the Gironde. From here you can take a ferry to Blaye *(p92)* and enjoy stunning views along the way.

Maison du Vin de Moulis
Jul-mid-Sep: Tue-Sat; mid-Sep-Jun: Mon-Fri moulis.com

Port de Lamarque
05 57 88 08 08

Barsac

C3 11 allée Jean-Jaurès, Langon; 05 5663 68 00

From the 18th century, Barsac, on the west bank of the river Ciron, was an important trade centre. It owed its wealth not only to wine production, but also to the local limestone that was used for building throughout the Bordeaux area. The church, which is dedicated to St Vincent, patron saint of Gironde vine growers, was rebuilt in the 18th century by the architect who also designed the Château de Malle, a Louis XIV-style wine estate in the Graves region (not open to the public).

The Barsac *appellation* applies to several châteaux, including **Château Climens** and Château Coutet. The Barsac white wines are slightly lighter and a little less sweet than the Sauternes wines.

Together, the vineyards around the villages of Arsac, Cantenac, Labarde, Margaux and Soussans produce the wines officially classed as "Margaux".

GREAT VIEW
Dune du Pilat

From the top of the Dune du Pilat, you can enjoy splendid views of the Atlantic Ocean to the west. Turning inland, you can see the Forêt Domaniale de la Teste, an ancient woodland that crosses Gironde and Landes.

Château Climens
Barsac Apr-Jul: by appointment only
chateau-climens.fr

Dune du Pilat

B3 Route de Biscarrosse, Pyla-sur-Mer; 05 56 54 02 22 or 05 56 22 12 85 (summer)

About 3 km (2 miles) long, 610 m (2,000 ft) wide and 110 m (360 ft) high, the Dune du Pilat is the highest sand dune in Europe. It overlooks the Banc d'Arguin and is covered with gillyflowers and convolvulus. Formed partly by the westerly winds, which blow the sand from the banks along the valleys, it grows by 1–4 m (3–13 ft) a year. The top of the dune offers great views.

A tree-lined road leading to the Château Margaux wine estate

Sauveterre-de-Guyenne

D3 · Place de la République; 05 56 71 53 45

In 1283, Edward VII, king of England, founded the *bastide* town of Selva-Terra. Later known as Sauveterre, it stood on the site of Athala, a small town founded in the 9th century. With its strategic location at the junction of roads running between Libourne and La Réole, and between Bordeaux and Duras, Sauveterre was long an object of dispute between the French and English, until it finally fell to the French in 1451. Sited at the heart of Entre-deux-Mers *(p94)*, the town no longer has its ramparts, which were destroyed in the early 19th century, though the four gates at the corners of the town remain. A vestige of Sauveterre's days as a defensive town is Tour Saubotte, on its west side, a tower with arrow-slits and a rampart walk.

The village of Castelviel, situated 7 km (4 miles) southwest of Sauveterre, has a church with a beautiful Romanesque doorway. The barrel vaulting is decorated with carvings of allegorical figures of the Virtues and Vices.

About 7 km (4 miles) southeast is Castelmoron-d'Albret. With 51 inhabitants, this is one of the smallest villages in France. This former seneschal town (the seat for royally-appointed governors) used by the House of Albret is set on a rocky outcrop with sheer cliffs 80 m (260 ft) high.

Lac d'Hourtin-Carcans

B2 · Place de l'Europe, Lacanau Océan; medoc-atlantique.com

Some 17 km (11 miles) long and with a vast surface area, the Lac d'Hourtin-Carcans is one of the largest lakes in France. Its shores are a good place to spot wildlife, such as herons, foxes, rabbits and hares. Plants include the rare aquatic flower *Lobelia dortmanna* and insect-devouring species, such as pitcher plants and sun-dews. The nearby resort of Carcans-Maubuisson offers tennis, cycling, horse riding and water sports. It also has a museum of local culture, the **Maison des Arts et Traditions Populaires de la Lande Médocaine**.

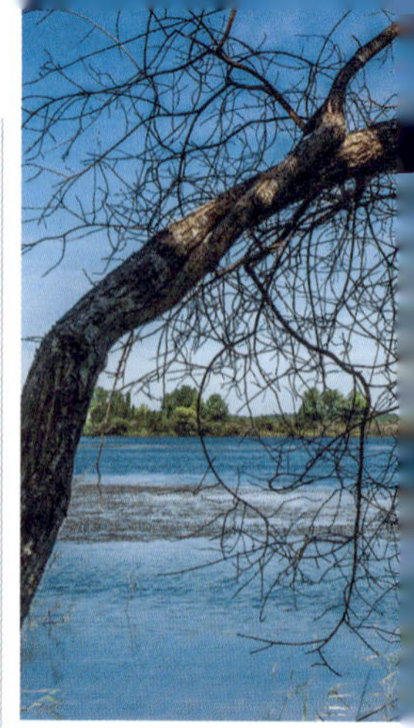

Maison des Arts et Traditions Populaires de la Lande Médocaine

129 avenue de Maubuisson, Carcans · Jul & Aug: Mon-Fri; mid-Jun-mid-Sep: 4:30-6:30pm Tue-Thu

Monségur

D3 · 3 rue Porte de la Réole; 05 56 61 39 44

This *bastide* town was founded in 1265 by a charter granted by Eleanor of Provence, wife of Henry III of England, who was also Duc d'Aquitaine. It was built on a promontory overlooking the valley of the river Dropt, and its strategic position gave the town its name (*Monségur* means "hill of safety"). The surviving medieval buildings include some half-timbered houses, a narrow alley known as the Ruelle du Souley, and a Gothic tower, the Tour du Gouverneur. In the northeast corner of the arcaded square stands the Église Notre-Dame, a late Gothic building that was restored in the 19th century.

↑ An old stone church peeking above grapevines in the *bastide* town of Sauveterre-de-Guyenne

←
Fishing on the Lac d'Hourtin-Carcans, one of the largest lakes in France

Did You Know?

The name "Monségur" derives from the Gascon "mont ségur" meaning "safe hill".

The cast-iron and glass market hall dates from the late 19th century. It was large enough to store 700 to 800 tonnes of *pruneaux d'Agen,* the famous local prunes. Today it is the setting for weekly markets and various festivals, such as the food and wine festival, the Foire au Gras, which takes place on the second Sunday of December and February. In July the town hosts the 24 Heures du Swing jazz festival.

A substantial amount of the town's original fortifications remains intact. The 2-km (1.2-mile) walk around the ramparts rewards you with views of the lush Dropt valley.

29

La Réole

D3 i 52 rue André Bénac; 05 56 61 13 55

Because of its strategic location on the banks of the Garonne, not far from the opening of the Dropt valley, this ancient walled town grew rich in the Middle Ages.

The town hall, founded by Richard the Lionheart at the end of the 12th century and superbly restored, is one of the oldest in France. The 13th-century Château des Quat'Sos is now privately owned and is currently closed to the public.

The town's Benedictine priory is now home to municipal offices. The grille over the central doorway of this jewel of 18th-century architecture was made by the master ironworker Blaise Charlut, who also made the banister of the inner staircase. The building is fronted by an elegant stone double staircase. The Église Saint-Pierre has a Romanesque apse and Gothic vaulting, which was rebuilt during the 17th century. A signposted walk around the town, with explanatory boards, lets visitors explore its architectural heritage. The town's ramparts were dismantled in 1629 by order of Cardinal Richelieu, but some remains can still be seen.

STAY

Amañi Hostel

Located in the historical centre of La Réole, this hostel has a wide range of rooms within its 12th-century building. Guests can enjoy a games area and a shared kitchen. It also offers bicycle storage.

D3 2 rue Peysseguin, La Réole 06 49 68 69 69

↑ The elegant cloisters of the Priory of Saint-Pierre de La Réole dating from the 18th century

La Brède

C3 3 place Marcel Vayssière, Martillac; tourisme-montesquieu.com

A wide avenue leads up to the **Château de la Brède**, where the philosopher and writer Charles de Montesquieu was born and lived. This rather austere Gothic building is surrounded by an artificial lake and moats. While the keep dates from the 13th century, the circular towers, chapel and other buildings date from the 15th century. Inside, Montesquieu's bedroom/study has been preserved. It was here that he wrote *De l'Esprit des Lois (The Spirit of Laws)*. His great library, with a barrel-vaulted ceiling, holds 7,000 books. The landscaped grounds in which the château stands were laid out by Montesquieu after a visit to England. Since 2011, wine has been produced on the property – a fitting tribute to Montesquieu, who was a keen promoter of the merits of Bordeaux wines.

Château de la Brède

Avenue du Château
Mar-Jun & Sep-mid-Nov: Wed-Sun; Jul & Aug: Tue-Sun
chateaulabrede.com

CHARLES DE MONTESQUIEU

Charles-Louis de Secondat, later Baron de La Brède et de Montesquieu, was born in La Brède in 1689. He became a lawyer but also had a keen interest in philosophy and science, and was also a "tireless promoter" of the merits of Bordeaux wines. In 1721, his *Persian Letters* - a political satire on the reign of Louis XIV and a brilliant critique of social mores - were published in Amsterdam, bringing him lasting fame. Elected president of the Parlement de Bordeaux, he also kept in touch with Parisian literary circles. He travelled widely, drawing on his observations to write *The Spirit of Laws* (1748), which laid the foundations of political science.

31

Saint-Macaire

C3 8 rue du Canton; 05 56 63 68 00

This medieval village on the edge of the Bordeaux region has some attractive buildings in ochre-coloured limestone. The priory church of Saint-Sauveur, in the form of a Latin cross, contains 14th-century frescoes, as well as a gilded wooden statue of the Madonna and Child. Place du Mercadiou, the ancient market square, is lined with fine 15th- and 16th-century merchants' houses. In summer, the village hosts Les Médiévales, with plays and concerts.

About 6 km (4 miles) northeast of Saint-Macaire is the wine-producing **Château Malromé**. It was home to artist Henri de Toulouse-Lautrec, who died there in 1901. He is buried in the cemetery at Verdelais, 3 km (2 miles) north of Malromé. The château is open to the public and also has a restaurant.

Around 3 km (2 miles) to the northwest is Saint-Maixant. The **Centre François-Mauriac de Malagar** here is devoted to the life and work of this French author and journalist (1883–1970) and Nobel laureate.

Château Malromé

Saint-André-du-Bois
Mar-Dec: Wed-Sun, by appointment malrome.com

← The idyllically set Château de la Brède, home of writer and philosopher Montesquieu

Centre François-Mauriac de Malagar
Domaine de Malagar, Saint-Maixant
Daily malagar.fr

Graves

C3

Graves is Bordeaux region's oldest wine-producing area. It stretches along the south bank of the Garonne river, south of Bordeaux on the Pessac and Léognan side. The soil here is gravelly *(graveleux)*, hence its name. There are no fewer than 350 vine-growing estates in Graves. Both red and white wines are produced, sometimes on the same estate, as at **Château Haut-Brion**. The Graves *appellation* covers an area of 31 sq km (12 sq miles), which produces about 18 million litres (over 4 million gallons) of wine a year.

Podensac, a major port on the Garonne in the 18th century, has some of the finest wine houses of this period. Lillet, a mixture of wine, fruit liqueur and cinchona bark, is the traditional apéritif here. The town's **Maison des Vins de Graves** illustrates the history of local winemaking and sells around 300 different Graves wines, both white and red. Podensac is also one of the best places to see the funnel-like steep wave, or tidal bore *(mascaret)*, that sweeps up the Gironde estuary with each incoming tide.

At Portets, in the heart of Graves, is Château Lagueloup. Along with the **Musée de la Vigne et du Vin**, the estate features vast wine cellars with wine presses and other devices that seem impressively sophisticated for their time.

> **Podensac is also one of the best places to see the funnel-like steep wave, or tidal bore *(mascaret)*, that sweeps up the Gironde estuary with each incoming tide.**

Château Haut-Brion
Pessac By appointment
haut-brion.com

Maison des Vins de Graves
61 cours du Maréchal-Foch, Podensac Jul-Aug: daily; Sep-Jun: Mon-Sat
vinsdegraves.com

Musée de la Vigne et du Vin
Château Lagueloup, Portets For tours, by appointment 05 56 67 18 11

Cadillac

C3 2 rue du Cros; 05 56 62 12 92

Set on the banks of the Garonne, the *bastide* town of Cadillac was established in 1280 to halt the progress of French troops, at a time when the Aquitaine region was ruled by the British. A surviving town gate, the Porte de la Mer, is a reminder of those warlike times.

The town is dominated by the **Château de Cadillac**. It was founded in 1599 by one of Henri III's favourites, who demolished the medieval fortress that stood on the site and built a sumptuous residence. Notable features of the interior include the decorated ceiling and eight monumental chimneypieces. The building was looted during the French Revolution, then in 1818 it served as a women's prison. From 1890 to 1952, it was used as a school for young offenders.

Rions, 5 km (3 miles) north of Cadillac on the D10, is a small town of Gallo-Roman origin and with medieval fortifications. A further 5 km (3 miles) northwest on the D10 is the impressive **Forteresse de Langoiran**.

↑ Cadillac's Porte de la Mer, a vestige of its medieval *bastide* walls

Château de Cadillac
4 place de la Libération Jun-Sep: daily; Oct-May: Tue-Sun
chateau-cadillac.fr

Forteresse de Langoiran
Le Château Jul-Aug: 11am-noon & 2-7pm daily; Sep-Jun: 2-6pm Sat & Sun chateaudelangoiran.com

DRINK

Maison du Lillet

This 19th-century distillery is the best place to discover Lillet - a regional apéritif that blends wine and liqueur, and is a component of the Vesper cocktail. The distillery offers Lillet tastings and has its own museum and shop.

C3 8 cours du Maréchal Foch, Podensac Sun & Mon lillet.com

↑ The magnificent Gothic cathedral of Bazas, and *(inset)* its soaring vaulted roof

Bazas

C4 1 place de la Cathédrale; tourisme-sud-gironde.com

Founded over 2,000 years ago, the town of Bazas later became a bishopric on the pilgrim route to Santiago de Compostela *(p226)*. Its magnificent Gothic cathedral was built between the 13th and 17th centuries, and has been restored. Particularly striking are the beautiful rose window and a triple Gothic doorway embellished with intricate carvings, both dating from the 13th century. Behind this majestic building lie the chapterhouse gardens. Place de la Cathédrale is a gently sloping square on which a market has been held for centuries. It is lined with arcaded 16th- and 17th-century houses, which have finely decorated façades.

The **Musée Municipal de Bazas** is devoted to the archaeology and history of the town. The **Apothicairerie de l'Hôpital Saint-Antoine de Bazas** contains a fine collection of pottery and glassware. For a pleasant tour of the town, pick up a map from the tourist office to explore its old streets.

The town of Captieux, 17 km (10 miles) south of Bazas, is one of the over-wintering sites of the migratory common crane. For information about these birds, contact the Ligue de Protection des Oiseaux Aquitaine in Audenge *(05 56 26 20 52)*.

Did You Know?

In Bazas, the speciality on the dinner menu is local Bazadaise beef, also celebrated in an annual festival.

Musée Municipal de Bazas

2 place de la Cathédrale 05 56 65 06 65 Jul & Aug: Tue, Thu & Sat

Apothicairerie de l'Hôpital Saint-Antoine de Bazas

1 place de la Cathédrale 05 56 25 25 84 By appointment

Château de Villandraut

C3 Rue Lafon Isoré Hours vary, check website chateaude villandraut.fr

This impressive château was built in 1305, both as a residential palace and for defensive purposes, on the orders of Pope Clement V (c 1264–1314) who was born in Villandraut. A huge building with an interior courtyard, it was – like the Château de Roquetaillade *(p76)* – defended by a rectangular line of ramparts set with six towers. From the top of these, there are fine views of the surrounding landscape. In July and August, torchlit explorations of the château are held on Wednesday evenings, and an atmospheric escape game can be reserved throughout the year.

Uzeste

C4 1 place de la Cathédrale, Bazas; 05 56 25 25 84

Consecrated in 1313 on the orders of Pope Clement V, the **Collégiale d'Uzeste** is one of the Gironde's finest Gothic buildings. Towering tall over the surroundings, this large abbey church was probably built to house the tomb of the pope (sited in the choir). The bell tower, in the flamboyant Gothic style, stands at the east end.

Collégiale d'Uzeste
Place de l'Église
06 09 92 20 23 9am-7pm daily

Sauternais

C3 14 place de la Mairie, Sauternes; 05 56 63 68 00

Lying along the south bank of the Garonne, the Sauternais area has a mix of siliceous, limestone and gravelly soil. The Ciron river, which flows through the area, gives it a favourable climate. The Sauternais is also dotted with prestigious châteaux, the most famous of which is the **Château d'Yquem**. Rated *premier cru supérieur*, the Sauternes wines produced there are some of the finest and most expensive in the world. Dating from the Middle Ages, Yquem is also one of the oldest wine estates in the area. Its vineyards cover just over 1 sq km (0.4 sq miles).

The Sauternes *appellation* covers five villages: Sauternes, Bommes, Fargues, Preignac and Barsac. These *grands crus* can be tasted and purchased at the **Maison du Sauternes**.

About 4.5 km (3 miles) west of Sauternes is the fortress at Budos, one of Pope Clement V's castles, built in 1308. Ruins of another of his castles lie at Fargues, 5 km (3 miles) east.

Château d'Yquem
Rue Château d'Yquem
By appointment
reservation.yquem.fr

Maison du Sauternes
14 place de la Mairie, Sauternes 05 56 76 69 83 Daily

SAUTERNES WINE

Grapevines used for Sauternes are produced like none other. Infected by a form of fungus known as "noble rot", they shrivel and are cut back severely. The grapes have a very high sugar content, resulting in the sweetness of the wine. The Sauternes grape harvest is a long and painstaking process, with every grape picked by hand. After fermentation, the wine matures in barrels for two years before being bottled. Sauternes is served well chilled. It can be enjoyed as an apéritif, or sipped at the end of a meal paired with a French fruit tart, especially apple and apricot.

↑ Wine tasting at Château Guiraud in the Sauternais, an area known for its sweet white wines

A DRIVING TOUR

THE MÉDOC REGION

Length 25 km (16 miles) **Starting point** Château Margaux **Stopping-off point** Join a Bordeaux River Cruise at Pauillac and dine on Île Patiras

This riverside drive takes in some of the most beautiful countryside of southwest France, as well as the Médoc vineyards, which produce some of the world's finest wines. The area sits between the Gironde estuary and an extensive forest, with the Atlantic Ocean to the west. It therefore enjoys a mild, humid climate that is ideal for grapevines. There is also a good mix of gravel, sand and clay soils. All this, combined with the expertise of local growers, accounts for the subtle wines created from traditional grape varieties, such as Cabernet Sauvignon.

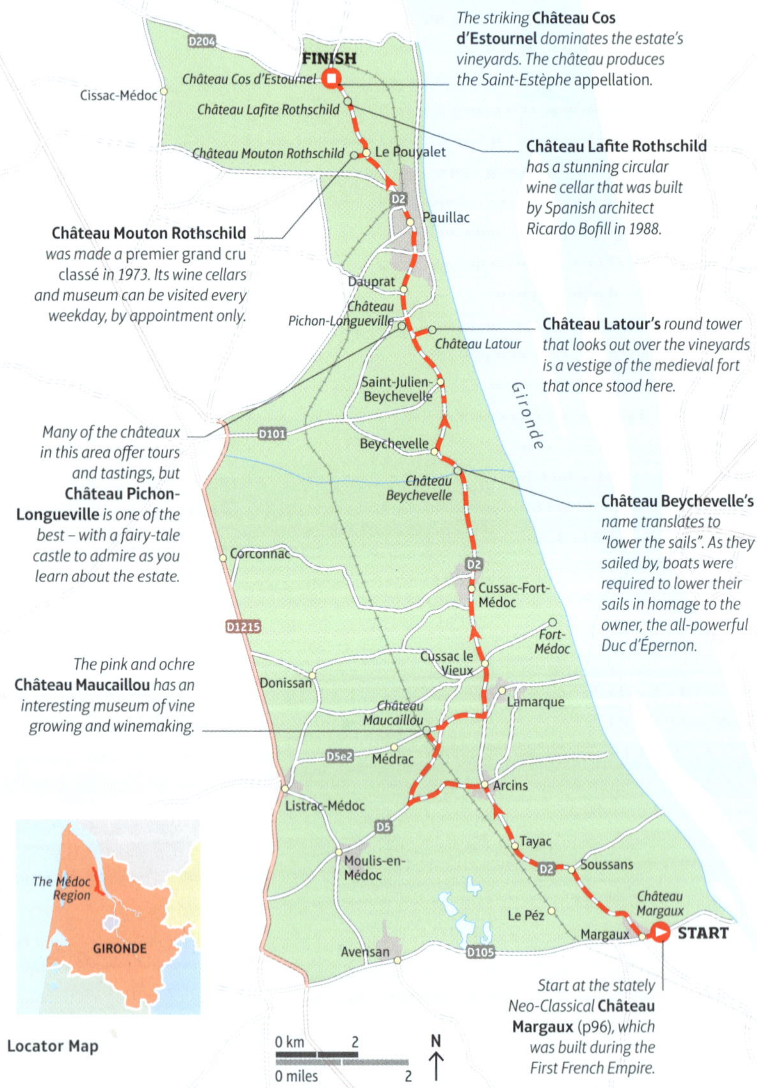

The striking **Château Cos d'Estournel** *dominates the estate's vineyards. The château produces the Saint-Estèphe* appellation.

Château Lafite Rothschild *has a stunning circular wine cellar that was built by Spanish architect Ricardo Bofill in 1988.*

Château Mouton Rothschild *was made a* premier grand cru classé *in 1973. Its wine cellars and museum can be visited every weekday, by appointment only.*

Château Latour's *round tower that looks out over the vineyards is a vestige of the medieval fort that once stood here.*

Many of the châteaux in this area offer tours and tastings, but **Château Pichon-Longueville** *is one of the best – with a fairy-tale castle to admire as you learn about the estate.*

Château Beychevelle's *name translates to "lower the sails". As they sailed by, boats were required to lower their sails in homage to the owner, the all-powerful Duc d'Épernon.*

The pink and ochre **Château Maucaillou** *has an interesting museum of vine growing and winemaking.*

Start at the stately Neo-Classical **Château Margaux** *(p96), which was built during the First French Empire.*

Locator Map

Did You Know?

Until 2025, the Médoc region almost exclusively produced red wines.

↑ A glowing sunset over the vineyards of the Médoc region

The buildings of Rocamadour illuminated against the rocky cliff

DORDOGNE AND LOT

The *départements* of Dordogne and Lot form a region known as Périgord-Quercy. Humans have left their mark here in a legacy going back to prehistoric times. The Vallée de la Vézère caves, Gallo-Roman sites, great castles that bore witness to centuries of war, and the many medieval *bastide* towns are just a few aspects of a local heritage that covers tens of thousands of years. Marrying the history with the region's famous natural beauty, the region's architecture sits in perfect harmony with the scenery – through stony fortress towers perched on rocky spurs, elegant Romanesque churches built of golden sandstone and troglodytic cliff-dwellings decorated with ancient artwork.

With the pride of local citizens tied to their history and serene landscapes, it's no wonder that this region is also home to no fewer than 18 of France's official Plus Beaux Villages (Most Beautiful Villages), almost 10 per cent of the entire list. The mix of landscapes offers something for everyone: to the north, meadows and forests; to the east, rugged limestone plateaus; to the south, vineyards, running down almost seamlessly into those of Bordeaux.

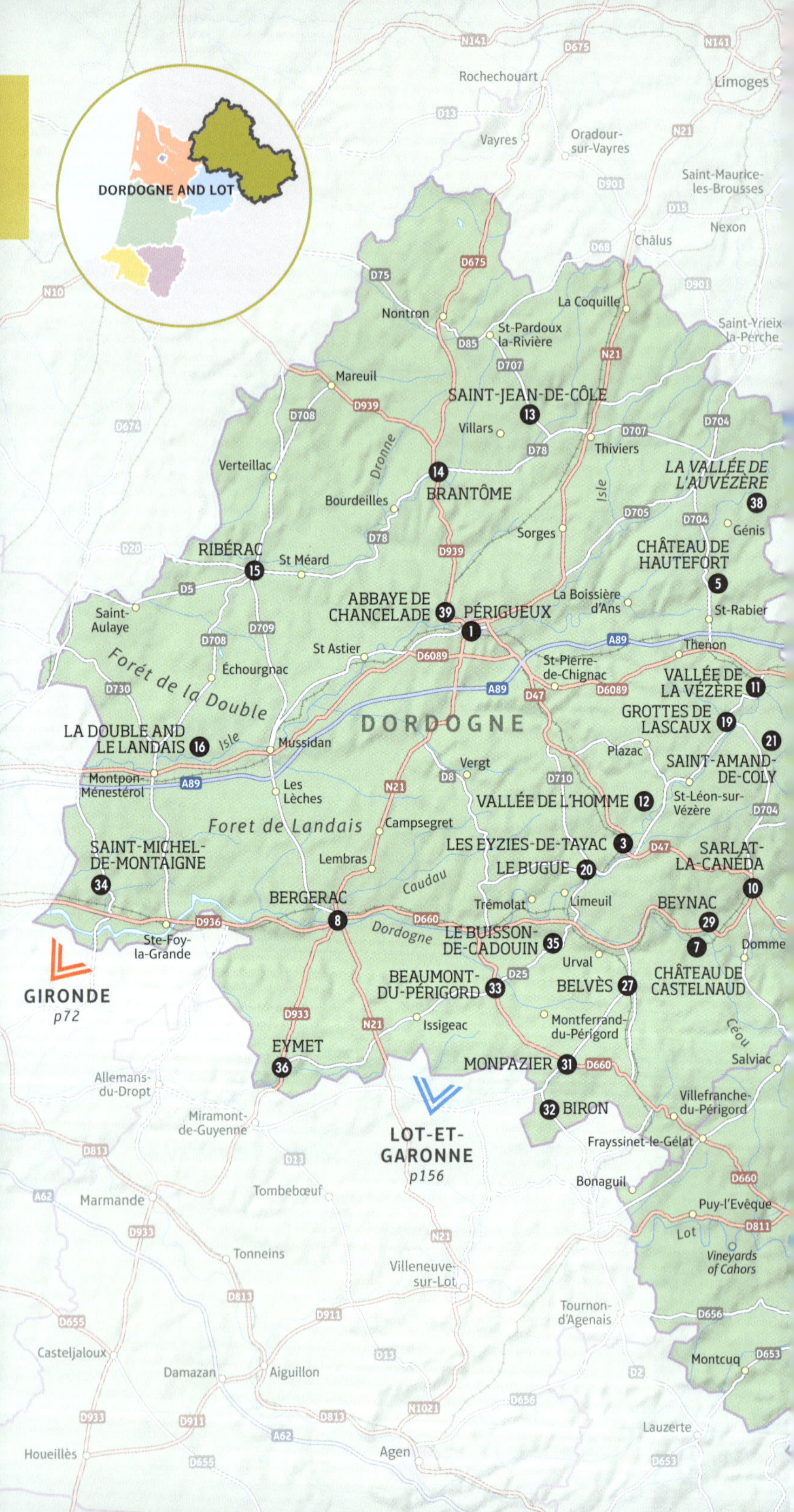

DORDOGNE AND LOT
DORDOGNE
Rochechouart
Limoges
Vayres
Oradour-sur-Vayres
Saint-Maurice-les-Brousses
Nexon
Châlus
La Coquille
Saint-Yrieix-la-Perche
Nontron
St-Pardoux la-Rivière
Mareuil
SAINT-JEAN-DE-CÔLE
13
Villars
Thiviers
LA VALLÉE DE L'AUVÉZÈRE
38
Génis
Verteillac
14
BRANTÔME
Bourdeilles
Sorges
CHÂTEAU DE HAUTEFORT
5
RIBÉRAC
15
St Méard
ABBAYE DE CHANCELADE
39
PÉRIGUEUX
1
La Boissière d'Ans
St-Rabier
Saint-Aulaye
Échourgnac
St Astier
Thenon
St-Pierre-de-Chignac
VALLÉE DE LA VÉZÈRE
11
Forêt de la Double
GROTTES DE LASCAUX
19
21
LA DOUBLE AND LE LANDAIS
16
Mussidan
Plazac
SAINT-AMAND-DE-COLY
Vergt
Montpon-Ménestérol
Les Lèches
VALLÉE DE L'HOMME
12
St-Léon-sur-Vézère
Foret de Landais
Campsegret
LES EYZIES-DE-TAYAC
3
SAINT-MICHEL-DE-MONTAIGNE
34
Lembras
LE BUGUE
20
SARLAT-LA-CANÉDA
10
BERGERAC
8
Trémolat
Limeuil
BEYNAC
29
Ste-Foy-la-Grande
LE BUISSON-DE-CADOUIN
35
7
Domme
Urval
GIRONDE
p72
BEAUMONT-DU-PÉRIGORD
33
BELVÈS
27
CHÂTEAU DE CASTELNAUD
Issigeac
Montferrand-du-Périgord
EYMET
36
MONPAZIER
31
Salviac
Allemans-du-Dropt
32 BIRON
Villefranche-du-Périgord
Miramont-de-Guyenne
LOT-ET-GARONNE
p156
Frayssinet-le-Gélat
Bonaguil
Marmande
Tombebœuf
Puy-l'Evêque
Vineyards of Cahors
Tonneins
Villeneuve-sur-Lot
Tournon-d'Agenais
Casteljaloux
Damazan
Aiguillon
Montcuq
Lauzerte
Houeillès
Agen
Dronne
Isle
Caudau
Dordogne
Céou
Lot
N141
D675
D13
N21
D901
D15
D68
D75
N10
D85
D707
D939
D708
D674
D704
D78
D705
D20
D5
D709
A89
D730
D6089
D47
D8
D710
D936
D660
D25
D933
D813
A62
D911
D655
D811
D656
D653
D2
N1021

DORDOGNE AND LOT
Must Sees
1 Périgueux
2 Gardens of the Manoir d'Eyrignac
3 Les Eyzies-de-Tayac
4 Rocamadour
5 Château de Hautefort
6 Figeac
7 Château de Castelnaud
8 Bergerac
9 Grotte du Pech-Merle
10 Sarlat-la-Canéda
Experience More
11 Vallée de la Vézère
12 Vallée de l'Homme
13 Saint-Jean-de-Côle
14 Brantôme
15 Ribérac
16 La Double and Le Landais
17 Terrasson-Lavilledieu
18 Castelnau-Bretenoux
19 Grottes de Lascaux
20 Le Bugue
21 Saint-Amand-de-Coly
22 Gouffre de Padirac
23 Martel
24 Souillac
25 Saint-Céré
26 Assier
27 Belvès
28 Saint-Cirq-Lapopie
29 Beynac
30 Gourdon
31 Monpazier
32 Biron
33 Beaumont-du-Périgord
34 Saint-Michel-de-Montaigne
35 Le Buisson-de-Cadouin
36 Eymet
37 Cahors
38 La Vallée de l'Auvézère
39 Abbaye de Chancelade
A20
D15
Saint-Germain-les-Belles
D901
Lubersac
D7
Vigeois
Brive-la-Gaillarde
17 TERRASSON-LAVILLEDIEU
Argentat
D940
D1120
D922
Montvert
N122
Salignac
D840
D820
MARTEL 23
2 GARDENS OF THE MANOIR D'EYRIGNAC
D1120
Aurillac
Carennac
18 CASTELNAU-BRETENOUX
D703
24 SOUILLAC
Autoire
Le Rouget
GOUFFRE DE PADIRAC 22
25 SAINT-CÉRÉ
A20
D920
Payrac
D673
4 ROCAMADOUR
D704
Gramat
D19
30 GOURDON
D840
Lacapelle-Marival
Maurs
Montsalvy
Le Bastit
D28
D673
ASSIER 26
D802
N122
Lamothe-Cassel
Causses de Gramat
FIGEAC 6
D920
LOT
Grèzes
Capdenac-le-Haut
D963
D653
D41
Espagnac-Ste-Eulalie
Célé
D840
Decazeville
Catus
D820
D22
GROTTE DU PECH-MERLE 9
Cabrerets
D662
D944
D840
Caillac
Cajarc
D922
37 CAHORS
Bouziès
28 SAINT-CIRQ-LAPOPIE
Lanuéjouls
D994
D988
A20
D911
D1
Rodez
Limogne-en-Quercy
D911
Villefranche-de-Rouergue
D911
Lalbenque
D926
D820
0 kilometres 20
0 miles 20
N
Castelnau-Montratier
Parisot

Ancient centre of Périgueux, built around the cathedral, on the banks of the River Isle

1

PÉRIGUEUX

E2 9 bis place du Coderc; tourisme-grand perigueux.fr

At the turn of every street, you travel through time in Périgueux. You will see a Byzantine cathedral, a Gaelic temple, a Roman amphitheatre and a marketplace once used for public executions. Medieval houses line the boulevards, and a Renaissance park is at its centre.

Vesunna

Parc de Vésone 05 53 53 00 92 Jul & Aug: daily; Sep-Dec & mid-Jan-Jun: Tue-Sun

A Gallo-Roman museum, Vesunna is named after the ancient city that occupied the site of modern Périgueux. Exhibits give an insight into the period's daily life. Nearby is the Tour de Vésone. At 24 m (80 ft) high with a diameter of 17 m (56 ft), it gives an idea of the size of the temple, long gone, of which it formed a part. The Jardin des Arènes has the remains of an amphitheatre.

Château Barrière

Rue de Turenne Daily

This 12th-century fortress served the aristocratic families of Périgord. Its oldest parts, a Gallo-Roman wall and a keep, can be seen at the rear. Its elegant five-tiered tower dates from the Renaissance.

Cathédrale Saint-Front

Place de la Clautre Daily

The Byzantine-Romanesque elements of Saint-Front were the design of Paul Abadie, the architect of the Sacré-Cœur in Paris. He also added domes and steeples to the structure. The interior has a magnificent 17th-century Baroque altar-piece and Stations of the Cross by Jacques-Émile Lafon.

Église Saint-Étienne-de-la-Cité

Place de la Cité Daily

Périgueux's first cathedral, a Romanesque, single-nave church, was built in the 11th century and remodelled in the 17th, when it also lost its cathedral status. It still has two of its four original domes.

Tour Mataguerre

Place Francheville 05 53 53 10 63 Jul & Aug: 10:30am-1pm & 2-5:30pm daily

Of the 28 towers that once surrounded the medieval district of Le Puy-Saint- Front,

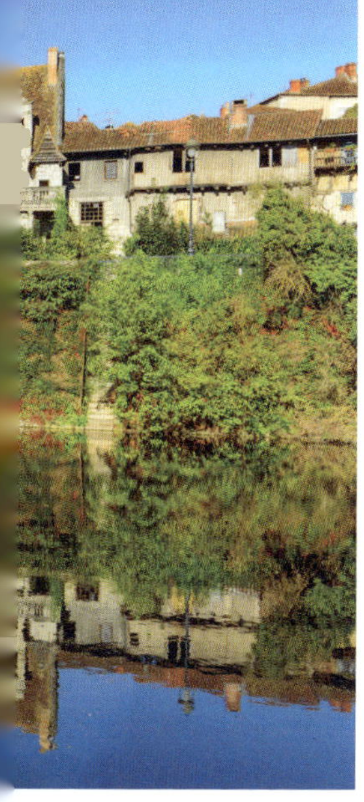

only this one stands. The tourist office next door organizes tours of this part of the fortifications that once encircled the city. A climb to the top is rewarded with breathtaking views.

Musée d'Art et d'Archéologie du Périgord

22 cours Tourny Hours vary, check website perigueux-maap.fr

This fascinating prehistoric collection includes the world's most complete Neanderthal skeleton, as well as glass, mosaics and earthenware from ancient Vesunna.

Musée Militaire

32 rue des Farges 05 53 53 47 36 2–6pm Mon–Sat

Exhibits at the Musée Militaire include a series of drawings made in the trenches during World War I by Gilbert-Privat (1892–1965), winner of the Prix de Rome. Medals, insignia and other wartime memorabilia help serve as a reminder of the sacrifices of those who fought.

TRUFFLES

The Périgordian truffle, *Tuber melanosporum*, is a highly prized delicacy for gourmets. An ingredient in many local specialities, this subterranean fungus is now scarce. In 1870, Sorges' limestone plateau alone produced 6 tonnes of truffles a year, which is equal to the yield obtained today from the whole of the Dordogne.

Écomusée de la Truffe

Sorges 05 53 05 90 11 Hours vary, call ahead

Northeast of Périgueux, Sorges is the Périgord's truffle capital. This museum features displays that showcase how truffles grow, the methods of finding them, and details of some spectacularly large examples.

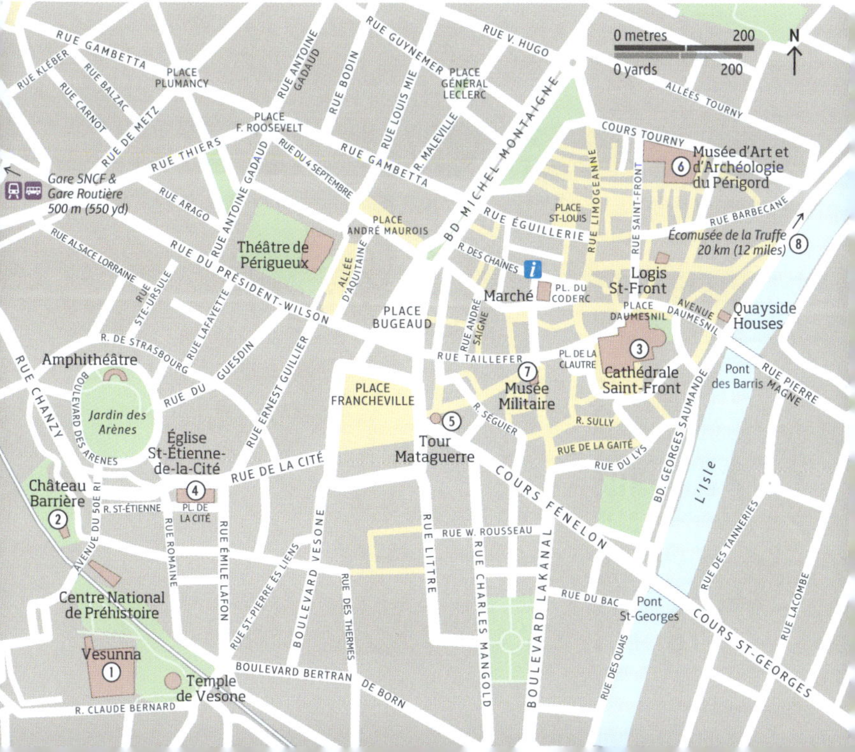

A SHORT WALK
PÉRIGUEUX

Distance 3 km (2 miles) **Time** 30 minutes
Nearest station Gare de Périgueux

The ancient centre of Périgueux is one of the largest urban conservation areas in France. A restoration programme, which began in 1970, has brought to life the narrow streets that run from the boulevards of the upper town down to the banks of the Isle river, and from the Mataguerre to the Plantier districts. Around the cathedral is the city's pleasant, pedestrianized, medieval area. On market days, place de la Mairie, place du Coderc and place de la Claustre buzz with activity. Place Saint-Louis, not far from rue Limogeanne, and the alleys leading off place de la Vertu, make for a fascinating stroll.

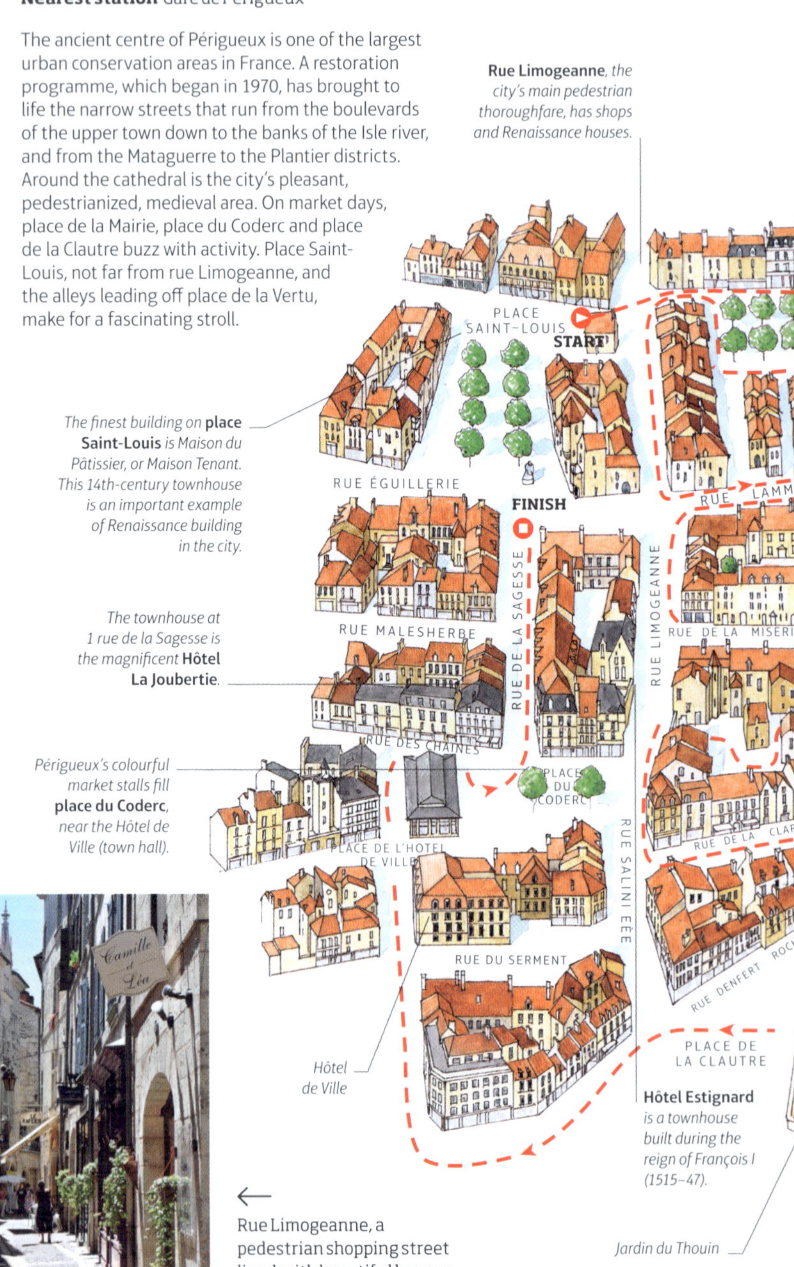

Rue Limogeanne, *the city's main pedestrian thoroughfare, has shops and Renaissance houses.*

The finest building on **place Saint-Louis** *is Maison du Pâtissier, or Maison Tenant. This 14th-century townhouse is an important example of Renaissance building in the city.*

The townhouse at 1 rue de la Sagesse is the magnificent **Hôtel La Joubertie**.

Périgueux's colourful market stalls fill **place du Coderc**, *near the Hôtel de Ville (town hall).*

Hôtel de Ville

Hôtel Estignard *is a townhouse built during the reign of François I (1515–47).*

Jardin du Thouin

← Rue Limogeanne, a pedestrian shopping street lined with beautiful houses

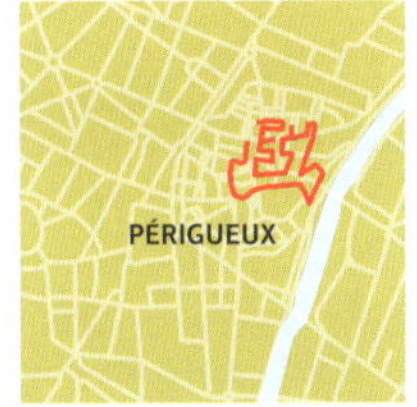

Locator Map
For more detail see p113

↑ Canoeing past the Cathédrale Saint-Front on the Isle river

RUE SAINT-FRONT
PLACE DE LA VERTU
RUE DES AUGUSTINS
RUE NOTRE-DAME
RUE DE LA CONSTITUTION
RUE DU PLANTIER
RUE SAINT-FRONT
PLACE DAUMESNIL
RUE DE TOURVILLE
AVENUE DAUMESNIL

The original masonic symbols on the **Freemasons' Hall** *were restored in 1987.*

Logis Saint-Front or Hôtel Gamensonn, *at 7 rue de la Constitution, consists of two houses, a half-timbered wing and a staircase tower.*

Did You Know?

The city is named after the Petrocorii, the Gallic people who first settled here.

The wonderful Renaissance quayside houses include the Hôtel Salleton, the Maison des Consuls and Maison Lambert.

Old Mill

0 metres 20
0 yards 20
N

Perigueux's original Roman-era church was destroyed by fire in 1120, and rebuilt as **Cathédrale Saint-Front** (p112) *in the form of a Greek cross.*

GARDENS OF THE MANOIR D'EYRIGNAC

F2 Salignac Souillac, Sarlat Hours vary, check website eyrignac.com

Enter Les Jardins du Manoir d'Eyrignac and explore seven unique gardens surrounding a 17th-century estate, family-owned for over 500 years. The grounds, complete with hand-clipped topiaries, vegetable patches and roses, create a paradise within the Dordogne.

First laid out in the 18th century, the gardens of this manor house form a cool oasis of greenery amid the dry, rocky limestone of the Périgord Noir region in southwest Dordogne. Watered by seven springs, they were built in the Romantic style in the 19th century, but within a century had fallen into such neglect that it took the owners – Gilles Sermadiras and later his son – nearly 40 years to restore them to their full glory. They finally opened to the public in 1987. Today, the gardens are a mix of the formal French and rustic Italian styles, with rolling lawns and a mass of mature trees and shrubs. The French garden, a masterpiece of symmetry and order, with topiary and carefully arranged parterres, stands in stark contrast to the more irregular "jigsaw" of the Italian garden. There are also many surprises to delight the visitor, such as secret nooks and unexpected vistas.

The "enchanted terrace" offers a fine view of the manor house and the French gardens.

Restaurant Côté Jardin

This long, grassy, hornbeam-lined avenue is a geometric masterpiece in a palette of harmonious greens.

Chinese pagoda

INSIDER TIP
White Picnic

Bring a picnic to join in the Pique-Nique Blanc (White Picnic). These fun open-air family parties are held on the lawns every Monday night in July and August and have a white dress code.

Walking down the shaded avenues in one of the estate's seven gardens

↑ The elegant, manicured grounds of the French-style Jardin Fruitier

EAT

Côté Jardin

Enjoy elegant regional dishes made with fine local produce at this restaurant located right in the gardens. There's also a separate tea room with a terrace for a quick snack or drink.

Gardens of the Manoir d'Eyrignac, Salignac
Apr–Oct: daily
eyrignac.com

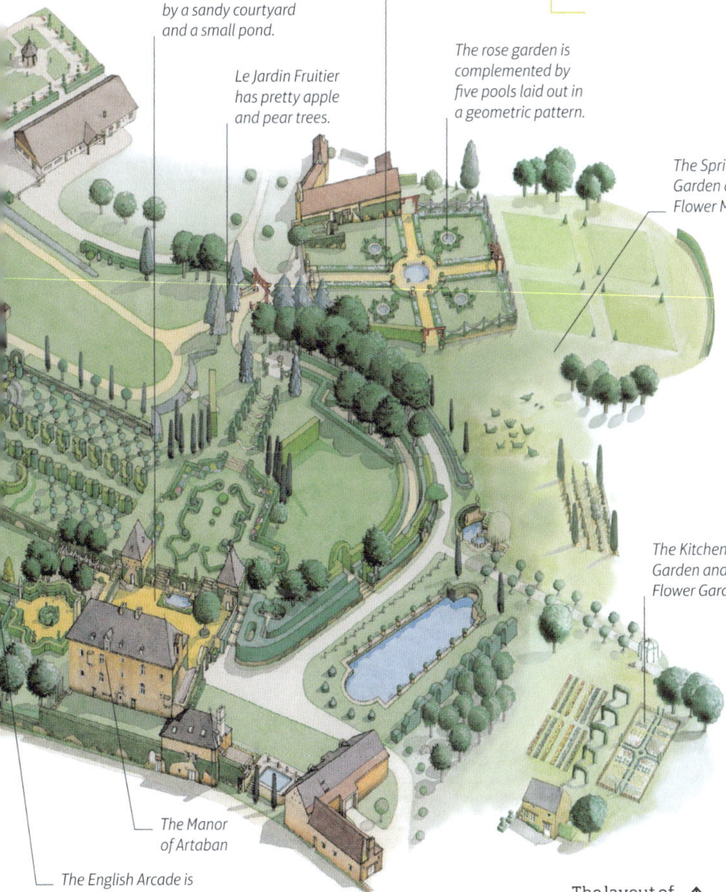

The terrace, which is laid out with flower-filled parterres, is fronted by a sandy courtyard and a small pond.

The White Rose Garden is planted only with white roses.

Le Jardin Fruitier has pretty apple and pear trees.

The rose garden is complemented by five pools laid out in a geometric pattern.

The Springs Garden and Wild Flower Meadows

The Kitchen Garden and the Flower Garden

The Manor of Artaban

The English Arcade is covered in vegetation that casts patterns of light and shade.

The layout of the Gardens of the Manoir d'Eyrignac ↑

LES EYZIES-DE-TAYAC

E2 19 avenue de la Préhistoire; lascaux-dordogne.com

At the heart of the Vallée de la Vézère, with its painted caves and rock-shelters, sits the village of Les Eyzies. Known as "the capital of prehistory", it stretches out along the foot of ochre-coloured cliffs that bear traces of some of the earliest human settlements. These sites are part of UNESCO's World Heritage List.

①  

Abri du Cap Blanc

Marquay Sun-Fri, by appointment via tourist office website

More than 15,000 years ago, early humans carved images on the wall of this rock-shelter. The result is a fine art display from the Magdalenian period.

②  

Abri du Poisson

On the D47 06 47 56 57 01 Jul & Aug: Tue, Thu & Fri

This small rock-shelter in the valley of the Gorge d'Enfer is named for the prehistoric fish relief found here. Carved in about 25,000 BCE, the relief of a salmon-like fish is 1 m (3 ft) long.

Abri Pataud

20 rue du Moyen Age 05 53 06 92 46 For renovation

This engraved rock-shelter contains traces of around 40 encampments dating from between 35,000 and 20,000 BCE. Below this is another rock-shelter whose ceiling features a relief of an oryx, made around 17,000 BCE.

Musée National de la Préhistoire

1 rue du Musée 05 53 06 45 45 Jul & Aug: daily; Sep-Jun: Wed-Mon

The exhibits in this museum make for an ideal introduction to the nearby painted caves, and also cover most of what is known about early humans.

Le Moustier, La Micoque and La Ferrassie

05 51 06 86 00 Mon-Fri; by appointment (call ahead)

The rock-shelter at Le Moustier, where a Neanderthal skeleton

INSIDER TIP
What to Wear When Caving

Touring dark and dank caves can be quite chilly, so be prepared with layered clothing, good sturdy shoes, and a sense of adventure as you head deep into the belly of the mountains.

Tucked beneath the rocks, the charming village of Les Eyzies-de-Tayac

was discovered, gave its name to the Mousterian culture (80,000–30,000 BCE). The oldest site in the Dordogne, La Micoque was inhabited from 300,000 BCE, while La Ferrassie contains evidence of Neanderthal burials.

6 

Abri de Laugerie Haute

On the D47 06 47 56 57 01 Mon-Fri; by appointment (call ahead)

This rock-shelter was inhabited from 22,000 to 12,000 BCE. It was abandoned when its ceiling fell in. Flint and bone tools, as well as a large number of harpoons, were found here.

7 

Grotte des Combarelles

On the D47 Sun-Fri, by appointment via tourist office website

Used during the Magdalenian period (around 15,000 BCE), this cave has engravings and drawings of horses, reindeer, mammoths, woolly rhinoceros and anthropomorphic figures.

8 

Grotte de Font-de-Gaume

Sun-Fri, by appointment via tourist office website

These cave walls are covered with coloured paintings dating from the Magdalenian period, and drawings and engravings of around 200 animals.

9 

Grotte du Grand Roc

1-4 avenue des Grottes 05 53 06 92 70 Feb-Dec: daily

This cave features fantastic mineral formations, including illuminated stalagmites and stalactites.

10 

Abri de Laugerie Basse

On the D47 Feb-Dec: daily abris-laugerie-basse.fr

This rock-shelter, dating from the Magdalenian period, chronicles the life of the Cro-Magnon people. The female figure of Venus Impudique (Shameless Venus) was found here in 1864.

EAT

Moulin de la Beune

Dine on local trout and porcini mushrooms at this converted water-mill by the river.

2 rue du Moulin Bas
moulindelabeune.com

11

Grotte de Bernifal

La Petite Beune 06 74 96 30 43 Jun-Sep: daily, by appointment (call ahead)

This small cave is accessed through the woods. Inside, tour guides use torches to light up the representations of mammoths and human figures, and signs and symbols dating from the Magdalenian period.

5 La Micoque
5 La Ferrassie 4 km (2 miles)
Le Moustier 4 km (2 miles) 5
0 kilometres 1
0 miles 1
N
D47
D706
D48
Le Fosses
La Cour
Les Guignes
6 Abri de Laugerie Haute
10 Abri de Laugerie Basse
9 Grotte du Grand Roc
2 Abri du Poisson
Vézére
Viregal
Viregal
Abri du Cap Blanc 2 km (1 mile) 1
Les Sables
Les Combarelles
7 Grotte des Combarelles
Les Fosses
Tayac
Beune
Les Girouteaux
Tremoulede
3 Abri Pataud
4 Musée National de la Préhistoire
8 Grotte de Font-de-Gaume
Moulin de la Beaune
Les Eyzies
La Rouquette
Beune
Les Granges
Grotte de Bernifal 11

4

ROCAMADOUR

F3 Rue Roland Le Preux; vallee-dordogne.com

Here history, legend, nature and religion converge. An important stop along the pilgrimage path to Santiago de Compostela, this famous town is a stunning cliff-hanging backdrop of old stone houses, Gothic churches and religious relics.

Sitting on a rocky plateau high above the Alzou valley, Rocamadour looks as if it is carved straight out of the limestone rock face. The town became one of the most famous pilgrimage centres in France because of the 12th-century statue of the Black Virgin and Child in the Chapelle Notre-Dame that was believed to have miraculous powers. An account dating from 1172 describes the 126 miracles granted by the Madonna, who is still honoured on 8 September each year during the *Semaine Mariale* (Marian Week).

INSIDER TIP

Going Up

There is a lift channelled into the rock face, which ascends (for a fee) from the base of the town to the sanctuaries and chapels that form the Cité Religieuse. A second lift travels (for a fee) up to the château.

↑ The spectacular town of Rocamadour carved into a cliff

↑ A vibrant pedestrianized street in popular Rocamadour

← Rocamadour's shrines and chapels perched on the cliff above the town

5

CHÂTEAU DE HAUTEFORT

F2 Le Bourg d'Hautefort Hours vary, check website chateau-hautefort.com

Hautefort Castle towers over the village below with a peacefulness that belies its tormented past. Rising more than once from the ashes, the castle has been the possession of French and English noblemen, a stronghold of the church and home to the Hautefort family.

Originally the site of a medieval fortress, the imposing residence that replaced it was built for the Marquis de Hautefort, who envisaged a classic building in the style of a Loire Valley château. Work began in 1630 and was completed in 1670. The castle was used as a prison during the French Revolution *(p54)*, and despite being recovered by the Damas family, the estate was later sold and fell into disrepair. The next owners, Baron and Baroness de Bastard, began restoring the main building in the 1920s, but this was brought to an abrupt end by a fire in August 1968, and the castle was left in ruins. Photographs showing the devastation of the fire are on view in the 14th-century Tour de Bretagne, the only surviving medieval part of the castle. Further phases of restoration were completed in 1995 and 2005.

Did You Know?

Guided tours on Wednesday nights in July and August include costumed actors and entertainers.

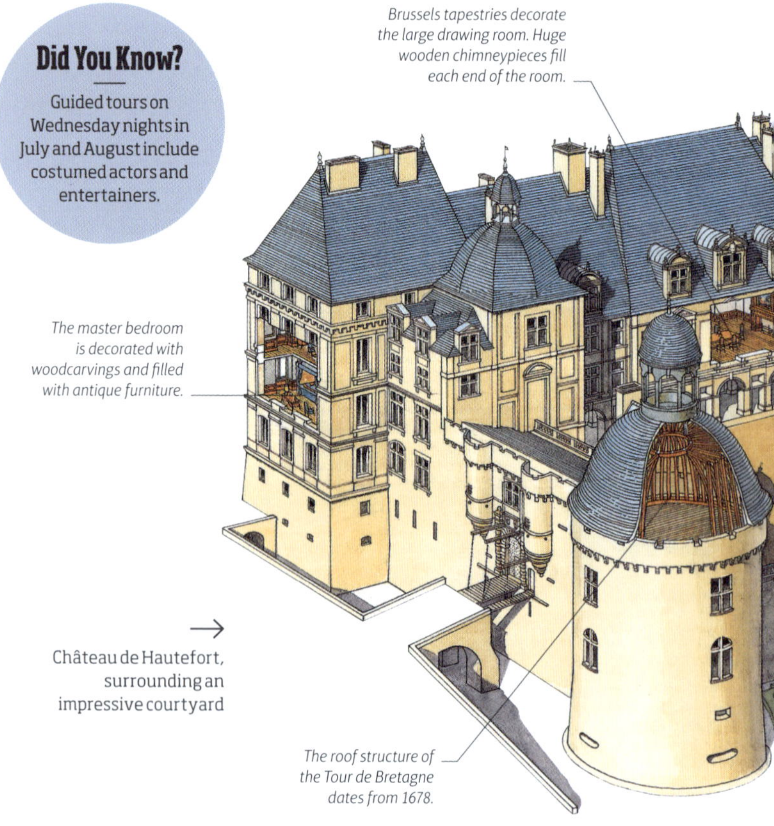

→ Château de Hautefort, surrounding an impressive courtyard

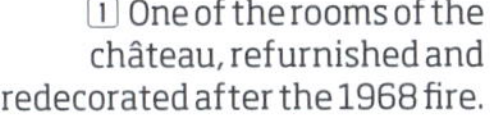

1 One of the rooms of the château, refurnished and redecorated after the 1968 fire.

2 The fabulous formal French garden was intended to marry the castle architecture with the natural beauty of the surrounding countryside.

3 The magnificent Château de Hautefort.

The Grand Staircase curves back on itself to lead to the upper floor.

The chapel ceiling, a trompe l'oeil coffered dome, looks down on a simple clay floor.

The terrace was rearranged in the 1930s. Box and yew have been clipped into domes.

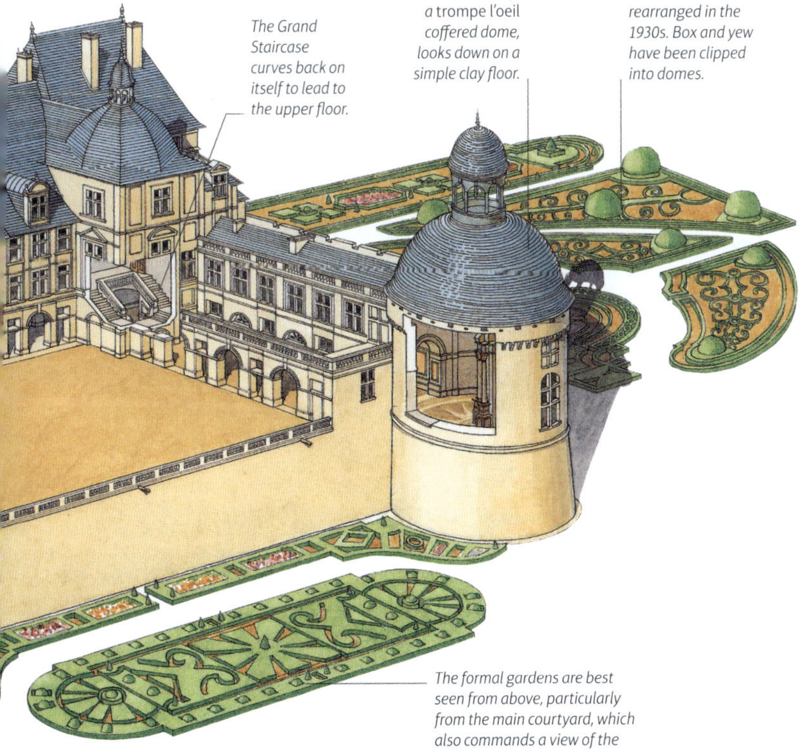

The formal gardens are best seen from above, particularly from the main courtyard, which also commands a view of the village on its southern side.

FIGEAC

G3 Hôtel de la Monnaie, place Vival; tourisme-figeac.com

"A flight of doves forming a cross in the sky over Saint-Sauveur" is the legend of the ancient abbey of Figeac and a reason this "town of art and history" is one of the "great sites of Midi-Pyrénées" to visit.

The town of Figeac, which sits clustered around its 9th-century abbey, grew and prospered as the result of trade. By the Middle Ages, its growing wealth enabled many inhabitants to build opulent houses here. Fortified in the 14th century, the town still has a medieval appearance, reflecting its past importance.

A place that delights in its medieval past, Figeac conceals stories of kings, pilgrims and religious armies within its narrow streets, timber-framed houses and stately mansions. With this incredible architectural heritage, Figeac offers a complete panoply of local urban architecture from the 12th century to the present day. Discover here, too, the history of mining, coin-making, and the secret code of hieroglyphics.

Hôtel de la Monnaie

Place Vival 05 65 34 06 25 Jul-Oct: daily; Nov-Jun: Mon-Sat

Constructed across the 13th and 14th centuries, this grand Renaissance residence, featuring an arcaded ground floor and gemelled windows, is known for its fine architecture. It presently serves as the Figeac tourist office.

Place Champollion

Place Champollion is one of Figeac's main squares. The building at No. 4, Maison du Griffon, dates from the Middle Ages and is adorned with carved Romanesque decorations. The 14th-century Gothic house at No. 5 has a stone *solelho* (open attic).

Abbaye Saint-Sauveur

6 rue Ferrer 05 65 34 11 63 Daily

The largest church in Figeac is one of the surviving elements of the abbey. It features a 13th-century chapter room, famed for its 17th-century panels and now known as the Chapelle Notre-Dame-de-la-Pitié.

Place des Écritures

This unusual area was laid out by Joseph Kosuth (1945–), a

INSIDER TIP

Medieval Gems

Other buildings in Figeac worth visiting include: Hôtel Galiot de Genouillac, with a spiral staircase; 14th-century Palais Balène, arranged around a courtyard; and Hôtel d'Auglanat, with a turret and 14th-century decorated doorway.

Restaurant tables set out in front of medieval buildings on place Champollion

pioneer of conceptual art. Part of his permanent installation here features an enlarged replica of the Rosetta Stone.

Hôtel de Colomb

5 rue de Colomb
05 65 50 05 40 10 Jul-15 Sep: daily; Apr-9 Jul & 16 Sep-3 Nov: Tue-Sun

With a restrained façade and a highly decorated staircase, this townhouse is typical of the 17th century. It has been the town hall since 1877, and houses the Espace Patrimoine, an exhibition on Figeac's history and heritage.

Musée Champollion: Les Écritures du Monde

Place Champollion
05 65 50 31 08 Jul & Aug: daily; Sep-Jun: Tue-Sun (Nov-Mar: pm only)

Set up in 1986, this museum is located in the house where renowned Egyptologist Jean-François Champollion (1790–1832) was born. Dating from the 13th and 14th centuries, its collection focuses on diverse writing specimens, including Egyptian hieroglyphics.

EAT

Commanderie des Templiers

Enjoy refreshments in the 13th-century courtyard of this former hostel for the Knights Templar.

41 rue Gambetta
commanderie-des-templiers.com

Video lounge at Musée Champollion: Les Écritures du Monde

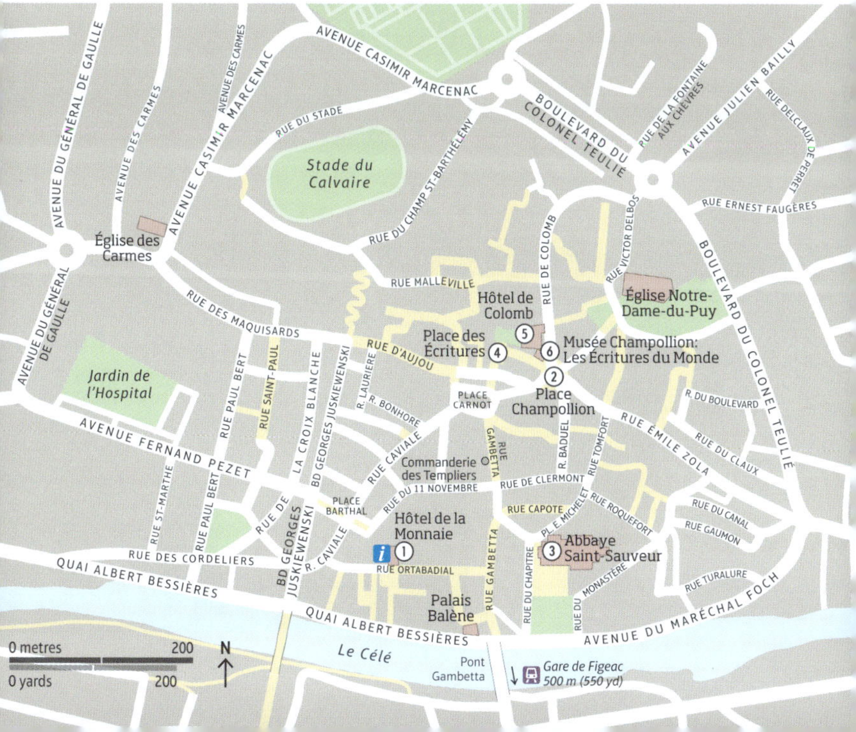

Did You Know?

The castle offers demonstrations of weaponry and blacksmithing on select days.

Château de Castelnaud, sitting above the hillside village of Castelnaud

7

CHÂTEAU DE CASTELNAUD

F3 Castelnaud-la-Chapelle Daily; hours vary, check website
castelnaud.com

Castelnaud Castle could easily take up a whole chapter in a book on French history. The prized possession of French and English kings, the castle saw battles that decided the fate of nations. Today, visitors delight over the building's authenticity, its war museum and its charming hilltop village.

Castelnaud has been an enduring presence in this region despite centuries of turmoil. It was destroyed by fire during an attack in the 13th century, besieged in 1442 by those seeking revenge during the Hundred Years' War *(p54)* and abandoned during the French Revolution.

After such a turbulent life, the castle gradually fell into ruin until the estate was bought in 1966 and classed as a historic monument. Visitors can now come to see impressive displays of medieval armour and weapons that evoke the war-torn history of the castle.

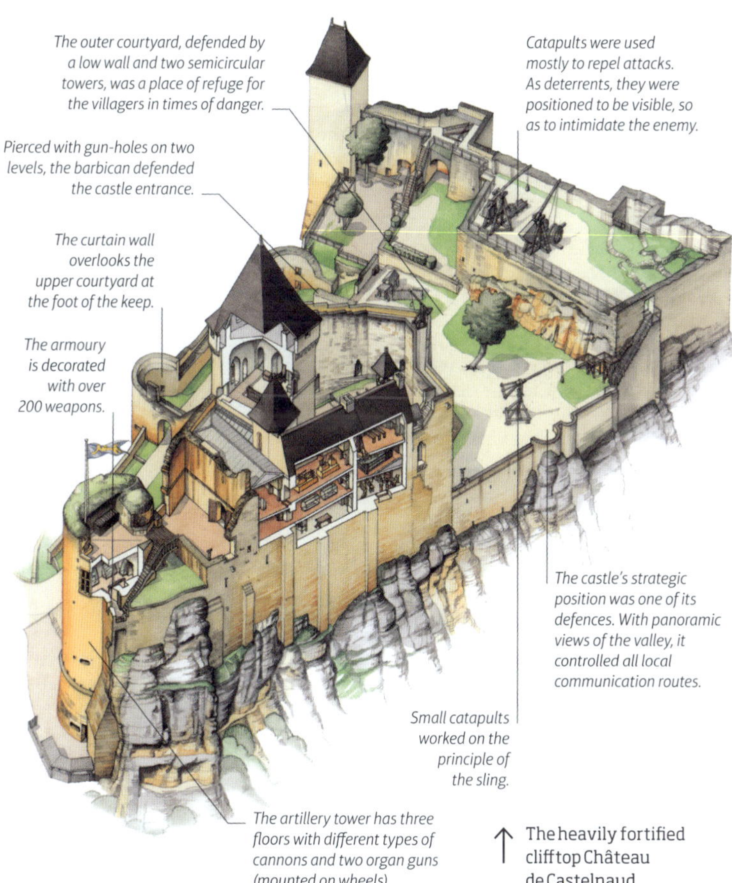

The heavily fortified clifftop Château de Castelnaud

BERGERAC

E3 Quai Cyrano, 1 rue des Récollets; pays-bergerac-tourisme.com

Bergerac blends the charm of the Dordogne and its half-timbered houses, squares, churches and stone bridges with the best of a busy city. Museums throughout the town tell of the area's association with tobacco and wine. At the centre of the Old Town, flower-filled place Pélissière is surrounded by shops and outdoor cafés.

Vieille Ville

The old, half-timbered houses of master-boatmen line place de la Mirpe, where there is a statue of Cyrano de Bergerac, Edmond Rostand's long-nosed hero. Rue Saint-Clar is lined with corbelled houses, with cob, brick and half-timbered walls. Place Pélissière, in a restored area of the town, is named after the skinners whose workshops once stood there. With the Église Saint-Jacques and Fontaine Font-Ronde, once a public washhouse, it forms a pretty enclave. Place Pélissière has another statue of Cyrano de Bergerac, which was erected in 2005. Rue Saint-James has interesting houses, including an 18th-century townhouse with a shop on the ground floor and bosses on its façade; a 16th-century house with mullioned windows; and 17th- and 18th-century half-timbered houses. Rue des Fontaines has two medieval houses.

Église Saint-Jacques

Place Pélissière

This 12th-century chapel on the pilgrim route to Compostela was enlarged in the 13th century when it became the medieval town's church with a single-wall belfry. Nearly destroyed during the Wars of Religion, it was later remodelled, with the nave rebuilt in the 18th century. The Neo-Gothic organ, built by Aristide Cavaillé-Coll in 1870, is listed as a historic monument.

Musée Costi

Via the inner courtyard of place de la Petite-Mission 05 53 63 04 13 Hours vary, call ahead

This museum fills two cellars of the Presbytère Saint-Jacques. It contains works donated by Costi, a sculptor who studied

↑ A *gabare*, a traditional barge, taking a tour on the Dordogne river, Bergerac

under Antoine Bourdelle. They consist of 52 bronzes and seven plaster casts, dated 1926–73.

Maison des Vins-Cloître des Récollets

1 rue des Récollets 05 53 63 57 55 Jun-Oct: daily; Nov-May: Mon-Sat

Cloître des Récollets was built in 1630 on the site of the former gardens of the Château de Bergerac. The 16th- and 18th-century galleries look on to the courtyard. It now houses the Maison des Vins de Bergerac, which offers wine tastings.

Musée du Tabac

Maison Peyrarède, place du Feu 05 53 63 04 13 Apr-Sep: Tue-Sun; Oct-Mar: hours vary, call ahead

Created in 1950 by the Direction des Musées de France, this museum occupies Maison Peyrarède, a townhouse built in 1604 and restored in 1982. The museum traces the history of tobacco over 3,000 years. Its collections illustrate the earliest use of the plant, its spread throughout the world, the ways that it was smoked, and its impact on society and the economy. Various smoking implements, with details of their manufacture, are shown. The importance of tobacco-growing in the Dordogne valley is also highlighted at the museum.

Temple de Bergerac

Place du Dr Cayla 05 53 57 02 73 Sat (mid-Jul-mid-Sep: daily during exhibitions)

This Protestant temple, constructed in 1788, bears witness to the Protestant Reform adopted by Bergerac in 1561. Today, it is still a place of worship and holds themed exhibitions during the summer. Leaflets explaining the architecture and history are available.

BERGERAC WINES

Bergerac wines were highly thought of in England during the Hundred Years' War, and in Holland when the town was a Protestant stronghold, but their renown goes back to the 13th century. Today there are 124 sq km (48 sq miles) of vineyards in the area, with 13 *appellations*, for red, rosé and white wines. For details on wine routes, contact the Interprofession des Vins de Bergerac et de Duras (IVBD): vins-bergeracduras.fr. You can also pick up the Wines of Bergerac map from the tourist office or the Maison des Vins-Cloître des Récollets.

GROTTE DU PECH-MERLE

F3 Peche-Merle Hours vary, check website; maximum of 700 visitors per day, book at least 3-4 days in advance pechmerle.com

Pech-Merle is one of the few original, ornate Palaeolithic caves open to the public. A fence protects paintings and engravings, yet visitors have the extraordinary opportunity to view hundreds of painted or engraved motifs of animals, humans and signs in their original prehistoric environment.

To visit this cave is literally to tread in the footsteps of early *Homo sapiens*. About 50 million years ago, a subterranean gallery was carved out over time by an underground river. The space, full of extraordinary natural rock formations, consists of several halls and chambers that contain hundreds of paintings, drawings and engravings showing animals, human figures and abstract symbols. Unique to Pech-Merle is the way in which these prehistoric images have been combined with the geological features of the cave. Because it was blocked up by a rockfall around 10,000 years ago, at the end of the Ice Age, the cave remained well preserved and fully intact until its discovery in 1922.

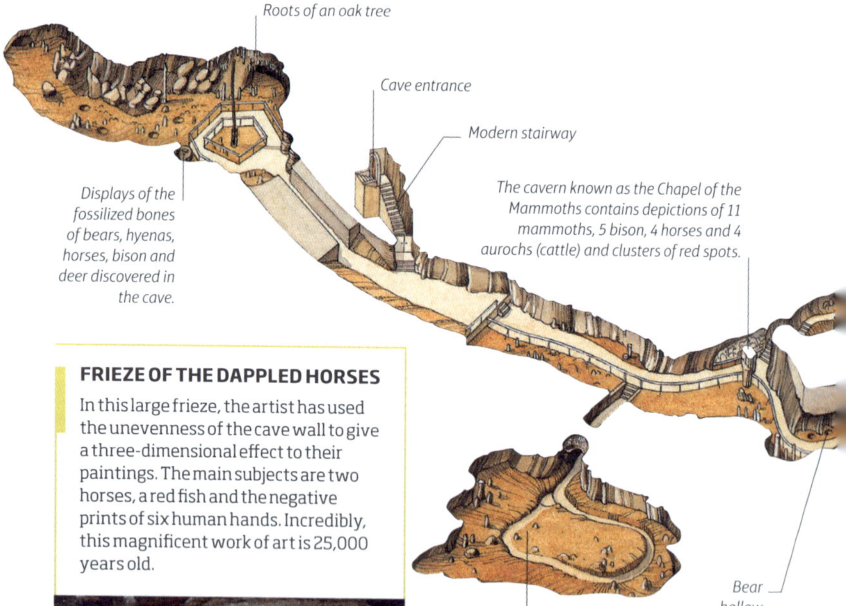

Roots of an oak tree

Cave entrance

Modern stairway

Displays of the fossilized bones of bears, hyenas, horses, bison and deer discovered in the cave.

The cavern known as the Chapel of the Mammoths contains depictions of 11 mammoths, 5 bison, 4 horses and 4 aurochs (cattle) and clusters of red spots.

Bear hollow

Ossuary closed to the public

FRIEZE OF THE DAPPLED HORSES

In this large frieze, the artist has used the unevenness of the cave wall to give a three-dimensional effect to their paintings. The main subjects are two horses, a red fish and the negative prints of six human hands. Incredibly, this magnificent work of art is 25,000 years old.

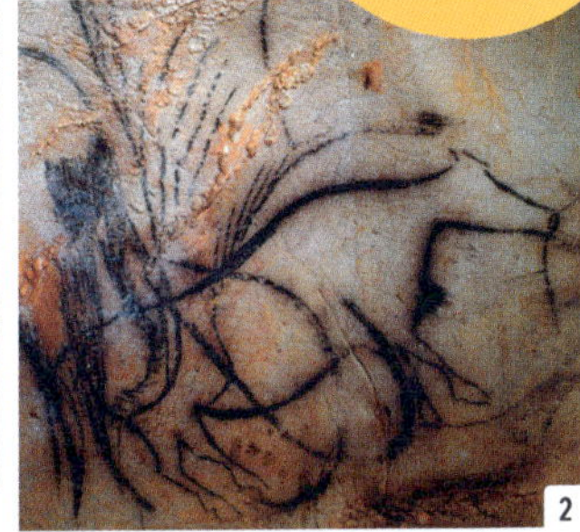

1 Visitors preparing to enter the caves.

2 Prehistoric paintings of an auroch, which used to live in this region.

3 The Hall of the Discs with its stunning calcite formations.

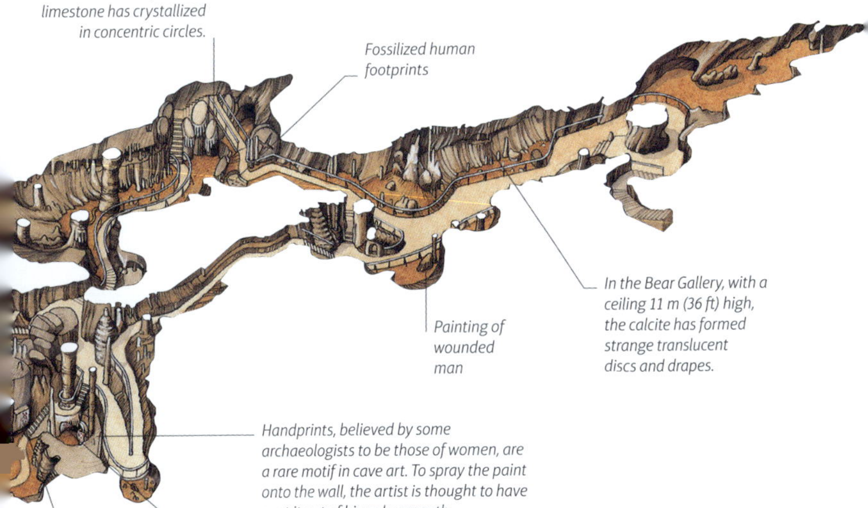

In the Hall of the Discs, the calcite from the limestone has crystallized in concentric circles.

Fossilized human footprints

In the Bear Gallery, with a ceiling 11 m (36 ft) high, the calcite has formed strange translucent discs and drapes.

Painting of wounded man

Handprints, believed by some archaeologists to be those of women, are a rare motif in cave art. To spray the paint onto the wall, the artist is thought to have spat it out of his or her mouth.

Red deer painting

The Frieze of the Bison-Women appears on the underside of an overhanging rock in the cavern with the Ceiling of the Hieroglyphs. It shows a mammoth and stylized female shapes drawn in red.

↑ The layout of the Grotte du Pech-Merle, showing the various chambers

Did You Know?

Ten other caves with prehistoric art have been discovered in the vicinity of Pech-Merle.

SARLAT-LA-CANÉDA

F2 · · 3 rue Tourny; sarlat-tourisme.com

Sarlat-la-Canéda, simply known as Sarlat, is a picture-book medieval town. With its cobblestone streets, sandstone buildings, elegant squares, and market days that are particularly colourful and bustling, it is no wonder that tourists flock here.

In summer, when it is closed to traffic, the heart of Sarlat's old town, with its architectural jewels, is a pleasure to explore on foot. On place de la Liberté is the Hôtel de Maleville (or Hôtel de Vienne), a townhouse in a combination of French and Italian Renaissance styles. Passage Henri-de-Ségogne, in the restored quarter of the town, is lined with 13th-, 15th- and 16th-century half-timbered corbelled houses with tiled roofs.

Cathédrale Saint-Sacerdos

Place du Peyrou · 05 53 59 03 16

Sarlat's cathedral was rebuilt in the 16th and 17th centuries on the site of an early Romanesque abbey church. The interior is arranged around a nave with four ribbed-vaulted sections. A stroll in the vicinity of the cathedral takes in the Cour des Fontaines and the Chapelle des Pénitents Bleus, the remains of the old cloister, and the Jardin des Enfeus, a former cemetery with burial niches carved into the wall. The purpose of the 12th-century Lanterne des Morts (Lantern of the Dead) is still unclear.

Western Sarlat

Half-timbered houses line rue des Armes, and can be seen from the ramparts. The

↑ Pretty restaurants on a charming cobbled street in Sarlat-la-Canéda

Chapelle des Pénitents Blancs is the remains of a 17th-century convent. Further on is the former Abbaye Sainte-Claire, also from the 17th century.

To the southeast of Sarlat is **Château de Fénelon**, where philosopher François de Salignac de la Mothe Fénelon (1651–1715) was born.

Château de Fénelon
Sainte-Mondane
05 53 29 81 45 Apr-Oct: Sun, Mon, Wed-Fri (Jul & Aug: Sun-Fri)

Eastern Sarlat

The former Présidial, in rue Landry, was the seat of the law courts in the 17th century, and is now a restaurant. The façade has a low arch with a loggia, containing a lantern, above. On either side of the town hall are old gabled houses. On rue Fénelon, opposite the alley leading to the Hôtel de Gérard, is a doorway framed by four columns decorated with fleurs-de-lis. It was once the town hall entrance.

Place de la Liberté

This picturesque square sits at the heart of Sarlat. The late medieval Manoir de Gisson, with tiled roof, is the hub of Sarlat's summer drama festival. Gargoyles stare down from the bell tower of the Église Sainte-Marie, now a covered market.

Rue des Consuls

This street is lined with many fine townhouses. Among them are the Hôtel Plamon, dating from the Middle Ages and modified in the 17th century, and Hôtel de Mirandol, near the Fontaine Sainte-Marie. Beyond the arch is the Hôtel Tapinois de Bétou with its wooden staircase dating from the *Ancien Régime* era.

EAT

Patisserie Massoulier
Indulge in one of this patisserie's gorgeous slices of cake, whimsical chocolate creations or fluffy pastries.

33 rue de la République
09 84 20 72 27

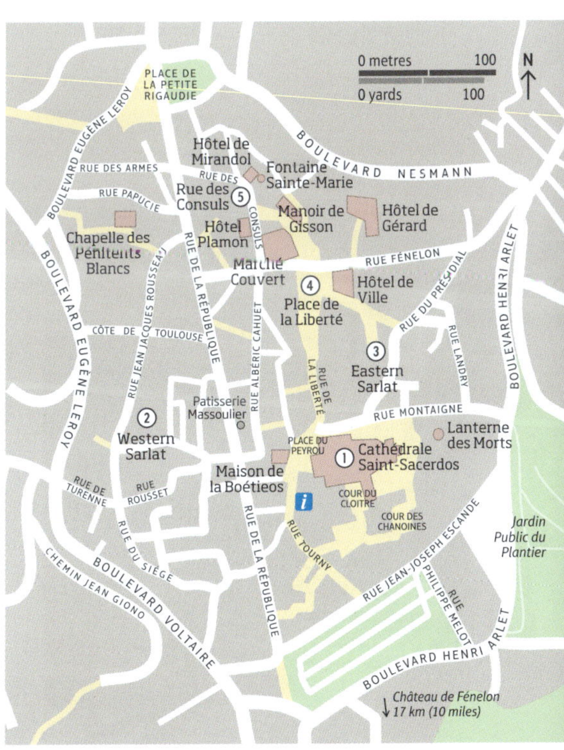

Collection of arms and armoury on display at Château de Fénelon

A SHORT WALK

SARLAT-LA-CANÉDA

Distance 1 km (half-a-mile) **Time** 20 minutes
Nearest station Gare de Sarlat

Nestling at the foot of a cluster of *pechs* (small hills), Sarlat-la-Canéda has undergone extensive restoration, returning its narrow streets and courtyards to their original splendour. A number of houses here consist of a medieval ground floor with Renaissance floors above. This centre of trade on the road to Santiago de Compostela *(p226)* grew rapidly in the mid- and late Middle Ages, when its splendid Renaissance houses were built. Rue de la République, laid out in the 19th century and nicknamed "La Traverse", runs between the picturesque medieval district and the town's other ancient streets. Although Sarlat's restored quarter is an architectural jewel that many come to admire, the town's seasonal truffle markets *(p31)* are also a big attraction for visitors today.

Did You Know?

Sarlat has been used as a location for many films, including Ridley Scott's *The Duellists*.

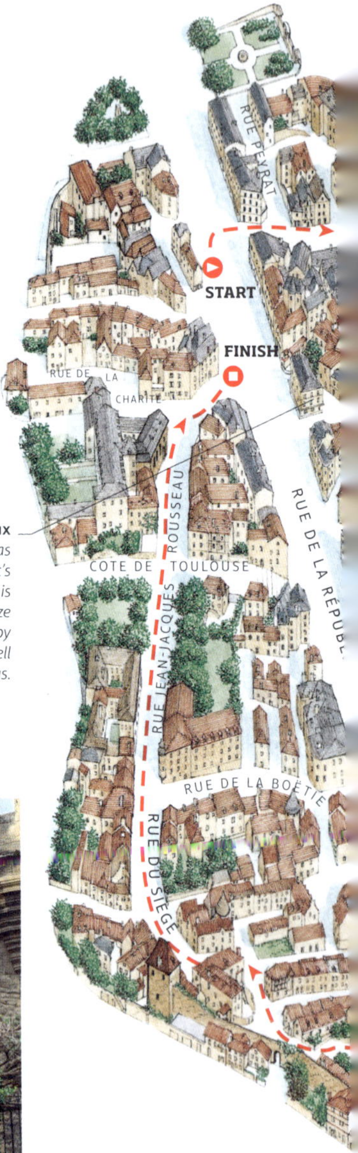

Place du Marché aux Oies *(Goose Square) was once the venue of Sarlat's live-fowl market. This is commemorated by bronze statues of geese by Lalanne. Sarlat is still well known for its foie gras.*

RUE PEYRAT
START
FINISH
RUE DE LA CHARITÉ
RUE JEAN-JACQUES ROUSSEAU
COTE DE TOULOUSE
RUE DE LA RÉPUBL
RUE DE LA BOÉTIE
RUE DU SIÈGE

Place du Marché aux Oies, a medieval area that was once used for busy markets

Lanterne des Morts (Lantern of the Dead) in the grounds of the Bishop's Palace

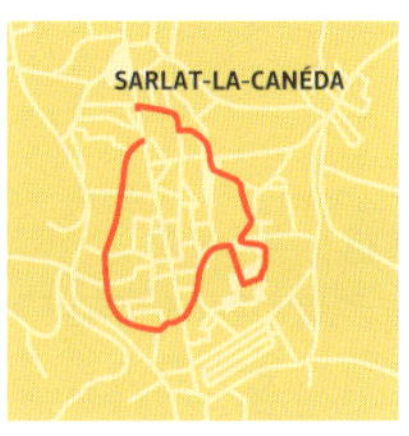

Locator Map

For more detail see p133

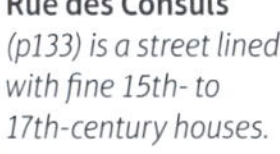

Rue des Consuls *(p133) is a street lined with fine 15th- to 17th-century houses.*

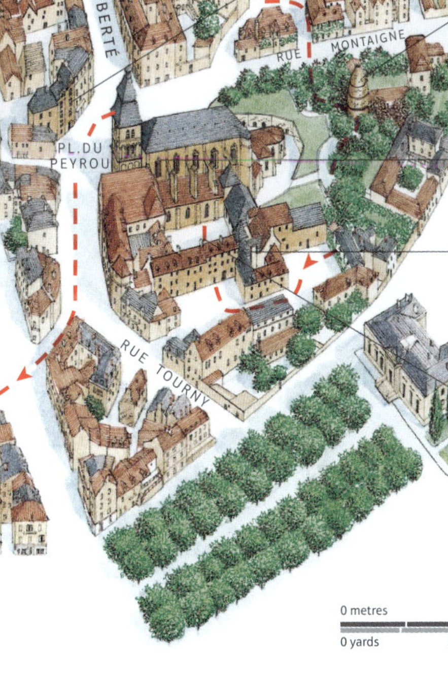

The hub of Sarlat, **place de la Liberté** *is lined with picturesque 16th- and 18th-century houses. The Église Sainte-Marie, in the background, was restored by the architect Jean Nouvel, and is now a covered market.*

The beautiful Renaissance **Maison de La Boétie** *was the birthplace of philosopher Étienne de La Boétie. The ornately decorated upper storeys have mullioned windows, and the building is crowned by an elegant tiled roof.*

The **Lanterne des Morts** *tower was constructed in the 12th century to commemorate a visit to Sarlat by St Bernard, a prominent abbot.*

Begun in 1504 and completed in the 17th century, **Cathédrale Saint-Sacerdos** *(p132) lacks stylistic unity, resulting in an eclectic mix of designs. A notable feature of the interior is the overhanging organ loft of 1770.*

Chapelle des Pénitents Bleus *is the only surviving element of an earlier Romanesque abbey church.*

The **Bishop's Palace** *has fine Gothic and Renaissance windows and an upper gallery. It now houses the tourist office, which puts on excellent exhibitions in the summer.*

EXPERIENCE MORE

Vallée de la Vézère

E/F2 19 avenue de la Préhistoire, Les Eyzies; 05 53 06 97 05

The Vallée de la Vézère is dotted with small picturesque towns. Condat-sur-Vézère, once a Templar town, stands at the confluence of the Vézère and the Coly. It has a Romanesque church and a castle with a square tower. The town of Fanlac, clustered round its church and bell tower, was the setting for *Jacquou le Croquant*, the 2007 film of the novel by Eugène Le Roy. The backdrop to the story was the Forêt Barade and Château de l'Herm, nearby. Set in woodland, these atmospheric ruins include a polygonal tower with a Gothic doorway that leads to a spiral staircase.

The town of Rouffignac was almost totally destroyed during World War II, although the church was thankfully spared. Nearby is the **Grotte de Rouffignac**, inhabited around 10,000 BCE and open to visitors since the 16th century. A little train takes visitors down 8 km (5 miles) of tunnels, which are covered with paintings and engravings, including 158 depictions of mammoths.

At Plazac, the 800-year-old keep was converted into a Romanesque church with a square belfry and an adjoining cemetery. The village of Saint-Geniès is filled with attractive ochre sandstone houses. The village also has a medieval church and a 17th-century château. The Gothic chapel at Le Cheylard, just outside the village, is decorated with biblical scenes completed during the Middle Ages. The château at Salignac, once a walled fortress, is now an elegant residence with a tiled roof. The 400-year-old **Manoir de Lacypierre** at Saint-Crépin is definitely worth a detour.

Crossing the Beune, the road leads from Tamniès to Marquay, a village with a fortified Romanesque church. Further on is the **Château de Commarque**, in a valley that has been settled since prehistoric times. The castle, partly in ruins, has a has a 12th-century Romanesque tower. The walk to the keep offers a fine view of the Château de Laussel. *Bories*, Périgordian dry-stone circular huts, can be seen around Sireuil. A group of these, the **Cabanes du Breuil**, form part of an open-air museum.

The **Château de Puymartin** is almost completely hidden by trees. It was built during the Middle Ages, rebuilt in the 15th century and restored around 1890. It contains period furniture, tapestries, ceiling frescoes and paintings.

Grotte de Rouffignac
Via the D82, Le Cluzeau, Villars 05 53 05 41 71 Apr-mid-Nov: daily

The former walled fortress of Château de Salignac

Manoir de Lacypierre
Le Bourg, Saint-Crépin May-Sep: daily chateaulacypierre.fr

Château de Commarque
Via the D48, Sireuil 05 53 59 00 25 Apr-mid-Nov: daily

Cabanes du Breuil
Via the D47, Saint-André-d'Allas 06 80 72 38 59 Apr-mid-Nov: daily

Château de Puymartin
Via the D47, Marquay, midway between Sarlat and Les Eyzies 05 53 59 29 97 Apr-mid-Nov: daily

Replica of part of the Lascaux cave at Le Parc du Thot, showing prehistoric animals such as aurochs

Vallée de l'Homme

E2 On the D706, between Montignac and Les Eyzies

This section of the Vallée de la Vézère, also known as the Vallée de l'Homme ("Valley of Mankind"), contains a large number of prehistoric sites.

The animal park at **Le Parc du Thot** contains species descended from the wild creatures that inhabited the region in the Upper Palaeolithic period, and whose likenesses can be seen on the walls of the prehistoric caves at Lascaux *(p140)*. Among them are reindeer, aurochs (long-horn cattle) and Przewalski's horses. There are also models of extinct species, such as mammoths and woolly rhinos. The museum features the re-creation of a prehistoric cave, showing methods used for painting the walls.

Offering reconstructions of daily life in prehistoric times, as well as workshops, the family-oriented **Préhisto Parc** takes visitors on a journey through time.

The rock-shelter at **Village de La Madeleine** gave its name to the Magdalenian society of hunter-gatherers that lived in the area from around 18,000–10,000 BCE. Excavations at this site brought to light an array of artifacts, including a fragment of engraved mammoth ivory. A child's grave, decorated with shells and red ochre, was also discovered here.

Roque-Saint-Christophe, a sheer rockface above the Vézère, is 80 m (260 ft) high and 1 km (half a mile) long. It has been inhabited since prehistoric times. The troglodytic fort and town carved in the rock here dates from the 10th century and could hold over 1,000 people.

A 15th-century carved cross stands at the entrance to the village of **Sergeac**, which was the Knights Templar's main base in the Périgord. Near the commander's residence, a house dating from the 14th–15th centuries, is a fortified church roofed with traditional Périgordian tiles.

Not far from Sergeac is the small valley of Castel-Merle, with rock-shelters that were inhabited from the Palaeolithic period to the Iron Age. Between Thonac and Sergeac is the magnificent Château de Blecayre.

The exhibiton at **Grottes du Roc de Cazelle**, one of the many rock-shelters in this area, tells the story of the human habitation of these caves from Upper Palaeolithic times to 1966. The tour includes the reconstruction of scenes from the lives of the early hunter-gatherers. Other displays show how houses here were cut out of the living rock.

Le Parc du Thot
Thonac 05 53 50 70 44 Feb-Dec: daily

Préhisto Parc
Tursac 05 53 50 73 19 Apr-mid-Nov: daily

Village de la Madeleine
Tursac 05 53 46 36 88 Mar-Nov: daily

Roque-Saint-Christophe
Peyzac-Le Moustier Daily roque-st-christophe.com

Sergeac
Place Bertran-de-Born, Montignac; 05 53 51 82 60

Grottes du Roc de Cazelle
Beyond Les Eyzies, on the D47 to Sarlat 05 53 59 46 09 Daily

HIDDEN GEM
Laugeral

In 1977, a hillside overlooking the Vallée de la Vézère was selected by a group of Buddhists as the site of a new community. All those who come in a spirit of peace are welcome to visit.

13 Saint-Jean-de-Côle

E1 Rue du Château; 05 53 62 14 15

One of France's prettiest villages, Saint-Jean-de-Côle sits on the banks of the river Côle. Its focal point is a late 11th-century priory, torched by the English during the Hundred Years' War and looted by Protestants in 1569 during the Wars of Religion. It was rebuilt in the 17th century. The 12th-century Byzantine-Romanesque church has an unusual plan: it forms a semicircle around the apse. Wooden carvings in the choir date from the 18th century.

The medieval bridge and the rue du Fond-du-Bourg, lined with 14th-century half-timbered houses, add to the village's picturesque appeal. The handsome 12th-century Château de la Marthonie, on place Saint-Jean, was rebuilt in the 15th century and enlarged in the 17th century.

The **Château de Jumilhac**, 26 km (16 miles) northeast of Saint-Jean-de-Côle, is a 13th-century castle. A magnificent roof set with pepperpot towers and skylights was added in 1600. The outbuildings and ramparts were demolished in the 17th century to make room for luxurious reception areas, including a drawing room based on the one at Versailles and a magnificent Louis-XIII-style staircase.

Château de Jumilhac
Jumilhac 05 53 52 42 97 Apr-mid-Nov: daily; mid-Nov-Mar: Sat & Sun

14 Brantôme

E1 Église Notre-Dame; 05 53 05 80 63

The pretty town of Brantôme sits on an island, encircled by a loop of the river Dronne. Its buildings cluster around the 9th-century Benedictine abbey. The bell tower, dating from the 11th century, is one of the oldest in France. A 16th-century bridge links the abbey to its gardens.

Brantôme makes an excellent base from which to explore other sights in the area. Around 10 km (6 miles) to the southwest stands the 13th-century **Château de Bourdeilles**, with an octagonal keep and fine Renaissance buildings. The nearby **Château de Puyguilhem** is a picture-perfect castle with equally impressive interiors. The **Grotte de Villars**, 15 km (9 miles) northeast of Brantôme, is a network of caves with 13 km (8 miles) of galleries, filled with fascinating rock formations and prehistoric paintings.

↑ A picturesque backstreet in the village of Saint-Jean-de-Côle

Château de Bourdeilles
05 53 03 73 36 Feb-Apr & Nov-Dec: Tue-Sun; Apr-Oct: daily

Château de Puyguilhem
Villars 05 53 54 82 18 May-Aug: daily; Sep & Apr: Tue-Sun; Oct-Mar: Wed-Sun

Grotte de Villars
Apr-Sep: daily
grotte-villars.com

15 Ribérac

D2 Place du Général-de-Gaulle; 05 53 90 03 10

Ribérac's medieval abbey church has 17th-century art and a dome above the choir.

Dotted around Ribérac are many more Romanesque domed churches, including the fortified church at Sioracde-Ribérac; the church at Grand-Brassac, with its splendid carved doorway; and the church at Saint-Privat-des-Prés, with an ornate circular arch.

Some 25 km (15 miles) northwest of Ribérac are the **Tourbières de Vendoire**, peat bogs where visitors can see extraordinary water-filled plant fossils.

Tourbières de Vendoire
05 53 90 79 56
Easter-Jun & Sep: Wed-Mon; Jul & Aug: daily

La Double and Le Landais

D2 Between Montpon and Ribérac, via the D708

The stunning, wild, marshy countryside here is covered with areas of dense forest, dotted with ponds and clearings. At the **Ferme du Parcot**, visitors can see local houses made with cob-filled wooden frames. Saint-Aulaye is a village known for its church, Cognac museum (open Jul & Aug) and riverside beach along the Dronne.

Ferme du Parcot
On the Saint-Astier road, Échourgnac 05 53 81 99 28 May, Jun & Sep: Sat & Sun; Jul-Aug: Tue-Sun

Terrasson-Lavilledieu

F2 Rue Jean-Rouby; 05 53 50 37 56

At the head of the Vallée de la Vézère, which leads down into the Périgord, the town of Terrasson-Lavilledieu grew up around a Merovingian abbey. The Pont Vieux, the town's old stone bridge, dates back to the 12th century. It was damaged during the Hundred Years' War and largely rebuilt in the late 15th century, as were the church and the monastery. Terrasson was a strategic town during the Wars of Religion (1562–98) and the French Revolution (1789–99). The enchanting **Jardins de l'Imaginaire** overlook the old town. These expansive gardens include a beautiful rose garden, a sacred wood, a water garden, a belvedere and scattered springs, all designed around historical and mythological themes. Created in 1996 by American landscape artist Kathryn Gustafson, these gardens portray the transition of human society from nature-based way of life to agriculture, and eventually to urban life.

Jardins de l'Imaginaire
Place de Genouillac; 05 53 50 86 82 Apr-Jun & Sep: Wed-Mon; Jul & Aug: daily

STAY

Logis Hôtel les Collines

A renovated farmhouse with spacious rooms, a swimming pool and delicious meals.

F2 Route des Crêtes, Terrasson-Lavilledieu
logishotels.com

←
Views over the town of Terrasson-Lavilledieu and the Vézère river

18 Castelnau-Bretenoux

G2 On the D43 05 65 10 98 00 Daily Sep–Jun: Tue

With a square keep and seigneurial quarters, this château is a resolutely defensive building and one of the area's best examples of military architecture. It was founded in the 12th century by the barons of Castelnau, and clear traces of its military past can still be seen in its elegant outline. Remodelled in the 16th and 17th centuries, then abandoned in the 18th and sacked in the French Revolution, the castle was restored in the late 19th century with funds provided by Jean Mouliérat, the famous tenor who sang at Paris's Opéra Comique. He built up a fine collection of paintings and furniture, which is now on display in the château's rooms. There are some wonderful views from the château's ramparts; the distant Chateau of Turenne is visible on a clear day.

At Le Buisson de Cadouin, 110 km (76 miles) south of Le Bugue, are the Grottes de Maxange, a cave system with some extraordinary rock formations.

19 Grottes de Lascaux

F2 Avenue de Lascaux, Montignac

The cave that became known as the "Sistine Chapel of pre-history" was discovered in 1940 by a young man out walking his dog. Its paintings, which date from around 18,000 BCE, provide a glimpse of that remote age. It is now known that the cave was never inhabited, but the precise meaning of the images on its walls remains unclear. The artists who created them used the relief of the cave walls to help breathe a sense of life into their depictions of bulls, deer, horses and ibexes that cover every surface from floor to ceiling.

The cave rapidly became a major attraction, but was closed in 1963 to prevent the deterioration of the paintings.

Lascaux II, a remarkable feat of scientific accuracy and artistic skill, opened in 1983. Executed by an artist using the same techniques and materials as her distant ancestors, the paintings are an accurate reconstruction of the originals, around 70 per cent of which have been replicated on the walls of two main cavities – the Diverticule Axial (Central Passage) and the Salle des Taureaux (Hall of Bulls).

Lascaux IV is part of the Centre International de l'Art Pariétal Montignac-Lascaux, designed by architect Duncan Lewis in partnership with Snohetta and SRA Architectes. Visitors walk along a landscaped path to a tunnel that leads into the replica of the original cave and paintings. Inside the main building, the Cave Art Theatre tracks the history of the work and shows videos of painted caves around the world.

Montignac itself is also worth a visit. A bustling town, it contains a number of fine 14th–16th-century houses.

Lascaux II and Lascaux IV

Hours vary, check website lascaux.fr

Lascaux IV, and *(inset)* a detail of one of the replica paintings

Le Bugue

E2 22 place de l'Hôtel de Ville; 05 53 51 82 60

An important tourist centre, this sizeable town offers a variety of attractions. One of them is **Parc du Bournat**. Here, scenes from the rural past of the Périgord region are re-created in a large open-air museum.

This is also the gateway to several more prehistoric cave systems. The **Grotte de Bara-Bahau** cave has a large gallery of unusual rock formations. This leads to a cavity with engravings of bears, horses and bison, as well as hands, a phallus and other symbols.

The cathedral-like domed interior of the **Gouffre de Proumeyssac** cave contains mineral formations in a huge variety of shapes. There is also a fascinating display on geological formations. By prior arrangement, visitors can descend into the chasm in a cradle suspended on cables, as the first people to explore this cave would have done.

Elsewhere in the local area, at the confluence of the Vézère and the Dordogne is the village of Limeuil. It has a pleasant riverside beach and many crafter's workshops. Narrow streets lead up to the grounds of the château and a botanical garden. Thomas à Becket once visited the Chapelle Saint-Martin here.

At Le Buisson de Cadouin *(p149)*, 110 km (76 miles) south of Le Bugue, are the **Grottes de Maxange**, a cave system with some extraordinary rock formations.

Parc du Bournat

191 allée Paul-Jean Souriau Apr-Sep: daily parclebournat.fr

Grotte de Bara-Bahau

Le Bugue Apr-Jun & Sep-early Nov: Tue-Sun; Jul & Aug: daily bara-bahau.fr

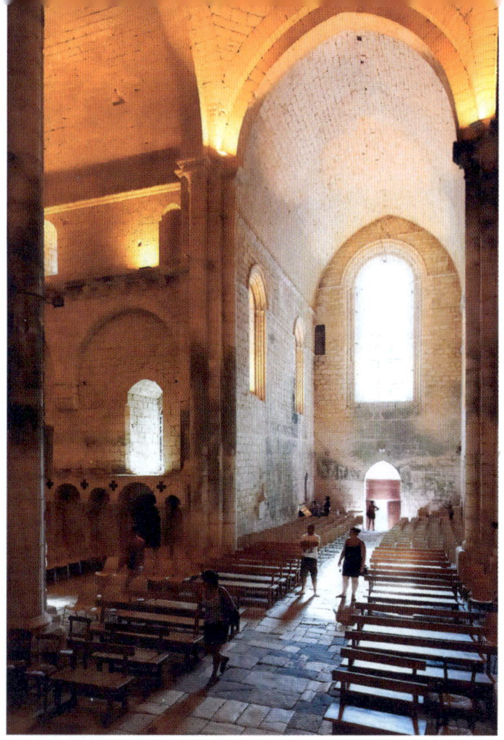

↑ The beautifully simple interior of Saint-Amand-de-Coly's abbey church

Gouffre de Proumeyssac

4 km (2.5 miles) from Le Bugue Hours vary, check website Jan gouffre-proumeyssac.com

Grottes de Maxange

Le Buisson de Cadouin Easter-early Nov lesgrottesde maxange.com

Saint-Amand-de-Coly

F2 Off the D704 or D62 Maison du Patrimoine (summer); 05 53 51 82 60

Originally part of a Romanesque abbey founded in the 7th century, the massive, fortified church here, with a nave 48 m (158 ft) long, still has defensive elements. Built on the plan of a Latin cross, it is enclosed by 300 m (985 ft) of walls. Its 30-m- (98-ft-) high belfry-keep is crowned by a garrison. The nave is lit by a stained-glass window set above the three-arched doorway. The floor of the beautifully empty interior slopes gently down towards the choir.

Concerts of classical music, forming part of the Festival du Périgord Noir, are held here and in the churches of Saint-Léon-sur-Vézère and Auriac. These beautiful Romanesque churches provide both a magical setting and fine acoustics.

INSIDER TIP
Vézère Fishing

There is excellent fishing to be had on the Vézère river. Salmon, sea trout, shad, lamprey, pike and other fish are plentiful. You can pick up a "fishing card" at the tourist office in Le Bugue or Les Eyzies.

↑ The dramatic entrance to the Gouffre de Padirac, a series of underground caverns and lakes

22  

Gouffre de Padirac

G3 Le Gouffre, Padirac Apr-mid-Nov: hours vary, check website gouffre-de-padirac.com

Viewed from above, the huge opening in the earth that forms the entrance to this series of underground caverns seems almost to be attempting to swallow up the sky. Discovered in 1889, the tunnels inside this geological curiosity were formed at least 1 million years ago, although the gaping hole in the ground that has made them accessible was probably created just 10,000 years ago. Reaching down to about 100 m (230 ft), the caves have a steady temperature of around 13°C (55°F). Tours consist of a short walk and a boat ride.

Some 10 m (33 ft) beneath the ground, under the 94-m (300-ft) Great Dome, is a group of giant stalagmites. Beyond this lies a lake, fed solely by water filtering through the rock, that sits "suspended" some 27 m (89 ft) above the level of an underground river.

23

Martel

F2 Palais de la Raymondie, place des Consuls; vallee-dordogne.com

Once the seat of the Vicomte de Turenne, the medieval town of Martel has seven towers, including the bell tower of its fortified Gothic church, which is pierced with arrow slits. Visitors can also see the remains of the old ramparts, the medieval Palais de la Raymondie – which houses temporary art exhibitions during the summer – and the 18th-century covered market. Vendors set up here twice a week, and a truffle market is also held in winter.

There is also a small railway museum on the first floor of the steam train terminal. On display here are various items from the railway's history, including lanterns, signals and uniforms, plus two model railways.

Some 7 km (4 miles) south of Martel on the N140 is the pre-Romanesque church at Creysse. It is unusual in having two identical apses against the straight wall of its east end. The nave follows the rocky spur's convex shape. The church's interior is not open to the public.

From 1681 to 1695, the controversial archbishop François Fénelon was prior of the fortified monastery at Carennac, 16 km (10 miles) southeast of Martel via the D803, then the D43. All that remains of the monastery are the dean's residence, now a local tourist office, the church, with an arresting depiction of the Last Judgment in the tympanum, and the cloister and chapter room. The village, opposite the Île de la Calypso, an island in the river, is dotted with interesting old houses.

With its lofty setting, the village of Loubressac, 20 km (12 miles) southeast of Martel, offers a wide view of the Cère, Bave and Dordogne valleys.

GREAT VIEW

Chemin de Fer Touristique du Haut-Quercy

Steam and diesel trains chug along a scenic stretch of old railway track from Martel to Saint-Denis *(trainduhautquercy.info)*.

Autoire's waterfall near Martel cascading down the limestone cliffs

From here the Château de Castelnau *(p126)*, Saint-Céré and the towers of Saint-Laurent *(p144)* can be seen. Inside the ramparts, narrow streets wind between the ochre-coloured houses.

Autoire, a village 30 km (19 miles) southeast of Martel, is best approached from the crest of the limestone plateau above a waterfall that crashes down for a sheer 40 m (130 ft). Flanked by majestic cliffs, here the rustic architecture of Quercy rubs shoulders with grand manor houses. The village is best explored on foot – you'll pass the ex-voto Chapelle Saint-Roch, which was erected after an outbreak of the plague in the 15th century, and the remains of the Château des Anglais, which was reduced to ruins during the Hundred Years' War.

24

Souillac

F2 Boulevard Louis-Jean-Malvy; vallee-dordogne.com

The town of Souillac lies between the Dordogne and the Borrèze. It grew up around a Benedictine monastery that was founded around 655 and became an abbey in the 16th century. Souillac later became a centre of trade, with goods such as wood, grains, cheese and wine, arriving by barge until the advent of the railway.

The **Abbaye Sainte-Marie**, the town's abbey church, was erected in the Middle Ages. It was built in a splendidly pure Byzantine-Romanesque style inspired by Hagia Sophia in Istanbul. Two notable features of the church are the doorway, which was reversed in the 17th century so as to face inwards, and the medieval carvings. The tourist office occupies a deconsecrated church, the Église Saint-Martin, which has a damaged belfry and Gothic vaulting. Art exhibitions are also held here. Parts of the town worth exploring include rue des Oules, rue des Craquelin and place Roucou.

Nearby are the **Grottes de Lacave**, limestone caves that were discovered in 1902. These caves were open to public in 1905. Riding on a small train, then taking a lift, visitors travel along 1.5 km (1 mile) of galleries and through a dozen caverns. The sheer variety of weird shapes formed by its stalactites and stalagmites, including some that suggest fantastic animals, makes this one of the most impressive of all such caves in France.

Abbaye Sainte-Marie
Place de l'Abbaye
05 65 32 71 00
8am–7pm daily

Grottes de Lacave
10 km (5 miles) southeast of Souillac
Early Feb–mid-Nov: daily vert-marine.com/grottes-de-lacave-46

The impressive Abbaye Sainte-Marie in Souillac

Saint-Céré

G3 3 avenue François de Maynard; vallee-dordogne.com

Saint-Céré's growth is thanks to the traffic of pilgrims visiting the tomb of St Spérie. In the Middle Ages, craftsmen settled and markets were established. The town suffered as a result of epidemics and wars, but it regained some of its splendour in the 17th century.

As in many places throughout the Dordogne, remains of past prosperity can be seen in many beautiful historic buildings, carefully preserved to give an old-world charm to the town. Highlights include buildings in the Place du Mercadial, on rue du Mazel, with the Renaissance-era Hôtel d'Auzier and Maison Queyssac, and in impasse Lagarouste, with its half-timbered corbelled houses. Hôtel d'Ambert, on rue Saint-Cyr, has turrets and a Renaissance doorway. Rue Paramelle leads to Maison Longueval and Hôtel de Puymule, in the Flamboyant Gothic style. The church contains an 18th-century marble altarpiece and has a Carolingian crypt. On a hill above the town is the Tours de Saint-Laurent, a keep dating back to the Middle Ages – and now all that remains of the castle. In 1945, Jean Lurçat (1882–1966), the painter and tapestry maker, acquired the property. It is now a museum-workshop, called the **Atelier-Musée Jean-Lurçat**.

Did You Know?

From late July to early August, the Festival Lyrique in Saint-Céré holds musical performances.

↑ Traditional half-timbered houses bordering place du Mercadial, one of the main squares in Saint-Céré

The **Château de Montal**, 3 km (2 miles) from Saint-Céré, was stripped of its finest architectural elements in the 19th century. However, thanks to the work of entrepreneur and arts patron Maurice Fenaille (1855–1937), the castle's original tapestries and furniture have been restored to their original setting. The medieval circular towers frame a beautiful Renaissance courtyard with a double staircase. A 17th-century Aubusson tapestry hangs in the guardroom. The upper-floor rooms have ceilings with exposed beams.

Atelier-Musée Jean-Lurçat

Apr-Sep: Tue-Sun
musees.lot.fr

Château de Montal

Saint-Jean-Lespinasse Mid-Jun-Aug: daily; Sep-mid-Jun: Wed-Sun
chateau-montal.fr

Assier

G3 Hôtel de La Monnaie, place Vival, Figeac; tourisme-figeac.com

This small town is best known for the remains of the **Château d'Assier**, which show that this was a Renaissance palace on a par with the finest châteaux of the Loire. It was built by Jacques Galiot de Genouillac (1465–1546), an artillery commander under Louis XII and François I. Of the building completed in 1535, only the entrance wing, with a spectacular portico doorway, survives. The decoration consisted of mythological and classical scenes, Renaissance figures and military emblems. The carved staircase is the finest feature of the interior.

Assier's church is unique in France for its dome over the burial chapel, which has triple-groined vaulting that forms an elaborate star pattern.

Near the village are two dolmens known as the Table de Roux and Bois des Bœufs. There are 11 of these burial chambers, dating from around 1500 BCE, in the vicinity.

Château d'Assier

05 65 40 40 99
May-Aug: Wed-Mon; Sep-Apr: by appointment
Public hols

Belvès

E3 1 rue des Filhols; perigordnoir-vallee dordogne.com

Set on a hilltop, this village was a fort in the 11th century. Its medieval heart centres on the castle and place d'Armes, where there is a 500-year-old covered market. Nearby is the 13th-century Hôtel Bontemps, with a Renaissance façade. The town has seven towers, some of them bell towers. These include one from the late-Middle Ages, the 11th-century keep (known as Tour de l'Auditeur) and the Tour des Frères. Église Notre-Dame, with its Flamboyant Gothic doorway, is all that remains of Belvès abbey. The troglodytic dwellings cut into the village's medieval fortifications were in use from the 13th century right up to the era of the *Ancien Régime*.

To the northwest, on the edge of Forêt de la Bessède, lies the village of Urval. It has a 13th-century communal oven, a rare vestige of medieval village life. Close by is a fortified Romanesque church from the Middle Ages.

Saint-Cirq-Lapopie

F4 Place du Sombral; tourisme-lot.com

Its exceptionally picturesque location and ensemble of attractive buildings make Saint-Cirq-Lapopie one of the jewels of the Lot valley. Rising in tiers up the limestone cliff face, it sits some 100 m (300 ft) above the river. Along its narrow streets are small courtyards and attractive stone and wooden houses. In the lower village, a 13th-century gate, Porte de la Pélissaria (or Porte de Rocamadour), opens onto Grand'Rue, where the medieval village begins.

Places of note include place du Carol, with a belvedere-dovecote, where the painter Henri Martin (1860–1943) lived; the 13th-century Maison Vinot; the 14th-century Maison Médiévale Daura; Maison Breton, once owned by the Surrealist writer André Breton (1896–1966); Maison Bessac, with double corbelling; place du Sombral with the 15th-century Maison Larroque and Maison Rignault, which houses the Musée Rignault; and Maison de la Fourdonne, which contains the Mairie. Near the ruined castle stands a late 16th-century fortified church.

The economy of the village, which had 1,500 inhabitants during the Middle Ages, was based on manufacturing, with crafters' workshops under the arcades along rue de la Pélissaria and Peyrolerie. Today, the work of *robinetaïres*, specialist wood-turners who make taps for the Cahors wine barrels, is a craft peculiar to Saint-Cirq-Lapopie.

From Bouziès, 5 km (3 miles) from Saint-Cirq, visitors can take a boat ride on the Lot with **Les Croisières de Saint-Cirq-Lapopie**.

Cajarc, 20 km (12 miles) east of Saint-Cirq-Lapopie, is a fine medieval village clustered around Maison de l'Hébrardie, a 13th-century former castle.

Les Croisières de Saint-Cirq-Lapopie
croisieres-saint-cirq-lapopie.com

SHOP

Le Moulin à Huile de Noix de Saint-Céré
At this ancient mill, organic walnuts are ground to produce walnut oil. After watching how the oil is made, head to the on-site shop, or to the one on place du Mercadial, to buy walnut oil and nut purées.

G3 55 rue Croix de Lagarde, Saint-Céré moulindesaintcere.com

Saint-Cirq-Lapopie stunningly perched above the Lot river ↓

Picture-perfect Beynac, magnificently set atop a rocky bluff overlooking the Dordogne river

29 Beynac

F3 La Balme; sarlat-tourisme.com

The village of Beynac, which clings dramatically to a steep cliff face, has attracted a clutch of artists and writers, including Camille Pissarro (1830–1903), Henry Miller (1891–1980) and the poet Paul Éluard (1895–1952), who spent the last years of his life here. The village is still filled with the artists' studios. The narrow street from the lower village up to the castle passes several ancient houses and offers expansive views.

Perched on a rock 150 m (490 ft) above the river, the **Château de Beynac** is visible from afar. The seat of one of the Périgord's four baronies, it occupies a strategic position, like its rival, Castelnaud *(p126)*. The castle repeatedly came under attack during the Hundred Years' War and again during the Wars of Religion. Restoration began in 1961.

Entry to the castle is via a double moat and through lines of ramparts. The 13th-century keep is flanked by the main building, dating from the same period but remodelled in the 16th century, and another building dating from the 14th and 17th centuries. The great hall, with vaulted ceiling, has a Renaissance chimneypiece. The castle was bought in 1962 by Lucien Grosso, who painstakingly restored the building. The exquisite 12th-century chapel, now a parish church, is roofed with traditional Périgordian tiles.

GREAT VIEW
Cazenac

Adjoining Beynac is the delightful hamlet of Cazenac. A walk along the road running down to the left of Cazenac, offers a stunning panorama of the valley, with the Château de Beynac in the distance.

Located around 4 km (2.5 miles) southeast of Beynac are **Les Jardins de Marqueyssac**. Here, there are over 6 km (4 miles) of walkways, lined with over 150,000 shrubs, surrounding a 19th-century château. Every Thursday evening during July and August the gardens are illuminated by thousands of candles (tickets must be booked online in advance).

Château de Beynac
05 53 29 50 40
Feb-Dec: daily

Les Jardins de Marqueyssac
Vézac Daily
marqueyssac.com

30 Gourdon

F3 20 boulevard des Martyrs; tourisme-gourdon.com

The town of Gourdon, which comes to life on market days (Thursday and Saturday), is the capital of the rural region of Bouriane. In the 16th century it grew rich from its weaving industry. The medieval heart of the town has a 13th-century fortified gate and some fine houses, including the

Beautiful old square in the *bastide* town of Monpazier

TOP 3 OUTDOOR EXPERIENCES

Canoeing
canoes-loisirs.com
From April to September, paddle down Dordogne river from Vitrac or Carsac to Beynac.

Hot-air Ballooning
montgolfiere-du-perigord.com
Soar over castles, the Dordogne river, and lush valleys.

Horse Riding
poneyclubarcenciel.fr
Tour Peyrac beaches and forests on horseback.

Maison du Sénéchal, Maison Cavaignac and Maison d'Anglars. Two particularly picturesque streets are rue du Majou, which was filled with drapers' shops in the Middle Ages, and rue Zig-Zag. The Église Saint-Pierre, a Gothic church with asymmetrical towers, has some splendid 16th-century stained-glass windows and Baroque wood-carvings. The town is dotted with other religious buildings. Among them are the Église des Cordeliers, built in the 13th century and altered in the 19th, Chapelle Notre-Dame-des-Neiges, Église Saint-Siméon and Chapelle du Majou. The medieval castle was destroyed in the 18th century, but the esplanade that fronted it remains and offers good views of the Bouriane river.

The **Grottes de Cougnac** at Payrignac, 3 km (2 miles) from Gourdon on the D17, are full of stalactites and stalagmites, and other interesting rock formations, which look magical when lit up. The Cro-Magnon people who used the cave 25,000 to 14,000 years ago decorated some walls with paintings of moufflon (wild sheep), human figures and symbols.

Grottes de Cougnac
Early Apr-Sep: daily; Oct-Nov: Mon-Sat
grottesdecougnac.com

31

Monpazier

E3 Place des Cornières; pays-bergerac-tourisme.com

Set on a hill overlooking the river Dropt, Monpazier is a classic *bastide* town. With a grid of streets and alleyways within its ramparts, it is one of the most attractive in southwest France. Founded in 1284 by Edward I, king of England, Monpazier has remained almost unchanged for 800 years, although only three of its original six fortified gates still stand. It has been used as a medieval location for several films. Its picturesque central square, the place des Cornières, is lined with arcades that are filled with shops. The square also has a 16th-century covered market, which still contains some antique grain measures. On Thursday mornings the square hosts a market, and in December truffles are sold here. Monpazier is the birthplace of the writer and explorer Jean Galmot (1879–1928).

Around 19 km (12 miles) southeast of Monpazier lies Villefranche-du-Périgord, another *bastide* town, established in 1261 at the meeting point of Périgord, Quercy and Agenais. From May to October, it hosts a famous *cèpes*, (a type of mushroom) market. This takes place on the town square. Arcaded houses stand opposite the market. The oak forests nearby are a pleasant place for a walk.

A further 8 km (5 miles) along the D57 lies Besse, a village with handsome ochre-coloured houses and a fortified church. The single-walled bell tower has an 11th-century doorway, with three archivolts that are covered with carvings of mythological animals.

Biron

E3 Place des Cornières, Montpazier; 05 53 22 68 59

Once the seat of one of the Périgord's four baronies, the massive **Château de Biron** dominates the surrounding countryside and straddles the border between the Périgord and the Agenais. With a 12th-century keep, Renaissance living quarters, a Gothic chapel and a small 14th-century manor house, decorated with 16th-century frescoes, it embodies a stunning medley of architectural styles spanning the 12th to the 18th centuries.

Having given asylum to Cathars in 1211, the castle was besieged by Simon de Montfort, and it changed allegiance countless times during the Hundred Years' War, suffering attack and damage as a result. It was largely rebuilt during the Renaissance and now towers over the attractive village of Biron, which has some fine houses around its covered market.

Château de Biron

Le Bourg, Vergt-de-Biron Hours vary, check website chateau-biron.fr

Beaumont-du-Périgord

E3 1 place Jean Moulin; 05 53 22 39 12

Since its foundation in 1272, Beaumont, a *bastide* town built by the English, has undergone much alteration. Of the 16 gates that once formed part of its fortifications, only one, the Porte de Luzier, remains, forming the present entrance into the town. The central square was remodelled in the 18th century and the covered market no longer exists. There are some fine medieval houses, particularly in rue Romieu and rue Vidal. The town's architectural jewel is its impressive fortified church, the Église Saint-Laurent-et-Saint-Front. One of the finest in southwest France, this huge, austere church is in a military Gothic style, with four belfry-like towers, linked by a wall-walk. The church was built from 1280 to 1330 and formed part of the town's defences. The doorway is decorated by a frieze filled with grimacing figures. The medieval village of Saint-Avit-Sénieur, 5 km (3 miles) east of the town of Beaumont, is visible from afar thanks to its church. This Romanesque structure was fortified in the 14th century, and a wall-walk connects its two towers.

Some 10 km (6 miles) east of Beaumont lies the village of Montferrand-du-Périgord. It has a splendid 16th-century covered market and the ruins of a castle with a 12th-century keep. A short walk up the hill from the village is the little church of St Christophe, set on its own and surrounded by a cemetery. The interior contains surprisingly well-preserved medieval frescoes.

The **Château de Lanquais**, 13 km (8 miles) northwest of Beaumont, has a 15th-century circular tower and polygonal staircase tower, as well as residential quarters dating from

PICTURE PERFECT
Château de Bannes

Near Beaumont-du-Périgord stands the turreted Château de Bannes sitting atop a grassy outcrop. Although it's closed to the public, it makes for a striking photograph.

the 16th and 17th centuries. It is also a *chambres d'hôte*, with elegant rooms.

Château de Lanquais
Apr–Jun & Sep: Wed–Mon; Jul & Aug: daily
chateaudelanquais.fr

Saint-Michel-de-Montaigne

D2 Place Clemenceau, Montpon-Ménestérol; 05 53 82 23 77

This village is best known for its associations with Michel de Montaigne, the Renaissance philosopher and writer. Of the impressive château where Montaigne lived, only the 16th-century **tower**, where he had his library and where he wrote his famous *Essais*, is original, while the rest has been rebuilt. The beams of his study, on the top floor, are inscribed with 57 Greek and Latin sentences and maxims, that represent the Epicurean, Stoic and sceptic ideas that influenced Montaigne. The views from the terrace stretch out over the Lidoire valley.

The village's Romanesque church has a doorway with columns and four intricately moulded arches. The interior features carved 17th-century furniture and the Stations of the Cross by the artist Gilbert Privat (1892–1969).

About 5 km (3 miles) from Saint-Michel-de-Montaigne on the D936 is the village of Montcaret. The Romanesque church here has capitals that may have been taken from an earlier Gallo-Roman building. Nearby are the remains of a large Gallo-Roman villa, discovered in 1827. It has fine mosaic flooring, an inner courtyard lined with columns, a 60-sq-m (645-sq-ft) main room with a pool with mosaics of aquatic subjects and baths with a sophisticated heating system. The quality of workmanship suggests that this was a place of luxury. Archaeological evidence suggests that the site has been inhabited since antiquity.

Tower
Hours vary, check website chateau-montaigne.com

Le Buisson-de-Cadouin

E3 Place de l'Abbaye, Le Buisson; 09 85 00 07 13

The village grew up round the 12th-century Cistercian **Abbaye de Cadouin** (a World Heritage Site), on the pilgrim route to Compostela. Until 1932, what was believed to be the Holy Shroud was kept here, and the village grew wealthy from the pilgrims who flocked to this sacred relic. Behind the abbey's imposing buttressed façade is the cloister, built in the 15th and 16th centuries in a mixture of Flamboyant Gothic and Renaissance styles. The carved finials and images, of both biblical and secular subjects, are a masterpiece of stone carving.

From the belvedere, at Trémolat, about 13 km (8 miles) northwest of Le Buisson-de-Cadouin, there are stunning views of the Cingle de Trémolat (the great loop in the Dordogne) and of the fertile plain. The fortified church, with its keep-like bell tower, is arrestingly austere.

Abbaye de Cadouin
Place de l'Abbaye
05 53 63 36 28 Mid-Feb–Oct: daily; Nov–Dec: Tue–Sun

Eymet

D3 45 place Gambetta; 05 53 23 74 95

This *bastide* town, built in the Dropt valley in 1270, retains its original square layout. Gargoyles look down from the keep, and the medieval houses have turrets with mullioned windows. A 17th-century fountain sits in the main square that is lined with half-timbered houses. Eymet is also known for its large British population who run many of the shops, cafés and local vineyards.

Some 20 km (12 miles) northeast of Eymet is the picture-perfect village of Issigeac, which dates back to Roman times. It has a spiral layout and is best known for its wonderful Sunday-morning food market. The Gothic church, with a bell tower over its entrance, stands on the site of a priory. The former bishop's palace, its two pavilions set with turrets, is now the tourist office, and the former tithe barn houses a shop.

↑ The Gothic cloisters of Abbaye de Cadouin at Le Buisson-de-Cadouin

The fine Gothic-Renaissance chapel in the grassy courtyard of the Château de Biron

Cahors

F4 Place François-Mitterrand; cahors valleedulot.com

Evidence of Cahors' ancient past can be seen in the ruins of the Gallo-Roman baths, now known as the Arc de Diane, which date back to the 1st century BCE. In the 13th century, trade brought prosperity, leading to the creation of the town's elegant mercantile sector (now rue du Château-du-Roi). The fortifications date from the 14th century and include the ramparts, set with 11 towers and two gatehouses. In the 19th century, Cahors began to spread out from this medieval core. This was when boulevard Gambetta, with the town hall, theatre and law courts, was built, and the quayside, walks and gardens were laid out.

Cahors' Vieille Ville (Old Town) is characterized by decorated courtyards, half-timbered houses with brick overhangs and houses with carved façades. Typical of the Renaissance is a form of decoration consisting of branches, roses and suns; particularly fine examples can be seen on the doors and chimneypieces. Later, in the 16th century, many windows were decorated in the Italian style, and in the 17th century many townhouses with ornate doorways were built. The most picturesque areas of the Vieille Ville are rue du Dr-Bergounioux, rue de Lastié, rue Saint-Urcisse, place Saint-James, rue de la Chantrerie, the Daurade quarter and the cathedral quarter.

Cahors' most iconic sight, the Pont Valentré, was built in the 14th century and never attacked. This impressive fortified bridge has six Gothic spans with chamfered piers. It was restored in 1879 by French architect Paul Gout and is the best-preserved medieval bridge in Europe. Cahors' other main sight is its cathedral, **Cathédrale Saint-Étienne**. A stopping place on the pilgrim route to Compostela *(p226)*, the building underwent several phases of construction from the 11th to the 17th centuries, and was restored in the 19th century. The result is a

Did You Know?

Almost all of the Lot's black truffles come from the countryside around Lalbenque, near Cahors.

A DEVILISH TALE

Pont Valentré took almost 50 years to build. According to a legend that grew up around it, the architect asked the Devil to help him complete this feat of civil engineering, in return for his soul. To escape the agreement, he tried to dupe the Devil, who took his revenge: each night the last stone laid in the central tower would mysteriously fall and had to be put back in place the next day. In 1879, while restoring the bridge, the architect immortalized this tale by setting a carving of the Devil on the central tower.

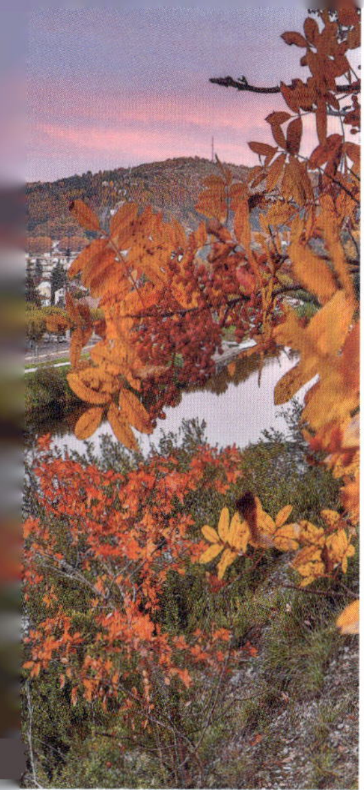

←
The graceful medieval Pont Valentré bridge, which has become a symbol of Cahors

beautiful, harmonious mix of styles, ranging from a Romanesque doorway, to a Flamboyant Gothic cloister.

Cahors makes a great base from which to explore other towns in the surrounding countryside. The village of Lalbenque, 17 km (11 miles) southeast of Cahors, is well known for its truffle market, which takes place on Tuesday from December to mid-March, and for its festivities celebrating this "black diamond". Some 32 km (20 miles) to the southwest of Cahors is Montcuq. The pretty streets here are lined with timbered houses and its 17th-century tower is the last surviving remnant of the ancient Cathar stronghold.

A lovely way to explore Cahors is to follow the garden trail. Pick up a map from the tourist office and head to the starting point at the foot of the Pont Valentré. The route winds through the narrow streets and criss-crosses the river Lot.

Cathédrale Saint-Étienne
17 place Jean Jacques Chapou Daily

GREAT VIEW
Mont St Cyr

Overlooking Cahors is Mont St Cyr, well worth climbing for spectacular views of the town. Cross Pont Louis-Philippe and climb up behind the statue of the Virgin. It takes about 30 minutes.

La Vallée de l'Auvézère

E/F1, E/F2 Place de l'Eglise, Hautefort; vezere-perigord.fr

Throughout this valley there are several interesting sights. The Chapelle d'Auberoche perches high on a cliff, offering dramatic views. Upriver, the Blâme cascades dramatically into the Auvézère at La Boissière d'Ans. Commanding views of the Loue and Auvézère valleys can also be had from the Colline de Saint-Raphaël. Two massive columns, in front of the church here, are the remains of a Benedictine priory. Génis is also set high up, on a granite plateau, looking down on the gorges of the river Dalon.

Upstream is an old mill, the Moulin du Pervendoux, beyond which are rapids and the Cascade du Saut-Ruban. A path (GR 646) leads down to this waterfall from the Église de Saint-Mesmin. At Le Puy-des-Âges, set on a quartz-rich spur, is the little chapel of Notre-Dame-de-Partout. The hilltop château close to Savignac-Lédrier looks down on a 17th-century forge, while at Payzac is the former Vaux papermill.

Abbaye de Chancelade

E2 Place de l'Abbaye, Chancelade Daily (except during services) abbaye-chancelade.com

Set in the Beauronne valley, the Augustinian Abbaye de Chancelade was founded in the 12th century and became an important centre of intellectual life. Having survived the Hundred Years' War and the Wars of Religion, it once again became influential in the 17th century. It is well preserved, with a washhouse, stables, workshops and a mill.

→
Carved choir stalls and medieval frescoes inside the Abbaye de Chancelade

A DRIVING TOUR
VINEYARDS OF CAHORS

Length 70 km (45 miles) **Starting point** Montcabrier
Stopping-off point Parnac, where you can sample local wine at Cave Coopérative du Vignoble de Cahors in summer

The vineyards around Cahors *(p150)* are among the oldest in Europe. Since the Middle Ages, Cahors wine has been noted for its excellent ageing properties, which stem from the high-quality vine-growing soil on the limestone plateau of the Causse. Vineyards stretch out for 60 km (37 miles) on either side of the Lot river, mainly in the valley below Cahors. While an exploration of the region offers many opportunities for wine tasting, the countryside itself provides a visual feast.

Locator Map

Set off from the bastide town of **Montcabrier,** *which has houses with magnificent façades and corbelled corner tiles.*

Duravel *has a wealth of wine estates – including Château La Gineste and Château de Rouffiac – so stop here for a tour and tasting to see why Cahors vineyards are so special.*

From the quayside to place de la Truffière, the narrow streets of **Puy-l'Évêque** *wind around medieval houses, passing the massive 13th-century keep and a fortified church.*

From **Bélaye** *there are stunning views of the Lot valley and Cahors vineyards. In the village are the remains of a bishop's castle and a church from the Middle Ages.*

Looking out at the Lot valley scenery from the village of Bélaye

Vineyards around the 15th-century Châteaux Lagrézette, in the town of Caillac

There are several châteaux in ***Caillac****: Laroque, Langle and Lagrézette, a medieval castle with a Renaissance flair.*

End with an overnight stay at the stunning ***Château de Mercuès****, once the summer residence for Cahors' bishops.*

D660
Les Junies
D50
D45
Ruisseau du Vert
D811
Labastide-du-Vert
Crayssac
D811
Espère
D8
FINISH
Château de Mercuès
Mercuès
Parnac
Caillac
Lot
D811
D820
D9
D8
Luzech
D8
Pradines
Albas
Saint-Vincent-Rive-d'Olt
Douelle
D8
Labéraudie
D12
Cahors
D620

Once a fort, ***Albas*** *overlooks the Lot from a clifftop. Stop here for another taste of Cahors viticulture at Château Eugénie. The shop has free wine tasting, and you can also book tours of the vineyards.*

In the shadow of the imposing medieval keep, ***Luzech*** *became one of Lot's four baronies. A walk around the peninsula leads to the 16th-century Chapelle Notre-Dame-de-l'Île. Maison des Consuls, built in the 12th century, houses an archaeological museum.*

A DRIVING TOUR DORDOGNE VALLEY

Length 35 km (22 miles) **Starting point** Cingle de Montfort **Stopping-off point** From the esplanade at Domme, the loop in the river at Montfort is a stunning sight

DORDOGNE AND LOT

Dordogne Valley

Locator Map

Probably no river in France crosses so varied a landscape and such different geological formations as the Dordogne. Starting in deep granite gorges in the Massif Central, the Dordogne is almost 3 km (2 miles) wide by the time it joins the Garonne. This drive takes in some of the Dordogne's classic countryside scenery, as well as fine châteaux that line this stretch of the river. You can stop to admire them from the river – either in a hired canoe or on a *gabare* (local rivercraft) tour.

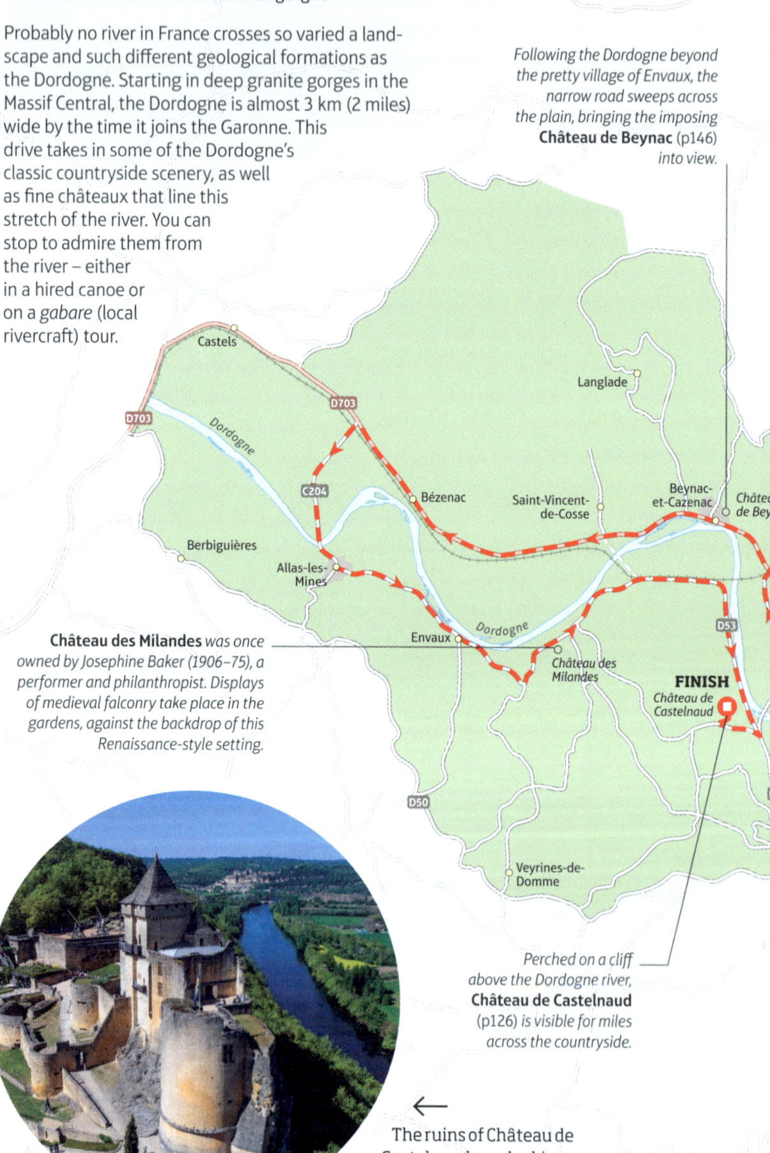

Following the Dordogne beyond the pretty village of Envaux, the narrow road sweeps across the plain, bringing the imposing **Château de Beynac** *(p146) into view.*

Château des Milandes *was once owned by Josephine Baker (1906–75), a performer and philanthropist. Displays of medieval falconry take place in the gardens, against the backdrop of this Renaissance-style setting.*

Perched on a cliff above the Dordogne river, **Château de Castelnaud** *(p126) is visible for miles across the countryside.*

← The ruins of Château de Castelnaud overlooking the Dordogne valley

←

Paddling along the Cingle de Montfort riverbend towards the cliff-top château in the town of Montfort

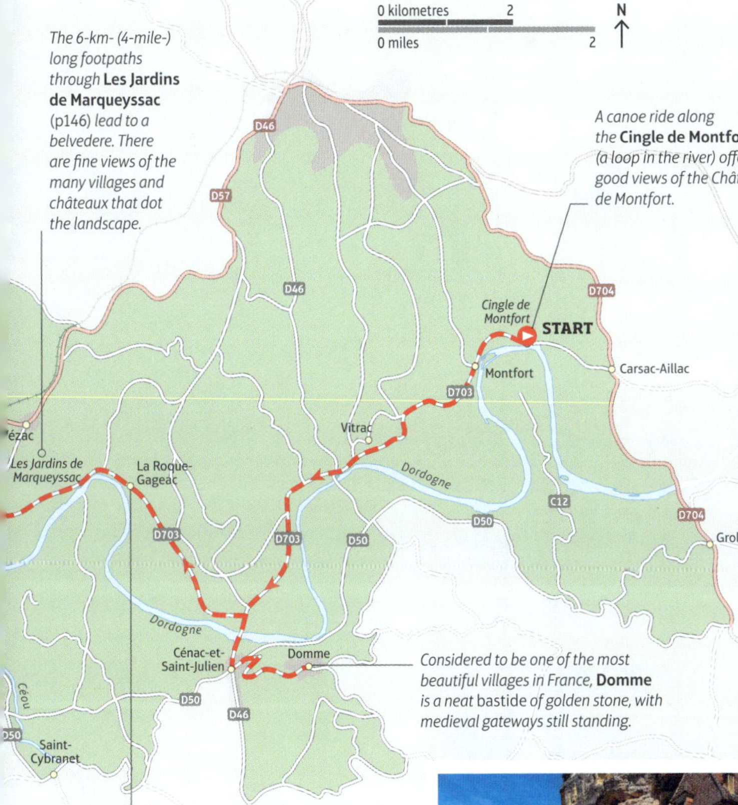

0 kilometres 2

0 miles 2

N

The 6-km- (4-mile-) long footpaths through **Les Jardins de Marqueyssac** *(p146) lead to a belvedere. There are fine views of the many villages and châteaux that dot the landscape.*

A canoe ride along the **Cingle de Montfort** *(a loop in the river) offers good views of the Château de Montfort.*

D46

D57

D46

D704

Cingle de Montfort

START

Montfort

Carsac-Aillac

D703

Vitrac

Vézac

Les Jardins de Marqueyssac

La Roque-Gageac

Dordogne

C12

D704

D50

Groléjac

D703

D703

D50

Dordogne

Cénac-et-Saint-Julien

Domme

D50

D46

Céou

D50

Saint-Cybranet

Considered to be one of the most beautiful villages in France, **Domme** *is a neat bastide of golden stone, with medieval gateways still standing.*

High on the cliffs above **La Roque-Gageac** *stands a troglodytic fort. The steep walk up to it is rewarded by a view of the valley.*

→

Picturesque brick houses in La Roque-Gageac

8

Exploring a narrow, red-brick lane in Agen

LOT-ET-GARONNE

Lot-et-Garonne lies between territories once held by the kings of France and the kings of England, and was the object of bitter dispute until it was finally won by France in 1472. In the 13th and 14th centuries, more than 40 *bastide* towns were built here on the orders of various French and English lords. With their central arcaded squares and streets laid out to a grid pattern, such towns were built as a response not only to a rapidly growing population, but also to the conflict between France and England that raged over southwest France until well into the 15th century.

With its fertile, rolling hills and valleys, and pine forests that encroach from Landes, Lot-et-Garonne is a region rich in pleasant, rural countryside. Miles of navigable waterways are provided by the Lot, the Garonne and the Baïse rivers, and the canal that runs alongside the Garonne. Today, as a prime producer of fruit and vegetables, Lot-et-Garonne serves as the orchard of Europe. Its fine wines compare favourably with those of neighbouring Bordeaux and are an important element in the bounty of gastronomic specialities to be enjoyed in this corner of France.

LOT-ET-GARONNE

Must Sees

1. Château de Bonaguil
2. Agen

Experience More

3. Gavaudun
4. Monsempron
5. Villeréal
6. Sauveterre-la-Lémance
7. Puymirol
8. Saint-Avit
9. Penne-d'Agenais
10. Tournon-d'Agenais
11. Pujols
12. Laroque-Timbaut
13. Villeneuve-sur-Lot
14. Prayssas
15. Casseneuil
16. Sainte-Livrade-sur-Lot
17. Monclar-d'Agenais
18. Clairac
19. Granges-sur-Lot
20. Duras
21. Castillonnès
22. Monflanquin
23. Lauzun
24. Marmande
25. Casteljaloux
26. Pays de Serres
27. Mézin
28. Aiguillon
29. Poudenas
30. Le Mas-d'Agenais
31. Laplume
32. Beauville
33. Saint-Maurin
34. Nérac
35. Vianne
36. Barbaste
37. Moirax
38. Aubiac
39. Layrac
40. Estillac

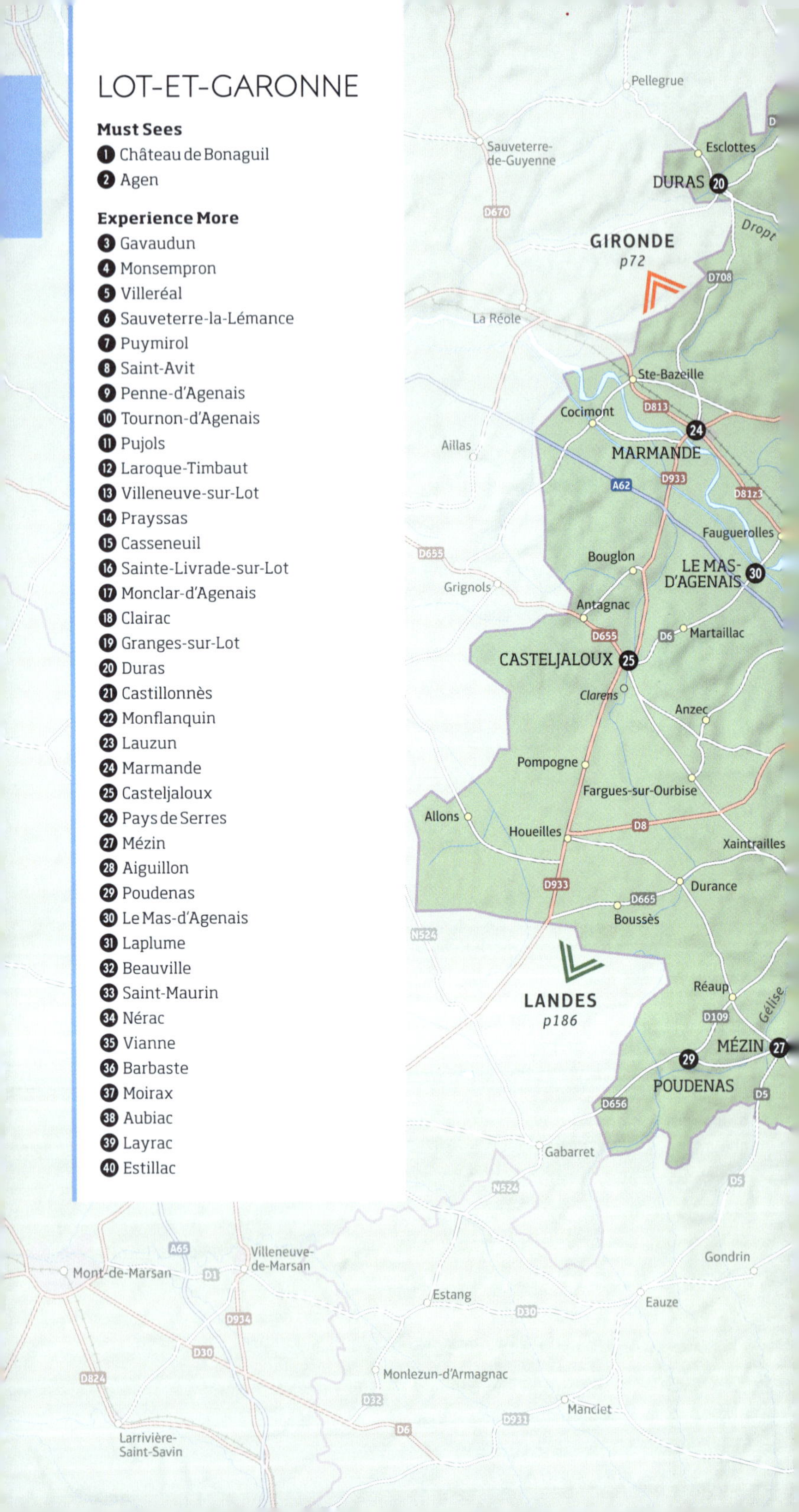

GIRONDE p72
LANDES p186

Pellegrue
Sauveterre-de-Guyenne
Esclottes
DURAS 20
Dropt
D670
D708
La Réole
Ste-Bazeille
Cocimont
D813
24 MARMANDE
Aillas
A62
D933
D81z3
Fauguerolles
D655
Bouglon
LE MAS-D'AGENAIS 30
Grignols
Antagnac
D655
D6
Martaillac
CASTELJALOUX 25
Clarens
Anzec
Pompogne
Fargues-sur-Ourbise
Allons
Houeilles
D8
Xaintrailles
D933
Durance
D665
Boussès
N524
Réaup
Gélise
D109
MÉZIN 27
29 POUDENAS
D656
D5
Gabarret
N524
D5
A65
Mont-de-Marsan
D1
Villeneuve-de-Marsan
Gondrin
Estang
D30
Eauze
D934
D30
D824
Monlezun-d'Armagnac
D32
Manciet
D931
D6
Larrivière-Saint-Savin

DORDOGNE AND LOT
p108
LOT-ET-GARONNE
1 CHÂTEAU DE BONAGUIL
2 AGEN
3 GAVAUDUN
4 MONSEMPRON
5 VILLERÉAL
6 SAUVETERRE-LA-LÉMANCE
7 PUYMIROL
8 SAINT-AVIT
9 PENNE-D'AGENAIS
10 TOURNON-D'AGENAIS
11 PUJOLS
12 LAROQUE-TIMBAUT
13 VILLENEUVE-SUR-LOT
14 PRAYSSAS
15 CASSENEUIL
16 SAINTE-LIVRADE-SUR-LOT
17 MONCLAR-D'AGENAIS
18 CLAIRAC
19 GRANGES-SUR-LOT
21 CASTILLONNÈS
22 MONFLANQUIN
23 LAUZUN
26 PAYS DE SERRES
28 AIGUILLON
31 LAPLUME
32 BEAUVILLE
33 SAINT-MAURIN
34 NÉRAC
35 VIANNE
37 MOIRAX
38 AUBIAC
39 LAYRAC
40 ESTILLAC
BARBASTE
Bouniagues
Beaumont-du-Périgord
Saint-Avit-Sénieur
Belvès
Issigeac
Bouillac
Loubès-Bernac
Fonroque
La Sauvetat-du-Dropt
Rives
Dropt
Montaut
Miramont-de-Guyenne
Seyches
Monbahus
Cancon
Lède
Lacaussade
Fumel
Puymician
Tombeboeuf
Canaule
Brugnac
Trentels
Lot
Port-de-Penne
Tonneins
Castelmoron-sur-Lot
Temple-sur-Lot
Dausse
Grotte de Lastournelle
Grotte de Fontirou
Pech-de-Berre
Garonne
Hautefage-la-Tour
Montaigu-de-Quercy
Bazens
Port Ste-Marie
Buzet-sur-Baïse
Colayrac-St-Cirq
Sérignac-sur-Garonne
Lavardac
Clermont-Soubiran
Caudecoste
Valence
Moissac
Baïse
Gers
Estressol
Francescas
Astaffort
Moncrabeau
Condom
Lectoure
Mouchan
Valence-sur-Baïse
D933
N21
D660
D19
D1
D2
D668
D710
D676
D667
D124
D127
D911
D102
D661
D656
D103
D118
D813
D215
D16
D953
A62
D931
D930
D7
D2
0 kilometres 15
0 miles 15
N
LOT-ET-GARONNE

1

CHÂTEAU DE BONAGUIL

E3 Saint-Front-sur-Lémance Hours vary, check website chateau-bonaguil.com

Bonaguil Castle is a monument to the Middle Ages and its defences. Its imposing fortifications were ahead of their time and remain intact on the well-preserved fortress, now renovated as a residence.

The colossal Château de Bonaguil stands majestically on a rocky spur, its ramparts and turrets fleetingly visible from behind lush greenery. Founded in the 13th century, it was eventually abandoned during the French Revolution *(p54)* before being sold to the town of Fumel's municipal authority. It is an impressive example of the transition between medieval military architecture and an early Renaissance noble residence.

↑ Overview of the fortification of Château de Bonaguil

800

The number of steps up to the top of the lookout post, from where there are stunning views.

↑ View from the ramparts, and *(inset)* a family exploring inside the castle

AGEN

E4 38 rue Garonne; destination-agen.com

Once a busy river port, Agen has several historic buildings that are still a part of the modern cityscape. Religious buildings of the Middle Ages that graced the old town sit alongside revitalized shopping boulevards and plazas. Old ramparts are now roadways, and the magnificent episcopal palace is the region's *préfecture*.

The largest settlement in the Garonne valley, Agen still has many fine buildings dating from its prosperous period as a manufacturing and trading centre. In the heart of town are narrow streets with half-timbered, medieval houses, grand townhouses and arcaded squares. There are also early Neo-Classical buildings. Between esplanade du Gravier and the canal running parallel with the river are pleasant green areas.

Vieille Ville

This part of town is crammed with many interesting features. These diverse buildings include the medieval Chapelle Notre-Dame-du-Bourg, on rue des Droits-de-l'Homme. Faced with red brick, the church has a single-walled pointed belfry that looks down onto an attractive small square. Also here is one of France's earliest reinforced concrete buildings, the 1908 Théâtre Ducourneau, in place du Docteur-Esquirol. The Neo-Classical theatre is renowned for its acoustics.

Rue Beauville, a well-restored, narrow thoroughfare, is lined with beautiful late medieval half-timbered houses with an overhanging upper storey. The Église Notre-Dame-des-Jacobins, which was once the chapel of a Dominican monastery built here in 1249, is now used for exhibitions.

Arcaded galleries line the nearby place des Laitiers. Ruelle des Juifs, a narrow alleyway, was, until the end of the 14th century, a street of bankers and merchants.

Rue des Cornières, on the other side of boulevard de la République, was a major thoroughfare for trade in the Middle Ages. It is now lined with attractive restored houses, set above rows of arcades in a variety of styles.

Other houses worth seeing are the beautiful 14th-century Maison du Sénéchal in rue du Puits-du-Saumon, and the 18th-century Hôtel Amblard, at 1 rue Floirac.

Cathédrale Saint-Caprais

Place du Maréchal-Foch
05 53 66 37 27 Tue-Sun

Originally built in the 12th century, the cathedral has been remodelled several

Boat on the canal at Agen, and *(inset)* boulevard de la République

times. It has a magnificent Romanesque apse and its walls are covered with richly coloured frescoes.

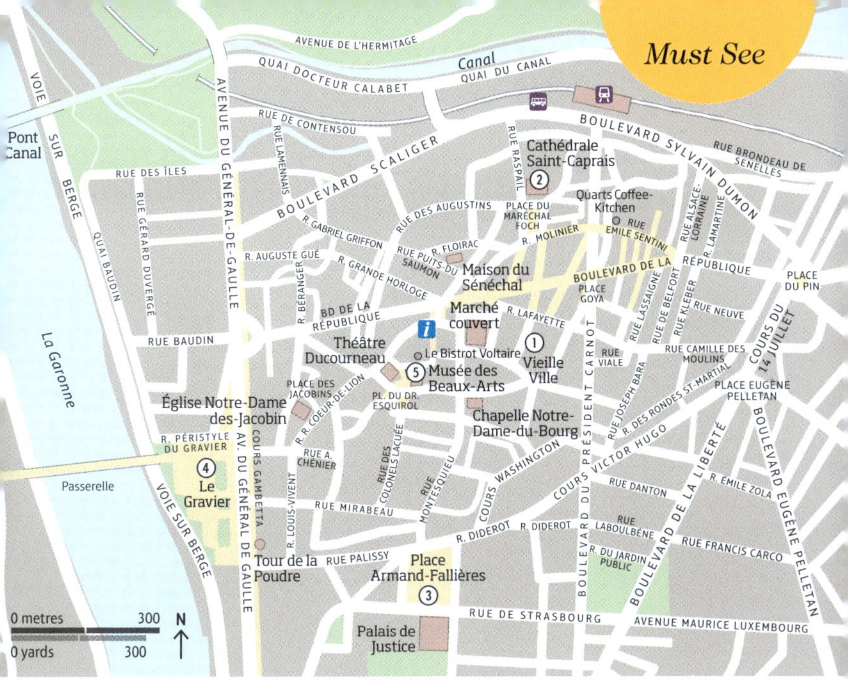

Place Armand-Fallières

The bishop's palace here, now used as the offices of the local council, was built in 1775 and added to later. A grand staircase, flanked by allegorical statues, fronts the Neo-Classical law courts.

Le Gravier

During the reign of Louis XIII, (from 1610 to 1643) this area near the river bank hosted regional fairs. The esplanade is now a popular place for strolling. On avenue Gambetta is Hôtel Hutot-de-Latour, an 18th-century, pink-brick building that was the tax collector's house. To its right is the Tour de la Poudre, once part of the medieval ramparts.

Musée des Beaux-Arts

Place du Docteur-Esquirol 05 53 69 47 23 Wed-Mon (excluding public hols)

Founded in 1876, this museum, one of the finest in southwest France, contains one of the most comprehensive overviews of life and culture in the Lot and Garonne valleys. The collections cover almost every period from prehistory to the 20th century.

The artifacts are displayed in four beautiful old townhouses. On show here is the *Vénus du Mas*, a Roman statue from Le Mas-d'Agenais *(p178)*, as well as Flemish, Dutch, French and Italian paintings of the 16th and 17th centuries and an important collection of Spanish paintings, including five works by Goya. Paintings by Courbet, Corot and Sisley cover the 19th century, and canvases by Roger Bissière and sculptures by Claude and François-Xavier Lalanne represent the modern era.

EAT

Quarts Coffee-Kitchen

This modern restaurant serves up fabulous and healthy breakfast bowls, smoothies and sandwiches.

3 rue Emile Sentini
05 53 96 63 74
Sun-Mon

Le Bistrot Voltaire

This highly regarded restaurant gives local dishes a twist and features a charming interior and a shaded terrace. The lunch menu changes weekly and the dinner options, monthly.

43 rue Voltaire
lebistrotvoltaire.com

A SHORT WALK
AGEN

Distance 1 km (half a mile) **Time** 15 minutes
Nearest station Agen

The French capital of rugby and prunes, Agen was originally a Gallo-Roman town known as Aginnum. It grew rapidly during the late Roman Empire, but suffered as a result of invasions in the 5th and 6th centuries. Control of the town passed between France and England during the Hundred Years' War *(p54)*. Agen later became a major manufacturing and trading base, exploiting its position on the Garonne river to export its produce. Today, it is an important administrative centre and university city. A stroll through the heart of town will reveal both modern hotspots as well as remnants of Agen's storied past.

↑ Outdoor dining at the charming place des Laitiers on the boulevard de la République

Hôtel Amblard

Maison du Sénéchal (14th century)

At **place des Laitiers** *is a statue of a pilgrim on the road to Santiago de Compostela (p226). It was made by Jean-Luc Toutain in 1998.*

Renowned for its acoustics, the Neo-Classical **Théâtre Ducourneau** *opened in 1908.*

The well-restored thoroughfare of **rue Beauville** *is one of the most picturesque in Agen. Both sides are lined with half-timbered houses with an overhanging upper storey.*

Cathédrale Saint-Caprais (p162) *has a fine Romanesque apse and its walls are covered with stunning frescoes.*

Locator Map

For more detail see p163

The exquisite, colourful interior of Cathédrale Saint-Caprais

Rue des Juifs *was a district inhabited by Jews expelled from Spain. In this narrow street, many worked as bankers, merchants and moneylenders.*

Faced with red brick, **Notre-Dame-du-Bourg's** *single-walled, pointed bell tower looks down onto an attractive small square.*

Hôtel de Ville

The displays at the **Musée des Beaux-Arts** (p163) *give a good insight into the cultures of the region.*

EXPERIENCE MORE

3 Gavaudun

E3 Place des Arcades, Monflanquin; 05 53 36 40 19

Perched on a hill, the village of Gavaudun stands above the wooded valleys around it. The ruins of the 11th–13th-century **Château de Gavaudun** are very impressive, particularly the keep with its limestone entrance. This stunning setting is regularly used for carnivals and musical events.

Château de Gavaudun
Le Bourg Mid-Apr-May & Oct: Wed-Sun; Jun-Sep: daily chateaude gavaudun.com

4 Monsempron

E4 Place Georges-Escande, Fumel; 05 53 71 13 70

Here, the imposing outline of the Benedictine priory of Saint-Géraud-de-Monsempron overlooks the confluence of the Lot and the Lémance. This fortified village has a beautifully proportioned Romanesque church. Although it was remodelled in the 16th century, the priory retains some earlier architectural elements, including a barrel-vaulted nave with carved capitals, a dome supported on stone columns above the central crossing and a minimalist doorway. The semicircular recesses of the apses overlap one another.

5 Villeréal

E3 Place de la Halle; coeurdebastides.com

Founded in 1265, the *bastide* town of Villeréal is laid out to a regular plan. The main square, at the centre of the town, is lined with arcades with corbelled houses above. The large, late- 14th-century covered market has an upper storey, with half-timbered cob walls, which housed the town hall and courts. The fortified medieval church, which once served as a place of refuge, has two turrets that are connected by a wall-walk. Up to the later years of the *Ancien Régime*, access to the town was still by drawbridge.

There is a cluster of interesting Romanesque churches in the villages sprinkling the countryside around Villeréal. The 12th-century church at Bournel, 7 km (4 miles) to the south, is dedicated to St Madeleine, whose statue can be seen above the arched main doorway. The medieval church at Rives, 2 km (1.5 miles) north, has an unusual triangular bell tower, with two arches and a round apse. The church at Montaut, 8 km (5 miles) to the southwest, was very important in the Middle Ages, being the seat of the archpriest with around

GREAT VIEW
Château de Fumel

Château de Fumel, near Monsempron, has splendid terraced gardens that offer stunning views over the Lot and the Vallée du Lot.

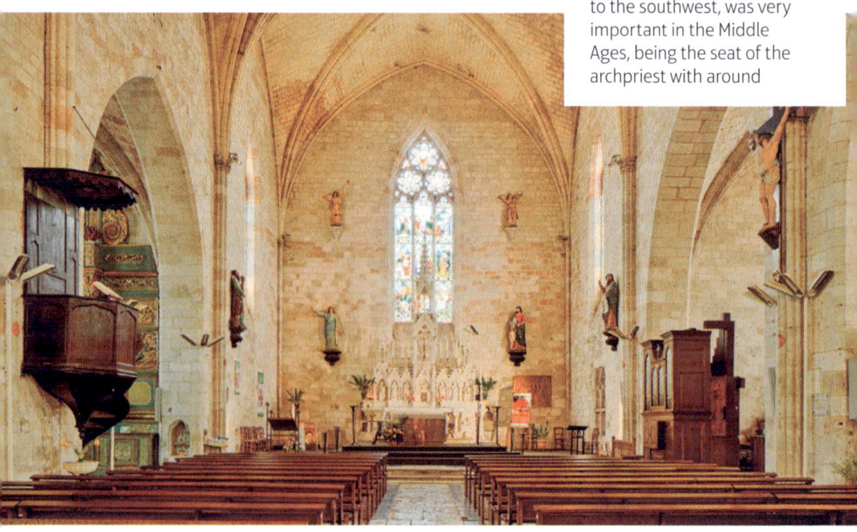

91 parishes. It has a five-arched bell tower, hung with two bells, astride two towers.

Sauveterre-la-Lémance

E3 Rue Notre-Dame, Villefranche-du-Périgord; perigordnoir-valleedordogne.com

This village, dominated by the privately owned Château des Rois-Ducs, gave its name to the Sauveterrian, a major period of the Mesolithic age. The small **Musée de la Préhistoire** displays objects found when excavations began in 1920 on a site known as Le Martinet.

At Saint-Front-sur-Lémance, 4 km (2.5 miles) southwest, there is an interesting 11th–14th-century fortified church.

Musée de la Préhistoire

Le Bourg Hours vary, check website sauveterre-prehistoire.fr

Puymirol

E4 La Mairie, 49 rue Royale; 05 53 95 32 10

Founded in 1246, Puymirol was the first *bastide* town to be built in the Agenais – an ancient region of France that is now part of the Lot-et-Garonne. It was well known for its fairs during the Middle Ages.

From the heights of the rocky spur on which it perches, the town looks down into the scenic Séoune valley. Puymirol is surrounded by ramparts with a wall-walk, and entry is via a gate known as Porte Comtale. The main street is rue Royale, and the main square, which is lined with arcades, still has its ancient well. The church, rebuilt in the 17th century, has a 13th-century doorway with a wide carved archway.

Some 8 km (5 miles) to the southeast is the hilltop village of Clermont-Soubiran, with stunning views of the rolling landscape all around. The Château de la Bastide houses a small museum, Musée du Vin et de la Tonnellerie, which has exhibits on local wine.

Inside the towering medieval Église Notre-Dame in Villeréal

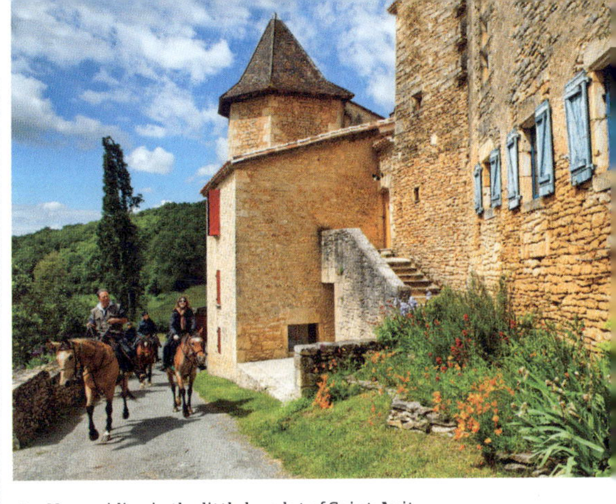

Horse riding in the little hamlet of Saint-Avit, best known for its Musée Bernard-Palissy

Saint-Avit

E3 Rue Notre-Dame, Villefranche-du-Périgord; perigordnoir-valleedordogne.com

This hamlet on a hillside in the Lède valley has just one street. The 13th-century Romanesque church is decorated with frescoes. Saint-Avit is the birthplace of Bernard Palissy, the famous potter, born in around 1510. He was known for his realistically modelled and painted dining ware, ewers and other vessels encrusted with "rustic figulines" in high relief, featuring reptiles, fish, shells and plants. He was patronized by the queen, Catherine de' Medici, but later imprisoned in the Bastille for his Protestant faith. He died in prison at the age of 80. The **Musée Bernard-Palissy** displays his work alongside contemporary ceramics.

Musée Bernard-Palissy

Saint-Avit May-Jun: Sun; Jul-Sep: Wed-Mon (Sep: closed Sat) museepalissy.net

STAY

La Maison Bleue

This restored stone building has five bedrooms, including one in a converted chapel, which has a private terrace.

E3 6 rue Saint-James, Villéreal
maisonbleuevillereal.com

Château Ladausse

Elegant rooms in a 17th-century manor house, which also hosts cooking classes and wine workshops.

E3 Monflanquin
ladausse.com

↑ The Basilique Notre-Dame de Peyragude, Penne-d'Agenais

9

Penne-d'Agenais

E4 Rue du 14 Juillet; tourisme-fumel.com

The history of Penne-d'Agenais is as tumultuous as that of the whole Aquitaine region. By turns a mighty base for Richard the Lionheart (1189–99), a possession of the counts of Toulouse and of Simon de Montfort's Crusaders, this town was held alternately by the French and the English during the Hundred Years' War (1337–1453), then passed from the Protestants to the Catholics during the Wars of Religion (1562–98). Filled with houses set on paved streets that run down the hillside, Penne-d'Agenais is crowned by the silvered dome of a great Neo-Byzantine basilica Notre-Dame de Peyragude, which was built from 1897 to 1947.

The remains of the medieval town include part of the 12th-century walls, as well as houses with Gothic doorways, and the keep of the castle, which was dismantled in the reign of Henri IV (1589–1610). Some houses on the main square have windows with intricate Gothic tracery. A restored gateway, the Porte de Ricard, is framed by buttresses. The defence tower on rue des Fossés once formed part of the ramparts. Place du Mercadiel and place Paul-Froment are lined with old arcaded merchants' houses. Beneath the town hall is the former "royal" prison.

INSIDER TIP

Penne d'Art

In the summer months, a contemporary art festival - the Penne d'Art - is held in Penne-d'Agenais. During the event, dozens of local artists display their artwork in various locations around town.

Tournon-d'Agenais

E4 Place de l'Hôtel de Ville; tourisme-fumel.com

Set in the Boudouyssou valley, this *bastide* town was built in about 1270, and soon after came under English control. Houses built into the ramparts look down from the high clifftop. Constructed from a mix of uncut boulders and dressed stone, some also have half-timbered walls. The medieval Maison de l'Abescat on rue de l'École housed the bishops of Agen during the Middle Ages. The bell tower in the square was built in 1637 and is crowned by a wooden steeple with a fine lunar clock that was added in 1843. Above place de la Mairie is a municipal garden, laid out on the site of a church destroyed in the 16th century during the Wars of Religion.

Pujols

E4 Place Saint-Nicolas; 05 53 36 78 69

Officially listed as one of France's prettiest villages, this heavily fortified town was dismantled several times in the course of its history.

Porte de Ville, the fortified gate, is the only entrance to this walled town. The gate also serves as the bell tower of the Église Saint-Nicolas, which dates back to the late Middle Ages. The main street is lined with half-timbered

and corbelled houses, many of which are over 500 years old. The Église Sainte-Foy, decorated inside with 16th-century frescoes, hosts temporary exhibitions.

A few minutes' drive south, the **Grotte de Lastournelle** is a cave system that features natural rock formations inside.

Grotte de Lastournelle
 1851 route des Grottes de Lastournelles, Sainte-Colombe-de-Villeneuve
Jul & Aug: daily; Sep–Jun: hours vary, check website
grotte-de-lastournelle.fr

12 Laroque-Timbaut

E4 Allée Federico Garcia Lorca; tourisme-villeneuvois.com

Laroque-Timbaut was founded on a rocky outcrop. The 13th-century covered market has a wooden roof supported on Tuscan columns.

Walking down the rue du Lô, visitors can see the foundations of a medieval castle and its old outbuildings. Outside the village is a memorial to its famous sons: the cyclist Paul Dangla (1878–1904) and Louis Brocq (1856–1928). The latter is famous for his work in the treatment of skin disorders. In the valley is a chapel dedicated to St German, where pilgrims gather on the last Sunday of May each year.

Hautefage-la-Tour, 5 km (3 miles) to the north, has a hexagonal tower, built in the 15th century. The church, completed several decades later, has a fine wooden roof. About 8 km (5 miles) northwest of Laroque-Timbaut is the fortified medieval village of Frespech. The **Musée du Foie Gras** in nearby Souleilles traces the 4,500-year-old history of the local speciality of *foie gras*.

Musée du Foie Gras
 Lieu Dit Souleilles
Daily Jan: Sun
souleilles-foiegras.com

13 Villeneuve-sur-Lot

E4 Allée Federico Garcia Lorca; tourisme-villeneuvois.com

Villeneuve was founded by Alphonse de Poitiers in 1264. It is the largest *bastide* town of the Lot-et-Garonne. The town's symbol is its bridge, Pont Vieux, which was built across the Lot in 1287 and restored about 400 years later. On the north bank of the river stands the Chapelle du Bout-du-Pont, dedicated to sailors and boatmen. A short walk from here is the **Musée de Gajac**, also situated on the riverside. Housed in an ancient mill, the museum's permanent collection highlights a series of etchings of Rome by engraver Piranesi (1720–78). Two majestic gates – Porte de Paris and Porte de Pujols – once formed part of the town's medieval ramparts. Markets are still held on place Lafayette, a square lined with arcades, and concerts held there animate the town centre.

The Église Sainte-Catherine was built in the 19th century on the site of an earlier building that had been demolished. In keeping with Byzantine-Romanesque style, it has stained-glass windows and wooden statues that date back to the *Ancien Régime* era.

In the Quartier d'Eysses, to the north of Villeneuve, is an archaeological site with a 1st-century CE Gallo-Roman villa. Amphorae and various other objects discovered here are displayed at the site's small **Musée Archéologique**.

Musée de Gajac
2 rue des Jardins
05 53 40 48 00 Tue–Sun

Musée Archéologique
Place Saint-Sernin-d'Eysses 07 88 16 83 50 Jul & Aug: daily

Did You Know?

French folklore claims Charlemagne's ailing army was healed by miraculous water from Laroque-Timbaut.

↓ Attractive half-timbered houses in the pretty village of Pujols

Prayssas

E4 Place de l'Hôtel-de-Ville; 05 53 95 00 15

Surrounded by low hills, this *bastide* town was built in the 13th century. The village of Clermont-Dessous, located 7 km (4 miles) to the south-west, is dominated by its castle. The town also features an 11th-century Romanesque church.

Casseneuil

E4 Allée Federico Garcia Lorca, Villeneuve-sur-Lot; 05 53 36 17 30

For centuries, this town relied on river transport and trade for its wealth. In 1214, it held out against the English under Simon de Montfort. Over-hanging houses line the river bank. The **Église Saint-Pierre** contains frescoes from the Middle Ages.

Église Saint-Pierre
21 place Saint-Pierre
05 53 41 07 92 (Mairie)
Jul-Aug: daily

Sainte-Livrade-sur-Lot

E4 Allée Federico Garcia Lorca, Villeneuve-sur-Lot; tourismevilleneuvois.com

The church in this *bastide* town was built in the 12th to 14th centuries. It has an attractive stone-built Romanesque tiered apse and contains a white-marble effigy of a 14th-century bishop. Another interesting feature of Sainte-Livrade is the Tour du Roy, a tower that formed part of a castle built here by Richard the Lionheart.

Monclar-d'Agenais

E4 Place Saint-Nicolas, Pujols; 05 53 36 78 69

Perched on a narrow spit of land, the *bastide* town of Monclar was founded by Alphonse of Poitiers in 1256. From its elevated site the town offers magnificent views of the Tolzac valley. One side of the town's main square is lined with arcades. The covered market abuts the Église Saint-Clar, which features a fine bell tower and a 16th-century porch.

Castelmoron-sur-Lot, 8 km (5 miles) to the southwest, has a pleasant human-made lake, beside which stands a Moorish town hall. The church at Fongrave, 7 km (4 miles) south, has a fine wooden sculpted altarpiece.

PICTURE PERFECT
Jardin des Nénuphars

Visitors can see nearly 300 varieties of water lilies in the beautiful water garden, the Jardin des Nénuphars "Latour-Marliac" *(latour-marliac.com)*, near Monclar-d'Agenais.

Clairac

D4 11 rue Touperie, Marmande; valdegaronne.com

Once a Protestant town, Clairac was besieged and its

fortifications destroyed by Louis XIII in 1621. However, several 15th-century half-timbered houses survive. The town's Benedictine abbey was established in the Early Middle Ages and by the 13th century it had become the most influential abbey in the Agenais. It is now closed to the public as it is privately owned. The handsome timbered Maison Montesquieu is where the writer of the same name *(p102)* is said to have written his famous political satire, the *Persian Letters* (1721).

The town of Tonneins, on the banks of the Garonne, was once the capital of ancient Gaul. This was a former tobacco manufacturing town, as is evident from the beautiful exterior of the Manufacture Royale des Tabacs (Royal Tobacco Factory), built in 1726.

Just 9 km (6 miles) south-east of Clairac, in a wooded valley, is the village of Lacépède. At the edge of the village is **Lac du Salabert**, a reservoir and nature reserve. There are observation posts along the lake for watching the local wildlife, and also the Terra Aventura, a 3.5-km (2-mile) botanical trail that runs around the lake.

Lac du Salabert
W sentier-lac-du-salabert.com

Granges-sur-Lot

E4 i 2 place du Café, Le Temple-sur-Lot; tourisme-lotetgaronne.com

Founded in 1291 on the banks of the River Lot, this *bastide* town was largely destroyed in the Hundred Years' War (1337–1453), during which Britain and France fought over the region of Aquitaine. The **Ferme et Musée du Pruneau**, 2 km (1 mile) away in the town of Le Gabach, is devoted to the history of the local prune industry. It features displays of ovens dating from the 19th and 20th centuries, drying cupboards and other equipment, as well as old documents that chronicle 100 years of the art of converting a plum to a prune. The museum is set in an orchard with more than 3,000 plum trees. Visitors can also enjoy tasting tours here.

At the **Chaudron Magique** farm at Brugnac, 11 km (7 miles) north, visitors can buy organic products, such as cereals, as well as angora goat hair.

Ferme et Musée du Pruneau
Le Gabach 05 53 84 00 69 Apr-Dec: daily; Jan-Mar: Mon-Sat Last two weeks Jan

Chaudron Magique
1219 route de Brugnac Hours vary, check website W chaudronmagique.fr

The Ferme et Musée du Pruneau, 2 km (1 mile) away in the town of Le Gabach, is devoted to the history of the local prune industry.

↓ The pretty town of Casseneuil, set on a peninsula in the Lot

Duras

D3 14 boulevard Jean-Brisseau; tourismeduras.com

Built on the plan of a *bastide*, this ancient fortified town looks down from a high promontory above the river Dropt. The **Château de Duras** was built around 1137 and later remodelled several times. By the late Middle Ages, it was a fortress set with eight towers; by the 17th century, it had developed into a grand residential château. During the French Revolution *(p54)*, it was almost reduced to a ruin. The state acquired it in 1969.

The castle is open to visitors, who can walk through almost 35 of its great rooms. These rooms include the Salle des Maréchaux (Marshals' Hall) and a barrel-vaulted ballroom dating from 1740. The castle tower offers a panoramic view of the Pays de Duras. The museum of local history, situated in the basement, documents life in the Duras, focusing on such aspects of the area as vine-growing, local crafts as well as other folk traditions.

Château de Duras
Place du Château
Feb–Dec: daily
chateau-de-duras.com

Castillonnès

E3 coeurdebastides.com

Founded in about 1259, the *bastide* town of Castillonnès is located on a rocky spur. During the Hundred Years' War *(p54)*, the town passed between the French and the English seven times, but was finally taken by the French in 1451. Two gates are all that remain of the original medieval ramparts.

On place des Cornières, the main square, is an unusual 20th-century covered market. On the other side of the main square is the former Maison du Gouverneur, graced with a Renaissance courtyard. The building is now the town hall.

The church, which was extensively rebuilt after the Wars of Religion, has a 17th-century Baroque altarpiece and stained glass by the master-craftsman Louis Franchéo.

About 22 km (14 miles) to the west of Castillonnès is Miramont-de-Guyenne. Founded in 1278 by Edward I, this *bastide* town was built on a site that was once used as a lookout post for the Knights Templar. A stroll around Miramont leads to the central square, with its reconstructed covered market and elegant arcades. The town also has a thriving shoe industry, which started in the 1800s with the creation of a unique, sheepskin clog.

Monflanquin

E3 Place des Arcades; coeurdebastides.com

This attractive, exceptionally well-preserved *bastide* town, officially listed as one of France's prettiest villages, is laid out to an oval plan. It clings to the hillside, rising sharply from the Lède valley. Built around 1240, with a grid pattern of streets, the *bastide* developed in 1252 under the leadership of Alphonse de Poitiers, but its defences were dismantled on the orders of

Did You Know?

Monflanquin's market has taken place every Thursday morning in the place des Arcades since 1256.

The arcaded houses of Monflanquin, a perfectly preserved *bastide* town

Cardinal Richelieu. The streets intersect at place des Arcades, at the top end of the town. The main square is lined with handsome arcaded houses, including the Maison du Prince Noir (House of the Black Prince), with Gothic rib-vaulting and moulded panels. The church, the beautiful **Église Saint-André**, has a single-wall bell tower, whose façade dates from 1927, and a relief-decorated medieval doorway.

Rue de l'Union, rue des Arcades and rue Sainte-Marie are lined with some fine stone houses, sporting arcades on the ground floor and old half-timbered façades above.

Overlooking the town on a rocky spur stands the Château de Roquefère, a fortified castle that is open to the public only on European Heritage Days (dates vary each year).

The **Musée des Bastides** shows how *bastide* towns were constructed, from the Middle Ages onwards, and how they served their purpose.

Église Saint-André
19 rue des Arcades
Daily

Musée des Bastides
Maison du Tourisme, place des Arcades 05 53 36 40 19 Apr-Jun & Sep: Wed-Sat; Jul & Aug: Tue-Fri

Lauzun

E3 5 rue Marcel Hervé; 05 53 20 10 07

The eventful life of the Duc de Lauzun, marshal of France and a courtier of Louis XIV, is conjured up in the rooms of the **Château de Lauzun**, which was built in the 13th century and remodelled around a hundred years later. The listed Renaissance wing has two monumental chimneypieces with carvings and marble capitals, and the vast *salle des gardes* ("guard room") still has its original 16th-century terracotta-tiled floor. The Gothic church, Église Saint-Étienne, in the village, opposite a house with caryatids, contains a Renaissance-era pulpit and altarpiece.

Château de Lauzun
06 74 25 16 65
Jul & Aug: daily

EAT & DRINK

Lot-et-Garonne has a rich food culture that revolves around its local farm produce and fine wines. Seek out one of these options to enjoy the best of the region's gastronomic traditions in a beautiful setting.

La Bastide des Oliviers
E3 1 Tour de Ville, Monflanquin labastidedesoliviers.fr

Chai et Rasade
D3 8 place du Marché, Duras 05 53 93 20 20

Hostellerie des Ducs
D3 Boulevard Jean-Brisseau, Duras hostellerieducs-duras.com

The distinctive towers of the 13th-century Château de Lauzun rising up over the historic town of Lauzun

The Lot-et-Garonne countryside around Monflanquin

Marmande

D3 11 rue Toupinerie; valdegaronne.com

The Marmande area has been a major producer of tomatoes for several hundred years, and now also grows strawberries. Rival factions fought over the town during the Hundred Years' War, but in 1580 it was finally won by France. The **Église Notre-Dame**, founded in 1275, has a listed organ built by Cavaillé-Coll in 1859. The church's Chapelle Saint-Benoît contains a 17th-century altarpiece with two carved scenes at the centre. Visitors can access the cloister through the gardens.

Rue Labat is lined with half-timbered houses and the old ramparts are decorated with a modern mosaic, depicting major episodes throughout the town's 800-year history.

Situated around 8 km (5 miles) northwest is the **Musée Archéologique André-Larroderie** at the Gallo-Roman site of Sainte-Bazeille. It features artifacts from the Iron Age to the time of Louis XIV, found at various digs in the Marmande area.

Église Notre-Dame

Rue de la République
Daily

Musée Archéologique André-Larroderie

Place René-Sanson
06 85 23 60 52 Apr-Jun & Sep-Oct: Sun; Jul & Aug: Wed-Mon

Did You Know?

The statue in front of Marmande's town hall is dedicated to the Marmande tomato.

Casteljaloux

D4 Maison du Roy; tourisme-coteauxetlandesdegascogne.fr

On the edge of the Landes forests, this spa town is closely associated with the Albret dynasty. Some 40 half-timbered corbelled houses, built in the 15th and 16th centuries, date from the period when the town was the capital of Gascony and a base for Henri IV's hunting expeditions.

The Maison du Roy (King's House) is a fine 16th-century residence associated with Louis XIII and Louis XIV. Tour Maquebœuf is one of the few surviving vestiges of the town's medieval fortifications.

At Clarens, 2 km (1 mile) south of Casteljaloux, is a vast lake surrounded by pine trees and fringed by sandy beaches. The lake is a popular local leisure spot where people come to enjoy a range of water sports, as well as treetop rope courses, which include a zip wire over the lake. Nearby, the town of Bouglon has a viewpoint that offers stunning vistas of the Forêt des Landes and the Garonne river valley. The Église Saint-Savin, 1 km (half a mile) south of Villefranche-du-Queyran, is a jewel of Romanesque architecture. Dating from the 11th–12th centuries, it has a beautiful 12-arched choir and 20 magnificently carved capitals.

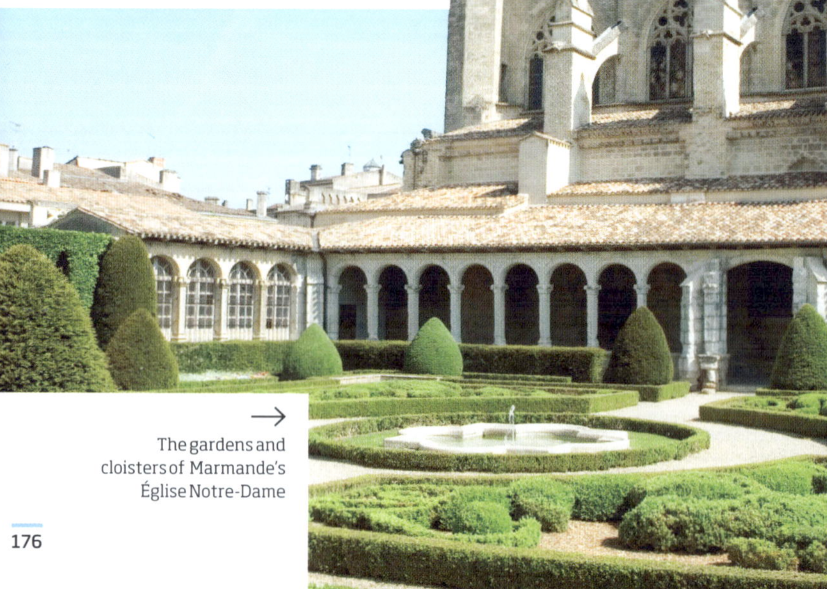

→ The gardens and cloisters of Marmande's Église Notre-Dame

26

Pays de Serres

D/E4 tourisme-pays-de-serres.fr

The steep valleys and plateaus of the Pays de Serres form a geologically distinct area of land, bordered by the River Lot to the north and the Garonne to the south. Narrow bands of limestone, known as *serres* ("long crests"), run right across this landscape, which is dotted with villages and old *bastide* towns that perch on the outcrops of rock. There are also many picturesque structures, such as dovecotes, farmhouses and a number of Romanesque churches and chapels.

27

Mézin

D4 7 avenue Mondenard, Nérac; 05 53 65 27 75

The town of Mézin grew up around its medieval monastery, of which nothing now remains, and its church. The main square is lined with picturesque arcades. In the narrow, winding streets all around stand half-timbered houses and a number of fine stone-built residences. The Gothic-arched Porte de Ville, a gateway also known as Porte Anglaise, is a vestige of the town's 13th-century ramparts.

In the square is the restored medieval **Église Saint-Jean-Baptiste**. Despite the rather functional, slightly leaning six columns that flank the nave, the church has an elegant interior. The climb up the bell tower's 90 steps is no longer permitted because it is too dangerous. The wrought-iron cross to the left of the main doorway into the church dates from 1815. It bears the instruments of the Passion, which are surmounted by the rooster that crowed when Peter denied

INSIDER TIP

Tourist Train

In the summer months a tourist train runs between Nérac and Mézin along a decommissioned stretch of railway *(chemin-de-fer-touristique-du-pays-de-l-albret.blog4ever.com)*.

Jesus. There are many gardens in the town and it is particularly pleasant to walk around the ramparts, in the rue Neuve quarter and also along the rue des Jardins.

The **Musée du Liège et du Bouchon** is devoted to the cork-making industry, for which the town was famous in the 19th and early 20th centuries. Exhibitions focus on the daily lives of workers, as well as the more unusual and modern uses of cork such as in aircrafts.

There are dozens of interesting Romanesque churches in the area. The fortified ancient churches at Villeneuve-de-Mézin, Lannes and Saint-Pé-Saint-Simon are especially notable and worth seeking out for lovers of architecture and history.

East of Mézin, the village of Moncrabeau is known as the "liars' capital". The local Liars' Academy, founded in 1748, hosts the International Festival of Lies on the first Sunday in August. French- and Gascon-speaking contestants compete by telling convincing lies in an effort to be crowned King of Liars. The village is also famous for Gascon cuisine that includes prunes, confit melons and goat's cheese.

Église Saint-Jean-Baptiste
Place Armand-Fallières
Daily

Musée du Liège et du Bouchon
Rue du Puits Saint-Côme 05 53 65 68 16
Apr-May & Oct-Nov: Tue-Fri; Jun-Sep: daily

Picturesque Poudenas, set on the river Gélise and overlooked by its château

Aiguillon

D4 30 rue Triers; 05 53 88 95 85

The small town of Aiguillon, at the confluence of the Lot and the Garonne, has been inhabited since Gallo-Roman times, and was a focus of conflict during the Hundred Years' War. The Château des Ducs was built by the Duc d'Aiguillon between 1775 and 1781. This luxurious residence was pillaged during the French Revolution, and in 1966 it was converted into a school.

The **Musée Raoul-Dastrac**, located in a deconsecrated church, showcases some of the artist's Post-Impressionist paintings and stages regular temporary exhibitions.

Pech-de-Berre, 4 km (2.5 miles) north of Aiguillon, offers expansive views of the Lot and Garonne valleys. Damazan, 7 km (4 miles) to the west on the Canal de Garonne, is a *bastide* town with elegant half-timbered houses and a covered market with the town hall on its upper floor. Around 8 km (5 miles) southwest of Aiguillon, houseboats can be seen on the canal at Buzet-sur-Baïse, which is noted for its vineyards. At Saint-Pierre-de-Buzet, 7 km (4 miles) southwest, is an attractive 12th-century fortified church.

Musée Raoul-Dastrac
Rue de la République
05 53 79 60 12 (Mairie)
Call ahead to check

Poudenas

D5 7 avenue Mondenard, Nérac; albret-tourisme.com

This medieval village was once a staging post frequently visited by Henri IV. With old stone buildings covered in ivy, historic architecture and a quiet, rural atmosphere, Poudenas is a great stop for those visitors who want to experience the quintessential French countryside.

It even has its own castle: the Château de Poudenas, built above the village by the lords of Poudenas, who were vassals of King Edward I of England. It is now a stunning luxury hotel. In the 1500s the castle, set in wooded parkland, was converted into a seigneurial residence. The château is fronted by arcaded galleries.

Le Mas-d'Agenais

D4 11 rue Toupinerie, Marmande; valdegaronne.com

The ancient village of Le Mas-d'Agenais spreads out along the canal that runs parallel to the Garonne. Evidence of Roman occupation has been discovered here, including a marble statue known as the *Vénus du Mas*, now displayed at the Musée des Beaux-Arts in Agen *(p163)*. The Collégiale Saint-Vincent, a beautiful 11th–12th-century abbey church, has 17th-century choir stalls and finely carved capitals. It also features a very small painting of *Christ on the Cross* (1631) by Rembrandt; the other six are in Munich. The 17th-century corn market in the square has a elegant wooden roof. The washhouse nearby, with its distinct five-sided roof, is also worth a detour.

Laplume

E4 64 Grande Rue; 05 53 95 16 67

Once the capital of the small Brulhois area located to the southwest of Agen, the village of Laplume looks out across the landscape from its vantage point, high on a rocky outcrop of limestone. Parts

The town hall on the central place de la Mairie in the old *bastide* town of Beauville

HIDDEN GEM

Lac de Lamontjoie

West of Agen, Lac de Lamontjoie is a peaceful spot for fishing (carp, in particular) and bird-watching. Visitors can camp here and, in summer months, dine at the lakeside restaurant.

of the medieval village still survive, including sections of the ramparts and two gates. The 16th-century Église Saint-Barthélemy was restored in the 17th and 18th centuries.

Just outside Laplume is the Lavoir de Labat, a curious five-sided washhouse that dates from the 17th or 18th century. Around 10 km (16 miles) north of Laplume, the village of Sainte-Colombe-en-Bruilhois is a good place to visit for its historic centre and its Gothic-Romanesque church.

32

Beauville

E4 **Place de la Mairie; 06 08 53 88 95**

Sheltering behind a row of trees, Beauville, an old *bastide* town, clings to the hillside, commanding an impressive view of the surrounding landscape. The attractive arcaded main square is lined with half-timbered houses. The Château de Beauville was built in the Middle Ages, with alterations made several hundred years later. The 16th-century church has a bell tower at the entrance.

33

Saint-Maurin

E4 **38 rue Garonne, Agen; destination-agen.fr**

This peaceful village, set in a lush valley, developed around an 11th-century Benedictine abbey which is dedicated to Saint Maurin; unusually, it's the only village in France of that name. The abbey was partly destroyed during the Crusades, then further damage was inflicted by the English in the 14th century. Now all that remains is part of the church and the abbot's house. Built on the plan of a Latin cross, this church has a semicircular choir with six exquisitely carved capitals, including a depiction of the martyrdom of St Maurin (he was decapitated). The nave once covered what is now part of the village square. Other vestiges of the abbey lie between newer buildings.

The abbot's house contains the **Abbey Château Museum**. Designed by the inhabitants of the village, and with the help of exhibits contributed by them, it documents daily life in the area in the early 20th century. There is also a model of the abbey as it was at the height of its splendour.

On the square in front of the abbot's house is a handsome covered market hall, restored in 1625, as well as several beautiful half-timbered houses.

The Église Saint-Martin-d'Anglars, above the village, was founded in the 13th century and rebuilt in the 16th. The furnishings inside it include a carved wooden altar from the Renaissance era and an 18th-century statue of St Joseph.

Abbey Château Museum

Palais Abbatial 05 53 95 31 25 (Mairie, Saint-Maurin) By appointment

The charming streets of Nérac, and *(inset)* the interior of the Église Saint-Nicolas

Nérac

D4 7 avenue Mondenard; albret-tourisme.com

The Baïse, now a navigable river, runs through the centre of Nérac, with the castle and the new town on one bank, and the district of Petit Nérac on the other. In the 14th century, Nérac – capital of the Albret region – was a favourite base of the Albret family. They had settled in the region around 200 years earlier and married into the Navarrese and the French royal family. Nérac was an important Protestant stronghold and, in 1621, its fortifications were dismantled on the orders of Louis XIII. The castle, built above the Baïse in the 14th to 16th centuries, reflects the importance of the Albret family at the height of their power. The castle once consisted of four wings set with circular towers. It was abandoned after the 16th century, and only the north wing now remains. It has an elegant corbelled gallery of twisted columns, built between 1470 and 1522. Since 1934 the wing has housed the **Château-Musée Henri IV**, with exhibits on the Albret family and life at court in Nérac.

The 18th-century **Église Saint-Nicolas**, with a Neo-Classical façade, is known for its frescoes and stained-glass windows, which show important figures, including patriarchs, prophets and kings.

The Maison des Conférences, a 16th-century townhouse on rue des Conférences, has its original tiered galleries and a façade decorated with Renaissance motifs. It is named for the meetings *(conférences)* that Catherine de' Medici and Henry of Navarre held here from 1578, to bring about a reconciliation between Catholics and Protestants.

Petit Nérac is full of pretty half-timbered houses. It lies along the Baïse, near the lock (dating from 1835). The district's main feature is the 19th-century Église Notre-Dame. The Maison de Sully, at the other end of the Vieux-Pont, rebuilt in the early modern era, was home to the young Duc de Sully in 1580. He later became first minister to Henri IV.

The Parc Royal de la Garenne, now a public park, stretches for 2 km (1 mile) along the river bank. It has

Did You Know?

Nérac is generally recognized as the place where the recipe for *foie gras* was invented.

several fountains, including the Fontaine du Dauphin, which was built in 1601 to mark the birth of Louis XIII, and the Fontaine de Fleurette, named after a young girl who drowned herself after being seduced and abandoned by the Prince of Navarre.

Chateau-Musée Henri IV
Impasse Henri IV 05 53 65 21 11 Jun-Sep: Tue-Sat

Église Saint-Nicolas
Place Saint-Nicolas
Daily

Vianne

D4 Place des Marronniers; 05 53 65 27 75

This *bastide* town was set up in 1284 on the banks of the Baïse. Its focal point is a 12th-century church. The nave, capitals and choir are Romanesque, while the doorway, decoration of the apse and bell tower fortifications are Gothic.

The glassmaker's workshop here has closed down, but the tradition is kept alive by local glass-blowers and engravers. Nearby, the town of Xaintrailles has a medieval keep. You can see how honey is made at the **Musée de l'Abeille** (Bee Museum). To the north is the 13th-century *bastide* town of Francescas. Here, sharing a building with the post office, is the surprising and quirky **Musée de la Boîte Ancienne en Fer Blanc** (Tin Can Museum).

INSIDER TIP
River Trips

Enjoy a leisurely trip from Nérac down the river Baïse aboard an old-fashioned *gabare,* a wooden boat that was once used to transport merchandise *(croisieresduprince henry.com).*

Musée de l'Abeille
Jeandouillard
Hours vary, check website
museedelabeille.wixsite.com/apicultrice

Musée de la Boîte Ancienne en Fer Blanc
Place du Centre, Au Bourg
05 53 65 42 78 9am-12:30pm Mon-Sat

Barbaste

D4 Rue du Moulin des Tours; 05 53 65 09 37

Built in the Middle Ages and set with four towers, the **Moulin des Tours de Barbaste** is a fortified mill that looks out over the Gélise river, onto a ten-span Romanesque bridge. In the late 19th century, the building was converted into a cork factory. It was damaged by fire in 1906 and again in 1937.

The *bastide* town of Lavardac, 2 km (1 mile) to the northeast, was founded in 1256. The harbour, on the Baïse, is a stopping place for pleasure boats. The medieval tower is all that remains of a medieval castle.

The tiny village of Durance lies 11 km (7 miles) west. This *bastide* village is surrounded by pine forest. All that remains of the fortifications is the south gate.

Moulin des Tours de Barbaste
Rue du Moulin des Tours Mid-Apr-early Nov: hours vary, check website moulindestours.com

←
Barbaste's Romanesque bridge spanning the Gélise river

Moirax

E4 Mairie, 11 voie César; 05 53 87 03 69

The ancient village of Moirax, which clusters around its majestic Romanesque church, looks out onto the flatlands of the Agenais.

In the early Middle Ages, the local baron, Guillaume de Moirax, donated land to the Cluniac order and a monastery was built here. Suffering at the hands of various warring factions, the monastery experienced turbulent times during the Middle Ages. Towards the end of the 17th century, a major programme of rebuilding work was started, but this was brought to an abrupt halt by the outbreak of the French Revolution in 1789.

The **Église Notre-Dame**, which was once part of the monastery, is an exquisite example of Romanesque architecture, and has been superbly restored. An arcaded bell tower now rises above the projecting central section of the façade. This is crowned by a limpet-shaped roof. A double tier of arches lines the buttressed aisles. The arches of the porch are decorated with beading and carved foliated scrolls, and rest on four slender columns. The Gothic arch above frames a semicircular window. Over the choir is a dome decorated with shingles and crowned by a lantern. The arched windows of the apse and side apses are decorated with further beading. The church is laid out to the plan of a basilica, having a nave that is flanked by aisles, a feature which is quite rare in the southwest of France. The only lighting for the nave comes from the window in the west wall.

The strictly symmetrical transept is divided into three equal sections. Each arm of the transept, which is lit by a set of double windows, has steps that lead up to a raised platform or stand. The dome that sits above the central crossing point has been rebuilt in a star shape.

The choir is lit by arched windows framed by slender columns. Four supporting arches rise up from its square base to the octagonal dome above. Five arched windows illuminate the vaulted apse. More than 100 ornate capitals decorate the various columns found in this church. As well as abstract geometric and plant motifs, the lion motif features on many of them, while birds, rams and all manner of fantastic monsters also appear. Thirteen capitals are carved with biblical scenes, including depictions of Adam and Eve in the Garden of Eden, St Michael killing the dragon and Daniel in the lions' den. The aisles are decorated with 17th-century woodcarvings, showing various scenes taken from the Old Testament.

Église Notre-Dame
10 Grand Rue Daily

Aubiac

E4 64 Grande Rue, Laplume; 05 53 95 16 67

Nestling in lush greenery, the impressive military-like structure of the Romanesque Église Sainte-Marie towers over the village. A significant architectural landmark, this church was built between the 9th and the 12th centuries on the site of a Merovingian building. Appearing as a square and severely plain fortress from the outside, the church has a contrastingly ornate interior, with rounded arches in the apse and barrel vaulting above the doorway. The dome over the square choir is decorated with 16th-century frescoes depicting the four Evangelists. The medieval castle next to the church belonged to a branch of the Galard family. It was rebuilt during the *Ancien Régime* era.

An important archaeological find from Aubiac is a Celtic bronze head of a horse, now featured in the Musée des Beaux-Arts in Agen *(p163)*.

Field beside the Église Notre-Dame, a Romanesque church in Moirax

One of the magnificently decorated rooms in the Château de Monluc

Layrac

E4 8 place du 11 novembre 1918; 05 53 66 51 53

Layrac commands stunning views over the Gers and Garonne valleys. The medieval Église Saint-Martin is crowned by an 18th-century dome, and it has a fine apse. The capitals on the church's façade bear carvings featuring monsters and demons. The church also contains a marble altarpiece and on the floor are traces of mosaics dating from the Middle Ages, depicting Samson overcoming the lion. Today, the bell tower is all that remains of the older church, which was destroyed in 1792. On place de Salens, visitors can admire a fountain and a washhouse, built against the remains of the ramparts.

Astaffort, a small town in the Brulhois area, is the birthplace of renownedthe singer and guitarist Francis Cabrel. Here, half-timbered houses and the remains of ramparts chronicle the town's past. The town's Romanesque church, Église Saint-Félix, was rebuilt in the 17th century. **Caudecoste**, on a hilltop, 8 km (5 miles) southeast of Layrac, was built in 1273. It is one of the few *bastide* towns to have been founded by a religious order. Half-timbered houses on wooden pillars cluster round its small arcaded square. The church, on the edge of the town, is also worth a visit.

Estillac

E3 05 53 67 80 36 (Mairie)

A stronghold in the Middle Ages, Estillac was once owned by Blaise de Monluc (c 1500–77), the writer and Maréchal de France (marshal of France) who led the Catholic armies in the 16th-century Wars of Religion. He also distinguished himself in the Franco-Italian wars, and is noted for his *Commentaires*, a treatise on soldiery. A white marble effigy of the former Maréchal is located in the grounds of Monluc's old home, **Château de Monluc**, in the nearby town of Saint-Puy. Visitors can enjoy guided tours here (for a fee), but the focus is more on the estate's wine production (and free tastings) than the château's former inhabitant.

Sérignac-sur-Garonne, on the canal northwest of Estillac, is very popular with visitors on boating holidays as well as cyclists and walkers. This *bastide* town has some half-timbered houses, a medieval church with a Romanesque porch and a spiral belfry, which was rebuilt in 1922 as a replica of the original 16th-century structure.

Château de Monluc
Saint-Puy
Hours vary, check website monluc.fr

EAT

Auberge Le Prieuré
Contemporary French dishes are served in a charming old village house at this Michelin-starred restaurant with a relaxed and friendly atmosphere.

E4 Le Bourg, Moirax auberge leprieure.fr

A DRIVING TOUR
PAYS DU DROPT

Length 55 km (35 miles) **Starting point** Sainte-Colombe-de-Duras **Stopping-off point** Dine at Hostellerie des Ducs (*p173*), a former convent that serves fine wines and traditional dishes

Locator Map

Occupying the northwestern corner of the *département* of Lot-et-Garonne, the Pays du Dropt is bisected by the Dropt river. It's a wonderful place for a relaxed drive – a region of gentle valleys covered with vines and plum trees, dotted with small, white stone Romanesque churches. The vineyards of the Côtes de Duras occupy some 20 sq km (8 sq miles), many of them part of small family estates. The Côtes de Duras area was granted its own *appellation* in 1937.

The picturesque, vine-covered church in the attractive village of ***Saint-Sernin-de-Duras*** *was restored in the 15th and 19th centuries.*

The village of ***Esclottes*** *is named for its clottes (boundary stones) that marked the borders of the dioceses of Agen and Bazas.*

This route will take you on a loop from ***Sainte-Colombe-de-Duras****. The choir of its small Romanesque church has carved capitals, and a fresco shows scenes from the life of St Colomba.*

Landerrouat
Villeneuve-de-Duras
D141
D708
D312
Esclottes
D15
Saint-Sernin de Duras
Savignac-de-Duras
D411
START
D312
D237
D203
Dourdèze
Sainte-Colombe-de-Duras
FINISH
D708
D134
D281
Duras
Dieulivol
Dropt
D234
D668
Pont-Neuf
D668
D708
D124
Taillecavat
Auriac-sur-Dropt
Saint-Pierre-sur-Dropt
D211
D228
Lévignac-de-Guyenne
D228

0 kilometres 3
0 miles 3
N

↑ An old *pigeonnier* (dovecote) in the fields around Esclottes

The ancient Église de Loubès in Loubès-Bernac

Loubès-Bernac *village has four churches. One of them, the Église de Loubès, has the coat of arms of Richard the Lionheart on its doorway.*

There are fine views from the remains of 12th-century ramparts at **Soumensac**.

In an ancient sauve (area of cleared land), the village of **La Sauvetat-du-Dropt** *has a large church with a 12th-century choir and a Romanesque bridge.*

The Église Saint-Eutrope in **Allemans-du-Dropt** *is decorated with beautiful 15th-century frescoes. They include depictions of the Last Supper and the Resurrection.*

Set above the Dropt valley, the charming 12th-century Romanesque church in **Monteton** *has finely carved capitals, featuring a host of fantasy beasts.*

Fresco of the Last Judgment in the Église Saint-Eutrope, Allemans-du-Dropt

Turquoise surf and golden sand on the Côte d'Argent near Hossegor

LANDES

Evidence of settlement in Landes goes back to prehistoric times, but the region's most visible historic legacy is the Hundred Years' War (1337–1453), during which many *bastide* towns were built up in strategic locations across the countryside. In this difficult, marshy terrain, life was hard. To keep watch over their sheep, local shepherds used to walk on stilts to make it easier to cross the muddy ground. During the Second Empire (1852–1870), the landscape changed as residents drained the marsh land and planted pine forests to produce resin and timber. Also at this time, the coming of the railways and better roads greatly improved communication between the towns and cities. However, the creation of the Parc Naturel Régional des Landes de Gascogne, in 1970, has helped to preserve Landes' traditional way of life. In the summer of 2022, the region's landscape, including that of the national park, underwent another significant change when forest fires destroyed over 70 sq km (27 sq miles) of pine forest. It is expected to take around ten years for the area to fully recover.

Today, thousands of visitors flock to the Landes region every year, drawn by the beauty of its forests and the long, sandy beaches stretching along its Atlantic coastline, a paradise for surfers. But it is also well worth exploring the picturesque hinterland, with its colourful festivals and many gastronomic treats.

LANDES

Must See

1 Parc Naturel Régional des Landes de Gascogne

Experience More

2 Hossegor
3 Mimizan
4 Biscarrosse
5 Courant d'Huchet
6 Pays d'Orthe
7 Sorde-l'Abbaye
8 Capbreton
9 Pomarez
10 Montfort-en-Chalosse
11 Dax
12 Labastide-d'Armagnac
13 Soustons
14 Mont-de-Marsan
15 Saint-Sever
16 Aire-sur-l'Adour
17 Grenade-sur-l'Adour
18 Peyrehorade
19 Brassempouy

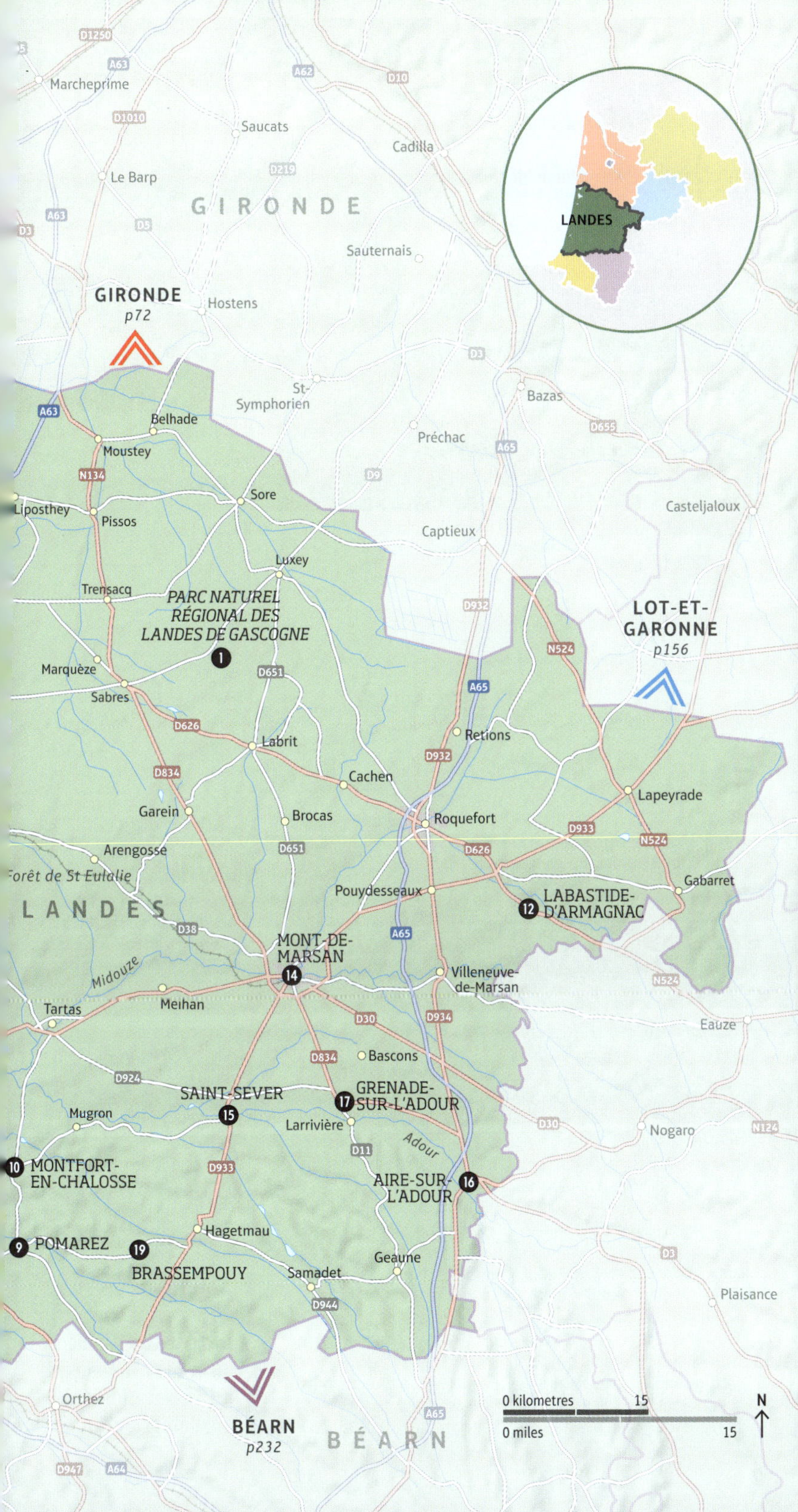

GIRONDE
GIRONDE
p72
LANDES
LOT-ET-GARONNE
p156
BÉARN
p232
BÉARN
LANDES
PARC NATUREL RÉGIONAL DES LANDES DE GASCOGNE
Marcheprime
Saucats
Cadilla
Le Barp
Sauternais
Hostens
St-Symphorien
Bazas
Belhade
Moustey
Préchac
Sore
Liposthey
Pissos
Casteljaloux
Captieux
Luxey
Trensacq
Marquèze
Sabres
Labrit
Retions
Cachen
Lapeyrade
Garein
Brocas
Roquefort
Arengosse
Forêt de St Eulalie
Pouydesseaux
Gabarret
LABASTIDE-D'ARMAGNAC
MONT-DE-MARSAN
Villeneuve-de-Marsan
Midouze
Tartas
Meilhan
Eauze
Bascons
SAINT-SEVER
GRENADE-SUR-L'ADOUR
Mugron
Larrivière
Nogaro
Adour
MONTFORT-EN-CHALOSSE
AIRE-SUR-L'ADOUR
Hagetmau
POMAREZ
BRASSEMPOUY
Geaune
Samadet
Plaisance
Orthez
0 kilometres 15
0 miles 15
N

Horse riding through the Parc Naturel Régional des Landes de Gascogne

PARC NATUREL RÉGIONAL DES LANDES DE GASCOGNE

C4 Maison de la Nature, 33 route de Bayonne, Belin-Beliet; parc-landes-de-gascogne.fr

Created in 1970 to preserve and enhance the land and culture of the Gascogne region, this park has three landscapes that live in harmony: "Pignada" or pine forests, the Leyre Valley and the Arcachon Basin.

This paradise for nature lovers lies between the Gironde and the Landes. The extensive plateau, stretching over 3,360 sq km (1,300 sq miles), is covered with forests of deciduous trees and evergreen pines, interspersed with large fields of maize. The farmland is irrigated by the river Leyre, which flows all the way through this conservation area. Besides these forested areas, the park contains many waterways and small lakes. From the unspoiled banks of the river Leyre, visitors can see picturesque villages, ancient farmhouses and splendid Romanesque churches.

Vallées des Leyre

The river Leyre, formed by the Grande Leyre and Petite Leyre, flows into the Arcachon Basin *(p86)*. As it is the source of 80 per cent of the basin's water, the river plays a key role in the important ecological balance of that watery expanse.

No roads run along its course, so the Leyre can only be explored by canoe or on foot. The forest, through which it flows for 100 km (60 miles), is surrounded by valleys and marshland with lots of wildlife.

Solférino

The charming village of Solférino was founded by Napoléon III in 1863. He and his wife, Eugénie, were very fond of southwest France and often travelled to the region's resort towns, such as Biarritz *(p216)* and Cambo-les-Bains *(p221)*.

Napoléon wanted to create an ideal model of rural life. To populate the region and promote agriculture, the Emperor purchased 70 sq km (27 sq miles) of flatland on which he built 10 farmhouses,

The charming village of Solférino was founded by Napoléon III in 1863. He wanted to create an ideal model of rural life.

28 family houses and 10 artisans' houses, as well as a church and a school.

Musée des Forges

Rue Tinarage, Brocas 06 75 35 19 43 Jun & Sep: Sat & Sun; Jul & Aug: Tue-Sun

In the 19th century, Brocas was an important ironworking centre. The museum, in a disused flour mill, shows the tools and techniques that were used in this industry, and also displays cast-iron objects such as firebacks. Next to the blast furnace are workshops, a barn and ironworkers' houses.

Écomusée de Marquèze

Route de Solférino, Sabres Apr-Oct: daily (Sep: closed Wed) marqueze.fr

The Écomusée de Marquèze is an open-air museum with three locations: Luxey, devoted to resin-tapping; Moustey, which focuses on local religious traditions; and Marquèze, which illustrates life in past times. To create the sense of going back in time, take a ride on a vintage steam train.

The Ecomusée, which opened in 1969, explores traditional rural and agricultural life in the Grande Lande, using the reconstruction of a small farming community from the late 19th century. Different types of buildings are represented, including a manor house, cottages and sheep barns. Specialist occupations, as well as other aspects of rural life, are demonstrated in an informative way.

Luxey

From the 1850s to the 1950s, the resin industry contributed to the economic prosperity of the Landes. A resin-processing workshop at Luxey still has its old buildings, dating from 1859, along with equipment used. Fires that ravaged the forests of the Landes severely affected the industry, and **La Maison d'Estupe-Huc** documents the difficult task of fighting these forest fires.

La Maison d'Estupe-Huc
06 70 88 81 24 By appointment (call ahead)

ROMANESQUE CHURCHES

Built during the early centuries of the second millennium, the churches of this area were important meeting places for the Santiago de Compostela pilgrims. Certain sanctuaries were built by the pilgrims *(p226)* themselves, who were almost the only people to cross the marshy flatlands of Les Landes during this period.

Moustey

Moustey has two churches, which stand opposite one another. The late 15th-century parish church of Sainte-Martin, to the north, is in the late Gothic style. The Église Notre-Dame, which was connected to a hostel, served pilgrims on their journeys across south-west France *(p226)*. It has an interesting 16th-century keystone. The village also has two rivers, which are good for kayaking in summer.

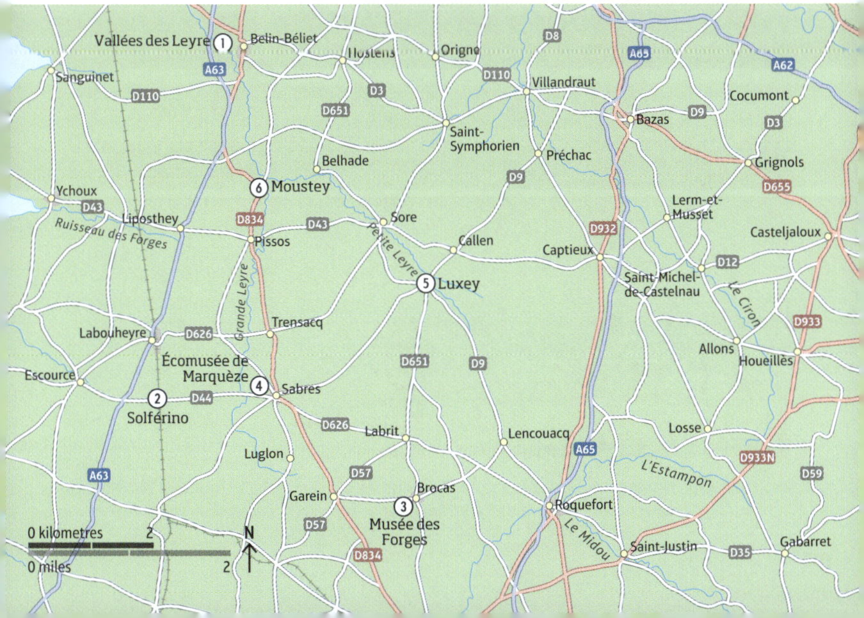

EXPERIENCE MORE

Hossegor

A5 🚌 i 166 avenue de la Gare; hossegor.fr

In the early 20th century, a number of writers – including Paul Margueritte and Rosny Jeune – fell under the spell of this picturesque village, surrounded by pine trees. Ever since, Hossegor has drawn a steady stream of visitors. In the 1930s, it became a coastal resort, and the **Sporting-Casino** was built, along with a traditional *fronton* where the ball game *pelote basque* is still played. The elegant villas around the golf course and the sea lake evoke the resort's heyday in the 1920s and 1930s. Built in a Basque-Béarn style, they have Basque features, such as white roofs and façades, as well as typical features of Landes buildings, such as low-pitched roofs and half-timbering. Hossegor is now also an international surfing hotspot. The Quiksilver Pro festival that takes place in September attracts some of the best surfers in the world.

Sporting-Casino
119 avenue Maurice Martin 10:30am-2am daily (to 3am Fri & Sat)
casino-hossegor.com

Mimizan

B4 🚌 i 38 avenue Maurice-Martin; mimizan-tourisme.com

In summer, the town of Mimizan attracts large numbers of visitors who come to enjoy its 10 km (6 miles) of beaches, as well as its vast forests, with their 40 km (25 miles) of cycle tracks. The town has an abbey church whose 13th-century bell tower is listed by UNESCO. A small museum in the abbey grounds, the **Musée du Prieuré à Mimizan**, illustrates life here during the Middle Ages. It also explores local geography and history as well as the area's changing relationship with the surrounding forest. Excursions organized by the tourist office introduce visitors to forestry in the area, with tours of local woodland and forestry businesses.

At Saint-Julien-en-Born, south of Mimizan, the Courant de Contis river flows down to the Plage de Contis, a beach with a lighthouse. At Lit-et-Mixe, a bit further south, is the **Musée Landes d'Antan**, which features a re-created period kitchen, and also documents local traditions.

Musée du Prieuré à Mimizan
Rue de l'Abbaye
05 58 09 00 61 Mid-Jun-mid-Sep: Tue-Sat; mid-Sep-mid-Jun: Tue-Fri

Musée Landes d'Antan
Lit-et-Mixe 05 58 42 70 14 Jun: Thu; Jul & Aug: daily; Sep: Mon-Fri

↑ Surfers on Hossegor beach, enjoying the excellent surfing conditions found along the Côte d'Argent

Biscarrosse

B4 🚌 i 55 place Georges-Dufau; biscarrosse.com

Biscarrosse, with a beach that stretches for 15 km (9 miles) – as far as the Adour river – marks the beginning of the Côte d'Argent (Silver Coast). Situated between the ocean and the forest, the town has two lakes, which offer a range of water sports.

Visitors with an interest in aviation will enjoy the **Musée Historique de l'Hydraviation**, devoted to seaplanes, with

Glorious sands at Moliets-et-Maa beach, at the mouth of the Courant d'Huchet

many crafts on display. The museum stands next to the Établissements Latécoère, which produced seaplanes from 1930 to the end of the 1950s. There's a fantastic seaplane airshow held biennially here in June (in even-numbered years).

The **Musée des Traditions et de l'Histoire de Biscarrosse** documents the town's history and the lives of resin collectors and shepherds on the Landes.

North of Biscarrosse is the Lac de Sanguinet. Its 56 sq km (22 sq miles) of clear, fresh waters are ideal for fishing and water sports. Sanguinet itself, on the site of a Gallo-Roman village, has an interesting archaeological museum, **Le Musée du Lac Sanguinet**.

Musée Historique de l'Hydraviation
332 avenue Louis-Bréguet 05 58 78 00 65
Feb, Jun & Sep–Dec: Tue–Sun; Jul & Aug: daily

Musée des Traditions et de l'Histoire de Biscarrosse
216 avenue Louis-Bréguet 05 58 78 77 37
Mid-Apr–Jun & Sep: Tue–Sat; Jul & Aug: daily

Le Musée du Lac Sanguinet
102 place de la Mairie
Hours vary, check website
musee-lac-sanguinet.fr

5

Courant d'Huchet

A5 Maison de la Réserve Naturelle du Courant d'Huchet, 374, rue des Berges du Lac, Léon; 05 58 48 73 91

The coast of Landes is dotted with watercourses, known as *courants*, that flow into the ocean. The best known is the Courant d'Huchet, a river with vibrant plants and wildlife to enjoy around the river banks. Since 1908, visitors have been able to travel on the water in *galupes*, flat-bottomed boats that are propelled along using a *palot* (punt). Starting from the Étang de Léon, the lake from where the *courant* flows, *galupe* tours follow a maze of watercourses, which are inhabited by a variety of birds, including teal, herons and woodcock. The banks are covered with cypresses, hibiscus, irises, gladioli and bracken, and in summer there are ducks, otters, wild boar, mink, crayfish and eels that come to spawn from the Sargasso Sea. *Galupes* owned by the Bateliers du Courant d'Huchet *(bateliers-courant-huchet.fr)* travel between Étang de Léon and the sea daily from April to October; the trip covers some 10 km (6 miles) and takes around two hours, with longer options in high summer.

STAY

Wood'n Sea Surf Lodge

Close to the best surfing spots in the area, this relaxed lodge has both dorms and private en-suite rooms.

A5 6 rue de Baye, Capbreton woodnsea-lodge.com

Hotel & Spa Villa Seren

Overlooking Hossegor Lake, this modern and stylish hotel has an outdoor heated pool.

A5 1111 avenue du Touring Club, Hossegor villaseren.fr

Les Echasses Golf & Surf Eco Lodge

Chic cabins surround a private forested lake, minutes from the beach.

A5 701 route des Bruyères, Saubion ecolodge-lesechasses.com

6

Pays d'Orthe

B5 147 avenue des Évadés, Peyrehorade; tourisme-orthe-arrigans.fr

South of the Landes lies the Pays d'Orthe, a region that has sat at the crossroads of travellers' routes through southwestern France since prehistoric times. The seat of the Orthe family from the 11th century until the French Revolution, the area has a wealth of magnificent châteaux and religious buildings. The *bastide* town of Hastingues, on the pilgrim route to Compostela and overlooking a bend in the river Gaves, was founded by the English in the 13th century. Its fortified gate once formed part of the town's original defensive ramparts.

The **Centre d'Exposition Saint-Jacques-de-Compostelle**, situated in a layby on the A64 motorway just south of Hastingues, documents the pilgrimage to Santiago de Compostela *(p226)*. East of Hastingues is the **Abbaye d'Arthous**, founded by Premonstratensians in the 12th century and remodelled in the 17th and 18th centuries. The Romanesque church here, built in about 1167, has Gothic elements, including pointed arches in its south aisle and capitals with superb carvings. A permanent exhibition, in the former monks' cells, documents the history of the abbey. There are also displays of prehistoric sculptures discovered at Sorde-l'Abbaye.

Saint-Étienne-d'Orthe, north of Hastingues, is the gateway to the alluvial plains of the Adour river, now a vast nature reserve. This stretch of land is home to a number of protected species, including white storks, European pond turtles and Landes ponies.

↑ Sorde-l'Abbaye's abbey on the Gave d'Oloron river; its boathouse opens onto the former millrace

Centre d'Exposition Saint-Jacques-de-Compostelle
Service area on the A64; also accessible from Hastingues Daily

Abbaye d'Arthous
785 route de l'Abbaye, Hastingues Apr-mid-Nov: Tue-Sun landes.fr/abbaye-arthous

Statue of St James at the Centre d'Exposition Saint-Jacques-de-Compostelle

7

Sorde-l'Abbaye

B6 Mairie; 05 58 73 04 83

The spot where Sorde-l'Abbaye now stands has been continuously inhabited since prehistoric times. The Falaise du Pastou, a cliff opposite the Gave d'Oloron, contains four rock shelters (not open to the public) dating from the Magdalenian period (around 12,000 BCE). For thousands of years, a natural fault in the cliff here provided a passage between France and Spain. From the early Middle Ages, it was regularly used by pilgrims on their way to Compostela, and the village became an important stopping point. In the Bourg-Vieux, the town's historic centre, is the **Abbaye Saint-Jean**, now a World Heritage Site. Benedictine monks, who settled here from around 975, founded it in the Middle Ages. Destroyed during the Wars of Religion, and rebuilt in the 17th century, and again by a Maurist community a hundred years later, the abbey was abandoned during the French Revolution. A medicinal herb garden has been re-created in front

INSIDER TIP
Paddle Power

Sorde-l'Abbaye is a picturesque starting point for kayaking and canoeing down the Gave d'Oloron, which rises in the Pyrénées. Trips range from easy-going paddles to more challenging rapids.

of it, which looks down onto the river. Next to the monastery buildings, now in ruins, is a Romanesque church with elements dating from the late Middle Ages, such as the mosaic floor in the choir, the apse, doorway and carved capitals. There is also an underground boat-house with a vaulted ceiling, which opens onto the river. This cellar, the only one of its kind in France, was used for storing cereals.

East of the monastery stands the 16th-century abbot's house, built on the site of a Gallo-Roman villa. Now privately owned, the house is not open to visitors, however, the remains of its 4th-century-CE baths and mosaic floors can be seen. As an interesting aside, Sorde-l'Abbaye is now the largest producer of kiwi fruit in France.

Abbaye Saint-Jean
Place de l'Église 05 58 73 09 62 Apr-Oct: Tue-Sun (Jul & Aug: daily); Nov: Mon-Fri

Capbreton

A5 Avenue Georges-Pompidou; capbreton-tourisme.com

Separated from Hossegor *(p192)* by an inlet of the sea, Capbreton became an important port in the Middle Ages and was also a stop on the coastal route of the pilgrimage to Santiago de Compostela. In the 16th and 17th centuries it was known as the "town of a thousand captains", dispatching its whaling and cod-fishing fleets to Newfoundland. Subsequently, the town lost business to rising Bayonne and sank into decline until Napoléon III ordered the Estacade to be built in 1858. This wooden pier with its lighthouse remains a beloved symbol of the town and a favourite place for promenades. In present times, Capbreton is still a fishing port as well as a highly acclaimed travel location.

Nearby, the **Marais d'Orx** is a nature reserve covering 8 sq km (3 sq miles). Every year, thousands of migratory birds of over 200 species, including the common spoonbill, stop here on their annual journey south.

Marais d'Orx
1005 route du Marais d'Orx Daily reserve-naturelle-marais-orx.fr

TOP 4 BEACHES IN LANDES

Biscarrosse Plage
Surf the waves or feast on seafood at little cafés along this wide beach west of Biscarrosse *(p192)*.

Lac de Sanguinet
A freshwater lake perfect for families, with bouncy castles and pedal boats *(p193)*.

Mimizan-Plage
A long stretch of coastline with plenty of beach houses for rent if you want to stay a while *(p192)*.

Plage Santocha
Dotted with WWII blockhouse ruins, this Capbreton beach is a surfer's paradise, with lessons available for amateurs.

← Capbreton's long wooden pier, stretching out to its weathered lighthouse

Pomarez

B5 28 rue Saint-Pierre, Amou; landes-chalosse.com

Although Pomarez, located on the Adour, is an old-established river port, few traces of its early history remain. It is now known as a major centre for *course landaise* (bull-leaping), a non-violent sport which has an enthusiastic following in the Landes.

West of Pomarez lies the 17th-century **Château de Gaujacq**. The Marquis de Montespan retired to the château to seek solace following his wife's liaison with the king, Louis XIV. The château has a pretty inner courtyard, and the view from the terrace shows the spectacular sweep of the Pyrenean mountain chain. Inside, there are several furnished rooms, including the dining room and the Cardinal's bedroom.

Château de Gaujacq
Gaujacq
05 58 89 01 01
Mid-Jul-Aug: Tue-Sun

BULL-LEAPING

This spectacle demands both courage and agility. The *écarteur* (bull-leaper) avoids the *coursière* (charging bull) by executing balletic moves of varying complexity. Working in teams, or *cuadrillas*, they leap and dodge, while wind bands play. The animal's horns are trimmed and the performance does not end with its slaughter. Although the anti-bull-fighting and bull-leaping movement is gaining momentum, France still allows these practices, which are classified as "uninterrupted local traditions".

Montfort-en-Chalosse

B5 55 place Foch; 05 58 98 58 50

This ancient *bastide* town lies in the heart of the Chalosse, a fertile area that produces high-quality beef, as well as ducks that are fed on maize grown on the Landes' flatlands to produce the area's famous *foie gras*. The fact that Montfort was an important stopping place on the pilgrimage route to Santiago de Compostela can be seen from its historic church, the Romanesque Église Saint-Pierre. It has a medieval nave and its tower dates from the late Middle Ages.

The **Musée de la Chalosse** is housed in an estate dating back to the *Ancien Régime* era, the manor house and its outbuildings providing a perfect setting for the re-creation of daily life in 19th-century Chalosse.

Just under 10 km (6 miles) from Montfort-en-Chalosse is the quiet and picturesque spa village of Préchacq-les-Bains, where the sulphur-rich thermal waters are used primarily in the treatment of rheumatism.

Musée de la Chalosse
480 chemin du Sala 05 58 98 69 27
Mar-Oct: Tue-Sun

Colonnaded courtyard that consoled a marquis, Château de Gaujacq, Pomarez

Dax

B5 11 cours Foch; dax-tourisme.com

Once a lake settlement, the town of Dax stretches out along the banks of the Adour between flatlands and the Pyrénées. Under Roman rule, the town grew, as it prospered from its thermal springs. In the 19th century, the arrival of the railways made Dax the foremost spa town in France. Today, Dax's resorts and hotels continue its ancient legacy, offering therapeutic and stress-busting treatments in beautiful settings. In the town centre, with its narrow medieval streets, Dax's famous therapeutic waters gush out of the Fontaine Chaude, also known as the Fontaine de la Nèhe.

The **Musée Jean-Charles de Borda**, named for a noted mathematician, scientist and mariner born in Dax, is housed in the Chapelle des Carmes, in the west of the town. The museum traces the town's past, from prehistory through the Middle Ages to present-day Dax. There is also an art exhibition devoted to Landais landscapes, and temporary exhibitions of modern art.

TOP 4 DAX SPA TREATMENTS

Pelotherapy
Uses mud from the Adour river mixed with algae from spring water.

Underwater Massage
A massage by a physiotherapist under a stream of spring water.

Floating Therapy
Feel weightless and calm in soothing saltwater pools.

Arobaths
Relaxing bubble baths in pure thermal water.

Statue of the polymath Jean-Charles de Borda in the pretty place Thiers, Dax

The **Musée Georgette-Dupouy** displays paintings by this 20th-century artist. In the north, along Parc Théodore-Denis, you can find the remains of Gallo-Roman walls, as well as the town's bullring, which was erected in 1913.

The **Parc du Sarrat** is laid out with an unusual mixture of formal, Japanese and vegetable gardens. Many of the plants and trees in the gardens are rare and protected species, and visits are by guided tour only. Further south is the **Musée de l'Aviation Légère de l'Armée de Terre (l'ALAT) et de l'Hélicoptère**, a museum of light army aircraft where the exhibits include vintage army helicopters. In addition, there is also a gallery of aviation photography.

The village of Saint-Paul-lès-Dax, which lies 2 km (1.5 miles) west of Dax, has an 11th-century church with carved reliefs. Also worth visiting here is the Forges d'Ardy, an old metalworks.

However, the main reason that visitors come to the peaceful town of Dax is still its curative thermal waters. There are four thermal spa centres, including **Espace Aquatique Sourcéo**.

Did You Know?

Dax's annual Feria in August lasts a mighty six days, filled with parades, music and dancing.

Musée Jean-Charles de Borda
11 bis rue des Carmes 05 58 74 12 91 Feb-Dec: Tue-Sat (Jul & Aug: Tue-Sun)

Musée Georgette-Dupouy
Passage de Presidial 05 58 56 04 34 Daily

Parc du Sarrat
Rue du Sel-Gemme 05 58 56 86 86 Mid-Mar-Nov: Tue, Thu & Sat

Musée de l'ALAT et de l'Hélicoptère
58 avenue de l'Aérodrome 05 58 35 95 24 Mar-Nov: Mon-Fri (Jul & Aug: daily)

Espace Aquatique Sourcéo
355 rue du Centre Aéré, Saint-Paul-lès-Dax Daily thermes-dax.com/sourceo

Interesting display of bicycle memorabilia in the chapel of Notre-Dame-des-Cyclistes, Labastide-d'Armagnac

Labastide-d'Armagnac

C5 Place Royale; 05 58 44 67 56

Set in verdant surroundings, the *bastide* was founded by Comte d'Armagnac, Bertrand VI, in 1291, at a time when the area was held by Edward I of England. Around place Royale, the town's arcaded central square, are 14th–17th-century half-timbered houses. In the 15th-century Gothic church is a painted wooden *pietà*, which dates from the same period. The fortified bell tower is a testament to the town's turbulent history.

The **Écomusée de l'Armagnac** is an open-air museum that showcases how Armagnac is made. It is said to be the oldest style of brandy in the world and has been exported from this area since at least the late 15th century or early 16th century.

Also worthy of interest here is **Notre-Dame-des-Cyclistes**, an 11th-century Romanesque chapel now dedicated to cyclists, both those following regional pilgrimages *(p226)* or general enthusiasts. This distinctive chapel has a museum, created by priest and avid cyclist Abbé Massie in 1959. The museum exhibits former cycling champions' jerseys and bicycles ridden in the Tour de France. The annual Fête de Notre Dame takes place on Whit Monday with a celebratory Mass in the chapel, followed by a bike ride and a concert.

The **Domaine d'Ognoas**, 12 km (7 miles) southwest of Labastide, is an estate of Armagnac-producing grapes. Visitors can see how Armagnac is distilled by traditional methods using the oldest distilling device in Gascony, and sample the results.

ARMAGNAC

Armagnac is a type of brandy, sipped from a wide-bowled glass so as to ensure the release of complex fragrances. Exported since the late Middle Ages, it has probably been made since ancient Gaul times. It was often consumed for its supposed health benefits, including enlivening the spirit and emboldening the wit. Experience it for yourself at Domaine d'Ognoas or at Chateau de Ravignan *(armagnac-ravignan.com)*, a 17th-century castle and Armagnac producer that offers daily afternoon tastings.

Écomusée de l'Armagnac
4 km (3 miles) southeast of Labastide
Hours vary, see website
ecomusee-armagnac.fr

Notre-Dame-des-Cyclistes
Labastide-d'Armagnac
May–mid-Oct: hours vary, check website
notredamedescyclistes.net

Domaine d'Ognoas
Arthez-d'Armagnac
May–Sep: Mon–Fri; Oct–Apr: Thu & Fri
domaine-ognoas.com

Soustons

B5 Grange de Labouyrie; soustons.fr

The main village of the Marensin district, Soustons stretches out along the banks of a large freshwater lake, which is popular with water-sports enthusiasts. In the centre of Soustons is a statue of François Mitterrand, the former president of France, who liked to spend time at his residence, Latché, situated 3 km (2 miles) from here.

The Marensin, an area that lies south of Soustons, is cut by rivers and dotted with lakes.

Gates and weirs regulating the confluence of two rivers in Mont-de-Marsan

Did You Know?

The area around Soustons is great for hiking and biking, with over 70 km (45 miles) of trails.

These include the **Réserve Naturelle de l'Étang Noir** and the Étang Blanc. Visitors can indulge in swimming, canoeing and fishing at the Étang Blanc. Classified as a nature reserve, the Étang Noir has a nature trail along raised wooden walkways, and pontoons to protect the environment, and facilitate the observation of birds such as the reed buntings, purple herons and black kites and local flora. Towards the coast, near Vieux-Boucau-les-Bains, is the resort of Port-d'Albret, clustered around a salt lake. Popular in summer, the resort can only be reached via the leafy Promenade du Mail.

Réserve Naturelle de l'Étang Noir
600 avenue du Parc des Sports, Seignosse Daily
reserves-naturelles.org/etang-noir

14

Mont-de-Marsan

C5 1 place Charles de Gaulle; montdemarsan-tourisme.fr

Mont-de-Marsan, the Landes' administrative centre since 1790, is set on the banks of the Midou and Douze rivers, which join to form the Midouze. Nicknamed the "Three-River Town", Mont-de-Marsan is a lively centre built on a history of trade.

The **Musée Despiau-Wlérick**, in the 14th-century Donjon de Lacataye fortress, is the only museum in France dedicated to French figurative sculpture of the first half of the 20th century. On display here is the work of Mont-de-Marsan artists such as Charles Despiau (1874–1946) and Robert Wlérick (1882–1944). It also features works by Alfred Auguste Janniot (1889–1969), a sculptor of the Art Deco period.

On rue Victor-Hugo, the Neo-Classical Église de la Madeleine, built in the early 19th century, features a high altar created by the Mazetti brothers in the 18th century.

Walking up towards the Douze river, visitors will see two Romanesque houses at Nos. 6 and 24 bis rue Maubec, built of the local shelly stone. An entrance on place Francis-Planté leads into the **Parc Jean Rameau**, named after the Landes novelist and poet (1858–1942). It was originally created in 1793 and now consists of sculptures and Japanese-style gardens.

Located in the east of the centre, in the Quartier Saint-Médard, is the 230,000 sq km (2.5 million sq ft) **Parc animalier de Nahuques**.

Musée Despiau-Wlérick
Donjon de Lacataye, 6 place Marguerite-de-Navarre
05 58 75 00 45 10am-noon, 2-6pm Mon-Fri

Parc Jean Rameau
Place Francis-Planté
05 58 05 87 37 Daily

Parc animalier de Nahuques
Avenue de Villeneuve
05 58 75 65 41 Daily

INSIDER TIP
Wild Swimming at the Lake

Surrounded by forest but just a short distance from Mont-de-Marsan, the Base de Loisirs du Marsan is a popular summertime spot for swimming at its white-sand beach. A shuttle from the city centre heads to the lake in summer.

Saint-Sever

C5 Place du Tour-du-Sol; landes-chalosse.com

Founded in 993, Saint-Sever is a strategically positioned town with a number of architectural jewels. Remains of the early settlement are clustered on the Plateau de Morlanne, which, with the town's former abbey and its surrounding streets, makes up one of Saint-Sever's two main districts.

The **Abbaye de Saint-Sever**, a World Heritage Site, stands on a square lined with fine 18th-century town-houses. First established in 988, the abbey was at its full glory in the 11th and 12th centuries. Damaged by fire, earthquakes and wars, the building was rebuilt on several occasions but was abandoned in 1790. In the 19th century, this architecturally important structure underwent some questionable restoration. Built according to a Benedictine plan, the church consists of 150 capitals. Their colourful painted decoration has been accorded a renewal.

At the Couvent des Jacobins, founded in 1280 and later remodelled, the monastery buildings are no longer open to the public, except for the west wing, which houses the **Musée d'art et d'histoire du Cap de Gascogne**. Among the exhibits in the museum of the history of the town is a copy of the *Beatus*, a commentary on the *Apocalypse of St John* (or Book of Revelations), illuminated by Stephanus Garcia. The original is placed at the Bibliothèque Nationale, Paris.

Abbaye de Saint-Sever
Place du Tour-du-Sol
05 58 76 34 64 Daily

Musée d'ar et d'histoire du Cap de Gascogne
Place de la République
05 58 76 34 64 Jul & Aug: daily; Sep & Oct: Sat & Sun

Aire-sur-l'Adour

C5 Place 19 Mars 1962; tourisme-aire-eugenie.fr

This picturesque town on the banks of the Adour also lies on the pilgrim route to Compostela, and is the gateway to the Tursan *(p202)*. The site was inhabited even before the Romans arrived in 50 BCE. The former bishop's palace, built in the early 17th century, now houses the town hall. Next to it stands the 14th-century Palais de l'Officialité, the old law courts. The Cathédrale Saint-Jean-Baptiste dates from the 12th century, with later alterations.

The **Église Sainte-Quitterie-du-Mas**, on the Colline du Mas, is a World Heritage Site. The church's large 11th-century crypt contains the tomb of the patron saint of Gascony. Other notable features are the arches of the 12th-century choir, above which is a brick-built bell tower, and the Baroque pulpit, carved in 1770.

Église Sainte-Quitterie-du-Mas
Rue du Mas 05 58 71 47 00 Jul-early Sep: daily

Grenade-sur-l'Adour

C5 14 place des Tilleuls; tourisme-paysgrenadois.fr

A *bastide* town founded by the English in 1322, Grenade-sur-l'Adour has 14th- and 15th-century houses and a beautiful church, with a Gothic apse, dating from the late 15th century. The **Petit Musée de l'Histoire Landaise** features a fascinating collection of pieces relating to popular traditions and a display of costumes.

Bascons, 6 km (4 miles) north of Grenade, is a *course landaise* (or bull-leaping, *p196*) centre. It even has a museum, the **Musée de la Course Landaise**, that displays exhibits chronicling the history of this popular regional sport. Displays include 19th-century posters advertising events, and a collection of early 20th-century postcards attesting to the exploits of the leading competitors.

Petit Musée de l'Histoire Landaise
20 place des Déporté
05 58 76 05 25 Wed-Fri pm

Musée de la Course Landaise
337 chemin de Guiret
05 58 52 91 76 For renovation; call to check

↑ Abbaye de Saint-Sever, chosen by UNESCO as part of the Santiago pilgrimage route

←

The four-towered Château d'Orthe, on the river bank at Peyrehorade

18

Peyrehorade

B6 🚉🚌 ℹ147 avenue des Evadés; tourisme-orthe-arrigans.fr

Located in the far south of the Landes between two rivers, the Gave d'Oloron and Gave de Pau, Peyrehorade is the largest village in the Pays d'Orthe. It is also the youngest, as it was only established in the 14th century as a result of trade between Bayonne and Toulouse. The village is dominated by the Château d'Aspremont, built in the 13th century by the Vicomtes d'Orthe on the site of an 11th-century fortress, of which only the ruins of the keep remain. The Château d'Orthe (also known as the Château de Montréal), which now houses the town hall, is another splendid building. Dating from the 16th century, it was remodelled by Jean de Montréal in the 18th century. It is not open to the public, but with its four towers, which look down on the Gave de Pau, it is an impressive sight.

EAT

L'Art des Mets

The menu reflects the region well at this restaurant, which is set in a former wine storage house. Try the local goat's cheese ravioli and the roasted lamb.

C5 19 rue Louis Sentex, Saint-Sever lartdesmetsaintsever.com

Brassempouy

C5 ℹ28 rue Saint-Pierre, Amou; landes-chalosse.com

Established in the 13th century, this ancient *bastide* town is associated with the famous *Venus of Brassempouy*, a Stone Age figurine of a woman discovered in the Grotte du Pape, a prehistoric cave near the town, in 1894. Carved in mammoth ivory more than 20,000 years ago, this figure is the earliest representation of a human face that has so far come to light. It is on display at the Musée des Antiquités Nationales de Saint-Germain-en-Laye, near Paris. A replica of the figure can be viewed at the **Maison de la Dame de Brassempouy**, next to the Château de Poudenx, along with other replicas of prehistoric figures from France and elsewhere dating from 35,000–15,000 BCE.

Maison de la Dame de Brassempouy

05 58 89 21 73

Mid-Feb–Jun & Sep–Nov: Tue–Sun; Jul & Aug: daily

→

The mammoth-ivory *Venus of Brassempouy*, sometimes called the "Lady with the Hood"

A DRIVING TOUR

TOUR OF THE TURSAN

Length 90 km (55 miles) **Starting point** Samadet **Stopping-off point** For lunch, sample some of the Tursan's excellent home made products at Les Halles market in Geaune

The Tursan is an area of lush green valleys, where maize – grown to fatten the many geese and ducks raised here – is the major crop. Tursan wine has been produced for centuries and, in the Middle Ages, Eleanor of Aquitaine *(p53)* had it exported to the English royal court. Light red, very dry white and rosé wines are made from grapes grown on 4.6 sq km (1.8 sq miles) of steep, terraced vineyards. The road over these hills follows a scenic route past wine estates, a spa town and picturesque buildings.

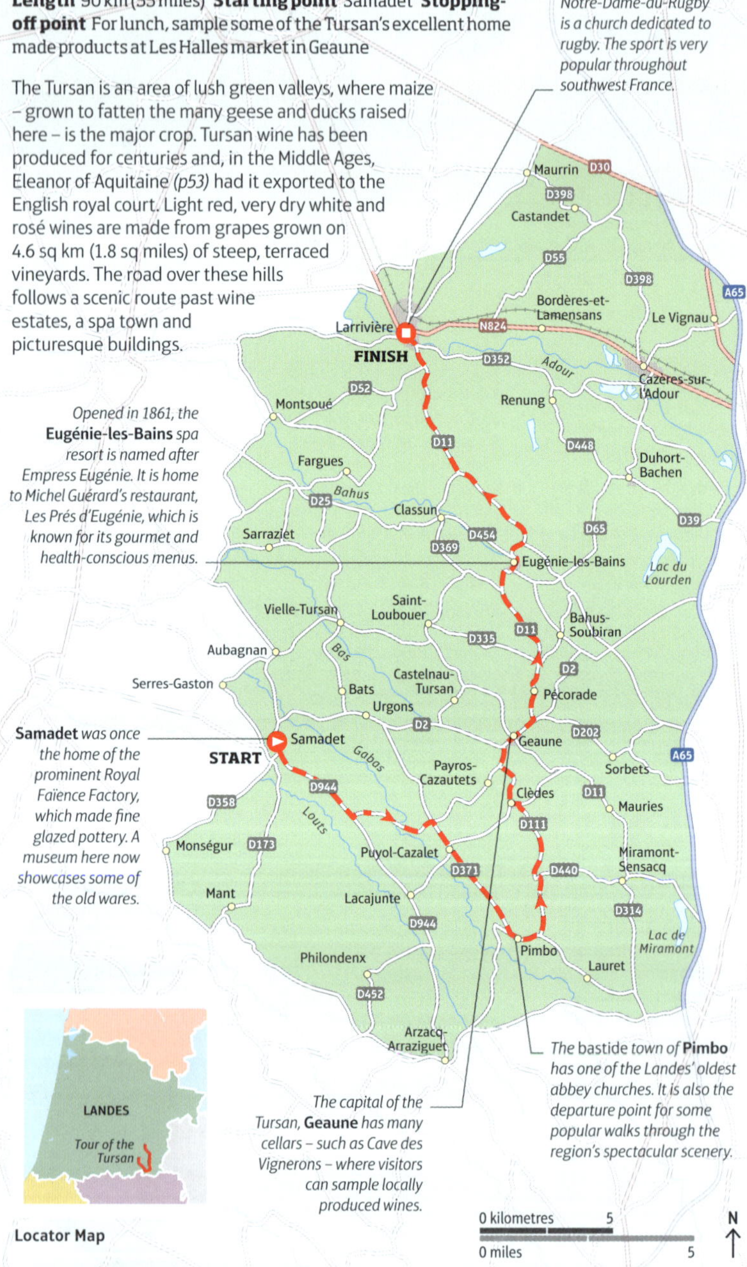

Larrivière's *Église Notre-Dame-du-Rugby is a church dedicated to rugby. The sport is very popular throughout southwest France.*

Opened in 1861, the **Eugénie-les-Bains** *spa resort is named after Empress Eugénie. It is home to Michel Guérard's restaurant, Les Prés d'Eugénie, which is known for its gourmet and health-conscious menus.*

Samadet *was once the home of the prominent Royal Faïence Factory, which made fine glazed pottery. A museum here now showcases some of the old wares.*

The capital of the Tursan, **Geaune** *has many cellars – such as Cave des Vignerons – where visitors can sample locally produced wines.*

The bastide town of **Pimbo** *has one of the Landes' oldest abbey churches. It is also the departure point for some popular walks through the region's spectacular scenery.*

Locator Map

↑ Vineyards of the Tursan, a prominent wine region in southwest France

The twin spires of Bayonne Cathedral rising above the rooftops

PAYS BASQUE

There is evidence of settlement in this part of France going back to Neolithic times. In the Middle Ages, the region was invaded by a series of peoples – including the Celts, the Romans and Germanic tribes – before becoming a part of the newly created Kingdom of Navarre in the mid-9th century. In the 16th century, the region was split between France and Spain, and the inhabitants endured many years of conflict between the two nations, until the Peace of the Pyrénées brought about a reconciliation in 1659. At the end of the 18th century, the Pays Basque entered a period of economic decline, which ended only with the birth of tourism.

Despite the many changes over the centuries, the Pays Basque has held on firmly to its identity, which is expressed as much in the use of Euskara, the Basque language, as in the region's architecture, festivals and food specialities. The western edge of the region is bordered by the Atlantic Ocean, with a coastline of beautiful beaches to which tourists flock year after year. Inland, picturesque villages dot the wide expanses of lush and unspoiled greenery.

Atlantic Ocean
Gulf of Gascony
Labenne
Orx
Biarrotte
LANDES
p186
Tarnos
Boucau
BAYONNE 1
Adour
Urt
BIARRITZ 4
Anglet
Biarritz Pays Basque Airport
Croix de Mouguerre
Briscous
Notre-Dame-de-Belloc
Bidart
Guéthary
Arbonne
Nive
LA BASTIDE-CLAIRENCE 15
Ouhabia
Forêt d'Hasparren
SAINT-JEAN-DE-LUZ 3
HENDAYE 2
21 CIBOURE
Ustaritz
HASPARREN 9
Urrugne
Ascain
Nivelle
St-Pée-sur-Nivelle
11 CAMBO-LES-BAINS
Bonloc
NIVELLE VALLEY 7
ESPELETTE 14
5 ITXASSOU
La Rhune
905 m (2,969 ft)
Sare
Louhossoa
Hélette
6 AINHOA
Artzamendi
926 m (3,038 ft)
Grottes de Sare
13 BIDARRAY
St-Martin-d'Arrosa
Ossès
Irouléguy
SAINT-ÉTIENNE-DE-BAÏGORRY 12
16 SAINT-JEAN-PIED-DE-PORT
Banca
Aldudes
Urepel
Espinal
Burguete-Auritz
Erro
Garralda
Zandueta
Abaurrepea/ Abaurrea Baja
Nagore
A63
A64
N10
D810
D817
D21
D22
D932
D918
D4
N121
D948
D15
N135
N140
PAYS BASQUE
Must See
1 Bayonne
Experience More
2 Hendaye
3 Saint-Jean-de-Luz
4 Biarritz
5 Itxassou
6 Ainhoa
7 Nivelle Valley
8 Larrau
9 Hasparren
10 Bidache
11 Cambo-les-Bains
12 Saint-Étienne-de-Baïgorry
13 Bidarray
14 Espelette
15 La Bastide-Clairence
16 Saint-Jean-Pied-de-Port
17 Saint-Palais
18 L'Hôpital-Saint-Blaise
19 Forêt d'Iraty
20 Sainte-Engrâce
21 Ciboure
22 Gorges de Kakuetta
23 Mauléon-Licharre
24 Massif des Arbailles
25 Tardets-Sorholus

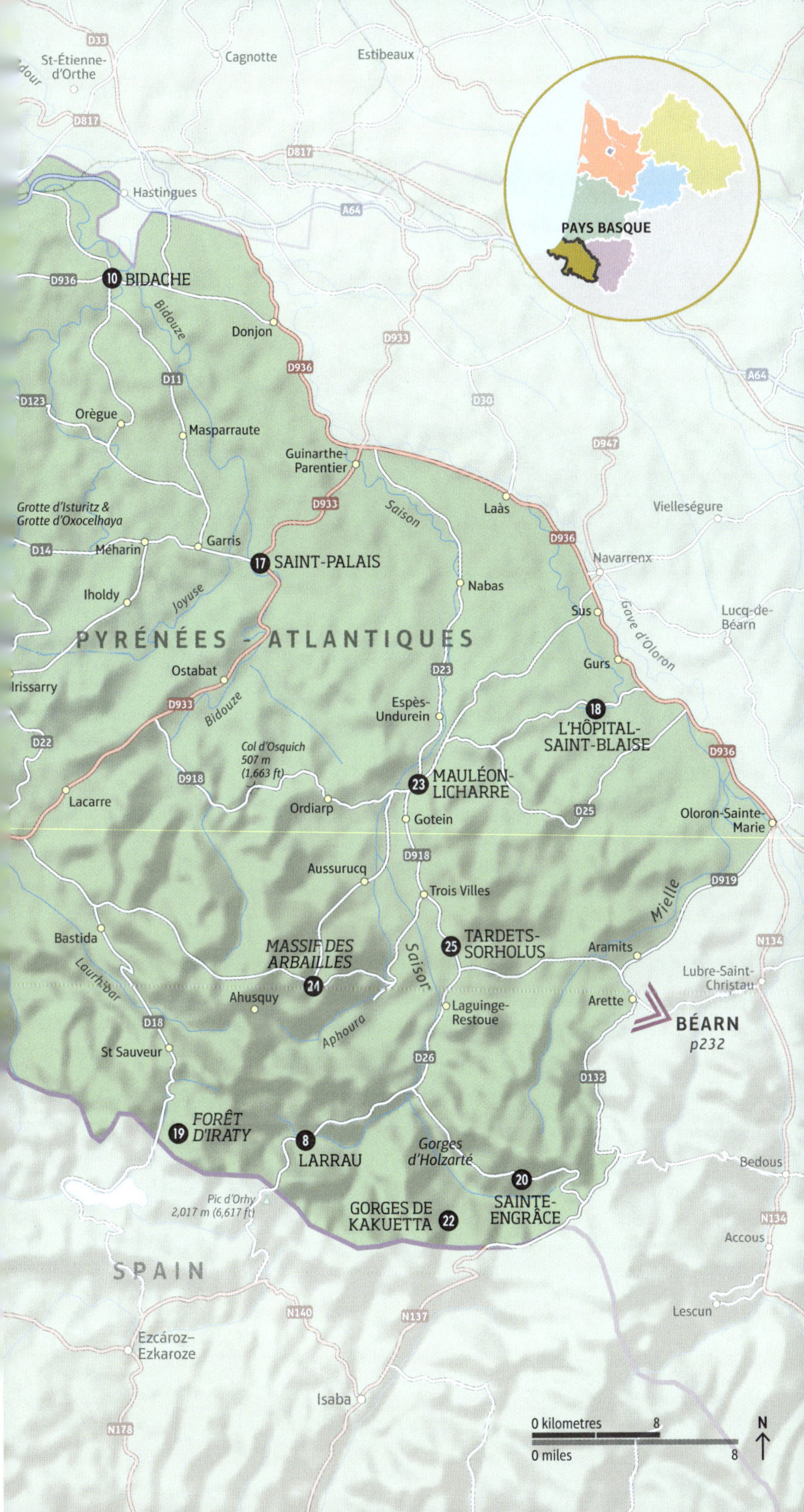

PAYS BASQUE
St-Étienne-d'Orthe
Cagnotte
Estibeaux
Hastingues
D33
D817
A64
10 BIDACHE
D936
Bidouze
Donjon
D11
D123
Orègue
Masparraute
Guinarthe-Parentier
D933
D30
D947
Saison
Laàs
Vielleségure
Grotte d'Isturitz & Grotte d'Oxocelhaya
D14
Méharin
Garris
17 SAINT-PALAIS
Navarrenx
Iholdy
Joyuse
Nabas
Sus
Lucq-de-Béarn
Gave d'Oloron
PYRÉNÉES - ATLANTIQUES
Ostabat
D23
Gurs
Irissarry
Espès-Undurein
18 L'HÔPITAL-SAINT-BLAISE
Bidouze
Col d'Osquich 507 m (1,663 ft)
D22
D918
23 MAULÉON-LICHARRE
Lacarre
Ordiarp
Gotein
D25
Oloron-Sainte-Marie
Aussurucq
Trois Villes
D919
Mielle
Bastida
MASSIF DES ARBAILLES
25 TARDETS-SORHOLUS
Aramits
N134
Lubre-Saint-Christau
Laurhibar
Saison
24
Ahusquy
Arette
Laguinge-Restoue
BÉARN p232
D18
Aphoura
St Sauveur
D26
D132
19 FORÊT D'IRATY
8 LARRAU
Gorges d'Holzarté
Bedous
20 SAINTE-ENGRÂCE
Pic d'Orhy 2,017 m (6,617 ft)
GORGES DE KAKUETTA 22
Accous
SPAIN
Lescun
N140
N137
Ezcároz–Ezkaroze
Isaba
N178
0 kilometres 8
0 miles 8
N

BAYONNE

A6 Place des Basques; visit bayonne.com

Two rivers converge on Bayonne and shape its very essence. From architecture to cuisine, the city will satisfy your appetite for the cultures of both France and neighbouring Spain. Only the summer festival interrupts the serenity of the place.

Nive Embankment

Starting at place de la Liberté, the Nive embankment runs past the covered market and open-air marketplace. Place de la Liberté is where the keys of the city are thrown into the crowd at the start of the city's July festivals. Quai Jauréguiberry, with its typical Bayonne houses, and rue Poissonnerie, further on, were hives of activity when Bayonne formed a major port for goods from the Americas.

A popular place for a stroll in summer, the embankment is lined with restaurant terraces and is filled with music and dancing in the festival season.

Historic City Centre

Until the 17th century, the old city, which clusters round the Gothic Cathédrale Sainte-Marie, was crisscrossed by canals. Some streets, like rue Port-Neuf, were created when the canals were filled in. Rue Argenterie is named after the goldsmiths and silversmiths who had their workshops here, while rue de la Salie was once part of the cloth and spice merchants' quarter.

Musée Bonnat-Helleu

5 rue Jacques-Laffitte Wed-Mon Tue museebonnat.bayonne.fr

Occupying a 19th-century building, the Musée Bonnat-Helleu contains over 5,000 works of art. These date from antiquity right up to the early decades of the 20th century. The galleries contain paintings, sculpture and ceramics, including works by Goya,

An attractive gallery displaying works of art at Musée Bonnat-Helleu

Aerial view of Bayonne, showing how the two rivers bisect the city

Rubens, Degas and other major artists as well as a set of 16th-century tapestries and a substantial collection of coins, medals and early photographs.

Château-Vieux

Rue des Gouverneurs

Built in the 12th century and extended in the 17th, the castle incorporates elements of a Roman fort. It was once home to Bayonne's English governor, and two French kings, François I and Louis XIV, stayed here. It is not open to the public, but visitors can walk into the courtyard.

Musée Basque

37 quai des Corsaires Tue-Sun (mid-Jul-mid-Aug: daily) musee-basque.com

The museum is housed in the Maison Dagourette, a superbly restored 16th-century house that is listed as a historic monument. The collections, which have grown since the museum's foundation in 1922, concentrate on Basque culture. Laid out in 20 rooms, they give an insight into the folk art and customs of Pays Basque. Displays cover a number of different themes, including local farm life and sea and river trade, as well as theatre, music, dance, games and sports, with a room devoted to pelota. There are also sections on everyday clothing and traditional costume, architecture, religious and secular festivals and burial customs. Among the paintings are depictions of typical local scenes and activities. Regular temporary exhibitions are also held here.

Place Paul-Bert

In July, when Bayonne's festival season is in full swing, this square in Petit Bayonne is the starting point for the traditional bull-running events. Nearby is the 19th-century Église Saint-André, where Mass is celebrated in Basque. Directly opposite the church is Château-Neuf, built in the 15th century during the reign of Charles VII. It forms part of the defences that were later built around the city. During the summer, the castle is the venue for large-scale temporary exhibitions mounted by the Musée Basque.

Quartier Saint-Esprit

This cosmopolitan district on the north bank of the Adour, east of Pont Saint-Esprit, remains largely working class. Immigrants, especially Jews driven out of Spain and Portugal, settled here from the mid-16th century onwards, helping build up sea trade. A synagogue and a Jewish cemetery located here are two vestiges of this period.

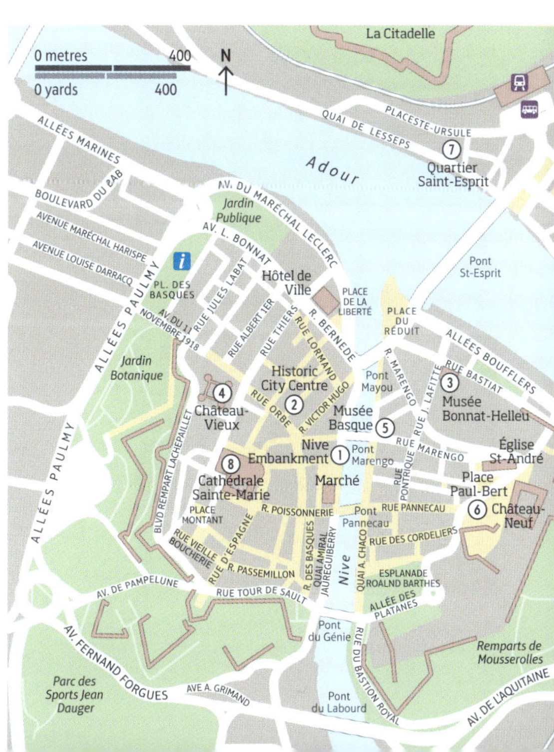

8

CATHÉDRALE SAINTE-MARIE

15 rue des Prébendes 8am-6:30pm Mon-Sat, 8am-7pm Sun
cathedraledebayonne.com

The impressive twin-spired Gothic cathedral dominates the skyline and is one of Bayonne's most iconic emblems. The Cathedral of Sainte-Marie – also known as the Cathedral of Notre-Dame de Bayonne or Bayonne Cathedral – is on the famed path to Santiago de Compostela.

Cathédrale Sainte-Marie was built in the 12th and 13th centuries on the site of a Romanesque cathedral. This imposing, northern Gothic structure, with its tall twin spires, can be seen from afar. Located in the heart of the old city, it was an important stopping place for pilgrims travelling to Santiago de Compostela in Spain *(p226)*. In the 19th century, it underwent extensive restoration after suffering damage during the French Revolution *(p54)*, meaning that the church that stands today is the result of around 800 years of continuous building work and renovation. Highlights to seek out in the cathedral are the choir – the oldest part of the cathedral – art by Nicolas-Guy Brenet and the beautiful stained-glass windows.

The twin spires of the cathedral beyond the shaded cloisters

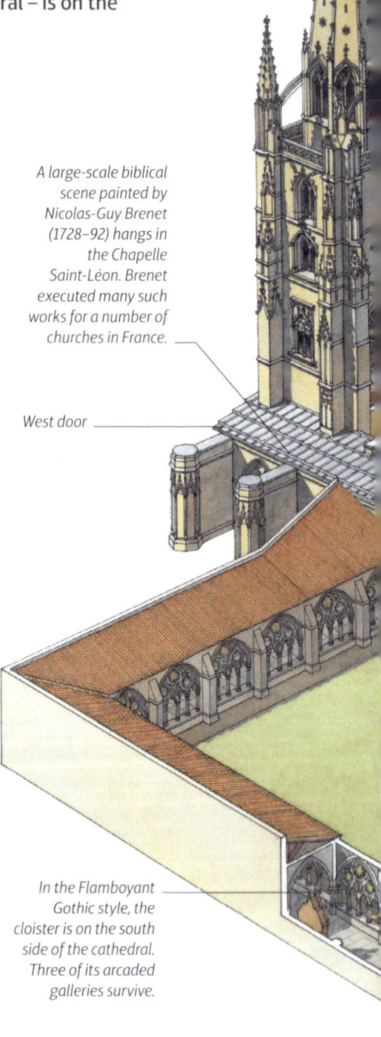

A large-scale biblical scene painted by Nicolas-Guy Brenet (1728–92) hangs in the Chapelle Saint-Léon. Brenet executed many such works for a number of churches in France.

West door

In the Flamboyant Gothic style, the cloister is on the south side of the cathedral. Three of its arcaded galleries survive.

The imposing Gothic Cathédrale Sainte-Marie

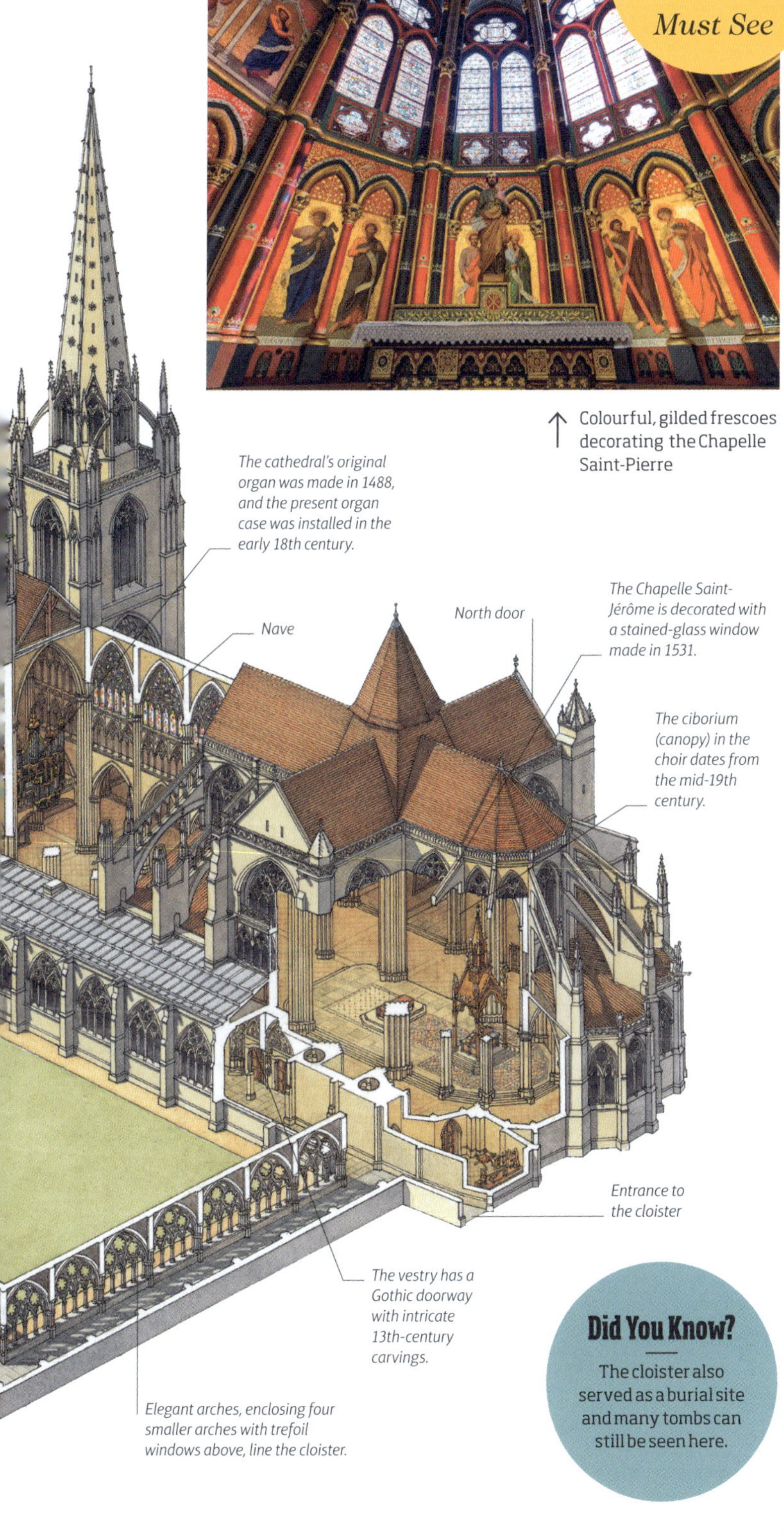

↑ Colourful, gilded frescoes decorating the Chapelle Saint-Pierre

Did You Know?

The cloister also served as a burial site and many tombs can still be seen here.

A SHORT WALK
BAYONNE

Distance 1.5 km (1 mile) **Time** 20 minutes
Nearest station Gare de Bayonne

The cultural capital of the northern Pays Basque, Bayonne grew and prospered from maritime trade and its strategic position near the border with Spain. It was long held by the English but was finally taken by the French in 1451. In the 16th century Bayonne also opened its gates to many Jewish refugees, who came here to escape persecution during the Spanish and Portuguese Inquisitions. At the confluence of the great Adour, near its estuary, and the smaller Nive, Bayonne has a remarkable architectural heritage that makes for a delightful walk around town. Try to time your visit for Bayonne's well-known July festivals.

In **place de la Liberté**, *the keys of the city are thrown into the crowd at the start of the city's July festivals.*

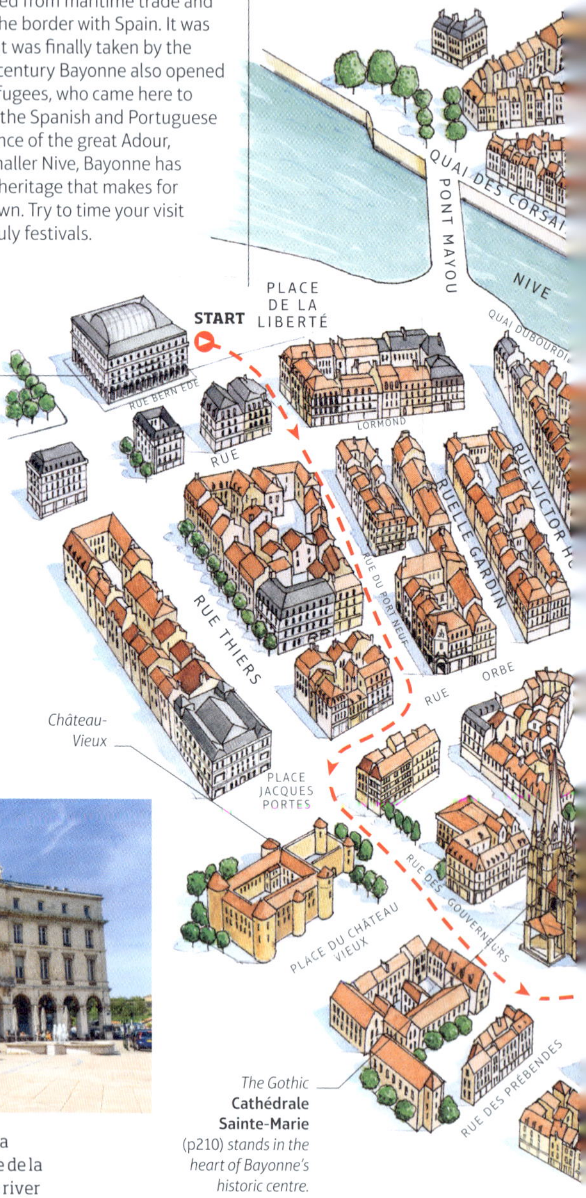

Set on the Nive, at the point where it joins the Adour, this former theatre was built in 1842. It now houses the **town hall**, *from whose balcony Bayonne's festivals are announced.*

Château-Vieux

The Gothic **Cathédrale Sainte-Marie** *(p210) stands in the heart of Bayonne's historic centre.*

↑ The *mairie* (town hall), a former theatre on place de la Liberté beside the Nive river

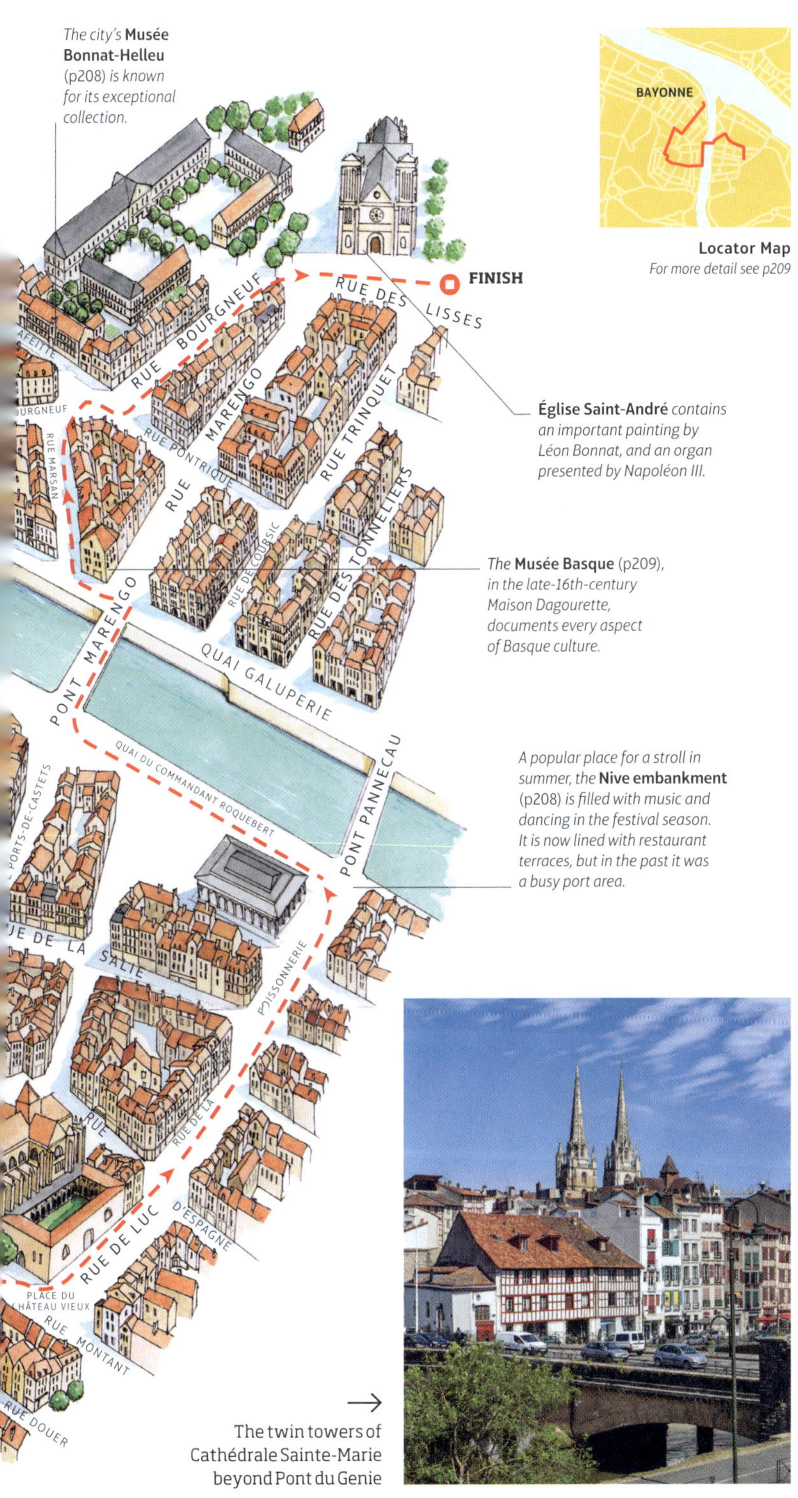

The city's **Musée Bonnat-Helleu** *(p208) is known for its exceptional collection.*

Locator Map

For more detail see p209

Église Saint-André *contains an important painting by Léon Bonnat, and an organ presented by Napoléon III.*

The **Musée Basque** *(p209), in the late-16th-century Maison Dagourette, documents every aspect of Basque culture.*

A popular place for a stroll in summer, the **Nive embankment** *(p208) is filled with music and dancing in the festival season. It is now lined with restaurant terraces, but in the past it was a busy port area.*

→ The twin towers of Cathédrale Sainte-Marie beyond Pont du Genie

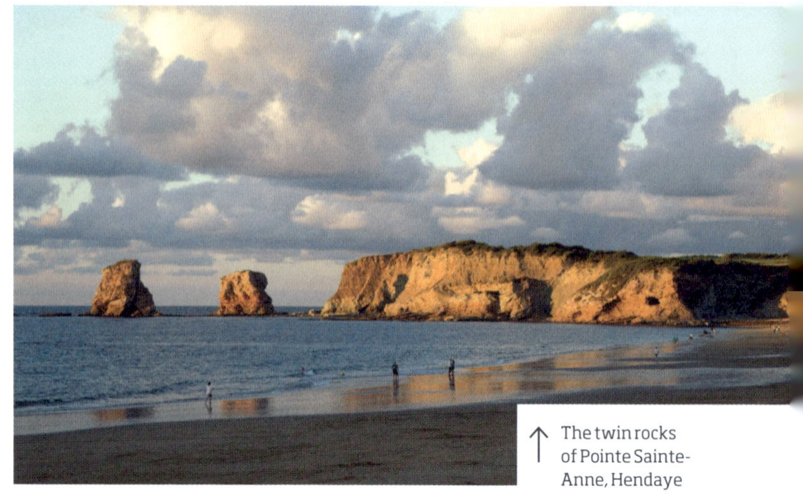

↑ The twin rocks of Pointe Sainte-Anne, Hendaye

EXPERIENCE MORE

Hendaye

A6 67b, boulevard de la Mer; hendaye-tourisme.fr

The family resort of Hendaye, at the mouth of the Bidassoa river, has two distinct areas, Hendaye-Plage and Hendaye-Ville. The Église Saint-Vincent is notable for its 13th-century crucifix and an alterpiece dating from the 17th century.

The two distinctive rocks of Pointe Sainte-Anne mark the entrance to the Baie de Fontarrabie.

Just 1.5 km (1 mile) from Hendaye lies the beautiful **Château d'Abbadia**, built by explorer Antoine d'Abbadia (1810–97). Here, quirky Asian-inspired touches blend with Gothic design.

Château d'Abbadia
Route de la Corniche 05 59 20 04 51 Apr–Oct: daily; Nov, Dec, Feb & Mar: Tue–Sun (call ahead to check opening hours)

STAY

Château d'Urtubie
Sleep like royalty at this fortified, 14th-century castle near Saint-Jean-de-Luz. Rooms are filled with antique furniture and paintings to admire.

A6 1 rue Bernard de Coral, Urrugne chateaudurtubie.net

Saint-Jean-de-Luz

A6 20 boulevard Victor Hugo; saint-jean-de-luz.com

Once a pirates' stronghold, Saint-Jean-de-Luz is located in a bay with the Fort de Socoa on one side and Pointe de Sainte-Barbe on the other. For centuries the town grew rich from the fortunes of traders and pirates – who were at their most active from the 16th to the 19th centuries – and from cod, sardine and tuna fishing as well as whaling. The harbour is still a lively place today, and this pleasant resort is popular with surfers. The coastline northeast of the town has a tempting choice of beaches: Erromardi, Lafitenia, Mayarco and Senix, shared with the neighbouring coastal resort town of Guéthary.

Place Louis-XIV, situated opposite the harbour and behind the tourist office, is lined with elegant residences. It is now filled with café terraces, laid out attractively in the shade of plane trees. Dominating the square is the **Maison Louis-XIV**, with an imposing façade of pale grey stone. This house was built in 1643 by Johannis de Lohobiague, a shipowner. Cardinal Mazarin (1602–61), the *de facto* ruler of France during the minority of Louis XIV, stayed here in 1660, as did Anne of Austria and Louis XIV himself, when he came here to marry the Spanish *infanta* Marie-Thérèse to fulfil the terms of the Peace of the Pyrénées. Next door are

Maison Saubat-Claret, with carved balconies, and the Hôtel de Ville (1654), which contains an equestrian statue of Louis by Bouchardon.

The handsome rue de la Republique leads from place Louis-XIV to the seafront and the Grande Plage. Having survived the fire of 1558, Maison Esquerrenea, at No. 17, is the town's oldest house. Like Maison Duplan at No. 10, it has a tower for observing ships entering the harbour. Curving around the harbourside itself is the quai de l'Infante, where Maison de l'Infante can be found. This house, also known as Maison Joanoenea and constructed in about 1640, belonged to the Haraneders, a shipowning family. Running parallel to the quay, rue Mazarin also has an array of beautiful townhouses, including Maison de l'Infante, the Maison des Trois-Canons at No. 10 and Maison de Théophile de la Tour-d'Auvergne at No. 18.

To the east of place Louis-XIV is rue Gambetta, which has beautiful houses at Nos. 18 and 20. On this street is the **Église Saint-Jean-Baptiste**. Having been destroyed by fire in 1419 and then rebuilt in several stages, this sturdy-looking church appears plain from the outside, but has a splendid 17th-century interior with a fine altarpiece. It was here that the marriage of Louis XIV and Marie-Thérèse took place on 9 June 1660.

The town of Urrugne, 5 km (3 miles) south of Saint-Jean-de-Luz, has an interesting church, the 16th-century Église Saint-Vincent. This church features a Renaissance doorway, a 45-m- (148-ft-) tall bell tower, an organ gallery as well as lofty wooden galleries.

Maison Louis-XIV
Place Louis-XIV
Apr-early Nov: Wed-Mon
maison-louis-xiv.fr

Église Saint-Jean-Baptiste
Rue Gambetta
05 59 26 08 81 Daily

Galleried altar in the Église Saint-Jean-Baptiste, Saint-Jean-de-Luz

GREAT VIEW
On Point

It's an easy walk from Saint-Jean-de-Luz, around the bay to the Pointe de Sainte-Barbe and its small white chapel. The reward is a stunning view back across the bay to Saint-Jean-de-Luz.

The Église Saint-Jean-Baptiste in Saint-Jean-de-Luz

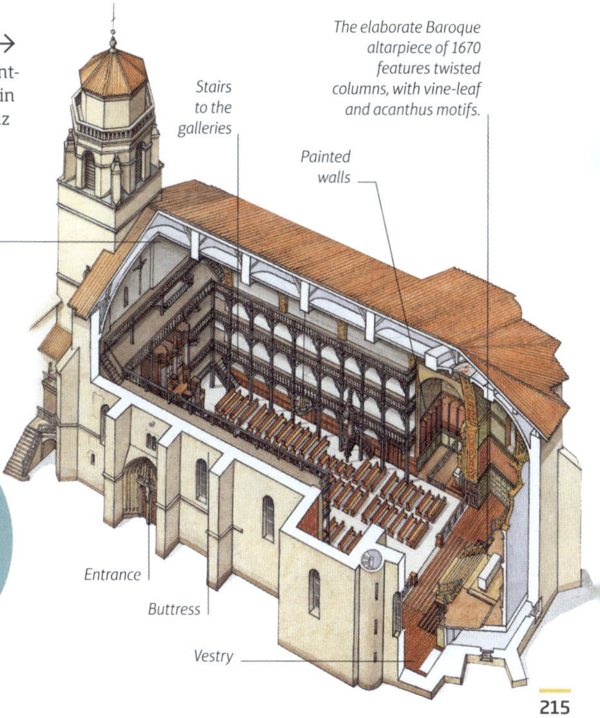

The elaborate Baroque altarpiece of 1670 features twisted columns, with vine-leaf and acanthus motifs.

Stairs to the galleries

Painted walls

As in many Basque churches, the interior is lined with tiered wooden galleries. Here there are three tiers on each side and four behind the organ.

Entrance

Buttress

Vestry

Did You Know?

Marie-Thérèse had been married to Louis XIV by proxy before even arriving in France.

4 Biarritz

A6 1 sq d'Ixelles; tourisme.biarritz.fr

Biarritz was just a small whaling port until the late 19th century, when seabathing came into vogue. This new trend, along with Napoléon III and Empress Eugénie's popularity, led to the town's discovery by the wider world. Expansion of the railway lines meant that new visitors could easily access the Emperor and Empress's favourite resort, and since then, Biarritz has drawn a cosmopolitan crowd.

The resort's famous Grande Plage (Great Beach) stretches out in front of the casino, an Art Deco building dating from 1924. To the right stands the impressive Hôtel du Palais, built in the early 20th century on the site of Villa Eugénie, the former imperial residence. In the distance is the **Phare de Biarritz**. The 248 steps in this lighthouse lead up to the lantern, from where there is a superb panoramic view. Plage Miramar, an extension of the Grande Plage, is backed by luxurious Belle Époque villas. The Russian Orthodox church on avenue de l'Impératrice was constructed in the late 19th century. The fishing harbour, built in 1870, sits in a sheltered inlet. Located above is the magnificent Église Sainte-Eugénie, built in a Gothic Revival architectural style.

The city's emblem is the Rocher de la Vierge, a rock formation jutting from the ocean, connected to the promenade by an iron walkway designed by designed by Schryvers workshops in Haumont. The rock is crowned by a statue of the Madonna.

On the esplanade is the handsome Villa Belza, a unique house with a turret and a peaked roof. The Plage du Port-Vieux, south of the rocks, leads on to the Côte des Basques.

SHOP

Chic beachwear is always *de rigueur* in Biarritz. Find your own style of funky, planet-friendly and individually designed pieces created by the local designers here.

Baigneuses Palace
A6 8 rue Lahontine
baigneusespalace.com

BTZ
A6 2 place Bellevue
btz-biarritz.com

SOWE Biarritz
37 rue Mazagran
05 59 43 41 62

Phare de Biarritz
Esplanade Elizabeth II 05 59 22 37 10 May-Sep: daily; Oct-Apr: Sat & Sun

The Grande Plage and casino, and *(inset)* the unique Villa Belza

↑ The Art Deco casino along Biarritz's Grand Plage in the 1920s

HIGH SOCIETY IN BIARRITZ

In the late 19th century, when Napoléon III and Empress Eugénie were putting Biarritz on the map as a coastal resort, the Second Empire gave way to the Belle Époque. It was then that Biarritz became an upper-class resort with a lively nightlife. Full of newly built Art Nouveau and Art Deco buildings, it held great allure for many prominent people, and throughout the early 20th century, the town's casinos and nightlife drew celebrities from France and around the world.

BATHING AT BIARRITZ

Bathing at Biarritz was at its most fashionable in the first half of the 20th century. The fashion for sea bathing was born in Biarritz thanks to Napoléon III and Empress Eugénie, who popularised sea-swimming in the mid-19th century. It remained a popular pastime with European aristocracy until seaside holidays were brought to an abrupt end by the Wall Street crash of 1929 and the economic hardship of the 1930s that followed.

↑ People sunbathing in Biarritz in the early 1920s, one of Biarritz's many heyday eras

FAMOUS VISITORS

The British Royal Family became regular visitors to Biarritz's sunny shores, following the lead set by King Edward VII, who spent many summer holidays in Biarritz in the early 20th century. Empress Elizabeth of Austria also came in search of a cure for her world-weariness. But as well as royalty, the city became a hotspot for entertainment and big-screen legends. Charlie Chaplin was one of a host of internationally famous people who regularly frequented Biarritz's many luxurious hotels, such as the Hôtel Miramar, in the 1930s and 1940s. Later, the Marquess of Cueva threw extravagant parties, entertaining royalty and film stars such as Rita Hayworth, Gary Cooper, Bing Crosby and Frank Sinatra.

↑ Edward, Duke of Windsor, and Wallis Simpson during a stay at a villa in Biarritz

Elaborate carpentry decorating the interior of the Église Saint-Fructueux

5 Itxassou

A6 Mairie; 05 59 29 75 36

Itxassou is set in the heart of a picturesque valley. In the Urzumu quarter of the village stands the 17th-century white-walled Église Saint-Fructueux, which is lined with galleries of turned and carved wood. The cemetery contains over 200 circular-topped funerary stones. Black cherries are a speciality of the area and are celebrated at a festival on the first Sunday in June. Either fresh or made into jam, these cherries are delicious with a slice of local ewe's-milk cheese.

Around 1.5 km (1 mile) from Itxassou, a winding road runs alongside the Nive river and the Gorges d'Ateka-Gaitz as far as Pas-de-Roland. According to legend, Roland pierced this great rock with his sword, Durandal. Here, Artzamendi (Basque for "Bear Mountain") soars up to 926 m (3,040 ft) and is within easy reach, by car or on foot. Another gentle walk along a marked path leads up to the summit of Mondarrain, at 750 m (2,461 ft), where there are ruins of a Roman fortress that was rebuilt in the Middle Ages.

EAT

Zuzulua

A traditional Basque restaurant and bar, right on La Nivele river, with a menu that's strong on grilled meats and seafood.

A6 Lieu-Dit Cherchebruit, Saint-Pée-sur-Nivelle Mon zuzulua.fr

6 Ainhoa

A6 Maison du Patrimoine; 05 59 29 93 99

Said to be one of France's prettiest villages, Ainhoa has rows of splendidly picturesque old houses with red or green woodwork. Some in the main street have carved lintels. The 14th-century church, in the main square, is lined with galleries and contains a gilt altarpiece. It also has a five-tiered bell tower and circular-topped funerary stones in the graveyard. More of these traditional Basque gravestones can be found at Notre-Dame de l'Aubépine, another church higher up at 450 m (1,477 ft). Views from here take in the Rhune peak, the Atlantic and the frontier district of Dancharia, in Navarre.

7 Nivelle Valley

A6

Set against the backdrop of three peaks – the Rhune, Mondarrain and Axuria – the landscape of this valley is a mix of rolling hills, open meadows and farmland, enclosed by neat hedges.

Ascain, 6 km (4 miles) from the coast, nestles in the foothills of the Rhune. The village was immortalized by French naval officer and novelist Pierre Loti (1850–1923) in his novel *Ramuntcho*. The old Labourd-style houses painted red, white and green on the main square make a picturesque sight. Consecrated in 1626 in the presence of Louis XIII, the church has an imposing west tower. Nearby is Saint-Pée-sur-Nivelle, which has 18th-century houses and a church, the Église Saint-Pierre, with tombstones – including one from the 16th century – set in the floor. Behind the church is the **Moulin Plazako Errota**, a 15th-century mill. It is no longer in use, but contains old grain measures that were used by Basque millers. The state-owned forest has footpaths and bicycle tracks, as well as strangely shaped pollarded oaks. The **Lac de Saint-Pée**, 2 km (1 mile) further on, via the D918, offers water-sports activities.

The summit of the lofty Rhune (905 m, 2,970 ft) can be reached on foot or by the **Petit Train de la Rhune**, which runs on a cog railway that dates from the 1920s. The mountainsides here are dotted with megalithic monuments dating from the Neolithic period. Visitors will also see shepherds with their sheep, as well as the little Basque ponies known as *pottoks*. Griffon vultures may be seen soaring overhead.

The old smugglers' village of Sare has some fine 17th- and 18th-century Labourd-style houses. Strolling through its various districts, visitors will come across 14 oratories dedicated to the Madonna and various saints, built in thanksgiving by fishermen from the 17th century.

Maison Ortillopitz, just outside Sare, is a stately 17th-century farmhouse. With half-timbered walls, a fine oak-beamed roof and thick stone walls, it is a typical *etxe*, or traditional Basque house.

The **Grottes de Sare** lie 7 km (4 miles) south of the village. Bones and flint tools that were discovered here show that these caves were inhabited in prehistoric times.

POTTOKS OF THE PAYS BASQUE

Since prehistoric times, the hills of the Pays Basque have been inhabited by a type of pony known as a *pottok* (pronouned "potiok"), meaning "little horse". *Pottoks* are hardy, having evolved in a harsh environment where food was scarce. They are typically bay or black and pot-bellied, with long manes, dainty legs and small hooves. These tiny horses are endangered but, in the 1970s, certain breeders began to take an interest in them. Once used for farm work or slaughtered for food, they are now protected and treated as the emblem of the Pays Basque.

Moulin Plazako Errota
Rue de l'Église 05 59 54 11 69 Jun-Sep: hours vary, call ahead

Lac de Saint-Pée
Rue du Fronton 05 59 54 11 69 Jul & Aug: daily

Petit Train de la Rhune
Col de Saint-Ignace Apr-Sep rhune.com

Maison Ortillopitz
La Maison Basque de Sare, Col de Saint-Ignace Mid-Apr-end Sep: Sun-Fri ortillopitz.com

Grottes de Sare
Hours vary, check website Jan grottes desare.fr

The summit of the lofty Rhune in the Nivelle Valley can be reached on foot or by the Petit Train de la Rhune, which runs on a cog railway that dates from the 1920s.

Shaped like a natural amphitheatre, the entrance to the Grottes de Sare in the Nivelle Valley

Larrau

B7 Rue Arhanpia, Tardets; 05 59 28 51 28

Larrau, a village of slate-roofed houses, clings to the sides of the Pic d'Orhy, a mountain that figures in local legends. On the edge of the Forêt d'Iraty *(p228)*, the village is the main centre of wood-pigeon hunting, a sport with a lively local following.

About 12 km (7 miles) south of Larrau is Col de Larrau, a mountain pass located at 1,573 m (5,163 ft). Having featured in the Tour de France, it's a major draw for mountain-bikers seeking a challenge. It's also a good place to stop on the way up to Pic d'Orhy, at 2,017 m (6,617 ft), 1.5 hours' walk away.

The Gorges d'Holzarté and Gorges d'Olhadubi, near Larrau, are two great canyons cut into the limestone by the action of water. There are dramatic views across the river valleys of both from the Passerelle d'Holzarté, a footbridge over the Gorges d'Olhadubi. Those who suffer from vertigo may find this bridge unnerving, but it is perfectly safe, and there are even picnic places where visitors can stop for lunch.

Hasparren

B6 2 place Saint-Jean; en-pays-basque.fr

Hasparren is surrounded by rolling hills and meadows grazed by flocks of sheep, and the landscape is dotted with villages and traditional half-timbered Basque farmhouses with white walls and red shutters. Once a centre for shoemaking and leather goods, Hasparren is now an industrial yet pleasant town.

The Chapelle du Sacré-Cœur, or Chapelle des Missionnaires, was built in 1933. The walls of the nave are covered in huge frescoes depicting 48 saints, some shown with the instruments of their martyrdom. A Byzantine-style mosaic, *Christ in Majesty*, adorns the choir.

Maison Eyhartzea, in rue Francis-Jammes, at the entrance to the village, was, from 1921 until his death in 1938, the home of the poet Francis Jammes, whose work celebrates traditional life in the Basque Country.

Between Cambo and Hasparren, the D22, known as the Route Impériale des Cimes (Mountaintop Road), offers panoramic views of the Nive valley, and of the Rhune, Artzamendi and Mondarrain mountain peaks. Turn off at a junction in the Pachkoenia district to return to Hasparren via Cambo-les-Bains and Bayonne-Saint-Pierre-d'Irube.

Nearby, at Ayherre, there is a panoramic view of the countryside. The Basque name for this village is *Eihera*, which means "mill". There were 14 mills, but now only one is in working order. On the edge of the village are the ruins of Château de Belzance.

About 13 km (8 miles) from Hasparren are the **Grotte d'Isturitz and Grotte d'Oxocelhaya**, caves formed by an underground stretch of the Arbéroue river. Paintings and engravings of deer and horses, as well as bones, tools and a musical instrument made of bone, were found here.

Grotte d'Isturitz and Grotte d'Oxocelhaya

Saint-Martin-d'Arbéroue Hours vary, check website grottes-isturitz.com

Bidache

B6 1 place du Fronton; en-pays-basque.fr

The fact that Bidache was once the seat of a dukedom gives some idea of the town's historical importance. This is also evident from the ruins of the Château de Gramont, built by the duke here in the Middle Ages. It was remodelled several times up until the 18th century and has both medieval and Renaissance elements. The Jewish cemetery in the village is one of the oldest in France, dating to the 17th century.

↑ The Passerelle d'Holzarté bridge over the Gorges d'Olhadubi, near Larrau

↑ Villa Arnaga, Edmond Rostand's house in Cambo-les-Bains, and *(inset)* the Great Hall

Cambo-les-Bains

B6 3 avenue de la Mairie; camboles bains.com

Well known as a spa resort, Cambo-les-Bains is set above the Nive river. Many people, including artists, writers and other famous figures in the 19th and early 20th centuries, have come here to sample the sulphur- and iron-rich waters of its two springs. Among them were Napoléon III and the Empress Eugénie, who acquired a holiday home in Biarritz in 1856; the Spanish composer Isaac Albéniz, in 1909, and the painter Pablo Tillac, in 1921.

In clear weather, there are panoramic views of the river valley and the Pyrénées from rue du Trinquet and rue des Terrasses. The Église Saint-Laurent has a Baroque altarpiece in gilded wood, with a central panel that depicts the martyrdom of St Laurence. In the graveyard are several examples of the circular-topped, Basque-style gravestones.

Avenue Edmond-Rostand leads to the hillside where Rostand, best known for his verse-drama *Cyrano de Bergerac*, built his home: the **Villa Arnaga**, which is set in extensive gardens. Every room is decorated in a different style, including Classical elements in the study. Displays relating to the writer's life and work fill the first-floor rooms.

In early October Cambo celebrates the *gâteau Basque*, a tart filled with cherries and crème pâtissière, with a festival that now attracts around 17,000 people. It was a baker here, Marianne Hirigoyen, who first thought to market this traditional Basque dessert to a wider audience, hence the connection between the delicacy and the town.

GREAT VIEW
Top Spot

Climb to the top of Mount Ursuia near Hasparren for sweeping views of the Basque countryside around it, the Pyrénées and the distant coast. The climb should take an easy three hours.

STAY

Rosa Enia Guesthouse

A historic mansion with rooms that include a treehouse. Basque meals are lovingly served.

B6 Avenue du Prof Grancher, Cambo-les-Bains 05 59 93 67 20

Villa Arnaga

Route du Docteur Camino 05 59 29 83 92
Apr–Oct: daily

Colourful interior of the Église Saint-Étienne, St-Étienne-de-Baïgorry

12

Saint-Étienne-de-Baïgorry

A6 i Place de la Mairie; 05 59 37 47 28

Saint-Étienne-de-Baïgorry is a traditional Basque town close to the Spanish border. From the central square there are fine views of Mont Buztanzelai and Mont Oilandoi, and over to Col d'Ispéguy.

Located on the banks of the Nive river, Église Saint-Étienne (St Stephen's church) was built on the site of the former chapel of the Lords of Etxauz. Next to this Romanesque church is the Porte des Cagots, a doorway for Baïgorry's *cagots* – villagers who were once set apart from the rest of the community for a reason that has now been lost in history. Their ghetto was in the Mitchelenea quarter, where there is a single-span bridge. Built in 1661, it is known locally as the Roman bridge.

With two medieval towers on its north side and two Renaissance parapets on the south, the Château d'Etxauz dominates Baïgorry. Its lords ruled here for 500 years.

Nearby, the vineyards of Irouléguy are the only ones in the northern Pays Basque region with their own **cave coopérative** (wine cooperative) to promote the wines produced here.

At Banca, just 8km (5 miles) south of Saint-Étienne-de-Baïgorry are the remains of an 18th-century blast furnace, a remnant of the mines that were once active.

Les Aldudes has Navarre-style houses featuring red sandstone. At Salaisons des Aldudes, a meat-curing factory, visitors can learn about the Basque pork industry and sample its produce. Pierre Oteïza, the owner, has almost single-handedly revived the art of making traditional hams from *pie noir*, a local breed of black-spotted pig.

PICTURE PERFECT

Ancient Aquitaine

Large prehistoric stone circles stand on the 907-m- (2,976-ft-) high Monte Argibel. Located in Spain, but easily accessible from Aldudes, Argibel has great hiking trails.

Cave Coopérative d'Irouléguy

On the D15

Daily (Oct–Mar: Mon–Sat)

cave-irouleguy.com

13

Bidarray

A6 i 14 place Charles-de-Gaulle, Saint-Jean-Pied-de-Port; 05 59 37 03 57

The village of Bidarray is divided into 12 districts, each with typical Basse-Navarre-style houses. On the square at the top of the hill stands a small 12th-century church with pink sandstone walls. Its graveyard contains circular-topped stones. The Nive river here is suitable for water sports, and several local centres organize activities on the river.

Being located on the GR10, a long-distance footpath running between Ainhoa and Baïgorry, also makes Bidarray a good starting point for scenic walks up the Iparla and Baygoura mountains and Mont Artzamendi.

Nearby, Ossès has elegant half-timbered houses, such as Maison Harizmendi and Maison Ibarrondo, and houses with decorated lintels, such as Maison Arrosa and Maison Arrosagaray. On the square stands the Église Saint-Julien, a Renaissance-style church with a seven-sided bell tower. The interior features carved wooden galleries, a spiral staircase and a magnificent Baroque altarpiece.

Saint-Martin-d'Arrosa, 4 km (2.5 miles) away on the opposite bank of the Nive, has several traditional houses with carved lintels. The church, on the promontory here, has a gilded wooden altar as well as moulded ceiling.

Irrissary, a village situated in the centre of the Pays Basque Nord, has a remarkable 12th-century priory hospital, which was once the seat of a commander of the Knights Templar, St Jean de Jérusalem.

14

Espelette

A6 Château; 05 59 93 95 02

Famous for its sweet red Espelette peppers, celebrated with a major festival in late October, this large village is also noted as the birthplace of Father Armand David (1826–1900). David was the first westerner to learn of the existence of the great panda in China when he received a skin as a gift, and also discovered a species of deer – *Elaphurus davidianus* – which is named after him. A plaque marks Maison Bergara, where he lived. Also worth a visit is the 11th-century **Château des Barons d'Ezpeleta**, which now houses the village hall and tourist office. The church, just outside, has a painted ceiling, wooden galleries, a 17th-century altarpiece as well as a large bell tower. In the cemetery are ancient circular-topped funerary stones.

Château des Barons d'Ezpeleta

145 route Karrika-Nagusia 05 59 93 95 02 Mon-Sat

15

La Bastide-Clairence

B6 Maison Darrieux, place des Arceaux; 05 59 29 65 05

This beautiful *bastide* town, on the border with Gascony, was founded in 1312 by the king of Navarre. Its location very near Béarn allowed it to control traffic on the Adour river. In the Middle Ages, the town grew as a result of its weaving and leatherworking industries, as well as trade. The town still has its original medieval grid layout, with two thoroughfares at right angles to six smaller streets, and half-timbered houses and arcades.

1650

The year in which a Basque sailor brought home chilli peppers from the New World.

The medieval Église Notre-Dame stands in a courtyard with gravestones set into it. Further up the hill is a graveyard consisting of about 60 headstones. Resting in this cemetery are members of the Sephardic Jewish community who arrived in the area from Portugal during the 17th century.

Located 3 km (2 miles) from La Bastide-Clairence is the Benedictine abbey of Nôtre-Dame-de-Belloc. Founded in 1875, it is inhabited by a community of monks who work the land and who publish books in Basque. The graveyard has a few circular-topped gravestones.

↑ La Bastide-Clairence, nominated as one of France's loveliest villages

Saint-Jean-Pied-de-Port

B6 14 place Charles-de-Gaulle; en-pays-basque.fr

As the final stopping place for pilgrims before the climb over the mountain pass to Roncesvalles, Saint-Jean-Pied-de-Port has been an important commercial town on the pilgrimage routes to Santiago de Compostela since the Middle Ages. Known as the Garden of Navarre, this town switched between sovereigns many times until 1589, when, under Henri IV, it became part of France.

Entry into the old town is from place Charles-de-Gaulle, through Porte de Navarre, a fortified gate with arrow slits and battlements. Steps lead up to the wall-walk near the 17th-century Citadelle. The medieval Église Notre-Dame-du-Bout-du-Pont has pink sandstone columns and pillars. Maison Mansart, also built in pink sandstone, houses the town hall.

Rue de la Citadelle is lined with beautiful stone houses, featuring carved lintels and eaves over richly decorated beams. One of the finest of these houses is Maison Arcanzola, built in 1510, with brick and half-timbered walls in its upper storey. Further up is the Prison des Évêques. In the 19th century it was used as a short-term prison, but the building dates from the times when the town was the seat of a bishopric – thrice between 1383 and 1417. Porte Saint-Jacques, the gateway at the end of rue de la Citadelle, is a World Heritage Site, and pilgrims still travel through it.

Crossing the Nive by the picturesque Pont Notre-Dame to the rue d'Espagne quarter on the opposite bank, you will arrive at the ramparts. A covered market is organized here on Mondays.

Situated around 28 km (17 miles) away, beyond Arnéguy and Valcarlos, in Spain, is Roncesvalles (Roncevaux in French). The town lies below Col de Roncevaux (or Puerto d'Ibañeta), a pass at an altitude of 1,507 m (4,946 ft). It is home to an 18th-century hostel, and the medieval Chapelle de Sancti Spiritus and Église de Santiago. The town is 800 km (500 miles) from Santiago de Compostela and, for the pilgrims arriving there, the most arduous part of their journey was over.

Did You Know?

Visit Saint-Jean-Pied-de-Port on a Monday and you'll catch both the weekly market and a pelota match.

Saint-Palais

B6 55 avenue de Gibraltar; en-pays-basque.fr

Founded in the 13th century, the *bastide* town of Saint-Palais later became the capital of the kingdom of Navarre. The former Franciscan convent, which now houses **L'Espace Chemins-Bideak**, stands at the crossroads of several pilgrimage routes. Several markets were held here. It is also where the region's first Estates General met in the 16th century. Visit the garden and the cloister,

The Nive river, flowing through Saint-Jean-Pied-de-Port ↓

and see the displays about Basque culture, which explore the impact of the Compostela route on the town.

The town has lovely old houses, particularly Maison des Têtes, which is decorated with carvings of heads, set within medallions. The **Musée de Basse-Navarre et des Chemins de Saint-Jacques** documents local history as well as that of the pilgrimages to Compostela.

Every year, on the first Sunday following 15 August, Saint-Palais hosts the Force Basque Festival, in which eight local teams compete in traditional Basque trials of strength, including tug of war, cart-lifting, splitting tree trunks and racing with huge sacks of grain slung across their shoulders. Parades and music add to the festivities.

The 16th-century **Château de Camou**, 5 km (3 miles) north of Saint-Palais, has models of Renaissance inventions. Ostabat, lying 12 km (7 miles) south of Saint-Palais, is located at the junction of several pilgrimage routes.

L'Espace Chemins-Bideak
55 avenue de Gibraltar
Apr-Nov: Mon-Sat (Jul & Aug: daily) chemins-bideak.com

Musée de Basse-Navarre et des Chemins de Saint-Jacques
7 rue Gambetta Jul & Aug: Thu-Sat amis-musee-basse-navarre.fr

↑ The rough stone exterior of the Église de L'Hôpital-Saint-Blaise contrasts with its magnificent interior

Château de Camou
06 44 30 04 57 By appointment only, call ahead

L'Hôpital-Saint-Blaise

B6 Mairie; 05 59 66 11 12

This tiny village, located 13 km (8 miles) northeast of Mauléon-Licharre, lies very close to the border with Béarn *(p232)*. It was once the seat of a commander of the Knights Templar, and had a hostel where pilgrims would stay and rest, before continuing on their journey up to Col du Somport, via Oloron-Sainte-Marie *(p244)* or Saint-Jean-Pied-de-Port.

The striking 12th-century **Église de L'Hôpital-Saint-Blaise** is in the Romanesque style with Moorish elements. These are particularly noticeable in the stone latticework of the windows and in the capitals of the doorway. Moorish influence is also apparent inside the church: the stone-built dome has groin vaults that intersect to form an eight-pointed star. The interior also has a Baroque altarpiece and traditional Basque-style galleries. Both these features date from a later period than the church itself.

Église de L'Hôpital-Saint-Blaise
Le Village
05 59 66 07 21
Apr-Nov: daily

BASQUE LINEN

Basque linen is traditionally woven with stripes, which served to identify different families' linen at the village washhouse. Originally woven from flax on wooden hand-looms, Basque linen is now made of both flax and cotton. Traditional patterns include variations on the Basque cross, although the background may be a solid colour, rather than just the traditional white. Linen cloth had a wide range of uses, from tablecloths and napkins to curtains. The largest pieces were used to decorate the interior of Basque houses. Today only a few workshops - Jean Vier in Saint-Jean-de-Luz and Lartigue 1910 *(p244)* near Oloron-Sainte-Marie, Béarn - keep this ancient skill alive.

PILGRIMAGE ROUTES OF SOUTHWEST FRANCE

The four main pilgrimage routes to the Spanish city of Santiago de Compostela all run through southwest France. Since the discovery of the supposed tomb of the apostle St James at Compostela in 813, many have embarked on the journey to visit it. James is believed to have preached in Spain, and it is thought that his body was taken there after his martyrdom in Jerusalem in the 1st century CE. After crossing the Pyrénées from France into Spain, pilgrims still had 800 km (500 miles) to travel before reaching the Cathedral of Santiago. The routes they used were added to UNESCO's World Heritage List in 1993 – one of only two pilgrimages to gain this status (the other being in Japan).

JACQUETS AND JACQUAIRES

In France, pilgrims travelling to Santiago de Compostela are known as *jacquets* (men) or *jacquaires* (women). The paths vary according to their point of departure – with the four main ones being Tours, Vézelay, Le Puy-en-Velay and Arles – but all pilgrim routes converge in the Pays Basque. Because of the spectacular scenery and the towns and villages that they pass through, these routes are still very popular to this day.

THE MARK OF THE PILGRIM

Scallop shells are a symbol of St James, and are therefore a common emblem of the pilgrimage. Many pilgrims carry a shell tied to their backpack. The symbol can also be seen carved into doorways of pilgrim-friendly hostels, on route markers along common pilgrimage paths, and even on street signs in cities such as Bordeaux, through which routes pass.

↑ Today's pilgrims carry a passport that is stamped to record their progress and the places they have stopped at

A map based on a 17th-century design, showing the various pilgrimage routes in France

Accounts of and guides to the pilgrimage routes date back to the 12th century

Pilgrims ascending the Pyrénées to enter Spain

LOCATIONS TO VISIT

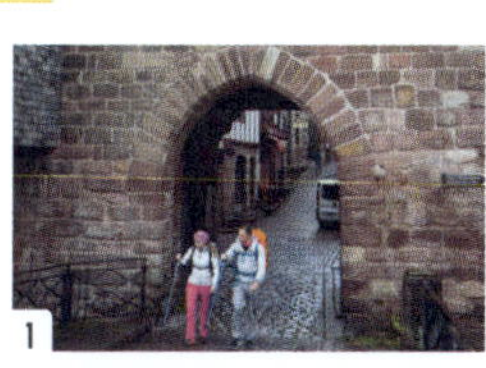

1 Porte Saint-Jacques

This gateway in Saint-Jean-Pied-de-Port *(p224)* is one of the many monuments on the route to Santiago de Compostela that are now listed as UNESCO World Heritage Sites.

2 Religious Buildings

Many churches, such as that shown here at L'Hôpital Saint-Blaise *(p225)*, are also World Heritage Sites. They testify to the strength of Christian faith in southwest France, as in the rest of Europe, during the Middle Ages.

3 Stèle de Gibraltar

In the picturesque village of Ostabat-Asme, near Saint-Palais, is the Stèle de Gibraltar monument. This column marks the symbolic convergence point of the pilgrim routes from Tours, Le Puy-en-Velay and Vézelay, all of which pass through this small town.

4 Pilgrim Sculpture

On the Spanish side of Col du Somport, this sculpture marks the route from Arles in France that later converges with four other pilgrim routes at Puente la Reina. From there, a single route known as the Camino Francés (French Way) continues straight to Santiago de Compostela.

Forêt d'Iraty

B7 en-pays-basque.fr

Straddling the border between France and Spain, the Forêt d'Iraty covers more than 170 sq km (65 sq miles). On the French side, altitudes range from 900 to 1,500 m (2,950 to 4,900 ft). The heavy annual rainfall results in luxuriant growth. Both pines and beech trees thrive here – this is Europe's largest beech forest. Like the Massif des Arbailles *(p231)*, the terrain is dotted with remains of ancient megalithic monuments.

The area also has many peat bogs. Because ancient plant matter is preserved by the airless conditions in the bogs, they act as a record of evolutionary change over thousands of years. The bogs are also home to most of the forest's wildlife, including wild boar, deer, foxes and squirrels. At Col de Bagargiak, there are several marked paths for circular walks of 1.5 to 4 hours, or for cross-country skiing in winter. The GR10, a long-distance footpath, crosses the northern part of the area. You can also drive through Iraty on the D18 from Larrau to Saint-Jean-Pied-de-Port.

INSIDER TIP
Local Cheese

Ossau-Iraty, an unpasteurized ewe's-milk cheese, is made in an area between the Forêt d'Iraty and the Pic du Midi d'Ossau. It has its own AOP and is often eaten as a dessert with black cherry jam.

Sainte-Engrâce

B7 Mairie; 05 59 28 60 83

In the heart of the upper Soule, at 630-m (2,068-ft), the shepherds' hamlet of Sainte-Engrâce lies on the border with Béarn and near Navarre, a province of the Spanish Basque Country. It consists of about 100 farmsteads, and "districts" spread out over a wide area of unspoiled countryside. At the confluence of the Gorges de Kakuetta and Gorges d'Ehujarre, it seems to stand guard over the great amphitheatre of hills all around. The 12th-century Romanesque abbey church is dedicated to Santa Gracia, after whom the village is named: a young Portuguese woman who was put to death around 300 CE, when Christians were being persecuted in Moorish Zaragoza. The original chapel on the site was built to house a relic of the saint – her arm, which was miraculously recovered. The chapel was later attached to the monastery at Leyre, in Navarre. It has a wooden pulpit and 21 capitals carved with a wealth of biblical scenes. The wrought-iron rood screen and Baroque altarpieces are noteworthy. The graveyard has several circular-topped Basque gravestones.

Ciboure

A6 5 place Camille Jullian; saint-jean-de-luz.com

Just south of Saint-Jean-de-Luz, on the other side of the Nivelle river, lies Ciboure. The town has numerous excellent examples of traditional Basque architecture, with its whitewashed houses, red woodwork and balconies. The Couvent des Récollets on quai Pascal-Elissalt was built

↑ Hiking through the verdant scenery of the Gorges de Kakuetta

in 1610 and, with the cloisters, it was used as a prison and tribunal during the French Revolution. You can peek at it through locked gates. On the quayside is a 17th-century house with a Dutch-style gabled façade: this is where the legendary composer Maurice Ravel was born. It now contains private apartments.

The 16th-century Église Saint-Vincent, in rue Pocalette, has a fortified octagonal bell tower. The church's interior has wooden galleries in three tiers, an impressive altarpiece and pictures from the Chapelle des Récollets. The lighthouse here was constructed in 1936 to a design by architect André Pavlovsky. The Fort de Socoa, built in the 1600s to defend the whaling port, stands at the tip of the harbour wall.

↑ Ciboure's harbour, protected by the harbour wall and Fort de Socoa

---

22 

Gorges de Kakuetta

B7 Sainte-Engrâce To the public; check website for details of reopening sainte-engrace.com/index.php

First explored by Édouard-Alfred Martel, a leading cave explorer, in 1906, these narrow gorges near Sainte-Engrâce were carved out of the rock by the action of water over thousands of years. You can walk all the way round the canyon in a 6.5-hour trek. You can also walk for 2 km (1 mile) right up into the gorge along metal walkways. Sturdy walking boots are strongly recommended.

The drop from the clifftops on either side to the bottom of the canyon is about 300 m (985 ft). Some of the narrow passages, including the Grand Étroit, which is one of the most magnificent in France, are no more than a few metres wide, but walking them is a thrilling experience.

TOP 4 HIKES IN THE FORÊT D'IRATY

Pic d'Orhy
At a height of 2,017 m (6,617 ft), this is an intermediate hike best done during summer.

Occabé
A well-marked trail leads to stone circles at this summit of 1,456 m (4,777 ft).

Urbeltza River
Follow an old road along the river to a waterfall and historic church ruins.

Pikatua-south
This fantastic winter route can be done in half a day but requires crampons and other winter climbing gear.

The moist conditions in these deep gorges allow lush vegetation to thrive. After walking for about an hour, you will come to a 20-m (65-ft) waterfall, whose source has still not been discovered. About 200 m (655 ft) further on, the walk comes to an end when you reach the Grotte du Lac, a cave with spectacular stalactites and stalagmites.

Mauléon-Licharre

B6 10 rue J B Hengas; en-pays-basque.fr

Capital of Soule, the smallest and the most sparsely populated of all the provinces of the Pays Basque, Mauléon-Licharre, also known as Mauléon-Soule, stretches out along the banks of the Saison river. In Mauléon, the upper part of the town, stands the 12th-century **Château Fort de Mauléon**. This small fortress, sitting on an outcrop of rock that towers over the valley, contains dungeons and old cannons.

The old *bastide* town of Mauléon was built in the 13th century, when Edward I of England ruled Aquitaine. Licharre, the lower town to the west, was the province's administrative centre. At the far end of the allées de la Soule, a long esplanade fronts the Hôtel de Montréal, a 17th-century building that now houses the town hall, a bandstand and a *fronton* (pelota court). **Château d'Andurain de Maytie**, built in the 16th and 17th centuries, has a shingle and slate, keel roof. Still inhabited by the descendants of Arnaud de Maytie, this residence has Renaissance-style decoration, including listed carved mantelpieces as well as antique furniture and rare books.

The town is renowned for its espadrilles, with several firms – some going back for generations – producing fine-quality, hand-sewn ranges of the traditional rope-soled slipper. Styling itself as "the espadrille capital of the Pays Basque", it holds an espadrille festival, on 15 August each year, with folk dancing and pelota contests.

The rest of the year you can visit the **Don Quichosse** espadrille workshop, where you can watch espadrilles being made.

Gotein-Libarrenx, 4 km (2.5 miles) from Mauléon-Licharre, has a 16th-century church, which contains an 18th-century altarpiece. Its bell tower, with three steeples each topped by a small cross, is typical of the Soule region. Ordiarp, 7 km (4 miles) further on towards Col d'Osquich, was a stopping place for pilgrims on the route to Santiago de Compostela. It has several medieval houses and a 12th-century church where Mass is held in Basque.

At Trois-Villes, 11 km (7 miles) away, is the **Château d'Eliçabéa**. Built in 1660 and surrounded by gardens, it belonged to the Comte de Tréville, captain of Louis XIII's musketeers. It features in Alexandre Dumas' famous novel *The Three Musketeers* (1844). The route leading to Les Arbailles passes a Soule-style church, with a Trinitarian steeple (a steeple topped by three points), at Aussurucq.

Grand salon in the *(inset)* Château d'Andurain de Maytie ↓

Château Fort de Mauléon
Rue du Fort
05 59 28 02 37 May: Fri-Wed; Jun & Sep: Wed-Sun; Jul & Aug: Sun-Fri

Château d'Andurain de Maytie
1 rue du Jeu-de-Paume 05 59 28 04 18
Jul-mid-Sep: Fri-Wed

Don Quichosse
Rue Jeanne d'Arc Mauléon-Licharre 05 59 28 28 18
9am-noon, 2-6pm Mon-Fri

Château d'Eliçabéa
Trois-Villes 05 59 28 54 01 Apr-Sep: Sat-Mon

The striking Chapelle de la Madeleine with sweeping views of the Soule Valley

Massif des Arbailles

B7 Rue Arhanpia, Tardets; 05 59 28 51 28

This region covers a mountainous area of limestone rocks. Heavy rainfall there has led to the formation of around 600 rock cavities. Pitted with sinkholes, crevasses and chasms, parts of the area resemble a giant Gruyère cheese. Because the terrain is often so uneven, walkers are advised not to stray from the footpaths.

The dense Forêt des Arbailles found in this region has a magical atmosphere that has inspired several legends. The forest is believed to be home to several creatures from Basque mythology, including Herensuge (a dragon) and lamina (wood sprites). From earliest times, the people of Les Arbailles have derived their livelihood from grazing sheep. Today, some local shepherds live in dry-stone huts known as *cayolars* and, from May to October, ewes are milked and cheeses – including the regional speciality of Ossau-Iraty cheese *(p228)* – are made.

The D117 leads to Ahusquy, where there is a spring whose pure, almost mineral-free waters are thought to have curative and diuretic properties. A steep scramble up the mountainside leads to a public drinking fountain at the source, should you wish to sample them. Ahusquy is a gateway to the Forêt des Arbailles, which is speckled with megalithic monuments, such as the Cercle de Pierre de Potto as well as the Dolmen d'Ithé.

In addition to livestock, this unspoiled natural environment is inhabited by deers and feral goats, and its cliffs are home to birds such as peregrine falcons, eagle owls, vultures and woodpeckers.

> **In the Massif des Arbailles, shepherds live in dry-stone huts known as *cayolars* and, from May to October, ewes are milked and cheeses, including Ossau-Iraty, are made.**

25

Tardets-Sorholus

B7 Rue Arhanpia; 05 59 28 51 28

The origins of Tardets-Sorholus go back to 1289, when it was founded as a *bastide* town. The central square, its focal point, is lined with 17th-century arcaded houses. In the town hall district is a *fronton* where games of pelota are played. Some of the houses along the banks of the Saison River have wooden galleries. The Soule-style farmhouses in the surrounding foothills are similar to the slate-roofed buildings of Béarn.

Around 8 km (5 miles) northeast of Tardets-Sorholus is the 16th-century Chapelle de la Madeleine. From here visitors can enjoy stunning views of the Soule and the Pyrenean mountain chain. A Latin inscription inside the church mentions an ancient Basque deity. The chapel can be accessed via car; however, outdoor enthusiasts are known to trek and cycle to the summit, too.

Lac Gentau at the foot of Pic du Midi d'Ossau

BÉARN

Béarn has a long and turbulent history to match the rest of Aquitaine. After Roman settlement, it was later incorporated into Spanish territory. By the 9th century, Béarn was under Gascon rule and, by 1290 had become an independent territory, despite treaties claiming it as part of France. Inheritance led to its inclusion in the kingdom of Navarre. In 1620 it was finally brought under the French Crown and, after the French Revolution, Béarn was linked with the Pays Basque to create a new *département* which was renamed the Pyrénées-Atlantiques in 1970. The modern world seemed barely to touch Béarn in the early 20th century. However, it changed enormously in post-war France thanks to the discovery of gas at Lacq, the cultivation of maize and the expansion of the capital, Pau. Improvements to the road network also helped to open up this breath-takingly beautiful, unspoiled region to visitors.

With the rugged Pic du Midi d'Ossau in the east and low-lying plains to the west, Béarn has a very varied landscape. Its cultural identity is clearly expressed by the use of its own language, Gascon, and by gastronomic specialities such as *garbure* (a ham and vegetable soup), ewe's-milk cheese and local wines.

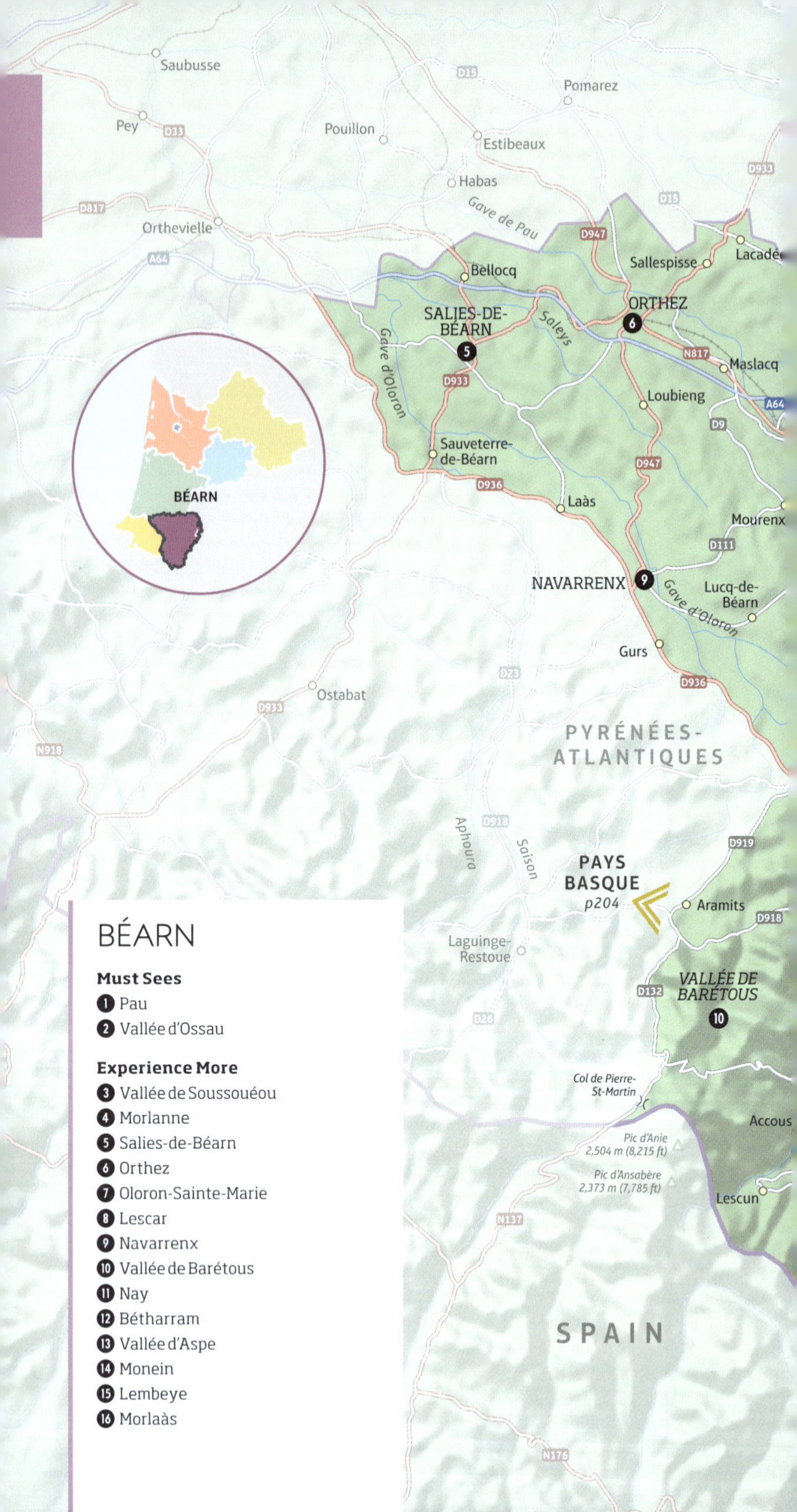

Saubusse
D15
Pomarez
Pey
D33
Pouillon
Estibeaux
D933
Habas
D15
D817
Gave de Pau
D947
Orthevielle
A64
Lacadée
Sallespisse
Bellocq
ORTHEZ
SALIES-DE-BÉARN
Saleys
6
5
N817
Maslacq
Gave d'Oloron
D933
Loubieng
A64
D9
BÉARN
Sauveterre-de-Béarn
D947
D936
Laàs
Mourenx
D111
NAVARRENX
9
Lucq-de-Béarn
Gave d'Oloron
Gurs
D23
D936
Ostabat
D933
N918
PYRÉNÉES-ATLANTIQUES
D918
Aphoura
Saison
D919
PAYS BASQUE
p204
Aramits
D918
Laguinge-Restoue
VALLÉE DE BARÉTOUS
D132
10
D26
Col de Pierre-St-Martin
Accous
Pic d'Anie
2,504 m (8,215 ft)
Pic d'Ansabère
2,373 m (7,785 ft)
Lescun
N137
SPAIN
N176
BÉARN
Must Sees
1 Pau
2 Vallée d'Ossau
Experience More
3 Vallée de Soussouéou
4 Morlanne
5 Salies-de-Béarn
6 Orthez
7 Oloron-Sainte-Marie
8 Lescar
9 Navarrenx
10 Vallée de Barétous
11 Nay
12 Bétharram
13 Vallée d'Aspe
14 Monein
15 Lembeye
16 Morlaàs

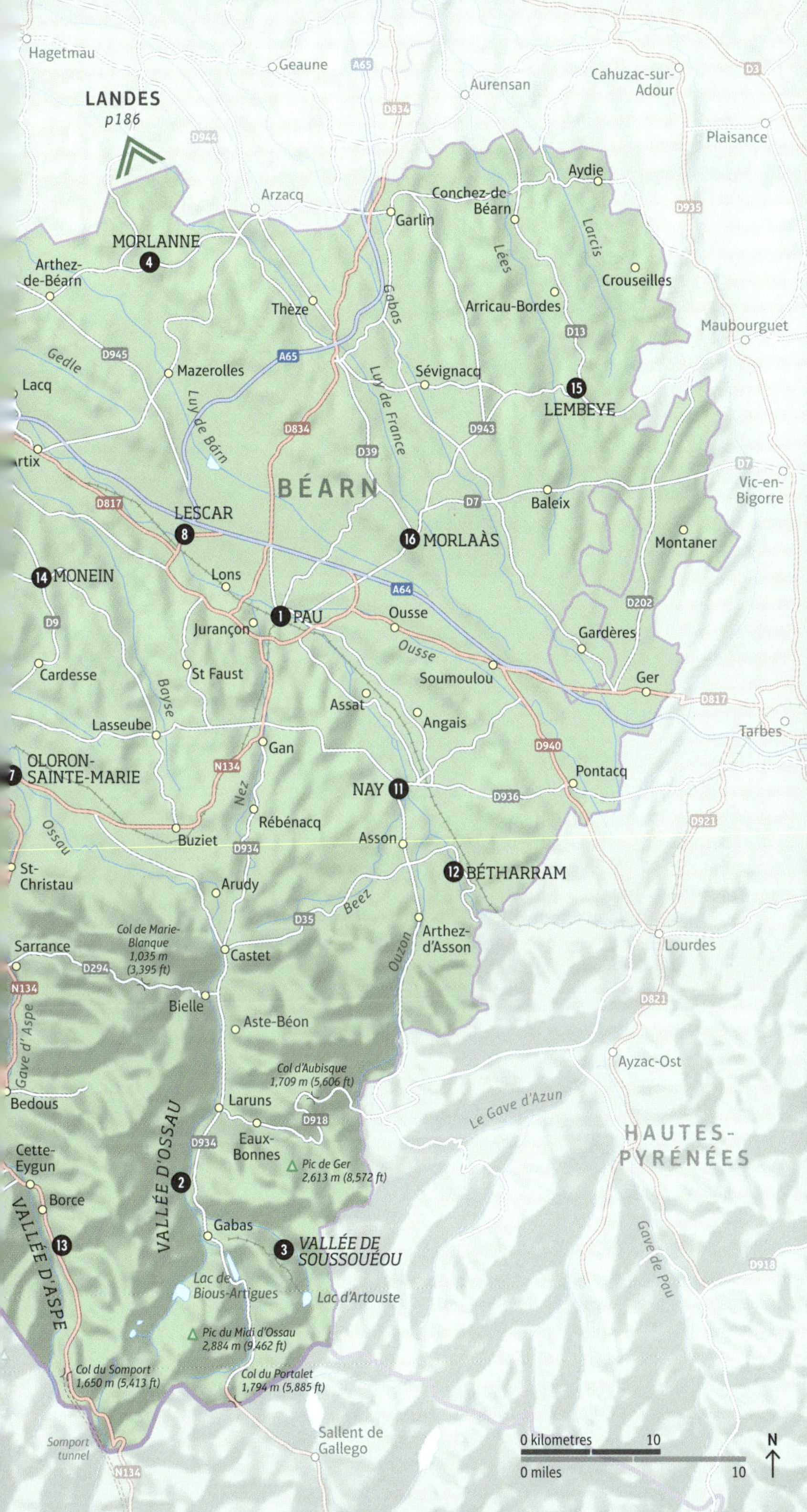

Hagetmau
Geaune
Aurensan
Cahuzac-sur-Adour
Plaisance
LANDES
p186
Arzacq
Aydie
Conchez-de-Béarn
Garlin
MORLANNE
Arthez-de-Béarn
Thèze
Crouseilles
Arricau-Bordes
Maubourguet
Gedle
Mazerolles
Lacq
Sévignacq
LEMBEYE
Luy de Béarn
Luy de France
Gabas
Lées
Larcis
Artix
BÉARN
LESCAR
Baleix
Vic-en-Bigorre
MORLAÀS
Montaner
MONEIN
Lons
PAU
Jurançon
Ousse
Gardères
Cardesse
St Faust
Soumoulou
Ger
Bayse
Assat
Angais
Lasseube
Gan
Tarbes
OLORON-SAINTE-MARIE
NAY
Pontacq
Nez
Rébénacq
Ossau
Buziet
Asson
St-Christau
BÉTHARRAM
Arudy
Beez
Col de Marie-Blanque
1,035 m
(3,395 ft)
Arthez-d'Asson
Sarrance
Castet
Lourdes
Ouzon
Bielle
Aste-Béon
Gave d'Aspe
Col d'Aubisque
1,709 m (5,606 ft)
Ayzac-Ost
Bedous
Laruns
Le Gave d'Azun
Eaux-Bonnes
HAUTES-PYRÉNÉES
Cette-Eygun
Pic de Ger
2,613 m (8,572 ft)
VALLÉE D'OSSAU
Borce
Gabas
VALLÉE DE SOUSSOUÉOU
VALLÉE D'ASPE
Gave de Pau
Lac de Bious-Artigues
Lac d'Artouste
Pic du Midi d'Ossau
2,884 m (9,462 ft)
Col du Somport
1,650 m (5,413 ft)
Col du Portalet
1,794 m (5,885 ft)
Somport tunnel
Sallent de Gallego
0 kilometres
10
0 miles
10
N

Stunning panorama of the picturesqe city of Pau

PAU

C6 Place Royale; pau-pyrenees.com

To discover the capital of old Béarn, a city of history and beauty, start your visit at place Georges-Clémenceau. From here parks, museums, regal châteaus and lively street life unfold. The historic district, with its Basque-style houses and cobbled streets, is a delight to explore. Steep passages and bridges span Pau's hilly terrain; from boulevard des Pyrénées and the funicular train, mountain views are legendary.

The capital of Béarn and seat of the royal court of Navarre, Pau is the birthplace of Henri IV of France and of the Bourbon dynasty. In the first half of the 19th century, the city's gentle climate attracted many visitors, including a number of wealthy English people, who came to spend their winters here. Soon luxurious villas were being built and splendid municipal gardens were laid out. In 1856, one of the first golf courses to be built on the continent of Europe opened in Pau, which also has an Anglican church, the Église Saint-Andrew, on the corner of rue O'Quin and rue Pasteur.

Villa Saint-Basil's

61 avenue Trespoey 05 59 84 73 87 Only during the journées du patrimoine in mid-Sep

Gathered in the Quartier Trespoey are several grand houses, almost all of them privately owned. The ground floor of Villa Saint-Basil's, built between 1885 and 1888 is set in beautiful parkland. Other privately owned villas north of the castle, beyond rue Gaston-Fébus, can be seen from the outside.

Quartier du Château and Quartier du Hédas

The old parts of the medieval and Renaissance town cluster around the castle *(p238)*. Rebuilt in the 18th century, the quarter has cobbled streets and several townhouses, including the Hôtel de Peyré, also known as Maison Sully, at 2 rue du Château. Its door knocker, in the shape of a basset hound, is said to be lucky.

Quartier du Hédas, the city's oldest district, has fine 16th-century townhouses in rue René-Fournets and at place Reine-Marguerite on rue Maréchal-Joffre.

INSIDER TIP

Nightlife Revived

For the best nightlife in Pau, head to the revived Quartier du Hédas. The formerly notorious alleys in the area, once used for sword duels, are now lined with cafés and bars that stay open till the wee hours.

③

Boulevard des Pyrénées

This pedestrian promenade was laid out in the late 19th century by Adolphe Alphand, a pupil of the great town planner Baron Haussmann.

About 1,800 m (1 mile) long, it lies on a natural terrace between Parc Beaumont and Parc du Château, and in clear weather offers glorious views of the Château gardens below and of the highest peaks of the Pyrénées, which are snowcapped all year round. Opposite 20 boulevard des Pyrénées, there is even an orientation table that names and indicates heights of the visible peaks.

The boulevard is lined with the terraces of cafés, restaurants and bars, which become lively on summer evenings, spilling out on to the pavement. The funicular, installed in 1908, carries passengers from place Royale to the railway station. Nearby is the Église Saint-Martin, next to a tree-lined square, with an impressive Neo-Gothic exterior.

④

Musée des Beaux-Arts

Rue Mathieu-Lalanne
05 59 27 33 02 11am-6pm Tue-Sun

Occupying a beautiful 1930s building, a stone's throw from the Palais Beaumont and boulevard des Pyrénées, this museum showcases some stunning examples of painting from the Dutch, Flemish, Spanish, Italian, French and English schools of the 15th to the 20th centuries. Among the museum's most famous works are *Portraits dans un Bureau de La Nouvelle-Orléans* (1873) by Degas, and works by artists including Rubens, Greco, Rodin and Morisot. Major temporary exhibitions are also regularly organized at the museum.

STAY

Hôtel Villa Navarre

Surrounded by a lush estate, this grand villa was built in 1865 and has luxurious and spacious rooms, plus an indoor pool and fine restaurant with mountain views.

59 avenue Trespoey
villanavarre.fr

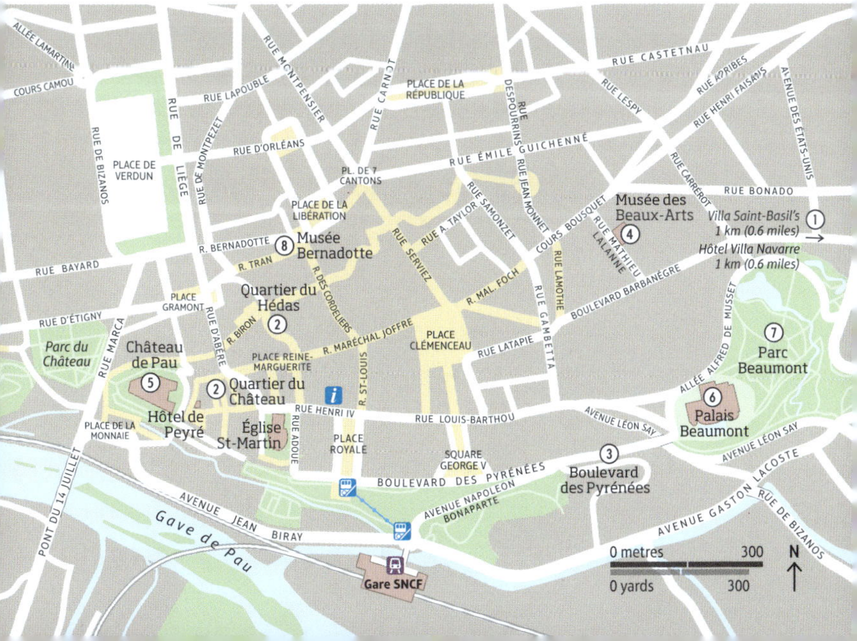

Château de Pau

Rue du Château
Hours vary, check website chateau-pau.fr

A fairy-tale castle that birthed a king, the château in the heart of Pau was originally a fortress built to ward off the French and English before becoming home to Henri IV. Louis-Philippe ordered a complete restoration in 1838 that

↑ The Château de Pau, perched on a hill above the city

Did You Know?

The tapestries in Château de Pau are some of the finest in all of France.

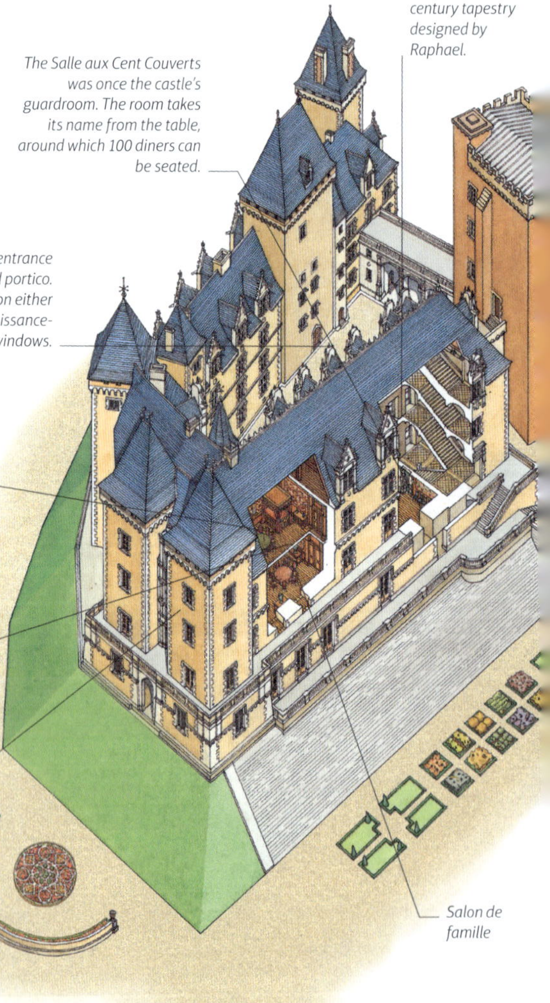

The castle contains a 17th-century tapestry designed by Raphael.

The Salle aux Cent Couverts was once the castle's guardroom. The room takes its name from the table, around which 100 diners can be seated.

The courtyard entrance is a three-arched portico. The buildings on either side have Renaissance-style windows.

The king's bedchamber has some of the richest furnishings.

The turtle shell used in decorations in the Chambre du Roi de Navarre is supposed to have served as Henri IV's cradle.

Jeanne d'Albret's bedchamber is hung with 18th-century tapestries of mythological allegories.

Statue of Gaston Fébus, the Count of Foix-Béarn

Salon de famille

survived the Revolution *(p54)*. Today it stands regally in the style of Versailles.

As it lay between his territory in Ariège and his court at Orthez, Gaston Fébus – who held the title of Comte de Foix-Béarn – chose Pau as a strategically located base. The original castle, built in 1370, was a fortress with a triple line of defences. During the Renaissance, it became the residence of the viscounts of Béarn, allies of the Albrets, rulers of Navarre, a Spanish kingdom. The birthplace of Henri IV, future king and France's first Bourbon monarch, it served as the centre of a Protestant state created by Henri's mother, Jeanne d'Albret *(p244)*. Later, the castle became a shrine to Henri, and in the 19th century, Louis-Philippe, himself a Bourbon, ordered a major programme of restoration, which was continued by Napoléon III.

A tour of the château lets visitors get up close to a beautiful piece of French history, and reveals many more works of art inside, including some of the finest Flemish and Gobelins tapestries in France.

Chapel

The historic and regal Château de Pau

Palais Beaumont

Allée Alfred de Musset 05 59 11 20 00 To the public

This winter palace, with a Neo-Classical south façade and decorative plasterwork, was built in 1900 to cater for foreign visitors and has since been restored. Set in the stunning parkland of Parc Beaumont, it also has a conference centre.

Parc Beaumont

Allée Alfred de Musset

The variant species of flora growing in the delightful Parc Beaumont, from Californian redwoods to the Himalayan cedars, is ample testament to the gentle climate of Pau – just about anything grows here. There is also a lovely rose garden, a lake and waterfall feature, and the open-air Théâtre de Verdure.

Musée Bernadotte

8 rue Tran 05 59 27 48 42 For renovation until 2026

The birthplace of Jean-Baptiste-Jules Bernadotte, one of Pau's greatest sons, is now a museum, documenting his phenomenal career.

Having joined the French army as a private in 1780, Bernadotte rose through the ranks to become a Maréchal d'Empire in 1804. He was made a royal prince of Sweden in 1810, succeeding to that country's throne in 1818, as Charles XIV.

> **The variant species of flora growing in the delightful Parc Beaumont, from Californian redwoods to the Himalayan cedars, is ample testament to the gentle climate of Pau.**

↑ Façade of the Palais Beaumont, the historic winter palace in Parc Beaumont

Skiers on the slopes at Gourette, a resort in the resort in Vallee d'Ossau

2 VALLÉE D'OSSAU

C7 Place de Laruns, Laruns; ossau-pyrenees.com

The Valle d'Ossau is a stark reminder of the indelible mark left on Béarn by the Ice Age. A bird's eye view of the valley reveals endless snowy vistas and incredible natural wonders that beckon adrenaline seekers.

Beginning south of Pau, the Vallée d'Ossau lies at right angles to the Pyrénées and runs right up to Col du Pourtalet on the border with Spain. Glaciers covered this whole area in the last Ice Age. The lower part of the valley stretches between the towns of Arudy and Laruns. In the upper valley, villages are sited in basins, amid deep gorges and broad plateaus encircled by rocky outcrops. The highest peak in this fine landscape is the 2,884-m- (9,465-ft-) high Pic du Midi d'Ossau. The collapsed cone of an extinct volcano, it serves as the emblem of the Haut Béarn. The Vallée d'Ossau has a strong cultural identity, reflected in traditional song and dance and in the use of the Gascon language.

① Castet

4 rue la Marque; 05 59 05 79 51 (Mairie)

This attractive village takes its name from the 12th-century fortified castle that guarded the valley. Dismantled by the valley's inhabitants in 1450, all that remains of the castle are two towers and the dungeon. A Romanesque church, the Église Saint-Polycarpe, stands on a promontory overlooking the village. Follow the road that leads down to the harbour, beside a lake on the Gave d'Ossau. Here there are marked pathways and an "espace naturel" devoted to the wildlife living in and around these waters.

② Arudy

Place Hôtel de Ville; 05 59 05 77 11

Arudy is famous for its fine marble. This ranges from a blueish-grey variety, the most common, to the rarest, which is veined with red or a mix of several colours. The Église Saint-Germain, dating from the 16th and 17th centuries, has a pointed dome and capitals carved with bears and cows, the emblems of Ossau.

③ Bielle

2 route de Pau; 05 59 82 60 36 (Mairie)

Bielle was the valley's political capital. It remained autonomous until the French

Did You Know?

In summer, flocks of sheep graze on the high-altitude pastures at Haut Ossau, watched over by shepherds.

Revolution in 1789. The records of the community's legal business were stored in a triple-lock chest, now displayed in the Église Saint-Vivien. The church's 16th-century tympanum is carved with symbols of Ossau. The town's richly decorated 15th–18th-century houses include Maison Trille and the former convent, which has a square pavilion and a circular tower, with an arched doorway.

Falaise aux Vautours

For renovation until 2027; check website for details
falaise-auxvautours.com

The cliffs at the villages of Aste and Béon are part of a protected nature reserve, known as Falaise aux Vautours. The visitor centre located at the foot of the cliffs displays details about griffon vultures. Hides inside the cliffs allow these birds to be viewed at close quarters.

Laruns

Maison du Parc National à Laruns, avenue de la Gare; 05 59 05 41 59

Laruns is home to the Ossau's tourist office and the Maison du Parc National. Here the valley's traditional culture is kept alive at the festival of music and dancing that takes place on 15 August each year. The Pon quarter, in the south of the town, features 16th- and 17th-century houses.

Route de l'Aubisque

This pass, which leads through stunning mountain scenery, lies beyond Laruns on the D918 to Gourette. Empress Eugénie instigated the construction of this "spa route", and encouraged the development of the health spa of Eaux-Bonnes along it.

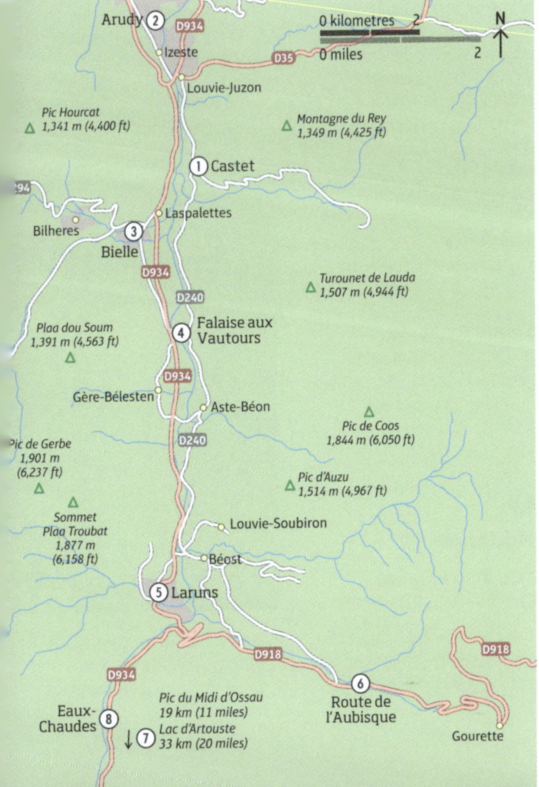

PIC DU MIDI D'OSSAU

Standing out like a giant shark's tooth, the Pic du Midi d'Ossau soars up to a height of 2,884 m (9,465 ft). Climbing to the top is safe only for experienced mountaineers, but its lower slopes are more easily accessible and offer long, pleasant walks as well as a number of family attractions. From the lakes and passes around the peak there are spectacular views of Béarn's mountains. Hikers should never set out without a good map and suitable equipment.

Lac d'Artouste

This picture-perfect lake makes for a lovely setting for a picnic. It is also the departure point for several good hiking routes.

High over the lake, along a narrow-gauge track laid out when the dam at Artouste was being built in 1924, runs a little train that takes visitors to Lac d'Artouste (late May–Sep, *p242*). This scenic journey, at an altitude of 2,000 m (6,564 ft), takes 55 minutes.

Eaux-Chaudes

Larun municipal district includes the spa town of Eaux-Chaudes, about 6 km (4 miles) to the south, which was at its peak during the 19th century. The village takes its name from the seven hot springs near the baths that made it famous and that were popular in the 19th and early 20th centuries. Various health treatments are still available here.

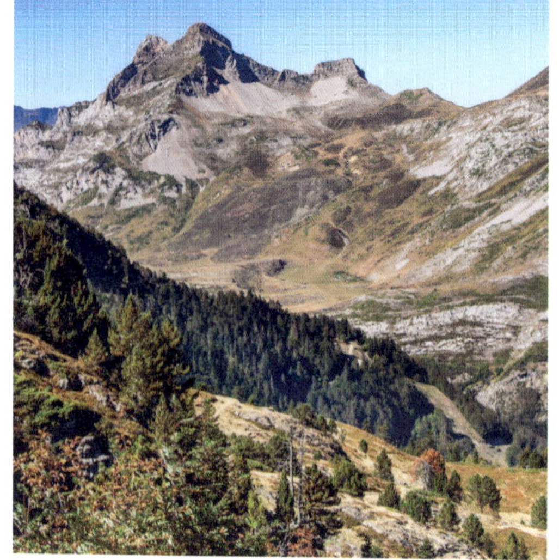

The view along the Vallée de Soussouéou from Lac d'Artouste as summer turns to autumn

EXPERIENCE MORE

3

Vallée de Soussouéou

**C7** **Maison de la Vallée d'Ossau; ossau-pyrenees.com**

The breathtaking Vallée de Soussouéou is about 10 km (6 miles) long. Information on hiking here is available from the tourist office at Laruns *(p241)*. If you intend to walk in the valley, drive out of Laruns on the Gabas road to the Miégebat power station; 2 km (1 mile) from there, take a left turn to Pont de Goua, a bridge near which you can park. From here a footpath leads through the undergrowth. A 30-minute walk brings you to the GR10, a long-distance path. From here, adventurous hikers can take a day's walk along this irregularly signed but well-used track to reach the Lac d'Artouste *(p241)*.

An alternative route up the valley is to drive through Gabas and park at the Lac de Fabrèges cable-car car park, 4 km (3 miles) further on. From here, a 12-minute ride will take you up to Col de la Sagette, where you can catch the **Train d'Artouste**, which follows a track up the side of the valley. The journey, in open carriages, takes 55 minutes, with splendid views of the Pic du Midi d'Ossau *(p241)*. From the terminus, it takes about 15 minutes to reach Lac d'Artouste on foot. You can also walk down from Col de la Sagette to the Soussouéou plateau and in summer there's a chairlift known as the Télésiège de l'Ours (Bear's Chairlift).

Train d'Artouste

 Station d'Artouste, Résidence Fario Late May–Sep: hours vary, check website artouste.fr

4

Morlanne

C6 **Carrère-du-Château; 05 59 81 42 66**

This characterful village has old houses in a style typical of northern Béarn. The village's main street runs from Maison Domecq, a 15th-century abbey, to **Château de Morlanne**. It was built in the Middle Ages, but its features were restored in the 1960s. On a guided tour of the castle, visitors will see medieval furniture, and art by Fragonard, Nattier, Canaletto and Van de Velde.

Arzacq-Arraziguet, 13 km (8 miles) from Morlanne, is a *bastide* town on the pilgrim route, built by the English. Its focal point is the arcaded place de la République. The parish church has a stained-glass window with a depiction of St James and a painted wooden Madonna and Child from the 16th century. Also here is the **Maison du Jambon de Bayonne**, a shop with a museum based on the history and production of Bayonne ham and other local specialities. **Château de Momas**, 14 km

Did You Know?

The Train d'Artouste is the highest open-top railway in Europe.

Resembling a toy castle, the fortified church of Saint-Laurant, Morlanne 

SALIES-DE-BÉARN'S SALTY FESTIVITIES

Although the legend of the wounded boar dates only from the Middle Ages, salt has been panned at Salies-de-Béarn since the Bronze Age. Today, salt is still at the heart of the town, with salty thermal baths, a salt museum, working salt marshes, and an annual salt festival. At the Fête du Sel, in the second week of September, over 10,000 people revel in music, parades, a cured foods market, and traditional races in which barrels of brine are rolled, carried and even borne on heads through the streets.

(9 miles) away, dates from the 14th to 16th centuries and was the residence of the lords of Momas. The present owner takes visitors on a tour of the garden here, planted with rare flowers, shrubs and vegetables.

Château de Morlanne
05 59 81 60 27
Apr-Oct: Tue-Sun

Maison du Jambon de Bayonne
Route de Samadet
Mon-Sat maison-du-jambon-de-bayonne.com

Château de Momas
9:30am-noon & 2:30-7pm Fri-Wed
chateaudemomas.com

5

Salies-de-Béarn

B6 8 rue de la Fontaine Salée; tourisme-bearn-gaves.com

Salies-de-Béarn's claim to fame is its saltwater spring, which led to its development as a spa resort. The town's historic district centres around the place du Bayaà, where stands the Fontaine du Sanglier, dedicated to a *sanglier* (wild boar) that legend credits with the discovery of the area's saltwater springs. The boar, wounded in the hunt, was discovered dead some time later, mired in a marsh and covered in salt crystals. Perfectly preserved, it tasted delicious – the first "Bayonne ham". The **Musée du Sel et Traditions Béarnaises** is a local history museum that is situated among 17th- and 18th-century houses and features a salt-panner's workshop. In front of the museum is a *couledé*, a stone trough, where water was kept after being drawn from the fountain and before being transferred to the reservoirs. The museum also showcases traditional costumes and tools of ancient trades.

Beyond Pont de la Lune, half-timbered houses on pillars flank the street. Also here is the headquarters of Maison de la Corporation des Part-Prenants, an organization founded in 1587 to oversee salt production in order to benefit the whole community. The old town ends at the spa quarter. The grand hotels here, such as the Hôtel du Parc (1893), were built during the spa's heyday at the end of the 19th century. Nearby are baths, built originally in 1857 and rebuilt in the Moorish style after a fire in 1888.

↑ Salies-de-Béarn town-houses, with shutters to keep out the sun

Musée du Sel et Traditions Béarnaises
14 rue des Puits-Salants
Apr-Oct: Mon-Sat
museedusel64.fr

Orthez

B6 1 rue des Jacobins; coeurdebearn.com

The emblem of Orthez, Béarn's "second capital", is the Pont Vieux, built across the Gave de Pau in the 13th century. The tower was added by Gaston Fébus, who inscribed it with a Gascon saying: *Toquey si gaouses* ("Touch it if you dare"). The **Château de Moncade** towers above the town. Built in the 13th and 14th centuries, it witnessed the flowering of Fébus's court, but was torched in 1569 during the Wars of Religion (1562–98). What remained was sold during the French Revolution, and it was finally restored in the 19th century.

On rue Bourg-Vieux is a 16th-century house with a stair-tower, mullioned windows and a formal garden. It was once the home of Jeanne-d'Albret, Queen of Navarre, who converted to Calvinism in 1560 and declared her whole territory officially Protestant in the years before the Wars of Religion between the Catholics and Protestants. Her old home now houses the **Musée Jeanne-d'Albret**, which documents the history of Protestantism in Béarn. **Maison Chrestia**, home of the Béarnese poet Francis Jammes from 1897 to 1907, illustrates his life and work.

Château de Moncade

Rue Moncade 05 59 69 36 24 Mid-Apr-mid-Sep: daily

Musée Jeanne-d'Albret

37 rue Bourg-Vieux Hours vary, check website museejeannedalbret.com

Maison Chrestia

7 avenue Francis-Jammes 05 59 69 11 24 Mid-Jan-mid-Dec: Tue, Fri & Sat

Oloron-Sainte-Marie

C6 Allée du Comte-de-Tréville; pyrenees-bearnaises.com

Situated at the confluence of the Gave d'Aspe and Gave d'Ossau, Oloron-Sainte-Marie is the capital of Haut Béarn and the gateway to the Vallée d'Aspe *(p248)*. In the 11th century, Oloron and the neighbouring bishopric of Sainte-Marie began to expand and merge, becoming a strategic point of trade with the Spanish kingdom of Aragon, as well as a major textile-weaving centre. Under Empress Eugénie, the two were officially united to create one city in 1858.

The most significant landmark is the magnificent Cathédrale Sainte-Marie, a UNESCO World Heritage Site. The building's 12th-century Romanesque carved doorway, covered by a porch, is arguably the finest and best-preserved such doorway in Béarn.

Basque textiles are still important to the town, although **Lartigue 1910**, in Bidos, 2 km (1 mile) from Oloron-Sainte-Marie, is one of only a few weaving workshops that still use traditional methods *(p225)*.

PICTURE PERFECT
Pilgrim Sculptures

Dotted around the streets and parks of Oloron are contemporary sculptures referencing the artistic activity associated with traditional pilgrim routes to Santiago de Compostela.

Lartigue 1910

2 avenue Georges-Messier 05 59 39 50 11 Mon-Sat

Lescar

C6 Place Royale; pau-pyrenees.com

Lescar, historically the capital of Béarn, is perched on a walled promontory that looks towards the Pyrénées. In the 12th century it became a fortified bishopric, with work on the Cathédrale Notre-Dame on place Royale commencing in 1120. A plaque set into the cathedral floor lists the tombs of some of the kings of Navarre who are buried here. Floor mosaics near the altar depict hunting scenes. The building also has fine 17th-century sculptures of Christ, the apostles and local saints. Around the cathedral stand the 14th-century Tour de l'Esquirette and two 16th-century towers, the Tour de l'Évêché and du Presbytère.

From the community centre *(salle des fêtes)*, a short walk leads along the ramparts to the upper town. The **Musée de Lescar** here is housed in the cellars of the old Episcopal Palace. Its archaeological collection explores the history of Lescar, from Iron-Age jewellery to everyday objects.

About 16 km (10 miles) from Lescar are the **Cave des Producteurs de Jurançon**, at Gan, and the Maison des Vins de Jurançon, at Lacommande.

The Pont Vieux, a 13th-century fortified bridge over the Gave de Pau at Orthez

At both, visitors can sample and buy local wines. The area's white wine was said to be a favourite of Henri IV, who first tasted it at his christening.

Opposite the Maison des Vins is a rare example of a 12th-century **Commanderie**, one of the hospitals founded by crusader Gaston IV. Nearby, the interior of the Église Saint-Blaise features capitals that are sculpted with biblical and mythological scenes.

Musée de Lescar

Place de l'Evêché 05 59 81 57 10 Jul & Aug: Mon-Sat

Cave des Producteurs de Jurançon

53 avenue Henri IV, Gan 05 59 21 57 03 Mon-Sat (Jul & Aug: daily) for tours and tastings

Commanderie

Rue de l'Église, Lacommande Jul & Aug: daily; Sep-Jun: Wed, Sat & Sun

Navarrenx

B6 2 place des Caserne; 05 59 38 32 85

Overlooking the Gave d'Oloron, this fortified town came under attack during the Wars of Religion and was besieged in 1569. The **Arsenal**, constructed in 1680, was originally the residence of the kings of Navarre. As its present name implies, it became a munitions and provisions store for the viscounts of Béarn. It operates as a cultural centre now.

In rue Saint-Antoine is a 16th-century house called the Maison de Jeanne-d'Albret after the ruler of Béarn in 1555. The 16th-century Église Saint-Germain has arches decorated with carved and painted heads.

Some 7 km (4 miles) from Navarrenx, on the D936 to Oloron, is **Camp de Gurs**. Here Spanish republicans were interned after the Civil War and Jews were held before deportation. About 16 km (10 miles) from here, at the 17th-century Château de Laàs, is **Musée Serbat**, a decorative arts museum.

View from the fortified town walls of Navarrenx

Arsenal

41 rue Saint-Germain, Navarrenx Mid-May-Sep: daily

Camp de Gurs

Impasse d'Ossau campgurs.com

Musée Serbat

Le Bourg, Laàs Hours vary, check website musee-serbat.com

SHOP

Maison des Vins de Jurançon

It is said that Henri IV's favourite wine was Jurançon, a Béarnese speciality. The area produces both dry and sweet white wine. Try some for yourself by buying a bottle or two at this large wine shop.

C6 Rue de l'Église, Lacommande 05 59 82 70 30 Tue-Sat

10 Vallée de Barétous

C7 45 avenue Marcel Loubens, Arette; pyrenees-bearnaises.com

Near the border between the Pays Basque in France and Navarre in Spain, the Vallée de Barétous is a region of sharp contrasts. Woodland, green hillsides and *estives* (summer pastures), grazed by sheep, mix with steep gorges, the lofty Pic d'Anie and the Col de la Pierre-Saint-Martin – a long, arid limestone chasm, thought to be the deepest in the world, that is a paradise for cave explorers.

Arette, with just over a thousand inhabitants, is the valley's largest town. On 13 August 1967, it was hit by an earthquake. The Centre Sismologique here registers earth tremors in the region, and tours can be arranged through the tourist office. The Maison de Barétous, at the tourist office, has an exhibition on life in the valley, and a feature on the Junte du Roncal ceremony.

Did You Know?

Two of Alexander Dumas's musketeers, Porthos and Aramis, hail from the Vallée de Barétous.

JUNTE DU RONCAL

On 13 July each year, at the Col de la Pierre-Saint-Martin, the Junte du Roncal - also known as the *Tribut des Trois Génisses* (Gift of Three Heifers) - commemorates a peace treaty that has been in force since 1375, between the residents of the Vallée de Barétous and those of the Roncal valley, in the Spanish province of Navarre. The mayors of each valley take an oath and, to mark it, the Béarnese present the Navarrese with three heifers. In exchange, they can graze their sheep on the *estives* (summer pastures) of their neighbours in the Roncal.

11 Nay

C6 Pl de 8 Mai 1945; 05 59 13 94 99

At the beginning of the 12th century, monks from Sainte-Christine in Gabas founded Nay (pronounced "Nye") to provide food and shelter for pilgrims travelling to the Spanish city of Santiago de Compostela. This small town, on the edge of the Hautes-Pyrénées, stands on the Gave de Pau, which becomes swollen with melt-water in spring. In 1302, Marguerite de Moncade made Nay a fortified *bastide* town. It began to prosper during the Middle Ages, thanks to the growth of the weaving industry, reaching the height of its prosperity in the 18th century with the manufacture of Basque berets and textiles. In 1543, Nay was severely damaged by fire. The Église Saint-Vincent, a single-nave church in the Languedoc Gothic style, originally from the 15th–16th centuries, was remodelled when the rest of the town was rebuilt.

The **Maison Carrée**, built by Pedro Sacaze – a wealthy merchant from Aragon – is

The lower Vallée de Barétous, a lush patchwork of fields and mixed woodland

a Renaissance-style town-house with Italian loggias and an inner courtyard. It fell into ruin in the 18th century but has been restored. The upper floors house the **Musée de l'Industrie**, which features a display on industry in Nay through the ages, with sections on local metalwork, weaving and quarrying.

The **Musée du Béret**, located in a former industrial building, traces the history of the most recognizable of all French fashions: the beret. After learning about the stages in its manufacture, visitors can pick up their own chic beret at the museum shop. Despite being associated with Pays Basque, this type of headgear in fact originates in the Vallée d'Ossau *(p240)*. From the industrial revolution onwards, its manufacture was a major source of income in Nay and Oloron-Sainte-Marie *(p244)*. However, beret-making is now in decline.

Maison Carrée and Musée de l'Industrie

Place de la République 05 59 13 99 65 Jul & Aug: Tue-Sun; Sep-Jun: Tue-Sat, open for exhibitions, check website for details maison-carree-nay.fr

Musée du Béret

Place Saint-Roch Hours vary, check website museeduberet.com

12

Bétharram

C7 13 place des Arcades, Saint-Pé-de-Bigorre; 05 62 41 88 10

The town's main attraction is the **Grottes de Bétharram**, a series of caves on five levels that visitors explore on foot, by boat and on a small train. An amazing array of draped, fringed and lace-like rock formations hang from the walls and ceilings of these great caverns.

Bétharram also features a Baroque chapel, the **Sanctuaire de Notre-Dame de Bétharram**, built in the 17th century. According to legend, the original chapel here was built in the 14th century after the Madonna had appeared on the banks of the Gave de Pau. A second chapel was destroyed by fire in 1569. The west front of the present chapel is of grey marble, with statues of the Four Evangelists and the Madonna and Child. The interior is opulent, featuring black marble pillars, a 17th-century altarpiece, paintings and gilded wooden sculptures.

The chapel is associated with Michel Garicoïts (1797–1863), a priest who is buried here. Founder of the Society of the Priests of the Sacred Heart of Bétharram, he was canonized in 1947.

Grottes de Bétharram

Chemin Leon Ross Mid-Feb-late Mar: Mon-Fri; late Mar-Oct: daily betharram.com

Sanctuaire de Notre-Dame de Bétharram

Avenue de Bétharram, Lestelle-Bétharram 06 73 09 91 70 Tue-Sun

A guide leads visitors around the Grottes de Bétharram caverns

Vallée d'Aspe

C7 Place Sarraillé, Bedous; pyrenees-bearnaises.com

The Vallée d'Aspe, south of Oloron-Sainte-Marie, is washed by the Gave d'Aspe. The railway viaduct here was built in 1910 to carry the now-defunct Pau–Canfranc line. Notre-Dame-de-la-Pierre, at Sarrance, is the first site of interest along a trail that makes up the **Écomusée de la Vallée d'Aspe**, the valley's open-air museum. This stop focuses on the legend of Sarrance and its pilgrims. Visitors can then see the 17th-century church and cloister. At Lourdios Ichère, the trail's next stop, an audiovisual presentation explains the daily life of the inhabitants of this mountain village. Bedous is the valley's commercial centre. The GR65, a long-distance path known as the Chemin de Saint-Jacques, runs from Bedous to Accous. Here visitors can taste cheeses made by the local farmers. Bedous' imposing Église Saint-Martin suffered severe damage twice in its history, first in 1569, then again in 1793. The Cirque de Lescun, at the head of the valley, is a huge green plateau dotted with barns and surrounded by high peaks. Cette-Eygun has a 12th-century church, the Église Saint-Pierre.

The **Maison du Parc National des Pyrénées** visitor centre at Etsaut has a fascinating exhibition dedicated to the Pyrenean brown bear. Just beyond Etsaut, the road joins the Chemin de la Mâture. This dramatic stretch of the GR10 is dug into the rockface above a sheer drop. In the mid-18th century, pine trunks to be used as masts *(mâture)* for French navy ships were dragged through here. The Chapelle Saint-Jacques at Borce, last of the Écomusée exhibition stops, once took in pilgrims. Inside are 16th-century frescoes as well as graffiti by Napoléon's soldiers. The main street has picturesque 15th- and 16th-century houses featuring mullioned windows, Gothic doorways and bread ovens. The commanding Fort du Portalet (1860), located above the Gorge d'Enfer, was used as a state prison during World War II.

Écomusée de la Vallée d'Aspe
Rue du Bourg, Sarrance 05 59 34 55 51
Apr-early Nov: Tue-Sat (Jul & Aug: also Sun)

Maison du Parc National des Pyrénées
Rue d'en Bas, Etsaut
05 59 34 88 30 During school hols

Monein

C6 58 rue du Commerce; 05 59 12 30 40

This town is set in the rolling hills of the Jurançon, a region that produces a renowned sweet white wine. On place Lacabanne is a 19th-century building with pillars and stone arches that houses the town hall and covered market.

Église Saint-Girons, built in 1530, is the largest Gothic church in Béarn. A thousand oak trees were needed to build its magnificent hull-shaped roof. The roof beams were originally dowled rather than nailed. Visits are by tour

↓ Herdsmen's dwellings on the lower slopes of the Vallée d'Aspe

The hull-shaped oak roof frame of the Église Saint-Girons in Monein

EAT

Restaurante L'Amandier

Proud purveyors of regional cuisine, from hearty *garbure* (local ham and vegetable soup) to roasted duck with Jurançon sauce.

C6 6 Place de la Hourquie, Morlaàs 05 59 33 41 38

only; a *son et lumière* (sound and light) show explains the roof's unusual construction.

Église Saint-Girons

 2 rue Saint-Girons 05 59 12 30 40 Hours vary, call ahead to book

15

Lembeye

C6 37 place Marcadieu; 05 59 68 28 78

Perched on a steep hillside, Lembeye was founded by Gaston VII of Béarn in 1286, and became the capital of Vic-Bilh ("Old Villages"), an area adjoining Bigorre and Gascony. Not far from place Marcadieu, near some old arcaded houses, is a fortified gate, known as Tour de l'Horloge (Clock Tower). Lembeye's large Gothic church has an interesting carved doorway.

About 19 km (12 miles) from Lembeye is the **Château de Mascaraàs**, featuring 17th- and 18th-century decoration. Note the château is open for guided tours only. Some 21 km (13 miles) away is the 14th-century **Château de Montaner** – built on the order of Gaston Fébus, the viscount of Béarn in the 14th century – and the **Église peinte de Montaner**, a church with remarkable 15th- and 16th-century frescoes.

Château de Mascaraàs

Mascaraàs-Haron 05 59 04 92 60 Apr, May & mid-Sep-Nov: Sat & Sun; Jun-mid-Sep: Wed-Mon

Château de Montaner

962 chemin Costa de Fébus, Montaner Hours vary, check website for details and to book chateau-montaner.fr

Église peinte de Montaner

 55 chemin Camin de la Gleisa 05 59 81 98 29 Hours vary, call ahead to book

16

Morlaàs

C6 Place Sainte-Foy; 05 59 33 62 25

The capital of Béarn from 1080 to 1260, and a stopping place on several of the pilgrim routes to the Spanish city of Santiago de Compostela *(p226)*, Morlaàs was once an important stronghold of Gaston Fébus, viscount of Béarn, and had its own mint.

Most of the town was destroyed during the Wars of Religion in the 16th century, and little remains of its past other than the **Église Sainte-Foy**, dedicated to St Faith, a French martyr. This church, built in 1080, has a Romanesque doorway, restored in the 19th century, carved with a depiction of St John's vision of the Apocalypse. The capitals in the apse are carved with scenes from the life of St Foy. The church is in a similar style to other buildings on the pilgrim route, particularly those in Jaca in the Spanish province of Aragon, on the other side of the Pyrénées.

Like Orthez, Salies-de-Béarn and other towns in the area, Morlaàs is also noted for traditional furniture-making.

Église Sainte-Foy

11 place Sainte-Foy 05 59 33 40 87 Daily

Carved figure of St James at the Église Sainte-Foy in Morlaàs

A DRIVING TOUR VINEYARDS OF MADIRAN

Length 40 km (25 miles) **Starting point** Lembeye
Stopping-off point The priory in the village of Madiran, where there is a Maison des Vins

Locator Map

The wines produced in this region are lesser known than their counterparts further north, but they are just as exquisite. Being at the intersection of Béarn, the Gers and the Hautes-Pyrénées also makes the area a wonderful place for a driving tour to visit some of the local vineyards for a tasting. Madiran's robust, dark red wine was long used as a communion wine, but became known to the wider world thanks to pilgrims who passed through the area on their way to Santiago de Compostela. Since then, as the quality of Madiran wine has improved, it has become even better known.

Between Béarn, Bigorre and the Landes, ***Aydie*** *is a major centre for the production of Madiran wine, as well as the wines of five other estates.*

Madiran*, a Gers town full of character, shares its name with the local wine appellation. A former priory here houses the Maison des Vins et du Pacherenc.*

From the 16th century, ***Conchez-de-Béarn*** *was the home town of Béarn's aristocracy.*

The magnificent ***Château Arricau-Bordes*** *is closed to the public, but visitors can explore the wine cellars in the former stables and take part in wine tastings.*

The Crouseilles-Madiran wine cooperative was founded here in 1950. The ***Cave de Crouseilles*** *is open to visitors for tours and wine tastings.*

The vestiges of ***Lembeye's*** *medieval history can still be seen around town (p249).*

The Madiran vineyards around Château Arricau-Bordes

NEED TO KNOW

The Miroir d'Eau reflecting pool in Bordeaux

BEFORE YOU GO

Things change, so plan ahead to make the most of your trip. Be prepared for all eventualities by considering the following points before you travel.

ELECTRICITY SUPPLY

Power sockets are type C and E, fitting C and E plugs. Standard voltage is 230v/50Hz.

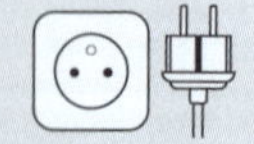

Passports and Visas

For entry requirements, including visas, consult your nearest French embassy or check the **France-Visas** website. Citizens of the UK, US, Canada, Australia and New Zealand do not need a visa for stays of up to three months but in future must apply in advance for the European Travel Information and Authorization System (ETIAS); roll-out has continually been postponed so check the website for details. Visitors from other countries may also require an ETIAS, so check before travelling. EU nationals do not need a visa or an ETIAS.

France-Visas
W france-visas.gouv.fr

ETIAS
W etiasvisa.co

Government Advice

Now more than ever, it is important to consult both your and the French government's advice before travelling. The **UK Foreign, Commonwealth & Development Office (FCDO)**, the **US Department of State**, the **Australian Department of Foreign Affairs and Trade** and **Gouvernement France** offer the latest information on security, health and local regulations.

Australian Department of Foreign Affairs and Trade
W smartraveller.gov.au

Gouvernement France
W gouvernement.fr

UK Foreign, Commonwealth & Development Office (FCDO)
W gov.uk/foreign-travel-advice

US Department of State
W travel.state.gov

Customs Information

You can find up-to-date information on the laws relating to goods and currency taken in or out of France on the official **France Tourism** website.

France Tourism
W france.fr

Insurance

We recommend taking out a comprehensive insurance policy covering theft, loss of belongings, medical care, cancellations and delays, and read the small print carefully. UK citizens are eligible for free emergency medical care in France, provided they have a valid European Health Insurance Card (EHIC) or UK Global Health Insurance Card (**GHIC**).

GHIC
W ghic.org.uk

Vaccinations

No vaccinations are required for France. For information regarding COVID-19 vaccination requirements, consult government advice.

Money

Most establishments accept major credit, debit and prepaid currency cards, but it's always a good idea to carry some cash too. Contactless payments are widely accepted almost everywhere in France. Tipping between 5 and 10 per cent of the cost of your bill in restaurants is polite.

Booking Accommodation

There is a range of accommodation across southwest France. Coastal areas are busiest in July and August, so book ahead if visiting at that time. Some smaller hotels close in low season.

Travellers with Specific Requirements

Various organizations are working to improve accessibility across France. **Jaccede** has details of accessible museums, hotels, bars and restaurants. Rail operator **SNCF** provides information about train travel, both online and in leaflets, and offers a booking service for free assistance. For advice, contact the French disability advocacy group **GIHP**.

GIHP
W gihpnational.org

Jaccede
W jaccede.com

SNCF
W accessibilite.sncf.com

Language

French is the official language, but English is widely spoken. The French are fiercely proud of their language, but don't let this put you off. Mastering a few niceties goes a long way. The Basque language (Euskara) is also spoken in the Pays Basque region.

Opening Hours

Situations can change quickly and unexpectedly. Always check before visiting attractions and hospitality venues for up-to-date opening hours and booking requirements.

Lunchtime Some shops and businesses close for an hour or two from around noon.

Mondays Some museums, small shops, restaurants and bars are closed, particularly in rural areas.

Tuesdays Most national museums and monuments are closed for the day.

Sundays Most shops are closed, or open for the morning only.

Public holidays Public services, shops, museums and attractions are usually closed.

School holidays To coincide with the end of the school term, attractions may have longer hours during summer, and shorter hours in late December.

PUBLIC HOLIDAYS

1 Jan	New Year's Day
Mar/Apr	Easter Monday
1 May	Labour Day/May Day
8 May	Victory 1945
May	Ascension Day
May	Whit Monday *(Pentecôte)*
14 Jul	Bastille Day
15 Aug	Assumption of Mary
1 Nov	All Saints' Day
11 Nov	Armistice Day
25 Dec	Christmas Day

GETTING AROUND

The towns of southwest France are well connected with trains and buses, but many visitors choose to explore the region by car or bicycle.

AT A GLANCE

PUBLIC TRANSPORT COSTS IN BORDEAUX

€1.90
Single journey
Bus, tram, Bato and coach

€3.30
Two journeys
Bus, tram, Bato and coach

€6.50
Unlimited 24-hour travel
Bus, tram, Bato and coach

TOP TIP
It is difficult to explore Bordeaux by car, as many areas are pedestrianized.

SPEED LIMIT

AUTOROUTE	DIVIDED HIGHWAY
130 km/h (80 mph)	110 km/h (68 mph)

RURAL ROADS	URBAN ROADS
80 km/h (49 mph)	50 km/h (31 mph)

Arriving by Air

The biggest airport in the region is Bordeaux-Mérignac Airport, with connections to more than 100 destinations. Shuttle buses operate between Bordeaux Airport and the city centre with departures every 8–20 minutes.

Biarritz Airport, Bergerac Airport, Brive Airport and Pau Airport are smaller alternatives.

Train Travel

International Train Travel

You can travel to France from many major cities in Europe by regular rail, or on the celebrated high-speed TGVs (Ouigo and InOui). **Interrail** and **Eurail** sell passes to EU residents and non-Europeans respectively, for international journeys lasting from five days up to three months. Both passes are valid directly via **TGV**, but do not include the mandatory seat reservation fee, which can be paid online in advance or at stations.

Eurail
W eurail.com
Interrail
W interrail.eu
TGV
W sncf-connect.com

Domestic Train Travel

The state-owned **SNCF** serves all regions of France. SNCF's regional TER trains can be booked online or at rail stations, while the longer Intercity and night trains usually require reservations. Tickets can be bought online at SNCF-connect, Trainline or **Raileurope**. Machines at stations also sell tickets, which must be inserted into yellow validating machines before boarding.

Railway buffs will also enjoy France's steam locomotive routes, including the route from Bergerac to Le Buisson and the Le Truffadou (Truffle Train) of Martel.

Raileurope
W raileurope.co.uk
Trainline
W thetrainline.com
SNCF
W sncf-connect.com

GETTING TO AND FROM BORDEAUX-MÉRIGNAC AIRPORT

Location	Distance to Airport	Journey Time by Car
Arcachon	66 km (41 miles)	45 mins
Bayonne	180 km (111 miles)	2 hours
Bergerac	110 km (68 miles)	1.5 hours
Biarritz	200 km (124 miles)	2 hours
Bordeaux centre	10 km (6 miles)	20 mins
Bordeaux Saint-Jean railway station	20 km (12 miles)	30 mins
Brive-la-Gaillarde	210 km (130 miles)	2.5 hours
Margaux	26 km (16 miles)	30 mins
Mont-de-Marsan	130 km (80 miles)	1.5 hours
Pau	220 km (137 miles)	2.5 hours
Périgueux	140 km (87 miles)	1.5 hours
Soulac-sur-Mer	100 km (62 miles)	1.5 hours

RAIL JOURNEY PLANNER

This map shows train routes between some of the region's major towns and cities. Journey times given below are the average time for each route.

Bordeaux to Arcachon	50 mins
Bordeaux to Biarritz	2 hrs
Bordeaux to Bayonne	2 hrs
Bordeaux to Bergerac	2.5 hrs
Bordeaux to Mont-de-Marsan	1.5 hrs
Bordeaux to Pau	2.5 hrs
Bordeaux to Périgueux	1.5 hrs
Bordeaux to Soulac-sur-Mer	1.75 hrs
Bayonne to Périgueux	4 hrs
Biarritz to Soulac-sur-Mer	4.5 hrs
Périgueux to Pau	4.5 hrs

Long-Distance Bus Travel

BlahBlahCar Bus operates a low-cost bus network that travels as far as Amsterdam and London and includes many stops in southwest France. **Flixbus** also has an extensive network across Europe and all over France.

Local bus companies in each region run frequent services between nearby cities.

Flixbus
W flixbus.fr
BlahBlahCar Bus
W blahblahcar.fr

Public Transport

Most urban areas are served by a bus system that can be used to explore the town. Smaller villages in the countryside may have no bus system, or the schedule may be infrequent and inefficient for tourists. As such, many visitors prefer to explore the area by car.

The **TBM** tram and bus network operates in and around Bordeaux, along with a network of self-service bicycles. Safety and hygiene measures, timetables, ticket and timetable information, transport maps, and more can be obtained from their website.

You can buy tram tickets for 1, 2 or 10 journeys, as well as travel cards valid for 1 day or 7 days.

TBM
W infotbm.com

Taxis

Official taxis are clearly identified. They can be hailed in passing, but not within sight of an official taxi stand. Billing begins from the moment of booking. Taxis are not usually seen in small rural communities, so visitors will need to find a local taxi company online and book in advance to ensure a ride.

Uber is popular throughout France, including in Bordeaux and Bergerac. **Heetch** is a late-night app-based service running in several cities, including Bordeaux.

Heetch
W heetch.com
Uber
W uber.com

Driving

With stunning views, well-maintained roads, and fast and spacious *autoroutes* (motorways), driving may be the best way to explore the Dordogne countryside. There are pros and cons, however. Congestion in the cities – particularly during July and August – may make train travel more appealing during those busy times. French cities also have many hard-to-navigate one-way streets, and parking can be difficult and expensive.

Car hire

To hire a car in France you must be aged 21 or over, have held a valid driver's licence for at least a year, and own a credit card which will be needed to pay the deposit. If visiting from the UK, you will also need to visit the **Share Driving Licence Service** on the DVLA website prior to departure to prove that you haven't exceeded 12 points on your licence.

Hire cars with automatic transmission will need to be booked in advance. Returning a car to a different location will incur extra charges. The major car-hire companies have branches in airports, and **HolidayAutos** has competitive rates in this part of France. Local companies are competitive on price but are not always able to offer one-way journeys.

HolidayAutos
W holidayautos.co.uk
Share Driving Licence Service
W gov.co.uk/view-driving-licence

Driving in France

To take your own foreign-registered car to France, you will need to carry the vehicle's registration and insurance documents, a full and valid driving licence, and a valid passport or national ID at all times. EU driving licences are valid here. If visiting from outside of the EU, or if your licence is not in French, you may need to apply for an International Driving Permit (IDP) through your government.

All French roads have national markings: A for *autoroute*, N for *nationale* (National Highway) and D for *département* (smaller country roads). *Autoroutes* have blue signs, and if there is a toll this will be marked. It's useful to carry cash at all times in case you use a toll road although most of them accept card and contactless payments; information on rates can be found on the **Autoroutes** website. Roads that cross country borders are labelled E for European routes, and these appear on a green sign. Rural roads appear on white signs, and are marked with C for communal or R for rural. Be aware that petrol stations can be scarce in rural areas and are often closed at night and on Sundays.

Restrictions exist across France to curb harmful emissions and improve air quality. Certain cities, including Bordeaux, now require drivers to show **Crit'Air** (clean air) stickers on windscreens. A map of low emission zones is available on the **Air Quality Certificate Service** government website, which can also be used to apply for Crit'Air stickers.

France has almost 50,000 charging stations for electric cars – the second-larget number after Italy. The **Open Charge Map** website plots charge point locations worldwide.

Air Quality Certificate Service
W certificat-air.gouv.fr

Autoroutes
W autoroutes.fr
Crit'Air
W crit-air.fr
Open Charge Map
W openchargemap.org

Parking

Parking is fairly easy throughout most of the region, but it can be hard to find spaces in Bordeaux. Traffic in the city centre is forbidden on the first Sunday of every month from 10am to 7pm in the summer and from 10am to 6pm in the winter.

Rules of the Road

Those aged 18 or over who hold a full driving licence are permitted to drive in France. An international car must display its national identification letters on a sticker (e.g. UK) unless the car has Euro-plates. Always drive on the right and remember that vehicles coming from the right usually have the right of way, unless signposted otherwise.

Seatbelts are compulsory, and children under ten must sit in the back seat with a booster seat. It is against the law to drive in a bus lane, to use a mobile phone (including hands-free) while driving, or to sound your horn in the city. It is also forbidden to have a Satnav or GPS system that can detect speed cameras, so disable this function on your device before your visit. French police can demand on-the-spot fines for traffic offences of up to €750.

France strictly enforces a blood alcohol content limit of 0.05 per cent. By law, drivers must carry a breathalyser – available for €1 at petrol stations – as well as a red warning triangle and a high-visibility vest.

In wet conditions, or if you have been driving for under three years, speed limits are reduced to 110 km/h (68 mph) on *autoroutes* and 100 km/h (62 mph) on divided highways.

Cycling

Many miles of scenic cycle routes wend their way through the Dordogne region. Bicycles can be taken on some boat and ferry services, and on the TER and Intercity trains, but non-folding bikes will incur a fee. On TGVs, bikes must be dismantled and stored in luggage spaces or carried in bags.

In Bordeaux, **TBM** offers a self-service bike-hire system with docks around the city, and with both manual and electric options. An interactive map is available via its app. You can purchase passes for 24 hours or 7 days. It costs €1 to release the bike (€2 for an e-bike), the first 30 minutes are free and after that the fee is 10 cents per minute.

Visit **Freewheeling France** for information on cycling around France, including bike-friendly accommodation, cycle routes, tours and hire.

Cycling in France is quite safe. According to the French Highway Code, it is only compulsory for children under 12 to wear helmets, although it is advisable that adults wear them, too. It is illegal to cycle while using headphones, and cyclists are subject to an alcohol limit of 0.05 per cent, the same as drivers. Bikes must have a bell or horn and working lights, and cyclists must wear reflective vests when cycling at night.

TBM
W infotbm.com/fr
Freewheeling France
W freewheelingfrance.com

Walking

The most rewarding way to experience the Dordogne is on foot. The **Visit Dordogne Valley** website has over 100 marked trails that can be explored, catering for a range of abilities. Note that it is forbidden to hitchhike on *autoroutes* and it is not recommended anywhere in France.

Visit Dordogne Valley
W visit-dordogne-valley.co.uk

Boats and Ferries

The southwest of France is laced with an extensive network of navigable waterways formed by Aquitaine's rivers and canals. They have been used for transporting people and goods for centuries and are still a great way to explore the region, as many of the most beautiful towns are accessible by water. Cruises can be booked through **Aquitaine Navigation**, and other companies exist throughout the region to serve river and canal routes. Various trips along the coast around Arcachon are offered by **Bateliers Arcachonnais**.

The city of Bordeaux lies on the Garonne river and where the Bato river shuttle, operated by TBM, has three routes connecting seven stations on both riverbanks. Boats can carry 67 passengers. There is always a captain on board and the boats are accessible for wheelchair users. A maximum of six bicycles can also be taken on each boat.

The marina at Arcachon is the second-largest in western France. It has 2,600 moorings with 250 for visitors. Each evening, the port authority posts the weather forecast for the next few days. You will need a licence to sail a pleasure boat yourself with an engine more powerful than 6HP.

Aquitaine Navigation
W aquitaine-navigation.com
Bateliers Arcachonnais
W bateliers-arcachon.com

PRACTICAL INFORMATION

A little local know-how goes a long way in southwest France. Here you will find all the essential advice and information you will need during your stay.

AT A GLANCE

EMERGENCY NUMBERS

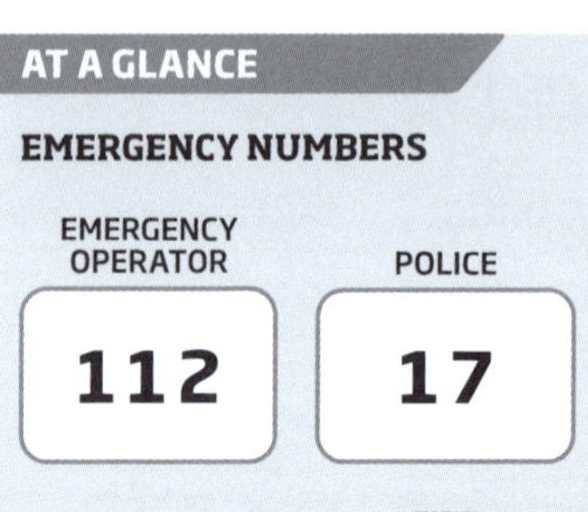

TIME ZONE

CET/CEST. Central European Summer Time runs from the last Sunday in March to the last Sunday in October.

TAP WATER

Unless otherwise stated, tap water and water from fountains in towns and villages is safe to drink.

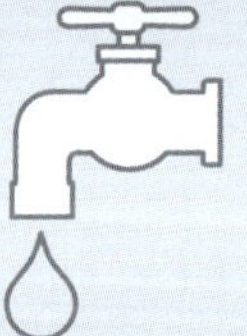

WEBSITES

France Tourism
Information and inspiration for travelling in France (*francetourism.com*).

Visit Dordogne Valley
Dordogne's tourist board website (*visit-dordogne-valley.co.uk*) with a useful calendar for the region.

Aquitaine Bike
Useful information on bike tours in the Dordogne region (*aquitaine bike.com*).

Personal Security

France is a safe country and visits are likely to be trouble-free. Take care of your belongings in busy tourist areas and on city buses during rush hour. It is also best to lock your car when leaving it, even if only for a few minutes. If travelling in a camper van or mobile home, be careful where you park at night so that you are able to seek help easily if required.

If anything is stolen, report it to the nearest police station. Get a copy of the crime report in order to make a claim on your insurance. Contact your embassy if you have your passport stolen, or in the event of a serious crime or accident.

France is a diverse, multicultural country. As a rule, the French are accepting of all people, regardless of their race, gender or sexuality. Same-sex marriage was legalized in 2013 and France recognized the right to legally change your gender in 2016. Bordeaux and other major cities have a thriving LGBTQ+ scene. **Le Girofard** in Bordeaux is a community centre and safe space for LQBTQ+ people, running a host of inclusive events and workshops.

Le Girofard
W le-girofard.org

Health

Pharmacists are an excellent source of advice when you are sick. They can diagnose minor ailments and suggest treatment. Private hospitals in major cities are more likely to have staff who speak fluent English.

EU and UK nationals holding an EHIC or GHIC are entitled to use the French national health service. Patients pay for treatment upfront and can reclaim most of the cost from the health authorities. The process can sometimes be lengthy so consider purchasing private travel insurance. Note that if you opt for private healthcare during your visit, this cannot be reclaimed under the EHIC or GHIC scheme.

For visitors from outside the EU and the UK, payment of medical expenses is the patient's responsibility, so it is important to arrange comprehensive medical insurance.

Smoking, Alcohol and Drugs

Smoking is prohibited in all public places but is allowed on restaurant, café and pub terraces, as long as they are not enclosed. The possession of narcotics is prohibited and could result in a prison sentence. Unless stated otherwise, alcohol consumption on the streets is permitted.

France has a strict limit of 0.05 per cent BAC (blood alcohol content) for drivers and cyclists.

ID

It is a legal requirement for foreign visitors to carry ID on them when visiting France, in the form of a passport or a national identity card. In the event of a routine check, which can take place on the roads, you may be asked to show your passport. If it is not with you, the police may escort you to wherever your passport is kept, or ask you to take your ID to a police station within four hours.

Local Customs

Etiquette is important in southwest France, but there are no strict rules – simple, basic manners go a long way. On entering and leaving a shop or café, say "bonjour" and "au revoir". Be sure to add "s'il vous plaît" (please) when ordering items, and say "pardon" if you accidentally bump into someone.

The French usually shake hands on meeting someone for the first time and when saying goodbye. Family, friends and colleagues who know each other well often greet each other with a kiss on each cheek. If you are unsure about what is expected, wait to see if you are offered a hand or a cheek.

Visiting Churches and Cathedrals

Dress respectfully when visiting a religious site: cover the torso and upper arms, and ensure that shorts and skirts reach at least to the knees.

Mobile Phones and Wi-Fi

For cheap calls to French numbers, it is advisable to use a French SIM card, which will work in unlocked phones.

A 5G network operates throughout most of France so mobile signal is strong here. Visitors on EU tariffs should be able to use their devices without being affected by data roaming charges, whereas many North American and Japanese phones aren't compatible here. It is best to check international rates with your service provider before using your phone abroad.

Free Wi-Fi hotspots are available in many public spaces. Cafés and restaurants usually allow customers to use their Wi-Fi for free. Bordeaux also has a Wi-Fi network that is available for free across the city.

Post

Stamps can be bought at post offices and *tabacs* (corner shops). Most post offices have self-service machines to weigh your mail. Vist **La Poste** for more information

La Poste
W laposte.fr

Taxes and Refunds

VAT is around 20 per cent in France. Non-EU residents can claim back tax on certain purchases over €175 if the claim is made within six months. Look out for the Global Refund Tax-Free sign, and ask the retailer for a form for a *détaxe* receipt. Present the goods receipt, *détaxe* receipt and your passport at customs when you leave the country to receive your refund.

Discount Cards

Entry to some museums is free on the first Sunday of each month. Under-18s and EU passport holders aged 18–26 are usually admitted free of charge to national museums, and there are sometimes discounts for students and over-60s with relevant ID.

The **Camping Card International** can provide savings of up to 20 per cent on campsite bookings. Bordeaux also offers a **CityPass** card, available for 24, 48 or 72 hours, which covers entry to local attractions, transport throughout the city and discounts on tours.

Bordeaux CityPass
W visiter-bordeaux.com/en/bordeaux-citypass
Camping Card International
W campingcardinternational.com

INDEX

Page numbers in **bold** refer to main entries.

PHRASE BOOK

IN AN EMERGENCY

Help!	**Au secours!**	*oh sekoor*
Stop!	**Arrêtez!**	*aret-ay*
Call a doctor!	**Appelez un médecin!**	*apuh-lay uñ medsañ*
Call an ambulance!	**Appelez une ambulance!**	*apuh-lay oon oñboo-loñs*
Call the police!	**Appelez la police!**	*apuh-lay lah poh-lees*
Call the fire brigade!	**Appelez les pompiers!**	*apuh-lay leh poñ-peeyay*
Where is the nearest telephone?	**Où est le téléphone le plus proche?**	*oo ay luh tehlehfon luh ploo prosh*
Where is the nearest hospital?	**Où est l'hôpital le plus proche?**	*oo ay l'opeetal luh ploo prosh*

COMMUNICATION ESSENTIALS

Yes	**Oui**	*wee*
No	**Non**	*noñ*
Please	**S'il vous plaît**	*seel voo play*
Thank you	**Merci**	*mer-see*
Excuse me	**Excusez-moi**	*exkoo-zay mwah*
Hello	**Bonjour**	*boñzhoor*
Goodbye	**Au revoir**	*oh ruh-vwar*
Good night	**Bonsoir**	*boñ-swar*
Morning	**Le matin**	*matañ*
Afternoon	**L'après-midi**	*l'apreh-meedee*
Evening	**Le soir**	*swar*
Yesterday	**Hier**	*eeyehr*
Today	**Aujourd'hui**	*oh-zhoor-dwee*
Tomorrow	**Demain**	*duhmañ*
Here	**Ici**	*ee-see*
There	**Là**	*lah*
What?	**Quoi, quel, quelle?**	*kwah, kel, kel*
When?	**Quand?**	*koñ*
Why?	**Pourquoi?**	*poor-kwah*
Where?	**Où?**	*oo*

USEFUL PHRASES

How are you?	**Comment allez-vous?**	*kom-moñ talay voo*
Very well, thank you.	**Très bien, merci.**	*treh byañ, mer-see*
Pleased to meet you.	**Enchanté de faire votre connaissance.**	*oñshoñ-tay duh fehr votr kon-ay-sans*
See you soon.	**A bientôt.**	*byañ-toh*
That's fine	**C'est bon**	*say bon*
Where is/are...?	**Où est/sont...?**	*ooay/soñ*
How far is it to...?	**Combien de kilometres d'ici à...?**	*kom-byañ duh keelo-metr d'ee-see ah*
Which way to...?	**Quelle est la direction pour...?**	*kel ay lah deer-ek-syoñ poor*
Do you speak English?	**Parlez-vous anglais?**	*par-lay voo oñg-lay*
I don't understand.	**Je ne comprends pas.**	*zhuh nuh kom-proñ pah*
Could you speak slowly please?	**Pouvez-vous parler moins vite s'il vous plaît?**	*poo-vay voo par-lay mwañ veet seel voo play*
I'm sorry.	**Excusez-moi.**	*exkoo-zay mwah*

USEFUL WORDS

big	**grand**	*groñ*
small	**petit**	*puh-tee*
hot	**chaud**	*show*
cold	**froid**	*frwah*
good	**bon/bien**	*boñ/byañ*
bad	**mauvais**	*moh-veh*
enough	**assez**	*assay*
well	**bien**	*byañ*
open	**ouvert**	*oo-ver*
closed	**fermé**	*fer-meh*
left	**gauche**	*gohsh*
right	**droite**	*drwaht*
straight on	**tout droite**	*too drwaht*
near	**près**	*preh*
far	**loin**	*lwañ*
up	**en haut**	*oñ oh*
down	**en bas**	*oñ bah*
early	**de bonne heure**	*duh bon urr*
late	**en retard**	*oñ ruh-tar*
entrance	**l'entrée**	*l'on-tray*
exit	**la sortie**	*sor-tee*
toilet	**les toilettes, le WC**	*twah-let, vay-see*
free, unoccupied	**libre**	*leebr*
free, no charge	**gratuit**	*grah-twee*

MAKING A TELEPHONE CALL

I'll try again later.	**Je rappelerai plus tard.**	*zhuh rapeleray ploo tar*
Can I leave a message?	**Est-ce que je peux laisser un message?**	*es-keh zhuh puh leh-say uñ mehsazh*
Hold on, please.	**Ne quittez pas, s'il vous plaît.**	*nuh kee-tay pah seel voo play*
Could you speak up a little?	**Pouvez-vous parler un peu plus fort?**	*poo-vay voo parlay uñ puh ploo for*
local call	**la communication locale**	*komoonikahsyoñ low-kal*

SHOPPING

How much does this cost?	**C'est combien s'il vous plaît?**	*say kom-byañ seel voo play*
I would like ...	**Je voudrais...**	*zhuh voo-dray*
Do you have?	**Est-ce que vous avez?**	*es-kuh voo zavay*
I'm just looking.	**Je regarde seulement.**	*zhuh ruhgar suhlmoñ*
Do you take credit cards?	**Est-ce que vous acceptez les cartes de crédit?**	*es-kuh voo zaksept-ay leh kart duh kreh-dee*
What time do you open?	**A quelle heure vous êtes ouvert?**	*ah kel urr voo zet oo-ver*
What time do you close?	**A quelle heure vous êtes fermé?**	*ah kel urr voo zet fer-may*
This one.	**Celui-ci**	*suhl-wee-see*
That one.	**Celui-là**	*suhl-wee-lah*
expensive	**cher**	*shehr*
cheap	**pas cher, bon marché**	*pah shehr, boñ mar-shay*
size, clothes	**la taille**	*tye*
size, shoes	**la pointure**	*pwañ-tur*
white	**blanc**	*bloñ*
black	**noir**	*nwahr*
red	**rouge**	*roozh*
yellow	**jaune**	*zhohwn*
green	**vert**	*vehr*
blue	**bleu**	*bluh*

TYPES OF SHOP

antique shop	**le magasin d'antiquités**	*maga-zañ d'oñteekee-tay*
bakery	**la boulangerie**	*booloñ-zhuree*
bank	**la banque**	*boñk*
bookshop	**la librairie**	*lee-brehree*
butcher	**la boucherie**	*boo-shehree*
cake shop	**la pâtisserie**	*patee-sree*
cheese shop	**la fromagerie**	*fromazh-ree*
chemist	**la pharmacie**	*farmah-see*
dairy	**la crémerie**	*krem-ree*
department store	**le grand magasin**	*groñ maga-zañ*
delicatessen	**la charcuterie**	*sharkoot-ree*
fishmonger	**la poissonnerie**	*pwasson-ree*
giftshop	**le magasin de cadeaux**	*maga-zañ duh kadoh*
greengrocer	**le marchand de légumes**	*mar-shoñ duh lay-goom*
grocery	**l'alimentation**	*alee-moñta-syoñ*
hairdresser	**le coiffeur**	*kwafuhr*
market	**le marché**	*marsh-ay*
newsagent	**le magasin de journaux**	*maga-zañ duh zhoor-no*
post office	**la poste, le bureau de poste, le PTT**	*pohst, booroh duh pohst, peh-teh-teh*
shoe shop	**le magasin de chaussures**	*maga-zañ duh show-soor*
supermarket	**le supermarché**	*soo pehr-marshay*
tobacconist	**le tabac**	*tabah*
travel agent	**l'agence de voyages**	*l'azhoñs duh vwayazh*

SIGHTSEEING

abbey	**l'abbaye**	*l'abay-ee*
art gallery	**la galerie d'art**	*galer-ree dart*
bus station	**la gare routière**	*gahr roo-tee-yehr*
cathedral	**la cathédrale**	*katay-dral*
church	**l'église**	*l'aygleez*
garden	**le jardin**	*zhar-dañ*
library	**la bibliothèque**	*beebleeo-tek*
museum	**le musée**	*moo-zay*
railway station	**la gare (SNCF)**	*gahr (es-en-say-ef)*
tourist information office	**les renseignements touristiques, le syndicat d'initiative**	*roñsayn-moñ toorees-teek, sandee-ka d'eenee-syateev*
town hall	**l'hôtel de ville**	*l'ohtel duh veel*
closed for public holiday	**fermeture jour férié**	*fehrmeh-tur zhoor fehree-ay*

STAYING IN A HOTEL

Do you have a vacant room?	**Est-ce que vous avez une chambre?**	*es-kuh voo-zavay oon shambr*
double room, with double bed	**la chambre à deux personnes, avec un grand lit**	*shambr ah duh pehr-son avek un gronñ lee*
twin room	**la chambre à deux lits**	*shambr ah duh lee*
single room	**la chambre à une personne**	*shambr ah oon pehr-son*
room with a bath, shower	**la chambre avec salle de bains, une douche**	*shambr avek sal duh bañ, oon doosh*
porter	**le garçon**	*gar-soñ*
key	**la clef**	*klay*
I have a reservation.	**J'ai fait une réservation.**	*zhay fay oon rayzehrva-syoñ*

EATING OUT

Have you got a table?	**Avez-vous une table de libre?**	*avay-voo oon tahbl duh leebr*
I want to reserve a table.	**Je voudrais réserver une table.**	*zhuh voo-dray rayzehr-vay oon tahbl*
The bill please.	**L'addition s'il vous plaît.**	*l'adee-syoñ seel voo play*
I am a vegetarian.	**Je suis végétarien.**	*zhuh swee vezhay-tehryañ*
Waitress/ waiter	**Madame, Mademoiselle/ Monsieur**	*mah-dam, mah-demwahzel/ muh-syuh*
menu	**le menu, la carte**	*men-oo, kart*
fixed-price menu	**le menu à prix fixe**	*men-oo ah pree feeks*
cover charge	**le couvert**	*koo-vehr*
wine list	**la carte des vins**	*kart-deh vañ*
glass	**le verre**	*vehr*
bottle	**la bouteille**	*boo-tay*
knife	**le couteau**	*koo-toh*
fork	**la fourchette**	*for-shet*
spoon	**la cuillère**	*kwee-yehr*
breakfast	**le petit déjeuner**	*puh-tee deh-zhuh-nay*
lunch	**le déjeuner**	*deh-zhuh-nay*
dinner	**le dîner**	*dee-nay*
main course	**le plat principal**	*plah prañsee-pal*
starter, first course	**l'entrée, le hors d'oeuvre**	*l'oñ-tray, or-duhvr*
dish of the day	**le plat du jour**	*plah doo zhoor*
wine bar	**le bar à vin**	*bar ah vañ*
café	**le café**	*ka-fay*
rare	**saignant**	*say-noñ*
medium	**à point**	*ah pwañ*
well done	**bien cuit**	*byañ kwee*

MENU DECODER

apple	**la pomme**	*pom*
baked	**cuit au four**	*kweet oh foor*
banana	**la banane**	*banan*
beef	**le boeuf**	*buhf*
beer, draught beer	**la bière, bière à la pression**	*bee-yehr, bee-yehr ah lah pres-syoñ*
boiled	**bouilli**	*boo-yee*
bread	**le pain**	*pan*
butter	**le beurre**	*burr*
cake	**le gâteau**	*gah-toh*
cheese	**le fromage**	*from-azh*
chicken	**le poulet**	*poo-lay*
chips	**les frites**	*freet*
chocolate	**le chocolat**	*shoko-lah*
cocktail	**le cocktail**	*cocktail*
coffee	**le café**	*kah-fay*
dessert	**le dessert**	*deh-ser*
dry	**sec**	*sek*
duck	**le canard**	*kanar*
egg	**l'oeuf**	*l'uf*
fish	**le poisson**	*pwah-ssoñ*
fresh fruit	**le fruit frais**	*frwee freh*
fresh lemon juice	**le citron pressé**	*see-troñ press-eh*
fresh orange juice	**l'orange pressée**	*l'oroñzh press-eh*
garlic	**l'ail**	*l'eye*
grilled	**grillé**	*gree-yay*
ham	**le jambon**	*zhoñ-boñ*
ice, ice cream	**la glace**	*glas*
lamb	**l'agneau**	*l'anyoh*
lemon	**le citron**	*see-troñ*
lobster	**le homard**	*omahr*
meat	**la viande**	*vee-yand*
milk	**le lait**	*leh*
mineral water	**l'eau minérale**	*l'oh meeney-ral*
mustard	**la moutarde**	*moo-tard*
oil	**l'huile**	*l'weel*
olives	**les olives**	*leh zoleev*
onions	**les oignons**	*leh zonyoñ*
orange	**l'orange**	*l'oroñzh*
pepper	**le poivre**	*pwavr*
poached	**poché**	*posh-ay*
pork	**le porc**	*por*
potatoes	**les pommes de terre**	*pom-duh tehr*
prawns	**les crevettes**	*kruh-vet*
rice	**le riz**	*ree*
roast	**rôti**	*row-tee*
roll	**le petit pain**	*puh-tee pañ*
salt	**le sel**	*sel*
sauce	**la sauce**	*sohs*
sausage, fresh	**la saucisse**	*sohsees*
seafood	**les fruits de mer**	*frwee duh mer*
shellfish	**les crustaces**	*kroos-tas*
snails	**les escargots**	*leh zes-kar-goh*
soup	**la soupe, le potage**	*soop, poh-tazh*
steak	**le bifteck, le steack**	*beef-tek, stek*
sugar	**le sucre**	*sookr*
tea	**le thé**	*tay*
toast	**pain grillé**	*pan greeyay*
vegetables	**les légumes**	*lay-goom*
vinegar	**le vinaigre**	*veenaygr*
water	**l'eau**	*l'oh*
wine (red)	**le vin rouge**	*vañ roozh*
wine (white)	**le vin blanc**	*vañ bloñ*

NUMBERS

0	**zéro**	*zeh-roh*
1	**un, une**	*uñ, oon*
2	**deux**	*duh*
3	**trois**	*trwah*
4	**quatre**	*katr*
5	**cinq**	*sañk*
6	**six**	*sees*
7	**sept**	*set*
8	**huit**	*weet*
9	**neuf**	*nerf*
10	**dix**	*dees*
11	**onze**	*oñz*
12	**douze**	*dooz*
13	**treize**	*trehz*
14	**quatorze**	*katorz*
15	**quinze**	*kañz*
16	**seize**	*sehz*
17	**dix-sept**	*dees-set*
18	**dix-huit**	*dees-weet*
19	**dix-neuf**	*dees-nerf*
20	**vingt**	*vañ*
30	**trente**	*tront*
40	**quarante**	*karoñt*
50	**cinquante**	*sañkoñt*
60	**soixante**	*swasoñt*
70	**soixante-dix**	*swasoñt-dees*
80	**quatre-vingts**	*katr-vañ*
90	**quatre-vingt-dix**	*katr-vañ-dees*
100	**cent**	*soñ*
1,000	**mille**	*meel*

TIME

one minute	**une minute**	*oon mee-noot*
one hour	**une heure**	*oon urr*
half an hour	**une demi-heure**	*oon duh-mee urr*
Monday	**lundi**	*luñ-dee*
Tuesday	**mardi**	*mar-dee*
Wednesday	**mercredi**	*mehrkruh-dee*
Thursday	**jeudi**	*zhuh-dee*
Friday	**vendredi**	*voñdruh-dee*
Saturday	**samedi**	*sam-dee*
Sunday	**dimanche**	*dee-moñsh*

ACKNOWLEDGMENTS

This edition updated by
Contributer Jon Bryant
Senior Editor Dipika Dasgupta
Senior Designer Katie Cavanaugh, Stuti Tiwari
Project Editors Eleanora Reeves, Anuroop Sanwalia
Art Editor Sulagna Das
Assistant Editor Pankhoori Sinha
Proofreader Kathryn Glendenning
Indexer Helen Peters
Assistant Picture Research Administrator Manpreet Kaur
Rights and Permissions Specialist Priya Singh
Deputy Manager, Picture Research Virien Chopra
Jacket Picture Researcher Diana Jarvis
Senior Cartographer Mohammed Hassan
Cartography Manager Suresh Kumar
Pre-Production Coordinator Tanveer Zaidi
Deputy Managing Editor Dharini Ganesh
Managing Editor Beverly Smart
Senior Managing Art Editor Priyanka Thakur
Editorial Director Hollie Teague
Art Director Maxine Pedliham
Publishing Director Georgina Dee

DK would like to thank the following for their contribution to the previous edition: Lisa Voormeij, Mike MacEacheran, Deborah Bine, Sophie Blackman, Gabrielle Innes, Suzanne Boireau-Tartarat, Pierre Chavot, Renée Grimaud, Wilfried Lecarpentier, Santiago Mendieta, Marie-Pascale Rauzier, Hilary Bird

The publisher would like to thank the following for their kind permission to reproduce their photographs:

Key: a-above; b-below/bottom; c-centre; f-far; l-left; r-right; t-top

123RF.com: Boris Breytman 123tl, 123tr; delcreations 10-1b; freeprod 10ca; Philippe Halle 117tl.

4Corners: Francesco Carovillano 78-9b, 126; Günter Gräfenhain 35tr, 96-7b; Laurent Grandadam 249tl; Carlo Irek 34t; Tim Mannakee 143b; Gianluca Santoni 98-9; Luigi Vaccarella 10clb, 16, 38-9t, 60-1, 67tr.

Alamy Stock Photo: ACTIVE MUSEUM / Le Pictorium / Collection 84bl; Kate After 54tr; Age Fotostock / Christian Goupi 124t, 125cra, / Felix González 80cl, / Ian Cook 173br, / J.D. Dallet 57cr, 102b, / Javier Larrea 47br, 51tr, 214t, / Kevin O´Hara 100bl, / Rafael Campillo 200bl; Agencja Fotograficzna Caro / Schwarz 49cl; Ajax News & Feature Service / COLLECTIONS / Caroline Beaumont 57tr; Jerónimo Alba 104cl, All Canada Photos / Ian Cook 26bl, 115tl; Andia / © Lux 32-3t, / Le Gal 248b; AOP / SCOPE-IMAGE 114bl, 118t; Art Kowalsky 8-9b; The Art Archive / Gianni Dagli Orti 227cra; Arterra Picture Library / Clement Philippe 131tl; Andy Arthur 176-7b; David Bagnall 38br; David Bertho / © XTU architects / La Cité du Vin 69crb; BIOSPHOTO / Georges Lopez 246-7t, / Laurent Lhote 35crb; Christophe Boisvieux 194tr, 249br; Andor Bujdoso 44-5t; Ed Buziak 225tr, 245tr; Cavan / Christophe Launay 30-1t; Nico Chapman 219tr; Chronicle 53tr; Liz Claire 6-7; Classic Image 42-3t; Simon Dack 152bl; Ian Dagnall 28cra, 140b, 155br; Daniel Valla FRPS 142tl; David Dunbar 242tl; dpa picture alliance 57clb; Keith Erskine 26crb; David Forster 155tl; Sioen Gérard 218t; Roberto Soncin Gerometta 135tr; Iurii Golub 8cla; Manfred Gottschalk 70bl; Granger Historical Picture Archive / NYC 33br, 131tr, 131cra; Sheila Halsall / Crédit Photo ASF 194bl; Hemis / Cedric PASQUINI 50cla, / Jean-Marc BARRERE 164cl, 166b, / Patrice Hauser 41crb, / Arnaud Chicurel 22cr, / Bertrand Rieger 151br, 215tr, 221cla, 222-3t, / Cédric Pasquini 12-3b, / Christophe Boisvieux 153tr, / Cintract Romain 239br, / Denis Caviglia 141tr, / Eric Bouloumié 65t, 101br, / Francis Leroy 149tr, / Franck Guiziou 89br, 90-1t, 91br, 104-5t, / Franck Guiziou / © XTU architects 69b, / Gregory Gerault 76-7t, / Jacques Pierre 145b, 244-5b, / Jean-Daniel Sudres 22crb, 24bl, 203, 223br, 230crb, 230b, / Jean-Marc Barrère 162clb, 162b, 167tr, 178tl, 179b, 180tl, 185tr, 195b, 240t, 243b, / Jean-Paul Azam 120bl, 227cl, / Laurent Moreau 105br, / Marc Dozier 32bl, / Pasquini Cedric 51crb, / Patrice Hauser 34bl, 89tl, 140clb, 190t, / Patrick Escudero 43bl, 211tr, / Romain Cintract 50cr; Marc Hill 226crb; Hemis.fr / Bertrand Rieger 132br; Historic Images 201br; Historimages Collection / Yolanda Perera Sánchez 54tl, 54br; The History Collection 52t; Robert Hoetink 143tr; Horizon Images / Motion 172-3t; Stephen Hughes 192bl; Ian Dagnall Commercial Collection 33cl; Image Professionals GmbH /

Fleurent 11br, / H et M 30bl, / TravelCollection 11t; Images of Birmingham Premium 35cla; incamerastock / ICP-UK 36-7b; Tom Irvine 48-9b; Ivoha 226-7t; JAUBERT French Collection 231tr; JBN / SCOPE-IMAGE 50clb; Jon Arnold Images Ltd / Walter Bibikow 121cra; John Keates 83br; John Kellerman 12t, 154bl, 165cra; David Kilpatrick 247bl; Piotr Krześlak 31br; Lebrecht Music & Arts 102ca; Hervé Lenain 81tr, 92cl, 144tr, 168tl, 168-9b, 170-1b, 198tl; K.D. Leperi 103tr; Look / Brigitte Merz 227bl; Julien De Marchi 148b; Martin Thomas Photography 128-9t; mauritius images GmbH / Klaus Neuner 83tr, / Walter Bibikow 93tr; MIKEL BILBAO GOROSTIAGA- TRAVELS 39crb; Jim Monk 71tl; Tim Moore 146-7b; Perry van Munster 210bl, 212bl, 216crb; Jean-Bernard Nadeau 65cra; Niday Picture Library 56tl; nobleIMAGES / David Noble 42br; Eva Ozkoidi 36-7t; Per Karlsson - BKWine.com 85cra, 50cl; Photononstop / Daniele Schneider 43c, 88bl, 90bl, 100-1t, 138t, 139b, 193t, 197tr, 229t; PjrTravel 66cra; PRISMA ARCHIVO 130bl; Profimedia.CZ a.s. / Kulinarni studio BAUER MEDIA 47c; Reciprocity Images 134bl; Fabrice Restier 51cr; robertharding / Adam Tall 31clb, / Alex Treadway 35b, / Ellen Rooney 13t; Ageev Rostislav 55bl; SAGAPHOTO.COM / Olivier Roux 94t, / Stéphane Gautier 208br; Science History Images / Photo Researchers 56crb; Kumar Sriskandan 19tl, 37cl, 39bl, 156-7, 160cra, 160-1; Neiliann Tait 49br; Paul Tavener 116bl; Claude Thibault 219bl; VPC Photo 53br; wanderworldimages 37crb; Belle Vue 136b.

AWL Images: Spani Arnaud 150-1t; Bertrand Gardel 66-7b; Hemis 174-5; Doug Pearson 12cl.

Bridgeman Images: Archives Charmet 227tr.

Château Lamothe Bergeron: Andy Julia 28tl.

Depositphotos Inc: ademyan 20, 204-5.

Dorling Kindersley: Philippe Giraud 182bl.

Dreamstime.com: Steve Allen 26t, 92b; Leonid Andronov 252-3; Annapustynnikova 45b; Oksana Ermak 68; Eric Cowez 96tl; Delstudio 46bl, 51cla; Pierre Jean Durieu 227clb (Stèle de Gibraltar); Sergey Dzyuba 213br, 238tl; Kevin Eaves 57br, 243tr; Iakov Filimonov 77cra; Freeprod 2-3; Freesurf69 11cr; Hans Geel 57cra; Javarman 123cra; Oleksandr Korzhenko 21, 196b, 232-3; Mekoufios 224b; Anton Petrus 180-1b; Renaud Philippe 8cl; Sylvain Robin 82bl; Rosshelen 13br; Saiko3p 208-9t, 236-7t; Sohadiszno 45cl; Travelling-light 18, 108-9; Xantana 29tr, 46-7t, 146tl.
Getty Images: 500px / Nigel Eve 184bl, 56bc; AFP / GAIZKA IROZ 221t, / Georges Gobet 44br, / GERARD JULIEN 50crb, / JEAN-PIERRE MULLER 41cla, / MEHDI FEDOUACH 13cr, 26cr, / PATRICK BERNARD 51tl; Archive Photos / ClassicStock / H. Armstrong Roberts 217cr; Bettmann 55cb; Corbis Documentary / Henrik Trygg 29tl, / Philippe Lissac 95br; Corbis Historical / Ipsumpix 53cb, / philippe giraud 251, /Photo Josse / Leemage 52bc; De Agostini / DEA / BIBLIOTECA AMBROSIANA 56-7t, / G. DAGLI ORTI 54cr, / C. SAPPA 183t; EyeEm / Arno Jannasch 86t, / Thomas Roess 198-9b; Melchior Feselen 53tl; Gamma-Rapho / Denise Sarlin 48tl; Hulton Archive / Apic 217t, / 54cla, / Print Collector 53cla; Icon Sport / Scoop Dyga 50cra; Lonely Planet Images / Simon Greenwood 180tr; Moment / Iñigo Fdz de Pinedo 220bl, / saulgranda 4, / ondacaracola photography 8clb; Paris Match Archive / Helene Pambrun 40-1t; Photononstop / Lionel Lourdel 85tl; Popperfoto 217br; Universal Images Group / Andia 58-59, 201t, / Bildagentur-online 52clb, / Christophel Fine Art 55t, / Kike Calvo 24crb; Roger Viollet / Boyer 54clb.
Getty Images / iStock:: Joel Carillet 227cla; Eric Cowez 28-9t; horstgerlach 17, 72-3; Max Labeille 24t, 29cla; syolacan 112-3t, 132-3t; Jane Tonal 228-9b.

Picfair.com: JJF arquitectos 22t; FreeProd 107.

Shutterstock.com: Mike_O 216b; Pjb / Sipa 51clb.

Robert Harding Picture Library: Robert Francis 185br; Javier Larrea 24cr.

Semitour Périgord: Dan Courtice 137tr.

SuperStock: Age Fotostock / Jerónimo Alba / © XTU architects / La Cité du Vin 38tl; Hemis / Jacques Pierre 40-1b, / Jean-Marc Barrère 49tr, / Hervé Hughes / © XTU architects / La Cité du Vin 22bl.

Unsplash: Pierluigi Ballandi / @pierballandi 19cb, 186-7.

Front Flap: 123RF.com: freeprod tr;
Alamy Stock Photo: Art Kowalsky bl; Hemis / Franck Guiziou t; John Kellerman br;
Dreamstime.com: Oleksandr Korzhenko cb;

Getty Images: Corbis Documentary / Henrik Trygg cla.

Cover images:
Front and Spine:
Depositphotos Inc: Jon_Chica

Back:
Alamy Stock Photo: BIOSPHOTO c; Photononstop tr; **Depositphotos Inc:** Jon_Chica b; **SuperStock:** Hemis / Jean-Marc Barrere cla.

First edition 2006

Published in Great Britain by Dorling Kindersley Limited, DK, 20 Vauxhall Bridge Road, London SW1V 2SA

The authorised representative in the EEA is Dorling Kindersley Verlag GmbH. Arnulfstr. 124, 80636 Munich, Germany

Published in the United States by DK Publishing, 1745 Broadway, 20th Floor, New York, NY 10019, USA

26 27 28 29 10 9 8 7 6 5 4 3 2 1

A CIP catalogue record for this book is available from the British Library.

A catalogue record for this book is available from the Library of Congress.

ISSN: 1542 1554
ISBN: 978 0 2417 2176 6

Printed and bound in China.

www.dk.com

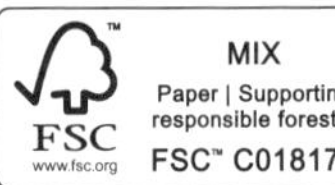

This book was made with Forest Stewardship Council™ certified paper – one small step in DK's commitment to a sustainable future.
Learn more at **www.dk.com/uk/information/sustainability**

A NOTE FROM DK

The rate at which the world is changing is constantly keeping the DK travel team on our toes. While we've worked hard to ensure that this edition of Dordogne, Bordeaux and the Southwest Coast is accurate and up-to-date, we know that opening hours alter, standards shift, prices fluctuate, places close and new ones pop up in their stead. So, if you notice we've got something wrong or left something out, we want to hear about it. Please get in touch at travelguides@dk.com